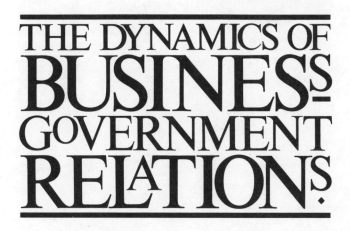

THE DYNAMICS OF
BUSINESS-
GOVERNMENT
RELATIONS

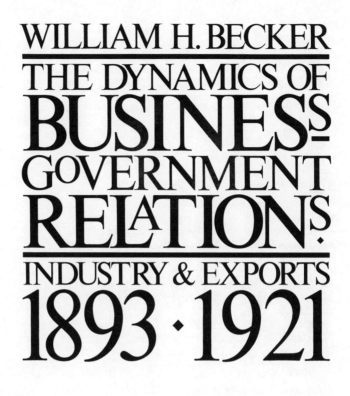

WILLIAM H. BECKER

THE DYNAMICS OF BUSINESS-GOVERNMENT RELATIONS

INDUSTRY & EXPORTS 1893 · 1921

94-41

The University of Chicago Press ◆ Chicago & London

To Ruth Anne and to Megan and Lauren

WILLIAM H. BECKER is associate professor of history
at University of Maryland Baltimore County and the
coeditor, with Samuel F. Wells, Jr., of *Economics and
Diplomacy: An Assessment.*

Publication of this work has been made possible
in part by a grant from the Andrew W. Mellon
Foundation.

The University of Chicago Press, Chicago 60637
The University of Chicago Press, Ltd., London

Library of Congress Cataloging in Publication Data

Becker, William H.
   The dynamics of business-government relations.

   Bibliography: p.
   Includes index.
   1. United States—Commerce—History. 2. Foreign
trade promotion—United States—History.
3. Industry and state—United States—History.
4. United States. Dept. of State—History.
5. United States. Dept. of Commerce—History.
I. Title.
HF3029.B38   382'. 63'0973   81-10318
ISBN 0-226-04121-2   AACR2

Contents

Preface

Between 1893 and 1921 exports of American manufactured products increased from $130 million to $1.627 billion. These exports were, at least before 1914, the most dramatic manifestation of America's growing international economic power. This book is the result of a study of the dynamics—the development and nature—of the relationship between manufacturers and government in the expansion of American foreign trade in manufactured goods.

Other historians have studied parts of American foreign economic expansion, and indeed in the last two decades the political economy of several aspects of American foreign policy has received close attention from, among others, William Appleman Williams, Walter LaFeber, Joan Hoff Wilson, Carl Parrini, and Burton I. Kaufman.[1] My analysis differs in several important respects from this previous revisionist work, which dealt wholly or in part with the political economy of American foreign trade in manufactured goods.

Significant attention is here focused on the changing economic structure and behavior of industries and firms that developed major foreign markets. An analysis of the economic factors in America and abroad that led to the expansion of manufactured exports is essential to an assessment of the way in which business-government contacts developed and to their significance for manufacturers. Other scholars have reached various conclusions about the role of government in foreign economic matters without paying sufficient attention to the economic basis of business decisions and behavior.

The one historian who has treated the subject of commercial expansion most fully, Burton I. Kaufman, has concluded that what needs emphasis in the Wilson years is "the coherence of purpose, the breadth of accomplishment and, indeed, the historical uniqueness that characterized business-government efforts at foreign trade organization."[2] This conclusion, as I will show, exaggerates the level of cooperation between business and government and its significance, at least to the largest American firms selling abroad.[3]

In addition, much of the important revisionist work on foreign economic policy pays insufficient attention to a competitive ideology that remained strong after World War I. The revisionists have overlooked the fact that the war reinforced the traditional fear of government intervention in private affairs. The conflict showed the ultimate dangers, many businessmen thought, of government politicizing American and international economic life.

Almost all students of foreign economic expansion have based their analyses of the business economy on what some business leaders thought and said. Attitudes and rhetoric—business' perception about the world—were important, and are treated in this study. But in the absence of a thorough consideration of fundamental structural changes in domestic industries and international markets, what business "spokesmen" said or thought was only part of the story. Business behavior did not necessarily reflect business rhetoric.[4]

This book is not exclusively an investigation into the business history of foreign trade. Export expansion did not occur in a political vacuum. Several departments of the federal government became involved in promoting the expansion of foreign trade. Many of the scholars referred to above have identified and studied the interaction between the government and business in foreign economic activities, but to understand fully the business-government relationship one needs to examine closely the workings of those agencies of government that sought to help business. This study, then, is in important respects also a bureaucratic history, especially of the Department of State and the Department of Commerce.

To establish, as others have done, that business and government at times worked together in foreign economic activities is not sufficient for an understanding of the dynamics of the relationship. I set out to assess the importance to business of relations with the government. In this analysis I also question the belief of many students of political economy who see growing business-government contacts as inevitable. In fact, as I will demonstrate here, there were ebbs and flows to business relations with different branches of the government bureaucracy. Relationships that were generally strong and mutually beneficial in terms of trade policy in 1914, for example, had eroded by 1920.

Finally, focusing on the behavior of market-seeking industrialists rather than on their rhetoric brings to the fore the differences within their community. The managers of small manufacturing firms perceived of the domestic and international economies in ways quite different from those who ran the largest manufacturing enterprises, the "big businesses" of the early twentieth century, and therefore behaved quite differently.

A key word in this book is "context." In this study I examined the development of business-government relations in foreign trade expansion in terms of the economic context of the industries that sold abroad and the institutional setting of the bureaucracies that sought to help them.

Attention to a broad economic and bureaucratic context provides a fuller perspective on business-government relations than does a narrow study of the points at which business and government intersect. A consideration of the economic context—the impact on industry of technological change and market conditions such as changing demand abroad—allows one to assess the significance of governmental assistance to foreign trade expansion. Previous work on the subject has usually focused on the business-government relationship alone. In the years before and after World War I contact increased and businessmen had greater access to Congress and the federal departments. More contacts did not necessarily mean that the contacts were more significant to business efforts. To assess the significance of government, one has to understand the operations of the mass production, mass distribution corporations and the role of business trade associations that provided services to their members seeking to begin or increase sales abroad.[5]

The government bureaucracy that grew up to promote the expansion of American commerce was not created simply in response to business pressures. American economic expansion was part of a larger bureaucratic struggle. The Department of State sought constituencies to support the extension and professionalization of a bureaucracy charged with overseeing the more complicated and demanding foreign policy that followed from the Spanish-American War. More directly a response to the desires of the business community was the establishment of the Department of Commerce and Labor. This agency appealed to business for support and initially came into conflict with the Department of State.

Bureaucratic rivalries were complicated further by congressional politics. Both the Department of State and the Department of Commerce faced a Congress unwilling to fund either agency at a level thought suitable by departmental leaders in each bureaucracy. Congress was essential to the development of relations between business and the federal bureaucracy in other ways too. Bureaucrats seeking constituencies for the work of their departments supported businessmen trying to effect changes in laws that manufacturers found inimical to overseas business.

Specifically, then, my argument is that between 1893 and 1921 market-seeking American manufacturers were primarily divided into two groups. The first was made up for the most part of the largest manufacturing companies in the country. These firms had cost, technological, and managerial advantages that made their products competitive in foreign markets, especially in the European and Canadian economies, which were similar to America's in terms of income and demand structures. Many of the largest firms first sold overseas in the late nineteenth century in response to a perceptible demand for their products. Generally they did not need government assistance to develop foreign markets. In the face of hostility abroad and foreign governmental restrictions these firms adopted private strategies to meet adverse conditions. Rising foreign tariffs drove them to build assembly plants and, in some industries, even factories abroad. Nationalistic hostility to the American "invasion" in some overseas markets persuaded American firms to hire foreign nationals for their overseas sales networks. Nationalistic sentiment abroad induced producers to deal with foreign officials through foreign employees. There was good reason indeed not to call on American officials for help, since to do so was just as likely to worsen as to improve a dispute over local taxes, trademarks, patents, tariffs, and the like.

At the outbreak of World War I, the largest industrial corporations in the United States—firms like Westinghouse, United States Steel, International Harvester—accounted for over 80 percent of American manufactured exports. They needed to deal with the American government primarily to get Congress to change legislation that they found inimical to their interests. And it was through their desire to change antitrust laws as they applied to foreign trade, to remove restrictions on American banks opening foreign branches, and to improve the merchant marine that these firms became involved closely with Congress and the federal bureaucracy.

Smaller manufacturers, those without the technological, marketing, and capital advantages of "big business" were major supporters of government assistance in the development of foreign markets. During the depression of the 1890s many comparatively small producers of homogeneous standard goods sought foreign markets as an alternative to the depressed conditions in the American economy. Many of these men concluded, as did some business journalists and politicians, that the depression only exacerbated a long-standing problem of "overproduction." What producers meant was that the American industrial economy produced too many goods and that the prices they received failed to provide the desired profit, even if they covered costs. To many of the smaller manufacturers the answer to this problem was an expansion of foreign sales.

Smaller manufacturers turned to the government for assistance in making their way into foreign markets, and it was among such businessmen that the greatest support developed for close cooperation with federal officials. There were difficulties, however, in getting what they wanted from Congress by way of changed legislation. And there were also limits to how far businessmen were willing to go in return for allowing the executive branch to interfere in what they considered their private business affairs.

In a capitalistic economy like that of the United States in the late nineteenth century, growth and expansion were celebrated goals. Few journalists, politicians, or businessmen opposed foreign economic expansion in principle. The difficulty for the smaller businessmen, however, was that their specific proposals to aid foreign market expansion often prompted the sharp opposition of other groups threatened by such proposed changes. Thus, protectionist businessmen and politicians opposed alterations in the tariff. While there was general agreement on the importance of upgrading the merchant marine, farmers and small businessmen objected to subsidies to ship operators. Attempts to professionalize the consular service of the Department of State encountered strong opposition in Congress, for politicians saw the proposals as further erosion of the patronage system, a source of revenue and discipline for the party controlling the White House.

To gain their legislative objectives in Congress, smaller market-seeking businessmen formed trade associations. These groups varied from those created to deal with one issue, such as the American Reciprocity Tariff League, to those more broad-based groups that addressed many issues of concern to expansion-oriented producers, such as the National Association of Manufacturers (NAM). This latter group proved significant in other ways. Its publications alerted members to foreign trade opportunities and its foreign department furnished legal advice and translation services. The NAM rivaled, at least until World War I, the major efforts of the Department of State and the Department of Commerce and Labor in assisting manufacturers looking for overseas markets.

One of the legislative successes that the NAM and other business groups finally achieved in 1903 was the creation of a Department of Commerce and Labor (which was divided into two departments in 1913). Congress charged the department with the responsibility of furthering the interests of domestic *and* foreign commerce. From its inception the department's secretaries sought to assist market-seeking smaller producers. In terms of congressional relations it made more sense for the Department of Commerce to align politically with the numerous and vocal, if economically less significant, smaller manufacturers than with the larger, decidedly more unpopular corporations. Under President William Howard Taft's secretary of commerce, Charles Nagel, the department tried to work out a close, almost formal arrangement with the National Council of Commerce to foster overseas sales. Formal ties never developed, but the eventually aborted National Council led to the creation of a U.S. Chamber of Commerce, which was willing to work in Washington on a broad range of issues, some of which concerned smaller market-seeking manufacturers.

In creating the Department of Commerce and Labor in 1903, Congress established a bureaucratic rival to the Department of State. By the turn of the century, the State Department had worked assiduously to identify itself with the aspirations of smaller producers seeking to begin or to expand sales overseas. The Department of State, unlike the Department of Commerce and Labor or the Department of Agriculture, did not have a "natural" constituency. Departmental leaders needed the sympathetic assistance of market-seeking producers in the years after the Spanish-American War, when the department faced increased worldwide responsibilities. Business support was necessary in order for the department to argue successfully for professionalization (that is, minimizing the role of patronage in appointments) before a Congress, and especially a House of Representatives, that tended to reflect the general public indifference to foreign affairs. With the creation of the Department of Commerce and Labor, the State Department redoubled its efforts to win favorable business opinion and to provide services to market-seeking businessmen. Before World War I, however, the Department of Commerce intruded more on the State Department's preserves abroad while making friends within the business community at home.

Bureaucratic rivalry between the two departments nevertheless had some positive effects for trade expansion. Smaller manufacturers usually showed interest in foreign trade overseas during downswings of the business cycle.

When domestic orders picked up, many smaller businessmen turned their attention almost exclusively to increasing their orders at home. Invariably at these times, they lost interest in consular reform, a tariff commission, changes in the antitrust laws, foreign branch banking, and the other issues that agitated market-seeking manufacturers. The bureaucrats in the two departments, however, because of the competition between them, continued to improve services to businessmen and to advocate in Congress the legislative changes that the business community thought necessary.

In the early twentieth century the Department of Commerce undermined the Department of State's efforts to identify with the interests of market-seeking manufacturers. A particularly bruising congressional battle in 1909 forced the Department of State to abandon its Office of Foreign Trade Advisors. But the State Department's efforts were most seriously eclipsed by the work of Woodrow Wilson's secretary of commerce, William C. Redfield. It is with Redfield's leadership at the Commerce Department, between 1913 and 1917 especially, that the relations between industrialists selling overseas and an agency of government were closest. Unlike his predecessors, Redfield enlisted the support of the largest corporations in order to change policies inimical to foreign trade interests. His department continued to provide services and encouragement to the smaller producers, indeed these services were markedly expanded, but the centerpiece of Redfield's cooperative activities was the creation of the National Foreign Trade Council (NFTC). Made up of a deliberately small number of representatives of the largest corporations and banks interested in foreign business, the group cooperated with Redfield to modify the antitrust laws and improve the merchant marine. The NFTC in return supported the department before congressional committees considering its budgets. More significantly, Redfield saw the department's duty as bringing together the hitherto separated and at times hostile smaller and larger producers. Working through the Commerce Department, they would launch a common effort to build public and congressional support for the notion that foreign trade was important to the nation's well-being and to pass legislation necessary to promote foreign trade.

The close collaboration between the Department of Commerce and industrialists interested in promoting foreign trade did not last long. The United States' entry into World War I eroded Redfield's efforts. Before 1917 the secretary had been able to use the European war as a pretext to bring about changes in merchant marine and antitrust policies, but U.S. involvement meant that foreign trade interests were subordinated to larger war-related goals. Wilson removed control over wartime trade from the Department of Commerce and gave it to the newly created War Trade Board (WTB). Redfield cooperated with the board, but found himself having to calm his businesss associates angered by some WTB policies.

The war fragmented responsibilities for foreign trade issues among a number of government agencies, undermining efforts to centralize in the Commerce

Department the promotion of foreign trade. After the war Redfield's efforts to reintroduce coordination through the Department of Commerce failed, and in 1919 he left government frustrated. The Department of State tried to take over the coordination of foreign trade promotion, but the department had many other responsibilities in the postwar years, not least of which was in phasing out wartime agencies in the transition from war to peacetime governmental operations. For coordination, the State Department relied on a fairly low-level committee, since the members of its higher-level committee, the Central Foreign Trade Committee, were too busy with other matters to meet more than once.

The war had other effects. It changed the perspective of some businessmen about foreign trade. For the most part, smaller businessmen continued to view overseas sales as a matter of international competition for a fairly steady market that was to be divided up and won by the most competitive. But many of the larger producers, with significant direct investments abroad, as well as significant foreign sales, began to take a different view of the world market. Instead of concern about competing with German and British manufacturers, many of the larger producers realized that the United States had to help reconstruct the European economies. They also realized that the United States' new status as a major international creditor required more than ever before that we buy from our foreign competitors in order to continue to sell to them. The war thus widened again the gap between the larger and smaller producers that Redfield had tried to close. Many of the smaller producers continued to think in terms of sharp competition with foreign manufacturers, of prying open foreign markets while keeping the American market protected. The larger producers who, because of oligopolistic organization, had greater control of prices in domestic and overseas markets were less concerned with foreign competition. And they were also more inclined to support those concerned with rebuilding the European economies. The smaller producers looked upon Europe with less sympathy, seeing there instead not much more than the homeland of their competitors. The Wilson administration, for its part, was not inclined to become directly involved in reconstruction. Government officials such as Secretary of the Treasury Carter Glass preferred to leave reconstruction to the private sector. Generally the administration learned from the war to fear the politicization of international economic issues.

Thus, by 1921 relations between business and government in the promotion of foreign trade had once again become distant. Between 1914 and 1917, the Department of Commerce had coordinated fairly well the occasionally different foreign trade interests of the larger and smaller producers. Taking advantage of emergency conditions brought about by the war in Europe, Secretary Redfield succeeded in changing policy toward antitrust enforcement. He began to work on the merchant marine problem and pushed for further changes in banking legislation to complete the work on foreign branch banking first made possible by the Federal Reserve Act in 1913. But his efforts at coordination broke down during the war. Redfield could not reassert control after the conflict, and the Department of State was not able to put the coalition together again. Moreover, the gap between the perceptions and interests of large and small producers grew again after the war over issues related to tariffs and postwar reconstruction.

In the 1920s Secretary of Commerce Herbert Hoover expanded markedly Redfield's efforts to make the department serve the interests of businessmen selling abroad, but he also worked on other issues abroad, since he was more concerned with assuring ample supplies of raw materials for the United States. And, unlike Redfield, Hoover and the Department of Commerce questioned the wisdom of the U.S. government encouraging the expansion of branch factories abroad, an issue that Redfield had ignored. Leaders in Hoover's department thought that such branch factories took jobs away from U.S. workers.

On balance, then, this analysis questions the revisionist view of the political economy of foreign trade expansion which sees the relationship between manufacturers and government growing closer, as businessmen became more dependent on government for services and assistance. In fact, the largest producers, who accounted for the bulk of foreign sales of manufactured goods, achieved and maintained their markets overseas without significant federal assistance. And the scale of their operations required them to keep in their own hands, as much as possible, the marketing of their products, since mass production and mass distribution required a constant flow of goods. The smaller producers relied more heavily on government than the larger ones did. But even their increasing reliance upon government as their source for information and representation abroad had limits. At least until 1914, private trade associations, especially the NAM, gave closer, more personal attention than government to the day-to-day legal, translation, and shipping services that were essential to making sales. Indeed the expansion of the exports of American manufactured goods between 1893 and 1921 is remarkable more for the lack of close government cooperation than for closer ties between business and government in the making of these sales.

My analysis begins in chapter 1 with a broad overview of the place the United States held in the international economy, and with the changing importance of manufactured goods in American exports. In chapter 2, I discuss the impact of the depression of the 1890s on those larger manufacturers who had already begun to develop foreign markets and on the smaller producers who first seriously began to seek them in the nineties. Chapter 3 constitutes an investigation of the early twentieth century and the way in which the larger and smaller producers cultivated foreign markets then. Chapter 4 is an analysis of the difficulties producers experienced in their attempts to influence legislation, in this instance, tariff legislation. The frustrations in dealing with Congress prompted the bureaucracy to seek allies among businessmen, and chapter 5 changes the focus of the study to a consideration of the way in which trade expansion was part of the battle to bring about professionalization in the Department of State. In chapter 6, I trace contacts before 1912 between the Department of Commerce and Labor and the business community, especially the abortive efforts to create a formal relationship between the department and a representative council of businessmen. Chapter 7 focuses on the way in which Woodrow Wilson's secretary of commerce, William C. Redfield, built a coalition between the Department of Commerce and small and large producers. It also examines the frustration of his efforts once the United States entered World War I. Chapter 8 is an examination of the changes in the postwar situation, especially the erosion of the Department of Commerce's power and Redfield's inability to regain the central role in promoting foreign trade. It is also an analysis of significant changes in the attitude of some of the large producers on the way in which to pursue trade expansion in the postwar years. Chapter 9 is an epilogue that briefly traces developments in the 1920s and beyond, with attention to the dynamics of business-government relations in trade expansion.

I would like to refer to the intellectual debts incurred in my study of business, government, and foreign policy. While I am critical of the methods of analysis and the conclusions of many of the revisionist historians who have studied aspects of the political economy of trade expansion, I also appreciate the importance of the studies that they have produced. Over the last twenty years William Appleman Williams's work, in particular, has prompted a new perspective on American foreign policy making. Others like Burton I. Kaufman have opened up an entirely new understanding of the interrelationship between business organizations and government agencies charged with responsibility for foreign policy. While I criticize his analysis and conclusions, I admire the pioneering nature of the questions he posed. Other scholars who do not necessarily consider their work "revisionist" have influenced this study too. Robert Hume Werking's extended analysis of changes in the Department of State covered areas that I have researched myself. But his work suggested new sources to explore and provided insights that proved invaluable. Michael J. Hogan's study of the ideology and politics of "cooperative competition" helped clarify my thinking about business and government. The masterful work of Robert D. Cuff on the War Industries Board was a model study of business-government relations, showing in detail just how intricate the interrelations between business and government were. Cuff's work alerted me to the possibilities of a cyclical pattern to the contacts between businessmen and government agencies. I benefited too from conversations with Bob Cuff, whose knowledge of the years of World War I and after is in my experience unmatched. I am, of course, solely responsible for what follows.

Finally, this book is informed by the work of Max Weber and Talcott Parsons and by students of the foreign trade–product life cycle, especially Raymond Vernon and Louis T. Wells, Jr. Parsons's analysis of the interaction of social groups alerted me to the importance of looking beyond the points at which two social actors (business and government) intersect and to analyzing what impact the contacts had for the social actors' other goals and behavior. Vernon and Wells provide invaluable guides to the historian because, unlike many other economists theorizing about foreign trade, they viewed it dynamically over time.[6]

It is a pleasure to acknowledge the institutions and individuals who helped make this work possible. I received a research grant from the Eleutherian Mills Historical Library, which allowed me to travel to Wilmington to use the excellent collections of the library, especially its extensive records and publications of the National Association of Manufacturers. The University of Maryland Baltimore County generously provided me with summer grants that gave me the time for research and later for writing. The cooperative staff at the Manuscript Division at the Library of Congress proved most helpful for my work there. And at the National Archives I should like to take note of the assistance, knowledgeability and many kindnesses of the staff in the Industrial and Social Department. The staff at the UMBC Library proved a model of efficiency and helpfulness. Mrs. Laura Justus undertook to decipher and type parts of earlier drafts and Mrs. Eleanor Latini cheerfully came to my aid to prepare a draft of much of the manuscript at a critical stage in its development. And Mrs. Mary Dietrich typed the last draft with her usual cooperativeness and efficiency.

My broader intellectual debts are many. In particular I remember those to Professors John J. Reed and Katherine S. Van Eerde at Muhlenberg College. They introduced me for the first time to the rigors and pleasures of professional historical scholarship. At Johns Hopkins University I had the good fortune to study with two outstanding students of the modern United States, Alfred D. Chandler, Jr., and Louis P. Galambos. Alfred Chandler was a model to all who worked with him for his knowledge and industriousness. His many studies of the history of the large corporation in the United States quite simply have made this work possible. And Louis Galambos provided me with another equally attractive model of hard work and lively intelligence. His studies of trade associations and later of changing public attitudes toward big business significantly influenced this analysis too.

Finally, this book is dedicated to my wife Ruth Anne and to my daughters Megan and Lauren, who provided the loving atmosphere which makes such scholarly efforts as this possible and worthwhile.

One
American Manufactures and the World Market: An Overview

To analyze the sentiment for and efforts at promoting America's foreign trade, we need first to understand the international context of American industrial activity. "Economic theory tells us," economist Mary Eysenbach has observed, "that we must explain trade not by absolute changes in any country but by relative changes changing the conditions of comparative advantage." We will consider in this chapter some of the basic trends of American export activity in relation to total world trade, the behavior of the other leading industrial powers, American economic activity (GNP), the relative growth within industries of foreign trade activity, and the geographical direction of American trade abroad.

The broad changes outlined here form the context of America's trade expansion. These pre-1914 alterations determined the way in which manufacturers, politicians and federal officials understood their economic world, although they would not necessarily have described their knowledge in the language used here.[1]

The changing international economic role of the United States in the three decades before 1914 influenced the behavior of both businessmen and government officials. By 1914 manufacturers surpassed the export of American agricultural products and raw materials. The largest proportion of our manufactured exports were in industry groupings influenced by chemical technology (steel and petroleum) and mechanical technology (machines), and the industries with the highest levels of concentration had the highest proportions of exports. Once war began in earnest after 1914, trade routes and levels of export activity were disturbed, as American producers sent more and more supplies of war-related goods to the Allied countries in Europe. Levels of prewar world trade did not return until 1924, and, as we shall see, several patterns had altered slightly by then. During the war the level of world commerce declined drastically, as the British blockade of Germany profoundly influenced the character and direction of trade. Before the United States entered the war, however, U.S. foreign commerce increased dramatically, for U.S. producers replaced those of the warring powers.[2]

A few words about terminology and data are in order here. In discussing industrial changes, my terminology conforms to that established in the Bureau of the Budget's *Standard Industrial Classification Manual* (Washington, D.C., 1957). The Standard Industrial Classification (SIC) assigned the products of all

1

American manufacturers to 430 *industries*. For the sake of simplicity, however, the SIC divided the 430 industries into 21 *industrial groups*. In short, industries are made up of *firms* (the largest of which in fact make products assigned to more than one industry), and industrial groups are made up of industries. (Table 5 makes explicit use of this classification scheme, and Appendix B lists the 100 largest firms in 1909 and 1919 by the SIC industrial classes.)

There are, however, other industrial classification systems. The most important for this study is the one adopted by Mary Locke Eysenbach in *American Manufactured Exports, 1879-1914: A Study of Growth and Comparative Advantage*. Her data (used in Tables 4, 6, and 7) are based on a scheme developed by the U.S. Bureau of Labor Statistics (U.S. Department of Labor, "The 1947 Interindustry Relations Study, Industrial Classifications Manual," revised, mimeographed). Like the SIC of the Bureau of the Budget, Eysenbach's scheme assigns "minor" industries to more "major" industrial groupings. Appendix A lists the industries included in the industrial groupings in Tables 4, 6, and 7.

The United States became a major actor in the world's exchange of manufactures at a time of profound change in the international economy. To be sure, America's growing role in the international market, especially during and after World War I, contributed to alterations in international economic relationships. But American manufacturers began to sell abroad much later than those in Britain and Germany. American exporters of manufactured goods entered an international economic system that itself had matured well before the United States became significant in the international trade of manufactures. United States businessmen were not entirely new to the world's markets, however, since they had been significant exporters of agricultural products and raw materials before the American Revolution.[3]

American manufacturers began to sell significant quantities of goods in world markets only in the 1890s, and especially in the first ten years after the turn of the century. By that time, international trade, finance, and exchange relations were well established. America, however, was to have a significant impact. By 1900 the international implications of the domestic economic activities of the major industrial countries were more pervasive than they had been fifty years before. Although well-developed exchange markets existed before 1850 and although merchant bankers in many nations were engaged in far-flung economic activities, the pace of international economic activity, the pervasiveness of its influence on the economies of European nations, and the complexity of its transactions were much greater in 1900 than half a century before. For most of the nineteenth century international trade had been confined to fairly distinct commercial areas; countries bought where they sold. Transportation was a major determinant in these relationships, although political (i.e., colonial) relationships played a part in marking out channels of trade. The major trading areas were roughly Western and Central Europe, Russia and the Baltic, the North Atlantic, and India and the Far East. Trading accounts were for the most part generally balanced within each of these areas, as credits or bullion were transferred from one country to another. To be sure, as the nineteenth century passed, and transportation and communication improved, contacts increased between one group of traditional trading partners and another. But the pattern that dominated the early nineteenth century continued into the later decades. There was a remarkable adherence to traditional channels, even for such an important trading country as Great Britain.

The United States increased its export of manufactures at about the time that the barriers among the basic trading areas were increasingly breached. One of the major reasons for trade across traditional channels was simply the marked increase in the volume of goods exchanged. Between 1875 and 1914 trade expanded at a faster rate than in any other previous period. Central to this change was the industrialization of key countries like Britain, Germany, France, and Belgium. As production increased, these economies diversified, altering the structure of their demand for goods and raw materials. Industrialization led to a greater volume of trade among the major commercial areas. Britain especially no longer sought only to sell where she bought. As exports moved beyond her traditional lines and imports came from outside the channels established earlier in the century, Great Britain and the other major European countries found themselves settling accounts on a truly multilateral basis. By the end of the nineteenth century, debits and credits were posted easily and frequently on trade accounts among many different parts of the world. At the same time, an increased volume of capital and labor moved more easily in the international economy and outside the traditional trading and commercial areas. These movements of the factors of production led to rapid changes in the productive capacity of different countries. As a result, it was much more common late in the century than earlier that industries, and indeed at times entire sectors of an economy, were affected by changes in economies far from home.

The internationalization of labor, capital, and trade was accompanied by the growth of a number of commercial, banking, and exchange institutions to service, monitor, and control the complicated activities of international economic life.[4] Great Britain became the center of international economic activities with major international insurance firms and commercial and investment banking houses headquartered in London. Britain's dominance of the international economic life was tied closely to the key role of the London money market. By World War I, Great Britain was the largest exporter of capital, accounting for about one half of international investment. The other major capital exporters were France and Germany, although Belgium and the Netherlands had substantial holdings too. The greatest flow of investment funds occurred in the sixty years before World War I. The United State began to export capital in the 1890s. Even so, until World War I the United States continued to be a net importer of capital as more was invested here than Americans invested abroad. About 70 percent of American foreign investment in the years before the war was in Mexico (about 40 percent) and Canada (30 percent). About 47 percent of British foreign investment was in the empire in 1913, 20 percent in the United States, and 20 percent in Latin America, half of that in Argentina. European foreign investment in the nineteenth century was usually in the purchase of government securities. Britain, France, and Germany thus helped Russia and countries in Central and Southeastern Europe to build their economic infrastructures, since often governments invested foreign funds in railroads, roads, and telegraph.[5]

These investments had another effect on the functioning of the international economy. In producing substantial foreign earnings for Great Britain, they helped make London the financial center of the world. As the nation with the largest volume of trade, Great Britain earned enormous sums, although the balance on her trade account was usually adverse, since she imported more than she exported. The earnings on investments abroad, however, turned the adverse merchandise balance into a positive total balance of payments, providing a surplus. By World War I foreign earnings provided 20 percent of Britain's total foreign income. Thus, the returns from these investments insured that Britain would have a surplus on current account, enabling her to ride out the waves of change in international trade in merchandise. The relative stability of Britain's earnings position made British currency one of great strength and reliability. And since the British continued to invest funds abroad—as well as carry on a large trade—sterling was readily available in the world's trading centers.[6]

Sterling played a dominant role in the short-term financing of international trade. Britain's large trade and her dominance of international long-term investment made her the major international supplier of short-term capital. As the largest trading nation, Britain under any circumstances would have been a major factor in the financing of international trade. But over the nineteenth century, British financial institutions developed international services that solidified the country's role in the world economy. Early in the century, merchant bankers built up large businesses which specialized in handling or accepting bills of exchange drawn on foreign banks and merchant houses. These British firms became expert in handling foreign exchange. By the last third of the century, the London money market had become more specialized as bill brokers borrowed money from banks to buy and discount foreign exchange. This became a large business by the 1870s, since the British banking system had a growing pool of funds available to lend the bill brokers. Improved communications and transportation allowed their services to be widely dispersed with relative ease and at competitive costs. Sterling was a good international currency, in short, because of its reliability and availability.[7]

British business, banking, and government leaders worked hard to maintain the stability of the system that had developed. Far from flawless, the arrangements worked because of British skill and experience, as well as considerable luck. Britain maintained its dominance in international finance because governments and major businesses in the international system agreed that the stability of exchange rates was one of the chief responsibilities of short-term banking policy. Governments, large banks, and major business houses sought to maintain stable exchange relations. They avoided as best as they could the sudden changes in policy or arbitrary behavior that would upset the value of debts and the predictability of future returns. Currencies came to have a fairly standard rate of exchange, defined in terms of a fixed content of gold. Governments and banks regulated currency and credit to insure a balance around the par value of gold. The exchange mechanism was by no means automatic, but the development of central banking systems in most major countries before World War I, as well as the better organization of commodity markets, allowed for a greater degree of "self-regulating" equilibrium. The institutions in London—with the tacit or explicit cooperation of banking and business leaders in major countries— thus financed trade with a relatively stable and abundant sterling currency, pegged to other currencies in terms of their gold content.[8]

American manufacturers thus entered a growing international economy served by a well-organized capital and money market in London. Many American merchants were familiar with international economic transactions, since the United States had been an important supplier of agricultural products and raw materials. World trade in primary products was about 70 percent higher than that in manufactured products in the late 1870s. World trade grew in spurts, with the most variability occurring in the exchange of manufactures. From about 1885 to 1914 world primary product trade grew at a volume of an average 17 percent every five years. Manufacturing trade grew more fitfully. The 1890s, when America entered international trade in manufactures substantially, was overall a period of rather slow growth, although it was followed by a decade of rapid expansion of the commerce in manufactures.[9]

American producers began to sell abroad in a period of increasing flux. German industrialists had begun to challenge Britain's leading position in international markets for manufactures. The United States was much less a threat than Germany, as we shall see. As the Germans challenged British markets in Europe and Latin America, Britain's trade began to shift to encompass more markets in India, the Far East, Australia, New Zealand, and East and West Africa. Despite the changes in the direction of trade, Great Britain still had in 1914 the largest share of the world's visible trade. And visible trade did not include interest earned on foreign investment. Between 1911 and 1913, Britain accounted for 14 percent of the world's trade, larger than that of any other major country, although this represented a decline from 1881–85, when she had 19 percent. Britain still had the highest percentage of manufactured exports in 1913, although she had lost significant ground to Germany (table 1).

America began to sell in an international economy dominated by British finance and a rapidly growing role for industrial Germany. The patterns of American manufactured export trade that developed before 1914 continued into

Table 1   **Shares of World Trade in Manufactures**

	1883	1890	1899	1913
United States	3.4%	3.9%	9.8%	11.0%
United Kingdom	37.1	35.8	28.4	25.4
Germany	17.2	17.2	19.5	23.0
France	14.6	14.5	12.6	10.6
Belgium	4.8	5.1	4.9	4.3
Canada	0.1	0.1	0.3	0.6
Japan	0.1	0.3	1.3	2.1
Others	22.7	23.1	23.2	23.0

Source: Lewis, "International Competition in Manufactures," *American Economic Review* 47 (May 1957): 579.

the years after the war, although Great Britain's financial position was altered significantly. The Great War at first appeared only marginally to affect international economic relations. Some capital invested abroad appeared to be unrecoverable, at least during the hostilities. Sources of short-term capital to finance trade dried up and uncertainty in commercial matters discouraged business, even for those who had funds available. In fact, however, the changes wrought by the war were profound and long lasting. The international economic system built up in the five decades before World War I was never restored. Channels of trade were disrupted permanently, and the levels of international commerce declined, not recovering fully to the trade of 1913 until 1924. The belligerents abandoned the international gold standard during the war, making exchange relations after 1918 very uncertain. Channels of trade altered as the major trading nations divided into two armed camps. By 1918 British production that went into export was half what it had been in 1913. And of great significance to international finance, Great Britain could no longer provide the foreign investment capital that she had before the war. In terms of capital and trade the United States took up some of the British slack, although much of the United States' trade became war-related even before entry into the conflict. British and German markets disappeared during the war. Especially was this the case in Latin America before 1917, as North Americans responded to the demand for goods in South American markets formerly supplied by the belligerents. With U.S. involvement in the war, however, Latin American nations again found themselves hard pressed for supplies of manufactured goods.[10]

Following the war, the international trading and financial system was subjected to further shocks and dislocations. The institutions and arrangements that had sustained the prewar international economy, as a result, did not revive themselves. Most European industrial areas were not severely damaged during the war, but their internal financial, commercial, and currency systems were so disrupted that it took several years in almost every European country before production again approached prewar levels. After the war many of the European countries were in financial chaos. The abandonment of the gold standard destroyed the relatively stable exchange relations that it had brought about before the war. The tacit general understandings on sound banking policy were pushed aside before the pressure of wartime and postwar conditions. Inflation destroyed savings which limited the investment that once stimulated production abroad, and Great Britain lost the extra earnings that helped finance the entire system of trade. Inflation undermined short-term commercial obligations, as lenders simply had no idea what some currencies were going to be worth when in several months repayment was due. Production could not begin without capital, and governments could not balance their budgets and stabilize their currencies until production again provided the revenues for governmental finance. Inflation and the dislocation of traditional channels of trade upset internal price levels (in France and Italy among others) in relation to the exchange value of their currencies. Many of these countries, to put it simply, needed large imports, but they could not pay for them because levels of production were so low that they could not produce enough for profitable export. Hence, some of the former belligerents needed foreign (American) loans in order to purchase the imports they needed, especially for food immediately after the war. Apart from loans that had been used to finance the war, then, the United States had become a major creditor by 1922.[11]

The political decisions of the war further disturbed the international economic system. The reparations exacted from Germany were serious enough, but the failure to announce the exact figure of reparations until 1 May 1921, when the report of the Reparations Commission was due, only led to further uncertainty in international transactions. The revolution in Russia literally took Russia out of the international economy for several years, and in central Europe the new political divisions cut up the comparative economic unity of the Austro-Hungarian Empire.[12]

The United States had become the major producing country of the world, as well as the major financial power by the end of the war. Trade in manufactures was greatly influenced by all of these changes. Americans had the capital to invest in rebuilding their markets in Europe and the short- and long-term capital to strengthen their position further in former German and British markets, especially in Latin America.

World War I, to be sure, contributed greatly to America's growing predominance in the international market for manufactured goods. But the growing importance of American manufacturers was built on more than Europe's ill fortune in war. United States trade in manufactures had begun to grow steadily in the two decades before the war, especially in several key industrial sectors. America's strength was in the production of what might be called newer as opposed to traditional industrial products. American machinery, electrical equip-

Table 2	Value of Finished Manufactured Exports, 1893–1921 (at Current Prices)		
Year	Value (in millions)	Year	Value (in millions)
1893	$130	1908	$489
1894	136	1909	440
1895	144	1910	499
1896	182	1911	598
1897	213	1912	672
1898	223	1913	776
1899	263	1914	725
1900	332	1915	807
1901	318	1916	2,625
1902	322	1917	2,706
1903	327	1918	2,069
1904	349	1919	2,564
1905	402	1920	3,205
1906	460	1921	1,627
1907	481		

Source: U.S. Bureau of the Census, *Historical Statistics of the United States, from Colonial Times to 1957* (Washington, D.C., 1960), p. 544.

ment, and processed food products all led the advance into foreign markets. The traditional textile products that had characterized industrial development, especially in Britain, were not an important part of American manufactured exports. In 1913 textiles were only .07 percent of U.S. manufactured exports. Sales of machinery put the United States in more direct competition with the Germans than with the British, although both Britain and the United States exported the traditional industrial goods made of iron and steel.[13]

By the middle of the 1890s—at the depth of the depression—the value of finished manufactured exports increased sharply, by almost 21 percent, for example, between 1895 and 1896. The rapid rate of increase continued at a faster pace after 1900, but on the whole the 1890s had been a decade of sharply rising American manufactured exports. In 1900, the value of finished exports $332 million).[14] These changes were accompanied by alterations in the relationships between industry and government.

The 1890s were the years in which Britain increasingly began to react to the well-organized German commercial campaign to expand exports by coordinating the efforts of government, banks, and industries. The British responded to the growth of German exports by continuing to concentrate on those products that had made Great Britain the first industrial power, but in new markets. Britain continued to export the older, standard, more traditional products of industrialization: textiles and iron and steel products. She conceded to Germany exports of goods based on newer technology in machinery, electrical equipment and the fruits of scientific research in chemistry. The Germans increasingly gained European industrial markets and the British continued their domination of the less-developed world.[15]

American producers came upon the world scene at a time when the Germans and British were working out through the international market a fairly rational division of the sales of manufactured goods. The United States was in more direct competition with the Germans than the British, because our strengths in international trade were in the steel, machinery, and electrical industries that led the German advance. But the United States also carved out for itself new markets, especially in the sale of durable and nondurable consumer goods for mass urban markets. American producers became leaders in the export of packaged foods and medicines, cigarettes, matches, sewing machines, office equipment, and eventually automobiles.

Although businessmen and government officials often appeared to think that trade was static, in fact the Americans and Germans were competing for a growing world trade in manufactured goods. This is not to say, however, that other countries did not suffer losses because of the American and German advance. France and Great Britain, while their trade grew, ended up having a smaller overall percentage of world trade in manufactures (see table 1).

The significance of the United States' growing export trade in manufactures must be seen from several different perspectives. Manufactured exports during peacetime were only a small part of total domestic output of manufactures, never achieving between 1879 and 1914 more than 6.6 percent.[16] This comparatively small proportion of domestic output of manufactured products helps to explain some of the difficulties promoters encountered in the efforts to expand foreign trade. Since exports did not directly affect large numbers of businessmen, market-seeking producers were hard pressed to convince a majority of the business community of the importance of what they advocated. But within particular industries and within the growing international economy, American export expansion was of greater significance.

America's role in the world industrial economy was the result of both domestic and international circumstances. In the course of structural change in the domestic economy, the increasing importance of industrial production, industries well suited to foreign selling were created. In 1860 over two-thirds of American exports were crude foodstuffs and raw materials. In the 1870s, a noticeable shift began as these materials dropped to 52 percent by 1872. By 1913 raw materials represented 42 percent of exports and manufactured exports made up a much greater proportion of American exports (35 percent) than in 1872 (.08 percent). Among industrial products, manufacturers of processed (manufactured) food, metals, and machinery predominated, accounting for 69 percent of American manufactured exports.[17]

Table 3	Exports of the United States (in millions of dollars at current prices)		
United States	**1872**	**1900**	**1913**
Food, drink, tobacco[a]	$187	$568	$ 513
Raw materials	250	542	1031
Metals manufactures	5	139	348
Machinery	7	72	186
Transport	3	15	64
Chemicals	11	35	69
Textiles	4	27	76
Others	13	55	149
Total	**479**	**1453**	**2435**

Source: Mary Locke Eysenbach, *American Manufactured Exports, 1879–1914: A Study of Growth and Comparative Advantage* (New York, 1976), p. 40.

[a]Includes unprocessed, as well as processed, food exports. Between 1900 and 1914 approximately one-half of "food, drink, tobacco" was processed food products (see table 4).

The average value of American exports between 1875 and 1880 had been approximately $664 million per year. Between 1909 and 1914 the average had risen to $2.131 billion. This change represented an increase in real value since average prices of all American exports were roughly equal in 1879 and 1914. The growing importance of finished manufactures in exports was not the result of price increases either. These changes represented increases in volume since the prices of finished manufactures were declining while those of crude foods, raw materials, manufactured foods, and semimanufactures were increasing.[18]

American products' growing importance in international markets was not simply a matter of growing supplies. Expanding industrial economies, especially in Europe, created a demand for many of America's goods.[19] The growth of U.S. trade and the shifts in its composition occurred in the context of a rapidly growing volume of exports from the industrial countries which accounted for 90 percent of world exports in manufactures. The United States, however, was not the world's major exporter, as we have seen, in terms of the percentage of world trade in manufactures. American production grew rapidly, giving rise to some concern in other industrial nations. But much of America's manufactured exports were in industrial groups that represented the fastest growing areas of the manufactured trade of the industrial countries. Between 1900 and 1913 total world trade in metals manufactures increased 91 percent, machinery 106 percent, and transport 126 percent. There were not significant increases in the U.S. share of world exports of these products. Transport had the greatest growth: in 1900 it was 14 percent of the total, whereas in 1913 it was 20 percent. Metals were 23 percent in 1900 and 25 percent in 1913; machinery actually declined from 27 percent in 1900 to 25 percent in 1913.[20] The magnitude of the change in the fastest growing areas of the world manufactured trade should caution historians against relying too heavily on expressions of European concern about the U.S. export "invasion." The rate of change of American exports as a part of world exports of these goods was not so rapid as the general increase in trade in these classes of goods.

The United States was, nevertheless, a formidable international economic entity. American industrialization had been so rapid in the late nineteenth century that the United States had become the leading industrial producer by 1913, alone accounting for one-third of the world's industrial production. As an overall percentage, however, American exports were less important a proportion of overall domestic output than in the European countries which with smaller economies had a higher percentage of trade in manufacturers entering into the international economy as exports. Between 1879 and 1914, 4.5 to 6.6 percent of American manufactured output was exported.[21]

Despite a fairly small and comparatively constant share of manufactured output exported (approximately 5.75 percent between 1879 and 1914), there were significant variations in industry groups. Between 1879 and 1914, a growing domestic economy took up a larger proportion of an increasing output in petroleum and manufactured foods, and exports declined as a percentage of domestic output. In 1914 petroleum and coal exports accounted for over 27 percent of total production in the industry, although that percentage had declined substantially from the 67 percent of 1879. Similarly, exports of manufactured food declined from 14.5 to 6.1 percent of total output between 1879 and 1914. In contrast, exports in the iron and steel and machinery industries more than doubled as a percentage of domestic output, and in transport exports tripled. But in none of these three expanding export industry groups—whose products accounted for more than 25 percent of all American manufactured exports—did exports represent more than 9 percent of total domestic output in 1914.[22]

At the same time that American producers expanded abroad, many industries were supplying more of the home market for manufactures, although on balance the United States continued to import more finished manufactures than it exported until 1898. Imports of manufactured goods, as a percentage of manufactured products consumed, fell from 14.0 to 5.9 percent between 1869 and 1909. To state it another way, the rate of growth of manufactured exports increased faster than the rate for manufactured imports. America imported most of its manufactured goods from Europe. Between 1905 and 1909, the value of American exports averaged $157 million and between 1910 and 1914, $209 million, an increase of 33 percent. For the same periods the value of imported finished manufactures increased from $255 to $309 million, an increase of 21 percent.[23] In some industries, however, the United States continued to import more than it exported. This was particularly noticeable in the textile

Table 4	Exports and Imports by Industry Group (at current prices)		
Industry Group[a]	1879[b]	1899	1914
Textiles	$ 13,864,200	$ 26,068,900	$ 74,653,000
	89,530,000	*107,058,000*	*249,430,000*
Chemicals	27,219,300	64,127,100	108,051,300
	21,277,000	*35,738,000*	*120,026,000*
Petroleum and coal	38,122,700	58,606,500	156,058,000
	21,000	*363,000*	*2,763,000*
Manufactured food	157,993,800	271,425,500	255,708,000
	83,926,000	*109,940,000*	*189,516,000*
Iron and steel	7,821,200	49,696,600	120,055,000
	18,467,000	*9,165,000*	*23,180,000*
Machinery	8,652,300	52,830,000	172,826,100
	550,000	*1,636,000*	*10,184,000*
Transport	1,968,600	14,654,500	56,331,600
			2,201,000

Source: Mary Locke Eysenbach, *American Manufactured Exports, 1879–1914: A Study of Growth and Comparative Advantage* (New York, 1976), pp. 271–75.

Note: Exports are shown in roman type, imports in italic.

[a]See Appendix A for the industries making up these groups.
[b]Fiscal year, for each year period.

industries (see table 4). Even though in 1914 exports of most manufacturing industries were not over 19 percent of domestic output, there was significant growth in dollar terms as the American economy continued to expand.

As striking as the growth of American manufactured exports, was the fact that the largest manufacturing firms dominated most of the industry groups that accounted for the largest share of American manufactured exports before World War I. Of the 100 largest manufacturing firms in 1909, 16 were in the manufacture of food, drink, and tobacco and almost 25 percent were in metals manufacture, which accounted for 23 of the 100 largest firms (see table 5). The textile industry was the only one with substantial exports but without an equally substantial percentage of the 100 largest manufacturing corporations. The three industry groups that accounted for 69 percent of manufactured exports in 1913 (food, drink, tobacco; metals manufacture; machinery) were made up of 48 of the 100 largest corporations, as determined by assets in 1909. If we add to that the firms in the other industrial groups that accounted for the bulk of American exports of manufactures (petroleum, textiles, chemicals, transport), we have another 19 of the largest 100 firms, for a total of 67 firms.

Table 5	Numbers of 100 Largest Firms in Industrial Groups Leading in Manufactured Exports	
Industry Group	**1909**	**1919**
Metals manufacture	23	24
Machinery (incl. electrical)	9	8
Transport	5	9
Chemicals	5	6
Textiles	1	1
Food, drink, tobacco	16	16
Petroleum	8	19

Sources: Alfred D. Chandler, Jr., "The Structure of American Industry in the Twentieth Century: An Historical Overview," *Business History Review* 43 (Autumn 1969): 291–93, and A. D. H. Kaplan, *Big Enterprise in a Competitive System* (rev. ed.; Washington, D.C., 1964), pp. 140–42.

Or to put it another way, 81 percent of manufactured exports in 1913 (see table 3) came from industry groups made up of 67 of the 100 largest industrial corporations in the United States in 1909.

Equally important was the fact that the industry groups that dominated manufactured exports were for the most part made up of industries in which there was a comparatively high level of concentration. Concentration is defined in terms of the percentage of the market controlled by a certain number of firms in an industry. An industry can be defined as "concentrated" (or oligopolistic) when up to 6 firms in an industry contributed 50 percent of the total product value or when up to 12 firms contributed 75 percent of the total product value. In 1909, the first year that adequate data have been compiled on concentration, in the industrial group machinery (excluding, for the moment, electrical machinery) 16 percent of the total product was produced by oligopolistic industries. The electrical machinery group contained 3 industries, 2 of which were oligopolistic; the 2 industries accounted for 68 percent of product value of the group. In the 8 industries of the transportation group, 2 were oligopolistic, and they accounted for 9 percent of the total product of that industry group. Primary metal industries contained 18 industries, of which 6 were oligopolistic, accounting for 35 percent of production value. In the industry group, "food and like products," there were 9 oligopolistic industries out of 30, and the oligopolies produced 24 percent of the group's total product value. Tobacco manufacturers' group was made up of one oligopolistic industry which accounted for 75 percent of production in the group. Chemicals' 25 industries had 8 oligopolies, which represented 9 percent of total production. It is important to note than in 9 of the 20 standard industry groups (as classified in the Standard Industrial Classification of the Bureau of the Budget's 1957 Manual) oligopolistic industries

13

accounted for 2 percent or less of total product value. Textiles were among the least concentrated industry groups; there were 6 oligopolies in 17 industries, but the oligopolists accounted for less than 1 percent of the product value of the industrial group.

In sum manufactured exports grew fastest in those industry groups made up of industries with the highest number of the 100 largest firms. Moreover, these industry groups contained industries with the highest percentages of output controlled by oligopolistic firms. To put it simply, "big business" dominated the industry groups with the largest percentages of manufactured exports. Only textiles, which represented 7 percent of manufactured exports in 1913, did not have industries in which oligopolies produced more than 2 percent of industry output. And only textiles had only one firm with assets to put it among the 100 largest manufacturing corporations.[24]

In 1919, the same major groups dominated American manufactured exports. And these groups included by then a larger number of the 100 largest firms (see table 5). Whereas in 1909 there were 67 of the 100 largest firms, in 1919 there were 83. Another important indication of the continued strength of the largest 100 firms was the increasing number of product lines these companies produced. In 1909 the largest firms in manufactured export produced 204 product lines; in 1919 the number was 259.[25]

The twenty years before 1913 witnessed not only changes in the composition of American export trade, but also the establishment of patterns in its direction. American export of manufactures was overwhelmingly directed toward Canada, Western Europe, and to a lesser extent Mexico (see table 6). American trade flowed to Western Europe because the European industrial economies had demand and income structures similar to our own. Europeans needed the machinery, metals, and transport equipment that we made. Because they had income structures similar to ours, they were able to purchase our products in large quantities. Canada and Mexico became important markets for the United States because their proximity cut transportation costs, making American goods competitive with similar European products.

By 1913, the basic patterns of American trade were established. These broad patterns formed the economic circumstances around which business and government came into closer contact over trade policy. Basic relationships, interests, and attitudes had developed by 1913, as we shall explore in greater detail in later chapters, among firms, trade associations, and bureaucracies interested in foreign trade.

World War I brought about a dramatic change in the value of American exports. It also disturbed the directions of trade, especially after 1917, when the United States entered the war. After the conflict, Germany and Britain took time to recover and so it was not until the mid 1920s (1924-25) that prewar trade patterns had returned. Asia, Africa, and South America had increased slightly in importance, although Europe and North America were still over-whelmingly the major areas to which the United States exported (see table 7).

The basic pattern of American manufactured trade had been established by 1913. In the 1890s and early 1900s businessmen's fundamental attitudes toward the export trade had developed determining what they expected by way of government assistance. By the time Europe went to war in 1914, moreover, institutional relationships among manufacturers, trade associations, and officials in the key Departments of Commerce and State bureaucracies had matured. The war and postwar period of readjustment tested these institutional arrangements.

Many scholars have argued that the depression between 1893 and 1897 was a critical turning point in America's relationship to the world economy. These troubled years were, as we shall see in the next chapter, important in that they stimulated great interest in foreign trade among small manufacturers. But in fact exports grew more rapidly after the depression than before and, again as we shall see in later chapters, important attitudes toward government and links with it developed after the turn of the century until World War I. To be sure, prices began to increase and this might explain the dollar growth after the turn of the century. But if we compare export quantities for products where data is available, a similar conclusion is warranted.[26]

The explanation for these changes is twofold. First, the industrial economies of Europe and Japan and the semi-industrial economy in Canada began a period of rapid economic expansion in the late 1890s. Railroads and suburban rail lines were added to existing networks; there was a burst of construction of bridges, roads, office buildings, factories, and warehouses; electricity was brought to cities; municipalities built sewer and water systems; telephone and telegraph wires spread across continents; and automobiles began to appear in increasing numbers.[27] At the same time, navies and armies grew, enlarging demand for armor-plated ships and guns. The demand created by all these changes, especially for capital goods, created opportunities for American producers of iron, steel, machinery, transportation vehicles, and electrical equipment. Furthermore, per capita income increased at the same time as urban and industrial populations increased in the major European countries.[28] The growth of city populations created potential markets for American consumer goods designed for the growing urban markets at home. The strength of American industries entry into the European and Canadian markets was related to the fact that marketing itself became one of the most indispensable skills for the makers of both producers' and consumers' goods. Many American manufacturers had great advantages because they dominated the American market by their marketing skills. The most dynamic of the consumer goods industries were those that developed in response to growing urbanization: cigarettes, processed food, bathroom (plumbing) fixtures. The marketing skills that had developed the significant markets for processed foods and cigarettes in the United States were transferred to the

15

Table 6	Exports by Region (at current prices)		
Industry Group			
Europe	**1879**	**1899**	**1914**
Textiles	$ 4,312,800	$ 2,192,100	$ 16,384,700
Chemicals	21,552,700	49,602,000	63,035,600
Coal and petroleum	29,467,500	40,319,700	83,070,000
Manufactured food	125,895,300	224,218,200	173,246,200
Iron and steel	1,345,800	17,136,700	19,876,900
Machinery	3,981,300	29,847,900	68,015,400
Transport	412,400	6,177,900	14,477,800
South America	**1879**	**1899**	**1914**
Textiles	$ 2,425,200	$ 3,556,400	$ 6,104,900
Chemicals	1,465,300	2,766,300	10,610,200
Coal and petroleum	1,142,600	3,400,800	18,208,500
Manufactured food	9,419,700	9,340,800	11,032,200
Iron and steel	1,399,700	3,770,200	17,990,200
Machinery	1,297,300	4,190,300	21,845,000
Transport	268,000	1,321,800	7,121,200
Oceania	**1879**	**1899**	**1914**
Textiles	$ 417,200	$ 1,138,900	$ 9,444,700
Chemicals	478,200	2,170,000	5,354,400
Coal and petroleum	492,600	2,005,600	8,513,200
Manufactured food	888,100	2,453,100	5,238,900
Iron and steel	1,286,500	5,017,000	12,205,700
Machinery	1,335,000	4,167,000	10,882,900
Transport	677,600	823,700	6,332,800

Source: Mary Locke Eysenbach, *American Manufactured Exports, 1879–1914: A Study of Growth and Comparative Advantage* (New York, 1976), pp. 276–82.

growing European urban economies. And, as W. Arthur Lewis observed in an analysis of international competition in manufactures:

> Every successful drive for trade in manufactures contains five elements: keen prices, a flood of salesmen, large-scale organization of selling, attention to customers' wishes, and liberal credit. Econometricians usually put all the emphasis on the first element, prices, because this is easiest to measure. Businessmen, however, usually attribute much greater importance to sales effort, and it is clear enough that success or failure in selling is not always attributable to prices.[29]

But the explanation for the continued growth of exports during and after

Industry Group			
North America	**1879**	**1899**	**1914**
Textiles	$ 3,955,400	$ 7,263,700	$ 32,208,500
Chemicals	2,428,500	8,043,600	25,967,400
Coal and petroleum	817,800	2,612,200	17,415,200
Manufactured food	19,297,800	25,894,000	53,433,000
Iron and steel	3,447,400	18,337,200	73,969,500
Machinery	1,820,800	10,804,500	48,321,800
Transport	482,000	3,096,500	23,539,300
Asia	**1879**	**1899**	**1914**
Textiles	$ 1,832,700	$ 11,435,300	$ 9,451,100
Chemicals	1,183,300	714,200	2,079,100
Coal and petroleum	5,419,300	8,936,000	22,560,900
Manufactured food	2,119,300	6,104,400	10,545,500
Iron and steel	188,000	4,415,200	10,177,600
Machinery	59,300	1,554,000	9,291,600
Transport	17,000	2,617,400	2,480,200
Africa	**1879**	**1899**	**1914**
Textiles	$ 938,900	$ 484,400	$ 1,060,600
Chemicals	111,300	829,900	952,700
Coal and petroleum	783,400	1,333,900	6,289,500
Manufactured food	512,500	2,397,900	1,591,300
Iron and steel	153,800	2,601,800	2,727,300
Machinery	140,900	1,533,400	4,820,200
Transport	111,600	617,900	2,378,800

the depression of the 1890s also rests, secondly, on changes within the domestic economy itself, in the supply of goods. As we have seen, the industries with the largest exports of manufactured goods had some of the highest levels of concentration. In industry after industry producers concentrated their efforts. Indeed, the period 1898-1901 saw the largest number of mergers in American history to that time. When the process was capped at the turn of the century with the formation of the U.S. Steel Company in 1901—the first billion-dollar corporation—American industry was concentrated as it had never been before. In the iron and steel industry, among the makers of electrical equipment, oil, chemicals, and processed foods, the 1890s were a period of increasing concentration. By World War I, as we have seen, many of the industries within these broader groups

17

Table 7	Percent of American Finished Manufactured Exports by Region (in millions)	
Region	**1910–14**	**1925[a]**
N. America	$241 (37%)	$587 (32%)
S. America	83 (13%)	291 (16%)
Europe	209 (32%)	525 (28%)
Asia and Oceania	106 (16%)	371 (20%)
Africa	16 (02%)	69 (04%)
Total	**$655**	**$1843**

Source: U.S. Department of Commerce, *Statistical Abstract of the United States for 1925* (Washington, D.C., 1926), pp. 449, 460.

[a]These values are in part a reflection of the 31 percent increase in prices between 1913 and 1925. The inflation, however, does not affect the calculation of percentages for the year 1925.

had become oligopolistic. Competition among these producers was based more on style, service, and advertising than price. The major firms had more control over pricing and production than the more numerous producers that many of these larger firms absorbed or superceded. The scale and complexity of operations, the volume and velocity of sales in many of these industries created significant barriers to entry and hence limited the possibility of new competition. In other industries, the depression of the 1890s provided producers with an opportunity to expand domestic facilities. Since prices and labor costs were low, it was a good time to expand vertically into marketing and into the control of raw materials if a firm was basically profitable. Many of these expanded firms had had foreign markets by the beginning of the depression of the 1890s. Producers of electrical equipment, transportation vehicles, agricultural machinery, elevators, and oil products had begun to sell abroad as early as the 1880s. For them, the 1890s opened up the possibility of more sales. The expansion of the late 1890s after the depression made such sales even more likely since they had strengthened their control within American industry and were confronted with opportunities by the growth of foreign economies. Using for the most part the retained earnings from a more concentrated industry and more prosperous period of growth at home, many of these producers were ready by 1900 to expand abroad even more aggressively than they had been in the depression.

Not every industry in the 1890s, however, experienced such vast changes. In the important machine tool industry—producers of these products were essential to industrialization—the highly specialized output of the manufacturers found ready markets abroad, but the firms remained small and did not for the most part engage in extensive marketing on their own. They found, however, ready

18

demand abroad, as did producers of products with special qualities of style. American hand tool makers, for example, developed a reputation for the durability and design of their goods. The same was true of ornamental builders' hardware—products which gained a reputation for the lightness of manufacture but also the attractiveness of their design. Makers of specialized instruments and scientific glassware also found ready markets for their output.[30]

Not all producers were able, however, to build foreign sales that lasted beyond the decline of American prices in the 1890s. Producers of lumber, leather, pottery, all found their overseas sales declining after the increase of prices in the domestic market. All of these manufacturers produced relatively standard industrial products, the output of labor-intensive manufacturing, with little opportunity to reduce costs substantially. Many of the firms in these industries abandoned foreign markets once prices improved in the domestic economy.

In summary, manufactured exports remained strong after the depression of the 1890s where the industry became concentrated and where, of more importance, firms integrated vertically to create their own marketing systems or improve marketing structures already in existence. Regular sales abroad, that is, sales beyond the depression of the 1890s, were also possible in industries in which Americans produced highly specialized products that had either before or during the depression begun to achieve recognition and popularity in foreign markets. Producers of the more traditional undifferentiated manufactures found sales dropping off once prices improved in the domestic market. Foreign sales became unlikely at prevailing prices, and indeed many of these producers found themselves having difficulty keeping up with burgeoning domestic orders.[31]

The depression of the 1890s, nevertheless, focused attention on foreign sales. And it was in response to the depression that some manufacturers began to think of the need to seek government assistance to help them expand their foreign sales. At the same time, the years of depression strengthened the advantages of other producers, making it possible for them to expand further their sales after the return of prosperity. Thus, the 1890s, to which we now turn, set out patterns of economic activity which influenced the attitudes of businessmen and government officials toward the world market, forcing some businessmen to examine the role that the United States government did and should play in the expansion of American trade.

Two

Depression and Foreign Trade in the 1890s

The depression of the 1890s stimulated an interest in overseas trade among a number of producers who had never before sought foreign sales. Businessmen's concerns were increasingly reflected in the statements of public officials, some of whom believed that government should help industrialists find markets abroad. Yet by the time the depression began in 1893, a pattern had already been set in American manufactured exports, a pattern that was to be firmly established by World War I. By the end of the depression of the 1890s, American manufactured exports were dominated by producers of a relatively few classes of goods—machinery, processed foods, oil, and metal products. The makers of these products had developed foreign sales before the depression of the 1890s, and their sales were more the result of substantial competitive advantages than of a need to solve short-run problems of production in excess of demand at prevailing prices in the depression of the 1890s. The firms in these industries had created overseas markets by producing new products (typewriters and cigarettes) or selling traditional products (meat and grains) in new packaged or processed forms. The firms making such products had substantial competitive advantages to exploit abroad. By mass production and mass distribution they had so well placed themselves in the national and then international markets that the entry of significant competitors into their industries was almost impossible. Many' of these advantaged firms found the 1890s to be a period of opportunity, a time to make the most of low costs and wages to build new plants and acquire new equipment. By the turn of the century, then, they were stronger than ever before. The depression also allowed firms in other industries (most notably steel and the fabricated products of iron and steel) to sell abroad for the first time as their products became more competitive in world markets. These large firms established their place in international trade well before the U.S. government took much interest in promoting expansion.

The depression of the 1890s, however, stimulated an interest in trade expansion among a large number of smaller firms that did not have the advantages of the mass production, mass distribution enterprises. The managers of these less advantaged firms believed that cooperative efforts among businessmen and assistance from government were required to make sales in world markets. These producers were never important economically in terms of the percentages of their foreign sales of manufactured goods. They were, however, numerous,

20

increasingly well-organized, vocal, and therefore effective in finding support within the Congress and the federal bureaucracy for policies to expand trade.

By the end of the 1890s, an effort began among businessmen organized into trade associations, especially the National Association of Manufacturers, to induce government to change the consular service, the tariff and policy toward the merchant marine in order to help businessmen without substantial competitive advantages to develop foreign markets. Unusually low prices in the United States in the 1890s had made possible foreign sales for producers who had not had them before. To many of these less-advantaged producers, export markets seemed to be the solution to the problems of temporary or long-term excess capacity, or a surplus. At the turn of the century, then, there were basically two experiences in world markets for American manufacturers: that of producers with substantial competitive advantages in terms of price, technology, and marketing and that of producers who might manufacture a large quantity of a product, but who had few if any long-term advantages to exploit abroad.

In the 1870s and 1880s mass production led to a substantial reduction in costs of production. The use of machines increased output and reduced costs in a number of industries producing standard goods: cloth, leather, and wood and products made from these materials. But maximum production from the application of these machines was quickly reached, since basically the machines replaced manual labor that shaped or cut wood, cloth, and leather. But in some industries machinery did more than replace labor. Machines also integrated processes and allowed for the development of continuous-process factories. Mass production occurred when by organization of factory and work force, and the application of technology, a vastly increased volume of output was possible. Because of organization for continuous-process manufacturing, the output at each stage of manufacture was greater than if these processes were carried on separately. In industries where technological and organizational innovations created a continuous-process manufacture, there was the greatest growth of output. These industries were able to produce one unit of output with a decreasing number of workers, as the ratio of capital, energy, materials, and managers to labor increased. In mining, basic agriculture, construction, and in the making of cloth, leather, and wood products, mass production was not possible. These activities did not lend themselves to the organization that made continuous-process, high-volume production possible. Continuous-process machinery and procedures led to an enormous increase in the output of cigarettes, products made from grain, canned foods, soaps, and film. In these various industries sharp increases in production were accompanied by a decrease in size of the work force required per unit of output.

Mass production was readily developed as well in the furnace, foundry, distilling and oil refining industries. In these industries where chemical processes were as important as mechanical, an intensified use of energy, improved technology, and greater attention to the organization of production yielded rapid increases of output per worker. In products made from petroleum, sugar, animal fats, and vegetable fats greater capacity in stills, superheated steam, and improved cracking techniques promoted the development of a high-volume production. Similarly, output in large batches was possible in the production of some chemicals and in the distilling of alcohol and the brewing of beer. In industries which used furnaces to produce iron, steel, copper, and other metals and glass, improved use of technology and organization of work brought a marked increase in output per worker. In all of these industries, what distinguished production was not only increased volume, but the increased speed at which products could be turned out. In metalworking industries, the application of improved machine tools to very complicated processes led to significant increases in output too. Mass production, therefore, brought about increased economies as much as by the speed and continuity of operations as by their scale. Innovators developed new machinery, improved the quality of raw materials, applied nonhuman energy more intensively to production, and developed an increasingly professional management to plan, coordinate, and monitor the processes from initial use of raw material to final product.[1]

The conditions that prompted these major changes in industry did *not* occur widely in the American economy. But where the conditions were right and where there were entrepreneurs and managers capable of making use of new technologies, the advantages brought to firms that adopted these new procedures were significant. A firm that adopted mass production or continuous-process, large-volume techniques produced a larger output at lower cost than competitors with perhaps larger facilities. And when these cost advantages were combined with similar achievements in marketing, such as mass distribution, manufacturers who mass produced and mass distributed their goods were for the most part the producers who dominated the American market for their products and also increasingly enlarged their share of world sales.

"Big business," the popular term for many of the firms combining mass production with mass distribution, developed other advantages too. When production was combined with control over raw materials, that is, vertical integration, an enterprise improved its competitive position. By bringing together raw or semifinished materials, manufacturing them, and then marketing products to the ultimate consumer, big business gained substantial advantages. Such enterprises could better coordinate supply with demand and they could plan the use of their work force and capital more efficiently than firms making a number of transactions in the labor, materials, and capital markets. Big business had lower unit costs because middlemen transaction costs were reduced. Moreover, because big businesses often had their own sales agents, they were able to reduce information costs about market conditions and consumer demand.

Big businesses had other advantages. A high cash flow generated by mass sales enabled them to finance their own expansion, providing their own working and fixed capital. The big businesses that grew in the 1880s tended to build their marketing operations from within one firm. In the depression of the 1890s another strategy developed, as firms merged and then integrated forward into sales and backward into control of raw materials. Those who succeeded in the 1880s and 1890s were also building managerial structures to coordinate, oversee, and assess the workings of their corporations. Thus, when the depression began in 1893, a number of firms that would dominate American manufactured exports at the time of World War I were already established in powerful positions in the domestic and international economy.[2]

Mass production began first to appear in industries processing agricultural products late in the 1870s and 1880s. The cigarette industry was one of the first to apply machinery to continuous-process manufacture. By the late 1880s one machine in one day could turn out 40 times as many cigarettes as the most skillful hand worker. The machine totally integrated the process of making a cigarette: assembling the tobacco and then shaping, rolling, pasting, and cutting the cigarette. Costs were further reduced in the 1880s, when among others James B. Duke developed machines to make boxes and put cigarettes in them. By the end of the decade, Duke's company dominated the American cigarette industry, since he was the first in America to use the new machinery aggressively. His machines' large volume of output impelled him to develop new marketing techniques. Wholesalers and jobbers were not capable of selling quickly the higher volume of cigarettes that he produced, and he needed to convince consumers to smoke cigarettes. Duke began in the mid-1880s to create a nationwide marketing system. He hired salaried agents in major cities to supervise salesmen who called on wholesalers and retailers in an effort to sell Duke's products. Duke also expected the sales manager to place local advertising to create a demand for the new product. In 1885, at the time he built a major New York factory, he sent a close associate abroad to develop contacts for foreign sales. As his sales system was established in the United States, he began to make agreements with foreign jobbers and wholesalers to sell his products abroad. By 1889, Duke's company dominated the American market and had substantial international sales. Duke enhanced his position at home and overseas when he and his four American competitors merged in 1890 to form the American Tobacco Company. The firm maintained high profits during the depression of the 1890s, being one of the most successful of the early mass production, mass distribution enterprises.[3]

Machines like those used by Duke appeared in other industries. In the manufacture of matches, four producers combined in 1881 to make a machine that produced and boxed matches, an achievement that gave the Diamond Match Company a dominant position in both American and international markets almost immediately. The Diamond Match Company took on its own distribution of the billions of matches produced because of the new machinery. The firm coordinated the flow of its product by a sales organization much like

23

Duke's, responsible for dealing with jobbers and larger retailers. The sales organization also coordinated advertising and foreign sales. The inexpensive production in the United States made the manufacturer a formidable competitor abroad, and to take even more advantage of low-cost production, in the 1890s Diamond Match built factories in Germany, Canada, Peru, Brazil, and England (near Liverpool, they built the largest match factory in the world). Despite the depression of the 1890s, Diamond Match continued to pay high profits and was able to consolidate plants at home and expand abroad.[4] Similar developments occurred elsewhere. In the 1880s and 1890s George Eastman invented and then perfected a continuous-process procedure for photographic negatives, using a gelatin emulsion rather than the glass plates standard at the time. Eastman's achievement in making film required the development of special marketing techniques. Eastman invented a camera that used his new film to tap the market for amateur photography. Professional photographers did not like the new film since it had to be developed in Rochester by Eastman. At first the camera had to be sent back so the film could be developed and reloaded—early cameras had films with 100 exposures. The market for Eastman's new camera, the Kodak, was enormous, and in response to the demand the company built a worldwide marketing network of branch offices. These offices supervised the work of salesmen, arranged demonstrations of the cameras, and stocked film supplies. The initial response to his camera was so encouraging that Eastman built a large production and servicing plant in England in 1890.[5]

Other American products reached world markets too. Improvements in the milling of wheat and other grains led to the invention of breakfast cereals. The need to find better ways of milling the hard-grain spring wheat of the northern prairies induced a series of changes in machinery and the organization of milling. The result was a great increase in the output of wheat and other grains. Millers replaced grindstones with several machines that first reduced the grain and then processed it further by multiple grinding. The plants that incorporated the many new processes mass-produced low-cost but high-quality flour. These elaborate mills first appeared in Minneapolis, adopted most successfully by the Pillsbury Brothers and their chief rival, Cadwallader Colden Washburn. The new continuous processing milling techniques were then applied to other grains: oats, barley, rye. Because the output of oats was so high, entrepreneurs sought other uses for them and created the new breakfast cereal industry. Henry P. Crowell was one of the first to adopt an aggressive marketing campaign to change the breakfast habits of the American public. Like Duke, he mounted a campaign that included contests, coupons, and premiums. In the 1880s, Crowell set up market organizations in the United States and abroad. His marketers abroad worked with jobbers, coordinating orders and shipments, and with journalists, creating advertising suited for local foreign tastes.[6]

Mass processing and distribution in meat-packing made the leading firms in the industry important sellers in the international market by the turn of the century. The innovating firm was that of Gustavus Swift, whose mass distribution technique made it the leading processor of beef in the United States in 1900. Swift had moved to Chicago from New England in 1875. Once in the Midwest, Swift, a wholesale butcher, began to process meat and through the development of an improved refrigerated railroad car sent dressed beef to eastern cities. At about the same time in the late 1870s, Swift built warehouses in eastern cities from which to deliver his beef to local retailers. After 1881, he began to build a nationwide warehouse system. Swift succeeded because he was able to provide high-quality beef at competitive prices. Before Swift processed and sent beef east in refrigerated cars, the cattle were sent east alive. Invariably some of the animals lost weight on the trip, others became ill, and still others died en route. By processing the beef in Chicago, Swift was able to overcome the damage to the product that came from shipment "on the hoof." Swift also paid attention to the slaughtering or "disassembling" process. By careful attention to each step in the slaughtering of the animals, Swift was able to create mass processing, which led to lower unit costs.[7]

To remain competitive, other major meat-packers followed the strategy set out by Swift. Thus, Philip D. Armour, Cudahy Brothers, and Nelson Morris built warehouse systems, purchased their own refrigerated rail cars, and introduced a more extensive division of labor in their processing plants. Armour became Swift's major competitor in the 1880s as Armour and Company began to follow Swift's strategy in 1882. These two major companies quickly moved into world markets, purchasing refrigerated ships and then building warehouses in major European port cities. By the turn of the century, the two largest firms and four smaller but significant competitors sold between 60 and 90 percent of beef in the United States and accounted for 95% of beef exports. The companies utilized their extensive processing to expand into processing pork and lamb as well as beef and then moved into the sale of by-products like soap and fertilizer. In 1900 American demand for beef and other meat products was so high that the major meat-packers began to look for supplies in Latin America. Eventually, they built packing plants in Argentina, Uruguay, and Brazil to process meat solely for the European markets.[8]

In refining, the achievements of the Standard Oil Company are well known. Early in its history Rockefeller's giant enterprise gained a dominant position in world markets; and even though challenged in the late 1890s by European rivals, Standard continued to maintain a significant place in overseas markets. Unlike other American manufacturing industries, the oil industry had as early as 1865 sold more abroad than at home. Between 1866 and 1885, foreign sales never fell below 64 percent of refined output. In 1871 they reached their highest point: 77 percent of the output of the American producers. The industry's major product was refined illuminating oils and by the 1870s its major market was Europe and England. By the 1890s, Standard Oil dominated the domestic and export markets for American crude oil and refined products.[9]

Lower unit costs and then improved marketing allowed firms in other refining industries to move easily into foreign sales. Improvements in technology increased production in refining cotton oil, linseed oil, alcohol, sulphuric acid, white and red lead, as well as other pigments. Changes in refining technology, however, were less revolutionary in some industries than others, and some refiners also had less difficulty than others in marketing their products through traditional wholesale channels. But in response to sharp competition in refining industries, producers combined first into trusts and then after 1889 into holding companies. Once consolidated, they developed a strategy of vertical integration that contributed to further cost advantages. As a result, large consolidated companies in the refining industries garnered significant shares of their domestic market and were able to secure foreign sales.[10]

By 1890, for example, the American Cotton Oil Company operated fourteen refineries. Formed in 1884 as a trust, the enterprise controlled supplies of cottonseed by a purchasing network throughout the south. The trust bought cotton gins and crude oil mills to take care of the initial refining of cottonseed oil. To speed the flow of its products, the company purchased its own tank cars, owning over 300 of them by 1891. In 1890 it began to expand into marketing by organizing sales offices here and abroad; it also purchased and constructed storage facilities abroad. The company concentrated at first on the Dutch and German markets, selling large quantities of margarine and food oils through a major depot in Rotterdam supplied by specially constructed tankers. The firm expanded its line of products in the early 1890s to include cattle feed and fertilizers, washing powders, lard, and soaps. The products and the marketing of the firm's goods were not so unique as to forestall competition, as was the case in a number of other refining industries. The Southern Cotton Oil Company was a major domestic competitor, producing a similar line of products and integrating backward and forward in the same ways that American Cotton Oil had. Both also faced competition from American producers of lard, soap, and fertilizers. Procter and Gamble and the major meat-packers were among the most notable of their competitors. Abroad Americans faced competition from large and vertically integrated foreign firms, most notably from the British Lever. Yet skill in marketing and the use of technology to develop tankers made foreign markets possible before the depression of the 1890s.[11]

A large number of the processors of lead formed a trust in 1889, National Lead. The firm soon dominated the industry in the chemical processing of white lead, red lead, and lead acetate. The fabrication of lead products (such as pipe and sheets) was in the hands of smaller firms. The company also became the country's primary producer of paint because of its ability to mass-produce linseed oil. The enterprise that grew out of the trust consolidated its purchasing operations and then built a national and global sales network. Although there was competition from the National Linseed Trust, National Lead's advantages in reducing costs in purchasing and in widespread sales operations, allowed it to dominate the industry at home and make significant sales abroad.[12]

In meeting the demand for products of metal in an industrializing economy, the metalworking industries adopted machine tools and improved raw materials to make high-quality products. Improvements were made in furnaces for tempering, and the machine tool industry improved its machines for cutting, grinding, and polishing. As a result, some manufacturers of simply fabricated products, such as castings, moldings, and tools like axes, hoes, saws, knives, and cutlery, gained excellent reputations for the quality of their products.[13]

American manufacturers gained real advantages, however, in the manufacture of more complex metalworked products. Attention to the precision of the tools and machinery employed, as well as to the organization needed to produce large quantities, made numerous products of American metalworking industries easily exportable. Attention to the interchangeability of parts used in manufacture, to factory organization, and to the movement and placement of workers within the factory cut the costs of production. Thus, products with simple assembly, such as stoves, and more complex metalworked machinery found ready demand abroad. Foreign sales early came to the American makers of harvesters, reapers, scales, and safes, and more complicated products like repeating firearms, sewing machines, typewriters, calculators, electrical motors, electrical machinery, and, after 1900, automobiles. By the 1880s and 1890s, factories making these products were giving attention to "scientific management" and, after 1900, to cost and factory accounting, which further helped them to reduce their costs.[14]

Many of the producers of machinery integrated forward into marketing. For the most part, traditional wholesalers and jobbers were not equipped to provide all of the necessary services for machinery producers: demonstration of the new machines; service of the equipment; replacement of parts; and credit to customers. The most extensive marketing operations were developed by I.M. Singer and Company. By 1859 Singer had created a domestic marketing system that helped him sell a high volume of output. A network of sales branches modeled on those in the United States were spread worldwide by the 1880s. By 1905 Singer had over 61,000 sales employees.[15]

Singer's need to build its own sales network was reflected in the experience of other manufacturers of machines. Like Singer, Cyrus McCormick's reaper found ready sales abroad, selling overseas as early as the 1860s. His firm too needed a strong branch marketing system because independent wholesalers did not "push" the McCormick brand, could not service the machines properly and could not provide the credit for farmers to finance them. Unlike Singer, however, McCormick had substantial competition. The depression of the 1890s and sharp competition eventually led McCormick to a merger in 1902, which created International Harvester, one of the largest American firms and one of the first truly multinational corporations.[16]

One of the first producers of office machines had an experience similar to that of McCormick's. E. and T. Fairbanks made weighing scales. Selling widely by the 1850s, the firm expanded after the Civil War, setting up sales branches in every region of the country and eventually Canada. The regional branch offices had salaried managers and salesmen to visit businessmen in their districts. Like those of McCormick and Singer, the sales branches provided consumer credit and service. As time went on, to make better use of the personnel in the sales branches, the firm broadened its line of office equipment.[17]

Manufacturers of other business equipment and machines followed a similar strategy. In the 1880s National Cash Register set up small but widely dispersed sales offices. The ability to provide credit and service, as well as an aggressive sales force working closely with retail customers, made National Cash Register a formidable force in both the domestic and international markets. The typewriter found its way into international markets in a similar way. The Remington Typewriter Company began from the first to sell in foreign markets as well as at home. Marketing was critical to this firm, as it was to many other machinery makers. Remington built sales branches that took care of the marketing, demonstration, and servicing of their typewriters. By the 1890s, Remington, along with National Cash Register and Singer Sewing Machine, were formidable sellers both at home and abroad. Their sales operations allowed them to sell their relatively new products in burgeoning markets, selling at a great volume. Initially, the sales branches were to provide services that traditional independent jobbers and wholesalers would not or could not provide. But once established, the sales branches allowed these firms to market a large output at low prices. Such sales made competition and entry into these industries difficult, if not impossible. The low-cost products that they produced and could market dependably, with the prospect of credit and service, gave them quick markets in America as well as abroad. The sales branches assured a high flow of cash back to the central offices. And a broad network of sales agents was an important source of information about market conditions and consumer tastes at home and abroad. The foreign branches also assured central management of information about local foreign economic and political conditions. Close and regular communication among branches, central sales offices, and factories eased the scheduling of a high and regular volume of products to customers. The increasing sales put pressure on the firms to improve methods of production, which reduced unit costs, making the operations more competitive and assuring these firms dominance in their industries for a long time.[18]

Other makers of machinery also did well at home and abroad, although producers who sold their machinery to other manufacturers did not have the same sales problems as those who sold to many buyers. The makers of specialized machinery and equipment needed special sales branches which housed the salesmen and engineers who helped in many cases to design equipment almost to order. In a rapidly changing technology like that of electricity in the late 1870s and 1880s, company executives had to assure that their salesmen and designers kept up with technological changes. Unique products designed, installed, and maintained by men informed about the latest technological developments helped major firms gain strong markets at home and overseas. Western Electric, the makers of telephones and telephone relay equipment, had substantial foreign sales by the 1880s. Similarly, Johnson Company, a major producer of electric streetcar rails and switches, and the Otis Elevator Company built strong marketing networks which helped develop overseas sales. With a more assured supply of electricity, Otis, a company dating back to the 1850s, expanded its business rapidly once it developed a high-speed hydraulic elevator. Starting in 1878 the firm began to build a branch office network that by the 1880s found Otis dominating both domestic and international markets.[19]

Other American firms of specialized machinery, or machinery that required some special design and engineering for each site, also built special marketing branches. Babcock and Wilcox sold steam boilers; Allis-Chalmers produced mining machinery; the Henry R. Worthington Company made pumps and hydraulic equipment for the sewerage and water systems of cities all over the world; the Norton Company produced grinding wheels and the machinery for grind wheels, as well as canning machinery.[20] These firms were able to maintain a dominant position in their industries for decades. The special sales branches kept the companies in close contact with their customers. The complexity of their machinery and equipment, and the importance therefore of their trained sales and engineering personnel, gave them a powerful competitive advantage.

Many of these companies also turned to formal research to improve their products. Singer and Eastman both devoted resources to improvement of their products, which in many instances gave them further technological advantages over their competitors, advantages often protected by patents. Most of the firms discussed here did have competitors, but rarely did competitors achieve a more significant portion of the market than the original firms.[21]

Nowhere were the connections among marketing, research, and patents more important than in the electrical industry. The application of advanced technology gave firms advantages that made competition difficult. George Westinghouse had by the 1890s established secure foreign markets for his unique air brakes at first and later for his innovative electrical equipment. In 1872 Westinghouse opened an export company to market the air brake. This subsidiary established a sales staff abroad which relied on a corps of technical personnel. He established his company firmly abroad when he had to manufacture his product in France because contracts for French railroads required that equipment and supplies be produced there. Eventually Westinghouse established factories in Great Britain, Germany, and Russia to manufacture brakes and signalling equipment for their railroads.[22]

Westinghouse, however, owed more to Europe and especially Britain than profitable markets for the air brake. It was in England, while establishing air brake manufacturing that Westinghouse turned his attention to electricity, as he studied the advanced signalling techniques of British railroads. The interest in signalling (he established a company to make and sell signalling equipment) stimulated research into broader questions of the transmission and use of electricity. Westinghouse first developed commercially safe and practical alternating current. Up to that time, direct current systems were possible so long as electricity did not need to be transmitted over great distances. Westinghouse made practicable high voltage transmission through the transformer which lowered voltage. The Westinghouse Electric Company developed the equipment to generate, transmit, and convert the electricity. As early as 1889, he set up a subsidiary in Britain to design and build such equipment on a contract basis. By the end of the 1890s Westinghouse had begun to manufacture in England. The production facilities set up there under a new corporation in 1899, British Westinghouse and Electric and Manufacturing Company, Ltd., paved the way for installations in Germany, France, Russia, and Canada.[23]

Westinghouse's innovative products found ready markets abroad in industrialized countries possessing a population with an income level similar to that in the United States. The major American competition in the electrical industry came from the Edison companies, later to become General Electric. As early as the 1870s Edison exploited ready foreign markets for his novel invention, the phonograph, and in 1879 the company planned to introduce the incandescent lamp to European markets. Edison had also been active in introducing telephone systems abroad. These efforts were not without risk. Both Westinghouse and Edison met sharp competition from European and American producers. Edison had to confront the sales of Bell Telephone interests; electric power competed with the producers of cheap gas. Yet Edison-inspired companies were established in England, France, and Germany. By the 1880s Edison had a branch network to sell and to install his products in Canada, South America, India, New Zealand, Australia, Japan, and Korea.[24]

Edison, however, turned his foreign interests over to others in the middle of the 1880s. He had made little money on his efforts abroad. He had expanded too far and with too little capital, becoming dependent on foreign bankers and investors. Indeed other lesser-known American companies had done better than Edison. Thomson-Houston Electric Company and Brush Electric Company successfully sold their unique products overseas. Thomson-Houston held patents in arc lighting which opened opportunities abroad, and Bush designed and manufactured constant-current high-voltage dynamos. Thomson-Houston set up an international subsidiary in 1884. When it acquired Brush Electric in 1887, it had already set up manufacturing facilities in Canada. By the beginning of the 1890s, Thomson-Houston had annual sales almost equal to Edison's General Electric Company. When Edison General Electric, Thomson-Houston Electric Company, and its subsidiary Thomson-Houston International Electric Company merged in 1892 to form General Electric Company, the firm started with substantial domestic and foreign business. The depression that began a year later slowed the growth of the firm, but it did not dampen its leaders' belief that rapid expansion would soon be possible again.[25]

These first big businesses, then, were also the first American firms to create substantial markets abroad. Success came to the mass production, mass marketing (or special marketing) firms that manufactured a high volume of standardized machinery, processed perishable goods, and produced low-priced packaged goods, or those that developed and marketed technologically sophisticated products. Most of the new enterprises that sold abroad were in the food processing and machinery industries in the 1880s, but they led the way in the coordination of goods from raw materials to final products. These modern corporations usually produced new products. For example, they manufactured machines for agriculture, sewing, and the office or products for urban consumers, such as cigarettes, breakfast cereals, canned products, roll film, or meat butchered and processed at a distance of time and space.[26]

In the 1890s, other firms followed similar patterns of development because, like the pioneers of the 1880s, they too found marketing unsuitable to the new products that they had to sell. As in the 1880s, the firms that developed their marketing operations in the 1890s tended to be in either the food processing or the machinery industries. In the consumer goods industries, the Boston Fruit Company, which became United Fruit in 1899, developed a refrigerated system of railroad cars in order to market bananas and later other tropical fruit throughout the United States and abroad. Wrigley's Chewing Gum, following the techniques of Duke's American Tobacco, began to market worldwide, and Asa Candler created a national and international sales force to sell Coca Cola.[27]

Office equipment producers followed the example of Remington and National Cash Register. In the late 1890s, for example, William S. Burroughs massproduced and marketed the adding machine, at home and then abroad. Companies of more complex, large, but standardized machinery followed patterns established by Otis Elevator. In the 1890s marketing networks were set up by Ingersoll Sergeant Drill, Merganthaler Linotype (the producers of new typesetting machinery), and the producers of dies, presses, and similar machine tool machinery. A new industry made widespread sales in the 1890s, as the Owens Bottle Machine Company produced machinery for high-speed, fully automatic bottling and Crown Cork and Seal provided the stoppers for the output of new mass-produced bottling machines.[28]

Some smaller companies in metal-making and metal-fabrication also turned to their own marketing in order to improve the scheduling of their output and the advertising of their products. Like so many others, new technology and the application of scientific management led to greater output, which strained the relations that producers had with their jobbers and wholesalers. As a result, producers set up regional sales offices which eventually made possible overseas sales, for example, to the leading producer of locks and building hardware, Yale and Towne Manufacturing Company. Likewise, Crane Company and American Standard needed a regional marketing apparatus to sell their plumbing fixtures.[29]

Size and vertical integration, especially when combined with mass production and mass distribution techniques, gave companies a decided advantage in selling at home and abroad. But the depression of the 1890s induced consolidations of other companies, some of which gained marketing and mass production advantages that made foreign sales possible.

The depression of the 1890s was less troublesome for the major mass production, mass distribution manufacturers than for smaller, unifunctional producers who did not have substantial technological or marketing advantages. Indeed for some of the mass production, mass distribution firms, the depression produced real opportunities. Depressions were often a time for the strong to expand and take advantage of low prices and wages to build new plants and install new equipment. Not all of these major firms were so fortunate. Yet in responding to problems created by the depression, some major corporations ultimately strengthened their position in the domestic and the international economy. And out of the merger movement precipitated in the depression years, a host of iron- and steel-related industries gained the marketing strength and cost advantages to begin by the turn of the century to sell in foreign markets.

The depression helped to solve one of the most persistent problems in the electrical industry. Patents proved critical in the founding of General Electric and in the competition with Westinghouse. In order for the two companies to produce the best railway, lighting, and power equipment, they needed to use the patents of the other. Tangled and expensive lawsuits had disturbed the electrical industry for years, since both manufacturers guaranteed to purchasers of their equipment protection against infringement suits. This was harder to do, however, as equipment became more complicated. Discussions about the joint use of patents had begun as early as 1889, although serious negotiations did not get underway until 1892. G.E. started in bad times and needed financial help from J.P. Morgan. The firm could not afford to pay expensive damages in litigation over infringements. By the middle of the 1890s, G.E. was willing to make an agreement with Westinghouse to share patents. Induced in part by the competition for shrinking markets in the 1890s, the firms finally agreed to share most important patents, allowing them to produce technologically advanced machinery and giving them further advantages abroad. Moreover, they followed their agreement by prosecuting other firms in the industry on patent infringement, eventually forcing smaller companies to sell out to one of the two major electrical producers. Even though disputes over patents and the interpretation of their agreement continued to occur, the patent agreement ultimately strengthened both companies. Their products were technologically superior to those of competitors because they could freely make use of the newest developments in electrical power, its transmission, and its usage in transportation equipment.[30]

Electrical equipment producers, however, were not the only makers of machinery to strengthen their competitive positions during the depression. During these same years, adverse economic conditions set in motion changes in the agricultural machinery industry that led to the formation of International Harvester in 1902. From as early as 1851 Cyrus H. McCormick, the inventor of the reaper, had shown an interest in exporting. He displayed his reaper at the Crystal Palace exhibition in London in 1851; soon after he licensed the manufacture and sale of his product in England. First efforts were far from profitable, but McCormick worked hard to convince European nobility and governmental officials of the significance of his invention. By the end of the century, the McCormick reaper and other of his agricultural equipment had achieved a worldwide market. At the time of McCormick's death in 1884, the company's catalog was published in twenty languages.[31]

McCormick, however, had not had a monopoly on the industry. And the competitive nature of the production of agricultural equipment led to the formation of the giant International Harvester Company in 1902. Conditions from 1884 to the formation of IH were such that observers referred to the "harvester war" in these years. As in other industries, the depression of the 1890s exacerbated already competitive conditions for the makers of agricultural equipment. Improved technology and the economies of large-scale production led to a general decline in prices for harvesters. It also reduced profits. To increase sales the major firms, McCormick and Deering, took greater control of marketing. By 1890 the companies replaced jobbers with their own branch sales offices which employed traveling agents to sell goods and to collect bills. Deering, McCormick, and others engaged in extensive and expensive advertising campaigns to sell their machines. The major firms also carried over their competition into foreign markets. The cost of selling harvesters was thus very high. In 1890 the six largest firms in the industry proposed a trust of eighteen firms. Public hostility to the idea and, more important, the inability of bankers to finance the new trust led to abandonment of negotiations early in 1891.[32]

The depression of the nineties only intensified the two major firms' competition at home and abroad. Even though conditions improved in 1897, McCormick and Deering had concluded that they could only gain higher profits through consolidation. Discussions began again in 1897. When these failed—the Deerings wanted too much money and the McCormicks feared that they would be unable to manage two large firms—both tried other means of competition. Both expanded their lines of products and integrated backward into controlling what were becoming ever more expensive supplies. Thus, Deering constructed a rolling mill and bought interests in blast furnaces, deposits of iron ore, coal fields, and timber lands. McCormick integrated backward too and continued to expand abroad, taking advantage of the company's vast experience.[33]

Difficulty in raising capital to build a steel mill, however, convinced the McCormicks of the need to eliminate the competition that in fact restricted the potential profits of the two largest producers. Vertical integration was so costly that profit rates were further undermined. While McCormick was able to expand abroad, the Deerings felt unable to compete with the experienced foreign operations of their chief competitor.[34]

Negotiations undertaken again in 1900 came to fruition in 1902 in the creation of International Harvester, which became a formidable factor in the export of a full line of agricultural machinery and tools. The new combination embraced not only Deering and McCormick, but also the other three major producers of harvesting machinery. Together the five firms accounted for the overwhelming bulk of the industry's output, producing the two principal types of harvesting machines, 90 percent of the grain binders and 80 percent of the mowers. Eliminating high selling costs and then carrying through plans for vertical integration gave International Harvester great strength in domestic and foreign markets.[35]

Of all the machinery producers, however, it was the Singer Company that had the most extensive worldwide markets by the 1890s. The depression helped the firm to secure its position in home and overseas markets, in which they accounted for almost three quarters of world sales of sewing machines. The 1890s saw the beginnings of a strong economic nationalism in Europe as Russia, France, Germany, and other European governments established protectionist tariffs. Singer, like many firms after the turn of the century, responded to these nationalistic policies by creating national sales companies in Germany in 1895 and in Russia in 1897. After the turn of the century, the company also built similar sales networks in Great Britain in 1905 and in the Scandinavian countries in 1901-2. Foreign sales companies allowed Singer to circumvent the higher taxes that some governments levied on foreign companies and to challenge in foreign courts violations of trade names and trademarks. Companies staffed and run by foreign nationals also reduced the force of foreign competitors' appeals to patriotism.[36]

The depression forced Singer's management to confront directly questions about the competitive position of the firm, as well as the efficiency of its operations. As a result, the company committed itself to continued technical improvement which strengthened the firm's hold on domestic and international business. By the 1890s, a younger generation of managers took over, and they devoted resources to an institutionalized quest for continuing improvements in the many different kinds of sewing machines. One manifestation of this effort was the introduction of the first electric-powered machine.[37]

The new managers at Singer also paid close attention to organization and efficiency. Singer's major strength had been its sales and marketing organizations. Practices and customs varied in different national markets, and standards of performance and return varied from branch to branch. The depression forced the central administration in the New York headquarters to pay close attention to the need to standardize procedures. They hoped to increase returns, make sales operations more efficient, and improve morale among employees who suffered from the apparent capriciousness of central headquarter's policies. To gain better control of the system, the central administration required weekly, monthly, and semiannual reports on salesmen on standard forms drawn up in New York. By the turn of the century, Singer's position in the industry was more secure than ever before. New York headquarters had standardized sales procedures in the field and it had increased the flow of information and data into the New York offices, creating greater control over current operations and future planning.[38]

The 1890s had different if equally profound effects on the oil industry. During that decade Standard perfected a strategy to deal with foreign competition in export markets. The company's major competitors in Europe in both crude and refined products were the Nobel and Rothschild interests. By the late 1880s Standard had concentrated many efforts on the Eastern seaboard to facilitate the refining and shipment of oil to Europe and England. The company had relied on agents and wholesalers abroad for the most part. In response to the competition of Russian supplies extracted, refined, and marketed by the Nobels and Rothschilds, Standard tightened control of its marketing operations abroad. At the same time, the company increased bulk distribution, beginning to employ tankers instead of barrels for distribution.

By the turn of the century, Standard had secured its position in the European markets for lubricants, illuminating oil, and crude oil. The use of gas and electricity for illumination, however, slowed the firm's growth. In response to this weakening in the European and American markets, Standard began to pay more attention to markets in the Middle East and Asia. Oriental markets were the most promising, since they were less urbanized and less likely to move quickly into adopting gas or electricity for illumination. At the end of the nineteenth century, then, the company faced decisions about building refineries in the Orient to compete with oil from Russia and Indonesia. It also negotiated market-sharing agreements with its chief foreign rivals in these years.[39]

The depression of the 1890s fostered a widespread merger movement that among the makers of semifinished and finished steel products led to advantages that allowed producers to begin to make substantial foreign sales for the first time. Producer's goods industries like steel had high fixed costs, a result of the heavy capitalization necessary for technologically complicated products. Higher costs of large-scale plant served as an incentive to cooperate. Firms needed to keep running to pay fixed costs of operation, but low prices often meant returns that paid little above those fixed costs.

Excess capacity had become a common problem among producers of light finished iron and steel products. The makers of semifinished steel and the heavier finished products were less troubled than the producers of the simpler and lighter products in the industry, but the makers of the semifinished and heavier steel products also faced these problems. As elsewhere in the American economy, the firms making iron and steel turned to cooperation to solve problems of low prices. Manufacturers relied for a long time on relatively informal gentlemen's agreements and pools. Most were short-lived, but short-run solutions were what for a long time suited manufacturers. The depth and length of the depression of the 1890s, however, induced producers to seek more permanent arrangements to insure price maintenance and production limitation. Thus, by the late 1890s producers began to form holding companies which succeeded in merging many former competitors. Important mergers in iron and steel concentrated price and production decisions in the hands of a very small number of managers as mergers allowed them to buy up and often shut down competitors.[40]

Mergers in iron and steel were part of a pattern that in the last years of the nineteenth century added up to the greatest merger movement in American history. The failure of pooling agreements, low prices, and underutilized capacity led producers to attempt to gain firmer control of numerous industries. These efforts did not always succeed, and many firms ultimately failed. But the combinations did succeed where entry into an industry was eliminated or sharply reduced. On the average, 266 firms disappeared annually into mergers between 1895 and 1907. In 1899, 1,208 firms were absorbed—the largest number ever— in every branch of almost every major industrial grouping. Such organizational changes altered the nature of the American industrial economy. In terms of the capitalization and control of markets, one giant corporation gained control of at least 62.5 percent of its market in 60 percent of the consolidations that took place between 1895 and 1904. In 10 percent of these consolidations, the large firms represented 42.5 to 62.5 percent.[41]

These combinations had a profound impact on American sales in foreign markets. The combinations in the iron and steel industries opened great new opportunities for American producers who had rarely sold abroad. The American iron and steel industry had grown rapidly in the late nineteenth century. High protection kept out significant competition, and the application of new technologies and a burgeoning domestic industrial market stimulated the industry in all its branches. Andrew Carnegie, the industry's leader in 1870-1900, controlled his own raw materials and transportation, bringing about by vertical integration lower costs as the years went on. His competitors were forced to compete by imitating Carnegie's strategies of vertical integration. The depression strengthened the Carnegie Company because Carnegie used bad times to buy or build new facilities at relatively low cost. He also expanded his efforts to cut costs of operations. His competitors in the making of semifinished steel followed in the 1890s, spreading Carnegie's cost-cutting techniques industrywide.[42]

Technological advances and improved plant design had made the American steel industry one of the fastest growing in the world in the 1870s and 1880s. By the late 1870s, Carnegie had combined many of the processes of steel making into single plants, designed by the leading engineers of the day for efficient operation and reduction of costs. A continuous flow of raw materials passed through these plants to the shipment of the final product. But improvements in the layout of steel plants was not the only reason for increased output. "Hard driving," the use of intense heat and powerful blast engines, helped too. The output of one of Carnegie's furnaces advanced from 13,000 tons in 1872 to 100,000 by the end of the 1890s. Others in the industry, by copying Carnegie's techniques, registered similar if not so dramatic increases in output. Carnegie's engineers also turned their attention to other matters. Materials flowed more quickly to the blast furnaces, ingots were rapidly cooled in special soaking pits, and improved rollers carried materials faster.

Each step in the steel-making process was more complicated and required a greater number of activities than in other industries adopting mass production techniques. Carnegie's concern for each part of the process—his desire to cut costs at every stage of production—made his firm a formidable competitor. Other companies followed Carnegie's lead, but there was no effective competitor before the turn of the century. The Carnegie Company was for the most part not interested in foreign sales, although its successor, United States Steel, was.[43]

Before the 1890s the rapidly growing domestic market provided ample opportunity for steel production. At first railroad construction provided a great stimulus, and then it was urbanization with heavy demand for structural steel, pipes, boiler plate, and equipment for street and suburban railways. Yet there were other reasons to concentrate on the home market. Foreign sales were costly to develop. Foreign buyers often required alterations in products which would have necessitated expensive adaptation in design and manufacture. Then, too, British, Belgian, and German producers had developed an experienced corps of sales agents. These foreign industrialists—more dependent and therefore more accustomed to foreign sales—had the contacts, the experienced help, the overseas warehouses and banking connections to sell worldwide.

Conditions during the depression of the 1890s, however, changed matters both at home and abroad. Falling secular prices in the United States combined with shortages and temporary price increases abroad to stimulate sales of American iron and steel products, as foreign buyers began to buy goods in the United States.[44] At home combinations in the late 1890s had created the conditions that permitted producers to seek foreign sales; the holding companies had enabled producers to overcome many of the obstacles that had stood in the way of earlier sales. Economies of scale allowed lower, more competitive prices, as did the lower costs of raw materials and distribution brought about by vertical integration. The new combinations were able to provide the venture capital to invest in developing foreign markets.[45]

The president of American Steel Hoop Company described succinctly why the new combinations went abroad. The company had been formed in 1899 out of the principal manufacturers of light hoops, bars, bands, cotton ties, etc. In testimony before the Industrial Commission, he outlined the advantages that the merger afforded in developing foreign sales. American Steel Hoop was "able to employ agents all over the world and go to the expense of pioneering for business as a smaller concern could not. They could not afford with a tonnage of 10,000 a month to send a man abroad, but with 60,000 or 70,000 tons a month we can send men all over the world and make money doing it." Like other combinations American Steel Hoop had been able to lower unit costs by closing down the most inefficient of its components and then centralizing production and distribution.

The head of American Steel and Wire Company observed similarly that the individual firms making up the combination could not alone have gained foreign sales; they simply did not have the capital resources to build overseas markets. But American Steel and Wire vigorously sought foreign markets once its highly competitive pricing had been controlled and returns on investment were more assured. Producers of primary steel products also sought foreign sales after merging. Federal Steel Company had integrated vertically in response to the competition of the leading firm in the industry, Carnegie Company. Second only to Carnegie in capacity, Federal soon after formation moved into cultivating foreign markets. It also had reduced unit costs through merging with raw materials suppliers. This vertical integration made planning easier and returns on investments more predictable than earlier, which then permitted the firm to expend resources in the risky business of seeking sales in foreign markets.[46]

Not everyone in the steel industry was convinced of the value of seeking foreign sales. The industry's leader, the Carnegie Company, had the lowest costs and the most extensive line of products. Carnegie only reluctantly sold abroad in the 1890s. While proud of the sales in markets traditionally controlled by the British, Carnegie thought it a sad day when he had to make foreign sales. He looked toward the further growth of demand in the domestic economy in the future as providing more than enough business for his firm.[47]

But Carnegie was not to remain active in the industry much beyond 1901. And the giant United States Steel Company formed out of Carnegie and other prominent firms was to become a major factor in American foreign sales. U.S. Steel was formed in response to a threat that the mergers of the late 1890s were not enough to assure stable prices and production. Problems arose when several of the large fabricating producers organized in the late 1890s announced plans to produce their own semifinished steel. While they had controlled large percentages of their own industry's capacity, they had nevertheless remained independent of the makers of primary steel. When in 1899 and 1900 American Steel and Wire and National Tube Company cancelled orders from Carnegie Company, Carnegie felt threatened. As the major producer of semifinished steel, his firm would lose much business if the firms made their own semifinished steel. Carnegie's response was to plan to manufacture wire rods, steel tubes, and steel sheets. If carried out, however, Carnegie's plans would have created a competitive storm that would have ended the relative tranquility brought about by the mergers of the late 1890s. Industry leaders and those with heavy investments in the new firms undertook to bring about an even larger amalgamation.[48]

After drawnout negotiations, the firm was established in 1901. United States Steel Company brought together the major manufacturers of semifinished products (Carnegie, National Steel, and Federal Steel) and some of the leading producers of finished goods (American Tin Plate, American Steel Hoop, American Bridge, American Sheet Steel, American Steel and Wire, and National Tube). The corporation controlled 45 percent of the country's production of iron ore and one-third of the blast furnaces in the United States. In its first full year of operation (1902) it accounted for 50.8 percent of the production of finished goods and 44.7 percent of pig iron output.[49]

Its first chairman of the board, Elbert Gary, set out to prevent a return to the "destructive" price competition of the 1890s. He wanted a good and "fair" return on capital of about 10 percent. He wanted to replace price competition with competition on service and quality. Gary worked out what economists would call an oligopolistic market in which a major firm by its position could dominate an industry of a few sellers. Gary insured comparative stability in pricing and greater flexibility in output, as the major firms could retain inventory more easily than the smaller firms of the 1890s. Some prices remained static, while others fluctuated less dramatically than in the 1890s, in the first two decades of the twentieth century.[50]

The new firm, as we shall see in the next chapter, used its strengths and advantages to dominate American exports of iron and steel products. Many of the firms' component enterprises had by 1901 begun to develop foreign sales of significance, and the new U.S. Steel set up a subsidiary company to sell these products abroad. The strengths of the combination in the market at home—high volume production, the economies of scale, relative price stability, and capital resources—were put to use to tap markets abroad.

By the turn of the century, then, producers in key industries of the American industrial economy had established or had begun to establish for themselves secure positions in world trade. After 1900 demand increased for many of these products, as the industrial economies of Europe expanded. The major American firms were ready to take advantage of these changes, since the 1890s had led to improvements in plant and equipment for some and better marketing arrangements for others. In the iron and steel industry, mergers created giant firms better able to compete abroad. Among machinery producers domestic conditions ultimately contributed to strengthen the position of the major firms in the electrical, agricultural equipment, and sewing machine industries.

But in the other industry groupings that eventually dominated American exports of manufactured goods, the combinations of the 1890s often helped to strengthen and enlarge foreign sales that had already begun before the 1890s. In the petroleum products, food products, and machinery industries, firms used advantages of technology and marketing at home to develop or increase sales abroad. Innovative technology, patents, advertising, and sales operations garnered foreign sales.

The depression of the 1890s had effects beyond changing the nature of industrial organization in the United States. It stimulated an interest in trade expansion among a number of manufacturers who did not have the technological or marketing advantages that the largest producers had. Before the 1890s these smaller producers paid little attention to foreign sales, concentrating on the burgeoning domestic economy instead. A good many of these industrialists manufactured undifferentiated products, homogeneous goods that would have had difficulty being sold abroad during "good" times. These products—textiles, dry goods, simple hardware—were similar to wares produced by other industrial countries. The American producers frankly thought of foreign trade as an outlet in hard times when domestic demand fell. During the depression small producers of specialized goods also began to seek markets abroad; they found a firmer demand for their products. At the end of the depression, they tried to keep markets developed earlier. These were producers mainly of machine tools and machinery makers specializing in light equipment for the textile, woodworking, printing, food processing, and paper-making industries; makers of high-quality hand tools and ornamental hardware also found ready markets for their products abroad.

Like the industrialists who had created the giant enterprises of the 1890s, smaller producers of both undifferentiated and differentiated products had faced in that decade persistent problems of overproduction at prevailing prices. Some of the industrialists concluded that permanent overseas markets were the solution to permanent excess capacity.

The first line of defense for many manufacturers in the iron and steel industry, as we have seen, was to form pools and horizontal organizations to control prices and limit production. Unless these informal horizontal arrangements became formal through the creation of a holding company, most of these agreements were relatively short-lived. And holding companies had little chance of success if they did not follow the path of mass production firms organized earlier. The cost advantages brought by vertical integration in securing raw materials and in marketing one's product were critical to the success of combinations. Holding companies that did little more than raise prices invited competition once they reached a level of reasonable profit. The failure to integrate vertically helps explain the failure of such combinations as National Cordage, American Biscuit, United States Leather, National Wallpaper, National Starch, and the firms that were formed after the reorganization of the Whiskey Trust.[51]

Mergers either failed or were not attempted in several industries: apparel, furniture, printing and publishing, lumber, and textiles. Combinations afforded these industries little advantage, since they were made up of labor-intensive firms which could not make use for the most part of mass marketing techniques. In industries that made machinery, mergers tended to fail when production technology was not complex and when specialized marketing was not required, the kind of marketing skills that gave advantage to the makers of more complex machines. Thus, mergers failed among the producers of laundry wringers, bicycles, shears, and woodworking machines, and among the makers of comparatively simple agricultural implements (forks, hoes, and the like).[52]

The manufacturers in industries in which mergers failed or were not attempted were those who showed the greatest interest in government assistance in the development of foreign markets. The inability to control their industries' output and prices forced them to seek other arrangements. To many of these producers in the distressed 1890s foreign markets seemed to be their salvation. During the depression many of the producers of homogeneous and undifferentiated goods made foreign sales for the first time. A comparatively sharp decline in American prices not matched in Europe made foreign sales possible for American "traditional" industrial goods. Before the 1890s, most of these standard products were not competitive with similar British and German goods. Overseas markets also proved attractive to manufacturers who did not want to join in combinations and mergers. Independent-minded producers in industries swept by mergers looked upon the foreign markets as a place of refuge, as a place to solve the problems of overproduction and at the same time to save one's enterprise.

But foreign markets also stimulated the interest of single-unit, unintegrated producers of specialized precision machinery, machine tools, and hand tools.[53] These manufacturers produced highly differentiated goods, often competitive in price and quality with those of Germany and Britain.[54]

These producers had competitive advantages, but they did not have the resources nor really the need to develop their own marketing apparatus. They depended upon traditional exporters here and importers abroad to market their products. Like those trying to break into world markets for the first time with undifferentiated goods, however, these producers of more competitive products supported changes in government policies and advocated governmental assistance.

The interest in foreign trade was not so widespread, however, as some historians have maintained. Indeed, it was only a strong interest of a distinct minority of manufacturers. But that is significant, for this minority was willing to create, support and devote time to associations that worked toward government aid in trade expansion. The National Association of Manufacturers (NAM) was the best organized and the largest association devoted to trade expansion, and in 1900 it had only about a thousand members. At about that time there were approximately 80,000 manufacturing corporations in the United States.[55] To be sure, it is difficult to determine accurately the interest in trade expansion. The New York *Journal of Commerce*, a major business publication, espoused the view that overseas markets offered the solution to the problems of the domestic economy. Its editors maintained that they spoke for general business opinion. This is clearly not the case, for there were other prestigious business journals that questioned whether such views were typical of business thinking at the time. *Iron Age*, a widely read journal of the iron and steel industry, observed that in the 1890s "some effort was made to stimulate interest among our manufacturers in seeking foreign markets, and a number of export journals were established, which may have conveyed to the casual reader the impression that the octopus of American enterprise was throwing out its tentacles to every corner of the globe and capturing everything in sight. Meanwhile the American manufacturer was not manifesting any great excitement.... Some imaginative promoter may have talked for publication rather more fully about the capture of the world's steel trade by his corporation than was altogether wise or modest."[56]

Some producers did not look upon foreign markets as a desirable solution to domestic economic problems. To many it indicated failure and sales at a loss, although better than no sales at all. The secretary of Tennessee Coal and Iron Company expressed this sentiment well in a paper delivered in November 1895 to the Alabama Industrial and Scientific Society. "It is obvious that distant markets can only be controlled by the sacrifice of profits, and that it is the development of the home market that we must look to for our profitable business." A manufacturer of one-tenth of the U.S. output of cut nails made similar observations when talking about the 25 percent of his output sold abroad. "To dispose of our surplus product," he said, "foreign goods are sold at loss; same must be made up in price of domestic article. Remedy suggested in order to equalize prices is limitation of production."[57]

Protectionist sentiment continued strong in these years too, and protectionists questioned the view that foreign markets were desirable. James Swank used the *Bulletin* of the American Iron and Steel Association to attack the idea of foreign trade expansion. He saw overseas markets as too costly in terms of what would have to be given up by reducing tariffs and opening the domestic markets to foreign producers.[58]

Even some of those who no longer saw high tariffs as entirely necessary remained skeptical about increasing export markets. Indeed Andrew Carnegie had shown real impatience with those promoting foreign expansion. He had referred to expansionist advocates as a "noisy" minority of the steel industry in 1889, and Carnegie himself regretted the need to sell abroad in the 1890s to dump some of his products. He wrote to a friend in Britain in September 1896 to lament that they were "bad days for us when we have to take foreign trade."[59] Fundamentally Carnegie believed that the future of American business lay in an expanding domestic economy. The steel industry had nothing to fear, he thought, when he contemplated the great demand for steel products to build cities, a market by the late 1890s of rapidly growing demand.[60]

Finally, a survey conducted by the United States Industrial Commission provides a wider perspective of manufacturers' thinking and shows that the views of those in the steel industry were typical. The poll suggested that there was a relatively small but committed group of smaller producers who believed that trade expansion was a solution to their problems. The Commission conducted a survey to determine whether those in foreign trade charged lower prices abroad than at home. Out of 2000 inquiries sent to manufacturers, 416 answered, and 300 of those indicated that they did not have export markets. Of the 100 or so that did have overseas sales, many indicated that they sold abroad because they were able to get higher prices there. Some indicated a desire to sell abroad to avoid a glutted domestic market, but theirs was not the general response. The survey, to be sure, was not scientific. Some responses were tabulated, while others were summarized in a paragraph. Yet the responses provide important insights into manufacturers' thinking about foreign markets.[61]

The survey also indicated that splits developed among the smaller producers who were to make up the most important pressure groups on trade expansion. There were those who clearly sought foreign sales to solve problems at home, as indicated. There were others who first sought foreign sales to deal with the depression of the 1890s, but who then found that they had real advantages to exploit abroad and the foreign market became important to their businesses. This was particularly true among the makers of machine tools and specialized machinery for industry. "Export trade is an extremely important factor for everyone engaged in building machine tools," one respondent observed. "The trade was saved from widespread disaster in the years from 1893 to 1897, during which there was great depression in the United States; but business was very good in Europe, and they took from 50 to 75 percent of all the output of the tool builders in the United States."[62] By 1898 improving prices at home made the American market more desirable, although some producers tried to hold foreign markets anyway. As a producer of machinery noted, "this [1896 export] campaign resulted in our gaining a firm foothold in the various markets of the world, which we have endeavored to since hold by meeting market conditions, whether higher or lower than the domestic market."[63]

This survey indicated that particular groups of smaller producers had a strong interest in foreign sales. On the one hand, there were producers who had done well when they went abroad; this was true of the makers of ornamental hardware, hand tools, and machine tools. It also included the makers of special machinery for the textile and printing industries and for the processors of coffee, rice and wheat. Manufacturers of these goods were and remained comparatively small in terms of employees and capital invested. Their products were specialized and highly differentiated, and they did not lend themselves to mass production or mass distribution. They used independent agents to market their products abroad. On the other hand, there were other producers who were interested in overseas markets in order to solve problems of long-term excess capacity. They possessed a technology simple to apply and made undifferentiated homogeneous products. Some makers of hats, textiles, clothing, clay goods, and leather products saw the foreign market as a solution to their domestic problems.[64]

It was the smaller producers of specialized machines, however, who led the way to the creation of the NAM, and it was among the makers of undifferentiated goods that they found their most willing members. The NAM was to become the largest, longest-lived business association devoted to foreign trade expansion. The association began with a small group of producers with a narrow set of interests. The organizers were primarily Ohio producers of machine tools and machinery. Their initial concern was the demise in 1894 of the provisions encouraging reciprocal tariff reductions, as outlined in the 1890 McKinley Tariff. Machinery makers feared retaliation against their own products because of generally high American tariffs. Reciprocity had left open the prospect of selective reduction in American rates in return for similar reductions abroad.[65]

The large response to the call for a meeting surprised the organizers. But producers of other goods like textiles also wanted to save reciprocity as a way in which to open up Latin American markets. At the organizational convention of the NAM, William McKinley, then governor of Ohio, delivered an enthusiastically received speech that expressed well the attitude of those attending toward reciprocity.[66]

Once formed, however, the NAM leadership and membership turned its attention to broader policy questions, although the early years saw as much attention paid to organizational matters as to the location of headquarters, staffing, and whether membership was to be opened to firms or individuals.[67] The broadening of concerns, however, was of great long-term significance. A wider spectrum of issues generated a larger base of support for the organization, so that, unlike many other business groups of the time, it was able to last beyond the enthusiasm over a particular issue. By 1900 the NAM had a thousand members, a full-time staff, and revenues of over $1,000,000. At first, in addition to reciprocity, the association advocated government-supported commercial expositions in South American capitals to display American products, increased government assistance to the merchant marine, and continued efforts to build the Nicaraguan or Isthmian Canal. In later years they addressed more issues. The NAM supported changes in banking legislation which would have permitted American branch banks abroad, and it cooperated in the movement to improve the Department of State's consular service. By 1898, the NAM's energetic president, Theodore C. Search, encouraged the membership to support the creation of a Department of Commerce and Industry to coordinate government efforts to increase foreign trade. Modeled after the Department of Agriculture, the new department was to be a departure from American federal administrative experience in which the executive departments were to do the public's business, but not serve a particular interest.[68]

The NAM, however, was more than simply a group designed to pressure Congress. The circular announcing the organizational convention stated that the NAM would serve as a forum for the exchange of information about developing foreign trade. The group was also to encourage the private collective activity of businessmen in expansion. Indeed, while the membership and leadership realized the importance of changing government policies, they also saw the need to adopt cooperative arrangements exhibited by European, especially German, businessmen.[69]

From the very first, then, the association tried to provide direct services to its members. Although the major elaboration and extension of these activities occurred after the turn of the century, the association began in the late 1890s to provide members information and assistance. One of its earliest efforts was to publish a trade index to introduce foreign buyers to the products made by members of the association who received free coverage in the book. The early editions were published in English and French; 7,500 copies were distributed free to leading merchants worldwide in the first year. By the second year, the editors had added a German and a Spanish edition.[70]

The association sponsored other publications to help its members expand their overseas business. *American Trade* (1897-1902), which later became *American Industries* (1902-1914), dealt with issues of foreign trade development, providing detailed information about the problems of selling overseas and foreign duties, currency, tariffs, ports, etc. The association devoted time, too, at national conventions to papers and discussions about how to seek and keep foreign markets. This information helped smaller producers most, since the larger manufacturers could afford to employ sales agents abroad to report on foreign conditions and opportunities.[71]

The NAM, however, did not confine itself to furnishing information. The growing staff began to provide direct services to its members. As with the NAM's publications, these efforts became more important after the turn of the century. Yet the tasks begun in the late 1890s were indicative of the importance the group placed on private collective activities. From the earliest years of the association, the leadership sought to engage display rooms and warehouses in foreign cities to introduce American goods to foreign buyers. Ideally, they wanted these to be government-supported, but there was little sentiment in Congress for such efforts and the NAM took it upon itself to rent facilities abroad to allow Americans to show and store their goods.

The first warehouse project was proposed for neighboring Mexico, where the NAM's president believed "a simple warehouse system" was necessary to garner a "share of her trade to which we seem to be entitled." Little came of the Mexican plans, and attention shifted southward. Eventually the association opened a warehouse in Caracas, Venezuela, in 1898. The executive committee continued to study sites in other Latin American cities, and some members dreamed of warehouses in the major European trading centers of London, Hamburg, Amsterdam, Antwerp, Copenhagen, and Berlin. While nothing came of these dreams, the association successfully established a warehouse and display rooms in Shanghai in 1900.[72]

Neither the warehouse in Caracas nor the one in Shanghai fared well. Unfortunately, the association chose places that soon faced political turmoil. A revolution toppled the government in Venezuela and an insurrection that followed against the new revolutionary government unsettled business conditions. Political turmoil and business depression led to liquidation of the Caracas warehouse in 1901. Similar problems arose in China, although the Shanghai warehouse did better for awhile than the one in Latin America.[73] Members exhibited great interest in these efforts because they confronted one of the smaller producers' major difficulties—the inability to employ traveling salesmen or set up foreign selling branches to gather information and assist in marketing.

The NAM helped its members in other ways. In 1899 the executive committee established an International Freight and Transportation Bureau to act as a forwarding agent. The bureau provided information about transportation rates, made arrangements for shipment, and, when necessary, helped members recover claims against shippers for overcharges. Of greatest significance, manufacturers often received lower rates than if they shipped themselves, since the bureau could combine shipments.[74]

These first efforts at providing information and direct services expanded greatly after the turn of the century. The late 1890s, however, demonstrated the ability of the association to attract and keep members by the assistance it gave and the issues it addressed. As a constant source of information about foreign trade expansion, the NAM provided continuity to those concerned about expansion because smaller producers' interests in foreign trade varied with conditions in the domestic economy. As the interest in trade expansion waned when conditions improved in the late 1890s, a minority interested in making the NAM a focus of antiunion activities prepared to take over, which they did in 1902. Foreign trade interests remained alive in the NAM and, as we shall see, the association expanded its activities to promote foreign trade. But the problems changed. Indeed, many struggled to hold their foreign markets, since their small operations could not handle the burgeoning domestic and foreign sales when domestic and foreign markets improved in the late 1890s. "We no longer find manufacturers striving to secure a market for their product," the president said in his 1900 report to the association's convention. "The most serious problem is to meet the demand for their goods and to make deliveries within the time specified by purchasers." Foreign trade expansion remained a concern of the association, but a minority antiunion faction were to take over and turn the association toward more national issues and more direct political activity.[75]

The NAM was not the only group to show interest in trade expansion. Some groups like the American Asiatic Association were equally interested, although they concentrated more on political pressure than service. Then, too, even more narrowly focused groups developed which devoted themselves to only one issue like the merchant marine or consular service. But the NAM was the most important of all the groups interested in trade expansion. It had the broadest base of support, the most professional staff organization, and the most extensive program to solve directly the everyday problems of creating foreign sales.

Thus by 1900 the largest producers were well established in foreign markets. The depression had helped some of them solidify their positions abroad as they consolidated or worked out patent agreements. Smaller producers without any of the substantial advantages of the major American corporations increased their interest in foreign sales and formed a major trade association to promote their interests through private collective activity and increasingly by lobbying in Congress for legislation to help smaller producers expand their foreign trade.

Efforts and programs begun in the late 1890s were expanded and intensified after 1900. At the same time, the NAM became more directly involved in politics in order to bring about legislation that the association and its members believed were necessary to promote trade expansion.[76] Yet in the decade and a half after 1900, the largest corporations strengthened their hold on America's export markets. As they responded to foreign competitors' and governments' attempts to limit their sales, the firms that had first established themselves in the 1870s and 1880s adopted policies that led to more secure foreign sales for the most part. By the time war broke out in Europe in 1914, a few of the largest American corporations accounted for the overwhelming share of American manufactured goods exported.

Three

Private Economic Power and the World Market, 1901–14

By 1914 major firms in key industries accounted for close to 90 percent of American manufactured exports.[1] Government policy toward foreign commerce (and the way in which smaller manufacturers related to the larger firms and to government) was closely tied to big business domination of exports. The largest American firms, giants like United States Steel, International Harvester, Standard Oil, Westinghouse, and Armour, did well abroad because of substantial advantages. The development of mass production and mass distribution techniques continued apace after the turn of the century, further strengthening companies that already had substantial power in key export industries a decade or two before 1900. The merger movement of the late nineteenth century created firms with even greater strength in already concentrated industries like steel and agricultural equipment. And companies with technological advantages and patents continued to develop new products and processes, leading to further control of markets at home and abroad.

But the response of foreign competitors and foreign governments to what was called the "American invasion" led to strategies by major American companies that gave them even greater advantages in export markets. To meet the demands of enterprises hard-pressed by American competition, foreign governments increased tariffs and passed stringent laws governing the use of American patents. To jump tariff walls and to qualify to use their patents abroad, American firms went beyond building foreign sales branches. They built assembly plants, which put together such goods as machinery, automobiles and electrical equipment from parts made in the United States. When these strategies were attacked through tariffs on the parts imported, some American firms simply began to make the parts abroad, thus beginning to manufacture overseas.

The sales of most American products abroad were made essentially through the private efforts of U.S. companies. At times firms turned to foreign-based officials of the American government for assistance. More often, however, U.S. corporate officials tried to mask or understate American ownership in a hostile environment by dealing directly with foreign government officials. Some U.S. companies, as we shall see, went so far as to hide their American nationality altogether, by establishing subsidiaries staffed and managed by foreign nationals.

Smaller American producers continued their interest in trade expansion in these years before the outbreak of war in Europe. In the early decades of the twentieth century the NAM expanded its services to members interested in foreign sales. The association's foreign department provided general information about foreign opportunities. In addition, the department provided direct assistance in translation, shipping, credit reports, and the like that helped members make sales abroad. NAM members were for the most part novices in foreign trade. Small producers of specialized products were members, but their export problems differed from those of the typical member of the NAM. Small producers with differentiated goods to sell abroad founded an association to serve their interests— the American Manufacturers' Export Association. Like the NAM, it eventually sought to press government to change foreign trade policies.

Large American firms' domination of the manufactured export market by 1914 was closely related to the rationalization of the late nineteenth-century mergers, to improving marketing structures, and in several industries to the further application of technology to production processes. The wave of consolidations in the late 1890s enabled many firms to expand operations at home and abroad. Most notably, enterprises in the steel industry first made overseas sales because of economic advantages brought about by mergers of the nineties. But firms in most of the other industries that had developed substantial overseas markets in the 1880s and 1890s continued to refine the mass production, mass distribution techniques that gave them significant advantages. As we have seen, specialized marketing structures created many of the major American industrial firms. Skilled marketing was a key factor at home and abroad, and it accounts for American firms' substantial selling in industrial economies much like that in the United States. Producers who had to provide special services of installation or marketing (like demonstration and credit) evolved large enterprises with extensive marketing arrangements. Likewise, those that had developed a high volume of output, often of a varied line of products, needed more assured marketing outlets than could be provided by traditional middlemen. These firms also integrated forward (and became large) in order to schedule their products regularly through marketing channels. The enterprises with substantial advantages in technology and marketing found ready markets abroad after 1900, as burgeoning European industrial economies provided ready demand. America could not only make the producers goods (the machinery and steel) but also the consumers goods (the cigarettes and processed foods) adapted for growing urban markets.[2]

The fundamental strength of the largest firms lay in their ability to limit and even prevent entry into their industries and into their markets at home and overseas. Following the merger movement of the late nineteenth century, many firms further coordinated their production and distribution processes. The resulting lower unit costs strengthened the market position of many of the largest firms in American industry. The increased capital expenditures for new and larger production and distribution facilities raised further barriers to entry into important industries. The structure of the modern industrial economy had been set then by the time America went to war in 1917. Of the 500 major industrial corporations in that year, nearly 90 percent were still in existence in 1967, either as independents or subsidiaries of other companies.[3] The American industrial economy was increasingly dominated in key sectors by oligopolistic patterns of competition. In many of the machinery, electrical equipment, chemical, explosive, meat-packing, steel, and oil industries, price competition was no longer the primary form of competition in the domestic market.

Lower prices and more intensive marketing made these firms better competitors abroad. Attention to marketing at home was necessary because the heavy expenditures for consolidation, new equipment and, in key industries, technology required a continuous flow of output to assure returns to meet high fixed costs. Increasingly extensive and sophisticated marketing techniques devoted to selling a large variety of goods to many different buyers were successful in foreign markets as well as at home. Of significance in some industries was a commitment to improve products through research. Thus in electrical, chemical, photographic, and some machinery industries the development of new products further strengthened market positions at home and abroad. Better marketing, the lower costs of mass production, and the constant attention to technological change created advantages and hence opportunities abroad. Relatively secure oligopolistic markets made the greatest American firms formidable competitors overseas.[4]

The relative control over prices and products made American firms serious competitors to foreign firms. United States companies faced sharp competition from German chemical and electrical producers. In some branches of the machinery industries, American firms faced vigorous competition from British, as well as German, producers. Generally, however, American manufacturers were able to hold their own in terms of the prices and quality of their products and the services that they provided to their customers.[5]

Foreign sales were achieved for the most part without assistance from the U.S. government. Even when challenged by foreign governments, American firms invariably relied on private efforts to cope with hostile government policy overseas. European competitors enlisted the support of their governments to fight what they perceived, early in the new century, as an "American invasion." Foreign governments turned to tariffs and patent laws to thwart American economic activity. Foreign manufacturers tried to appeal to nationalistic sentiments in order to keep their countrymen from buying American goods. Ironically, these challenges led to American responses that in a number of significant cases helped strengthen the foreign operations of American firms. Tariffs and patents contributed to the need for American companies to market more intensely and to develop branch manufacturing abroad. Among such leading industrial firms as those making Kodak cameras and Singer sewing machines, constant attention to improved technology and new products secured more markets for American manufacturers and kept American producers in advance of their potential foreign competitors in key industries.[6]

The histories of several of the major industrial firms of the early twentieth century illustrate how strengths developed in the domestic economy secured markets abroad. United States Steel, as we have seen, grew out of the late nineteenth-century merger movement and provides an excellent example of the relationship between mergers and increased foreign trade.[7] At first, United States Steel remained a holding company. To coordinate the overseas sales of its member firms, the executives of U.S. Steel set up an export subsidiary, U.S. Steel Products Company. The first man in charge of the export company was James A. Farrell. An excellent example of the self-made man, he would one day become president of U.S. Steel. In 1899 he had become the president of American Steel and Wire, a company that under his direction had developed significant sales overseas. Farrell was convinced that America needed foreign markets, and he set about to take advantage of the great strengths that U.S. Steel had. Because it controlled almost 50 percent of the industry's capacity in pig iron, steel ingots, steel castings, and rolled iron and steel, U.S. Steel had enormous control over prices and production at home. To break into foreign markets, U.S. Steel Products was able to undersell competitors abroad, even at the expense of short-run losses.[8]

Marketing steel abroad required less investment and attention to demonstration, service and credit facilities than in the sale of products like sewing machines. Yet Farrell wanted foreign purchasers to have access to an assured supply of the company's products, and he had built warehouses in cities like Valparaiso, Lima, Sydney, and Johannesburg. He then turned his considerable energies to transportation problems. Shipping products presented particular problems when U.S. Steel tried to sell in Latin America. The American merchant marine had languished after the Civil War, and to cultivate markets in Latin America often required costly transshipment which undermined some of the price advantages that U.S. Steel and other producers would otherwise have had. To get to remote places in Latin America, therefore, U.S. Steel Products purchased its own steamship line. U.S. Steel thus joined the ranks of other American producers in the meat-packing, brewing, and cotton oil industries who had developed their own transportation when private arrangements proved too costly.[9]

The result of U.S. Steel's efforts was domination of American sales of steel products abroad. By 1909, the company estimated that it controlled 90 percent of American iron and steel exports. Domination continued past 1914 and into the United States' war years. By the 1920s, however, U.S. Steel began to drop out of the world market, as foreign prices declined and domestic construction and auto manufacturing created a growing demand for steel products.[10] But until then, the firm was a major exporter of American products. Farrell's experience at U.S. Steel convinced him of the importance of export markets. He became a prominent leader of efforts to encourage commercial expansion, as we shall see in later chapters.

Many firms expanded operations after the turn of the century. The end of the depression of the 1890s stimulated the electrical manufacturers to greater efforts at foreign sales. New construction at home and overseas, especially in Europe, led to growing foreign sales. Westinghouse continued patterns of foreign sales developed much earlier. In the early years of the new century, the company established production facilities in Germany, France, Russia, and Canada. Patents were important for Westinghouse's operations in Britain. To begin manufacturing, Westinghouse set up the British Westinghouse Electric and Manufacturing Company, Ltd. The concern, a wholly owned subsidiary corporation, was granted exclusive rights to use Westinghouse patents. Similar patterns were followed after 1900, when Westinghouse made substantial investments in large manufacturing facilities in Germany, France, Russia, and Canada. Ultimately, Westinghouse overextended itself, as became clear after World War I, although the company was hard pressed in 1907, when some of the foreign companies went into receivership.[11]

Westinghouse's great American rival, General Electric, proceeded more modestly at first, as befit a company not so well endowed financially as Westinghouse. But General Electric expanded abroad after the depression of the 1890s. General Electric's predecessor firms Thomson Houston and Edison Electric both had had substantial foreign sales. Patents played an important role in General Electric's sales overseas, as they had with Westinghouse. Basically, General Electric formed or gained control of "associated" firms abroad. Through these companies General Electric granted exclusive rights to use its patents or to work licenses. In return, the parent American company required that the affiliated foreign firm would not sell outside of its territory. All of General Electric's patents, for example, were given to its English affiliate. General Electric, however, retained the right to produce and sell its products outside of the British firm's exclusive territory. Similarly, General Electric made patent agreements with Japanese firms in 1904 and 1909. The company gained greater control of the Japanese firms by providing capital for the expansion of the Japanese plants to work the patents in the manufacture of electric lights and electric power equipment. Similarly, patents proved significant for the expansion of General Electric's operations in France. In fact, the company simply followed understandings made by its forerunner company, Thomson Houston, when it established an affiliated company in France to use patents and exercise exclusive rights to sell in the French market. Arrangements were different only in Germany. General Electric made agreements with Germany's Allgemeine Elektrizitäts Gessellschaft to divide markets. Allgemeine Elektrizitäts Gessellschaft received much of central Europe, Turkey, and Eastern Russia, in return for which General Electric had exclusive rights in Canada and America. South America, Central America (including Mexico), and Japan were considered neutral areas and open to competition of both firms.[12]

Patents played another important part in General Electric's corporate strategy. General Electric began to exploit systematically the advances in formal knowledge of physics at the end of the nineteenth century. General Electric founded a research laboratory in 1900, one of the first in American industry. Management started hesitatingly and then moved substantially, employing in its research facilities a staff of over one hundred by 1906. By the war General Electric had attracted scientists with advanced degrees and substantial reputations in order to conduct research on Xrays, electric lighting, metallurgy, and radio. Expenditures for research were modest by today's standards, but the $100,000 spent for the development of an effective process to manufacture tungsten filaments for lamps was substantial for the day. And the management of General Electric clearly thought of patents as a decided competitive advantage abroad, since competition came from German producers who also spent large sums on research in electrical equipment.[13]

But research on new products occurred elsewhere in American industry too. Between 1900 and 1910 DuPont began to make expenditures on research and development. In the photography industry, Kodak saw research as a way to maintain its market positions by gaining new patents. But even in industries where innovation and technology were comparatively simple, market leaders tried to keep their leading positions by attention to improved technology. Singer improved old models and expanded its line of machines. In the 1880s, management established an engineering department to improve machines in order to maintain the company's competitive position.[14]

But advantages gained from mergers and the use of patents were not the only reasons American firms expanded abroad after 1900. The behavior of foreign companies and their governments played an important part in the way that American firms did business abroad. International Harvester provides a good example. The companies that combined to form International Harvester in 1902 had had more significant stakes and experience in overseas sales than had the enterprises collected together into U.S. Steel. Like other successful mergers of the 1890s, International Harvester rationalized production and distribution. In terms of marketing, the company established fairly distinct patterns of distribution at home and abroad based on the extensive foreign operations of McCormick Harvester Company. At home, they expanded operations to include a full line of products. Such diversification and expansion of related activities strengthened the position of the firm in the industry. Sharp price competition in one line of products and short-term losses were offset by increased prices in other less competitive lines. A full range of products helped reduce distribution costs, as dealers sold more and more kinds of goods.

The harvesting machine companies that made up International Harvester had produced several special machines: binders, reapers, mowers, rakes, and corn binders. International Harvester expanded operations to include tillage implements and eventually wagons, thrashers, and tractors. The full-line strategy at home eventually found its way abroad.[15]

But International Harvester's foreign expansion also resulted from foreign conditions. The policies of foreign governments forced the company to build manufacturing plants abroad. High foreign tariffs would have offset the advantages International Harvester achieved through its marketing operations. As a result, by 1900 the firm had built plants in Canada, France, Sweden, Germany, and Russia, a reflection of the fact that foreign sales represented 40 percent of the firm's entire business, and at times the firm's most profitable business. Generally, these foreign operations were created privately without government assistance. In building plants in Russia, however, International Harvester had to work closely with Russian government officials. The czar's government feared that Russia would be weakened through the unsupervised investment of Western European capital. American investments were small by comparison to those made by European capitalists, but International Harvester and other American firms like Westinghouse Air Brake had to work under close Russian governmental supervision to allow them to operate at all. As such, International Harvester occasionally had to turn to American State Department officials to help deal with the Russian bureaucracy, although the company relied mostly on its own dealings with czarist officials.[16]

Like International Harvester, other American firms abroad expanded their operations in response to foreign hostility. Investments in marketing were followed by the construction of branch factories overseas. American Radiator built a number of branch factories to offset the negative effects of high tariffs. Like Singer, American Radiator tried to mask its American ownership by taking on foreign names for its overseas subsidiaries. The decision to hide an American corporate identity allowed the corporation to eschew assistance from American officials, since to turn to American consuls to defend an American business opened the company to criticism by foreign nationalists.[17]

It was not always easy, however, to mask a corporate identity by choosing foreign names and officials for subsidiaries. This was especially true in Germany. Of all the European countries, German laws and practices were the most hostile to American enterprise. High tariffs and stringent patent laws often forced American firms to build branch factories to protect their stakes in German markets. The German patent laws, at least until a modification and relaxation in 1909, required the holders of foreign patents to utilize them in Germany or face having the patents voided. France was not so overtly hostile to foreign interests, but tariffs in the prewar years were high enough that American firms had to build factories there too. Like the European industrial leaders, Japan tried to protect its own manufacturers. After 1899, with the end of treaties restricting its tariff autonomy, Japan was able to set its own tariffs, and did so in such a way as to keep foreign products out. Firms most affected by tariffs, patent laws, and intense nationalistic feelings were those in the oil, tobacco, electrical equipment, automobile, and fertilizer industries.[18]

Not every American manufacturer, however, responded to foreign challenges by building branch factories. Some American firms cooperated with and made peace with their European competitors to secure the markets these firms had established themselves. European business had fewer restrictions on cartel agreements than American firms had at home. At times, major American companies joined in cartels to set prices or more typically to parcel out markets. From time to time Standard Oil came to terms with some of its foreign competitors. Standard continued to market competitively at other times and to meet foreign competition with further investments in foreign facilities. One such understanding supposedly took place in 1907 among Standard Oil, Deutsche Bank-Shell and Nobel-Rothschild interests to divide the European market. In the Far East, Standard Oil of New York, which had substantial markets selling kerosene, came to terms with a primary competitor, Royal Dutch-Shell. Agreements made in 1905 lasted only until 1911, when sharp price competition resumed. The breakup of Standard Oil in 1911 did not halt foreign business for 9 of the 34 component companies of Standard Oil. These new firms continued to sell abroad through marketing facilities, and some retained foreign refineries. Despite increasing competition most of these companies were able to establish or maintain previously established markets, although they cooperated less frequently with foreign competitors.[19]

Oil was not the only industry that at times secured its export markets by agreement with foreign cartels. In the aluminum and copper industries there were also agreements. And there were hints of such cartel arrangements in the iron and steel industry. The fear of antitrust prosecution, however, restrained full-scale efforts to divide markets formally. A visit by leading men in the European steel industry in 1913, sponsored by the American Iron and Steel Association, provided the opportunity for discussions of cartel understandings, but nothing came of these meetings. Leaders of U.S Steel, especially Elbert H. Gary, were most sensitive to and indeed fearful of antitrust prosecution.[20]

Copper producers, however, did participate in foreign cartels. As early as 1888, a large American producer, Calumet and Hecla of Michigan, took part in a scheme organized by the French to control the world output of copper. By 1891 the effort had clearly failed. Calumet and Hecla then approached foreign competitors themselves with plans to curtail American exports in return for reduced imports. These plans met with only limited success. Greater control of the world's copper market became possible when the Rothschilds bought Anaconda Copper Company. With the acquisition of the largest American company in the industry, the Rothschilds had about 40 percent of the world's output under their control. They met some success in controlling prices, but Anaconda returned to American hands in the late nineteenth-century wave of mergers when Anaconda became part of Amalgamated Copper Company in 1899. In 1900 the new firm helped reorganize a major dealer in copper to distribute the firm's products better abroad. Meanwhile, Amalgamated Copper faced increasing competition from the Guggenheim brothers. These major companies, despite their firm control of the domestic market, were not able to stabilize prices because European buyers were able to form buyers' combinations which forced prices down. John D. Ryan, of Amalgamated, became a leading spokesman for changes in the antitrust laws to allow Americans to combine in retaliation. He wanted a change in the

Sherman Act, instead of special permission from the Federal Trade Commission. The latter, he feared, would allow only the smaller firms an opportunity to combine, when in fact it was a serious problem for the larger ones as well.[21]

All these manufacturers looked upon such collaboration as a necessary response to European conditions and as following foreign practices. The forerunner of Aluminum Company of American (Alcoa) was Pittsburgh Reduction Company (the name was changed at the beginning of 1907). As early as 1895, the company had engaged in arrangements to divide products with European competitors. The firm, organized in 1888, had built a plant in France in 1891 to capture some of the European market. These efforts at direct manufacturing abroad proved unsuccessful. Thus a few years later Pittsburgh Reduction entered into a market-sharing agreement with a large Swiss enterprise. The Swiss were to keep out of the American market in return for Pittsburgh's keeping out of Switzerland, Germany, and Austria-Hungary. The agreement did not last; the American firm began to sell widely in Europe afterwards and by the turn of the century had a substantial trade. In the meantime, Pittsburgh Reduction had entered into business in Canada, completing a plant there in 1899-1900.[22]

The company had to participate in European cartels, however, or face the united competition of European producers. Pittsburgh's management feared prosecution under the Sherman Act and thus formed a wholly owned Canadian subsidiary to act on behalf of the American parent. The Canadian subsidiary manufactured for Canada and also handled all exports, making agreements with European producers to divide the European market and essentially to protect the American from European imports. The accords first signed in 1901 were strengthened in 1906 and 1908. But Alcoa faced prosecution for violations of the American antitrust laws. In 1912 the company signed a consent decree, which prohibited agreements about imports and exports from the United States. Alcoa, however, was able still to participate in foreign cartels through its Canadian subsidiary. The Justice Department understood that Alcoa would make those agreements from Canada; its only concern was that the American market remain open. In effect, the U.S. government allowed Alcoa to regulate the market outside of the United States with its European competitors.[23]

The foreign environment affected the operations of other American exporters in other ways. Cigarettes had grown in popularity in the United States in response to changing markets. City dwellers preferred cigarettes to chewing tobacco and cigars which were suited to a less urban environment. Urban Europeans quickly adopted cigarettes and James B. Duke, the leader in the American industry, exported as early as the 1890s. But Duke's American Tobacco had to respond to tariffs and other foreign discriminations. High duties on manufactured tobacco prompted Duke to acquire a British firm in 1901, but in response his British competitors combined to form Imperial Tobacco. Following sharp competition Duke and Imperial reached an agreement to divide markets between the United States and Britain. American Tobacco joined with Imperial in 1902 to form another company, British-American Tobacco, to divide the rest of the world's market.

A 1911 Supreme Court decision broke up American Tobacco. The decision in *U.S.* v. *American Tobacco* also required the American firm to break its foreign understandings about divisions of the market. The four American companies to emerge from this decision were not inclined to look to foreign business. Duke himself, however, remained as chairman of the board of British-American Tobacco, and that company, headquartered in London, continued its hold on the world market outside of the United States.[24]

Not everyone needed such agreements. In many other American industries, unique products, often the result of new technologies, secured markets for American producers in the early years of the century. In equipment for business and commerce, American firms took an early lead. National Cash Register sold abroad for many years before the turn of the century, expanding its operations thereafter. But other companies that specialized in office machines had also begun to market broadly in Europe in the early years of the century. The forerunner of IBM, Computing-Tabulating-Recording Company, was formed out of a merger of three major firms making business equipment. These companies, International Times Recording Company, Tabulating Machine Company and Computing Scale Company, all had foreign sales at the time the company was created in 1911. These predecessor firms had responded to foreign competition by building a marketing organization and eventually plants abroad, as well as coming to terms with competitors and licensing foreign manufacture of their goods. Computing-Tabulating-Recording Company became IBM in 1924.[25]

New technologies adapted for mass selling continued to strengthen American producers' positions in a number of other industries. The automobile is an excellent example. Ford Motor Company sold from the first in export markets. Indeed, the fourth car produced was exported. Henry Ford was by no means the only producer of motor cars. He was, however, one of the first producers to concentrate on making an automobile for the ordinary citizen. Before Ford, especially abroad, automotive pioneers concentrated on making cars for a wealthy and aristocratic clientele. The machines produced were excellent and often beautifully hand-finished. But Ford devoted his efforts to a practical, inexpensive, relatively light product, and increasingly he found a large market both at home and abroad for his cars.

Like many major American firms, Ford and other American auto producers turned to foreign assembly and eventually manufacturing of parts. Assembly plants were the first response to tariffs, since it was less costly to ship parts than a completed automobile. Once a market was established, further savings became possible simply by making most parts abroad. The first assembly plants were in Canada. Ford began to manufacture his cars in Canada in 1904 through a subsidiary company that gave Ford a controlling interest in exchange for patents and Henry Ford's services if needed. This Canadian enterprise could sell to the entire British Empire, with the exception of England and Ireland. There, Ford established a sales branch which employed agents to sell the company's automobiles. In 1911-12 the company constructed an assembly plant, and by 1914 Ford's Model T had become the most popular auto in England, outselling all competitors. By the same time, Ford was assembling cars in France and had established the first direct Latin American sales outlet in Argentina.[26]

Other American automobile manufacturers were making significant inroads in foreign markets at the same time as Ford. When General Motors was formed in 1908, it acquired Olds Motor Works and Buick, both of which had begun to sell and make automobiles in Canada. These producers, like Ford, had so early gone to foreign manufacturing because of the high Canadian tariffs. *Horseless Age* announced proudly in 1904, however, that American automobiles were sold on five continents, although clearly Europe and North America were the major sales areas. Exports of the American machines had begun early, as makers of the Cadillac, Pope, White, Waltham, and Locomobile and Duryea sold in foreign markets. By 1903, about one-third of the output of American automobiles went into foreign sales; the bulk of these exports were of the less expensive models.[27]

Thus, by 1914 some of the largest firms in the American industrial economy had secured for themselves significant foreign markets. In some industries technology and in others marketing accounted for these gains. Others solidified their positions by cartel agreements with foreign competitors, understandings that at times resulted in federal litigation. Many of the most successful enterprises were those that had developed an oligopolistic market structure at home. They had relative control over production and prices, and this strength helped meet and surpass foreign price competition. These firms also responded to hostile foreign government opposition by increased attention to controlling foreign operations. Producers with heavy investments in plants needed an assured flow of products to insure returns adequate to meet the costs of investment. The need to keep up such a flow encouraged firms to gain greater control of their foreign sales through direct selling, assembly, and manufacturing. The ability to compete abroad was in many cases closely tied to the strong oligopolistic markets at home, where the sharp price competition of the 1880s and 1890s had been significantly reduced. As we shall see, these large firms were not unconcerned about government policy. But they were interested in policies that were consistent and rational, policies that did not undermine the foreign markets that these largest producers had attained because of advantage.

While the major producers firmly established their markets abroad, smaller manufacturers continued their interest in overseas sales. Sales abroad were easily attainable for those smaller manufacturers who made highly specialized products (machine tools and laboratory glass, for example) or produced goods with distinctive design (builders' hardware) or utilized special advertising (patent medicines). But many smaller industrialists whose goods had no particular advantage in foreign markets also wanted to keep the markets gained in the depression of the 1890s. Industry trade associations, local chambers of commerce, and boards of trade sponsored informational programs about the problems of trade expansion. For the most part, organizations such as the Cincinnati Board of Trade and similar groups in Baltimore, Rochester, and Columbus provided general advice and encouragement to their members. Widespread interest in trade expansion, however, was not translated into significant direct assistance to businessmen until the National Association of Manufacturers expanded its services to members after 1900.

Local chambers of commerce distributed government publications to their members. These groups also tried through petitions and testimony in Congress to gain support for changes in the tariff and in merchant marine policy. Many local chambers of commerce participated in national campaigns, like that of the National Reciprocity Conference, to gain support for changes in federal policy. Direct assistance to producers was provided by groups like the Machine Tool Builders Association that were able to furnish specific information to their members about how foreign conditions affected a particular industry. Of all the efforts of businessmen, the most significant private collective activity was that of the NAM. This group went beyond providing general information and hortatory statements about the benefits of foreign trade. At the same time, the NAM stepped up its lobbying efforts in Congress, establishing an office in Washington for that purpose. As important as lobbying was, direct attention to the industrial needs of businessmen was equally important. As the assistant secretary of the NAM noted in 1912, concern in 1900 for issues of reciprocal trade relations, an isthmian canal, merchant marine, and a department of industries were significant, but the association's collective efforts were important too. "While all these measures were in themselves important and deserving of the support of the manufacturers of the country," the assistant secretary observed, "the individual manufacturer who essayed for the first time to sell his wares abroad by his own efforts found that he was in need of a great deal of detailed information and advice which he was at a loss how to secure and with assurance as to its reliability. Therefore, from the beginning, the Association attempted—and we think its subsequent history shows attempted successfully—not only to advocate in resolutions and addresses this or that great measure, but at the same time to become a practical organization in working efficiently for the promotion of those measures and providing that information and expert assistance which the individual manufacturer required."[28]

The NAM increased its membership in the early years of the century. It almost doubled between 1902 and 1903, increasing by nearly one thousand members. Between 1903 and 1904 there was another increase of about a thousand, reaching a total of almost 3000 members. This increase in numbers, combined with an increase in dues, allowed the association to expand its services. Membership increased slightly after that, until in 1914 there were about 3,400. In 1905 the

NAM's president observed that the growth of membership was tied in large part to the work of the NAM in expanding trade, although the association's leadership of an antiunion movement also played its part. From the first tentative efforts at direct assistance to its members in the late nineties, the NAM expanded its private collective efforts to expand trade in the early years of the century. The department chiefly responsible for this aid was the foreign department, formerly the bureau of information, although other branches of the NAM provided assistance at times.[29]

The NAM's foreign department became the most important division of the association, even in the years when the executive officers focused on, and gained public attention for, their antiunion activities. An expanding foreign department staff provided an increasing variety of services to members. In the years before the war, expenditures on the department increased rapidly. The department provided the direct, almost day-to-day assistance that was essential to the smaller unifunctional (unintegrated) producers in the NAM. These were the men who for the most part did not employ their own foreign sales agents and had little chance of ever establishing branch selling or manufacturing abroad.

Of similar importance, the NAM increased the number of its publications. By 1900, NAM publications had gained a wide readership and attention for the NAM both at home and abroad. Information about foreign opportunities and foreign ways of doing business was clearly one of the most important kinds of general assistance the NAM could provide to smaller producers seeking to expand their foreign markets. The largest producers set up sales branches through which agents reported from the field. Information was critical to both the large and small. While the agents and sales branches of the larger manufacturers reported back to home offices, it was the publications of the NAM that apprised the smaller producers of opportunities for sales abroad, as well as of some of the problems that might be encountered in trying to make sales overseas.

The publications of the NAM provided another important service too. The association tried to publicize to foreign businessmen what was available from American producers, and so the publication strategy of the NAM was two-pronged: to inform Americans about foreign opportunities and to notify foreign buyers about American products.

The publication program that first attracted members to the NAM before 1900 expanded in the new century. *American Trade* was changed to *American Industries* in 1902, its scope expanded and its distribution abroad widened. By 1905, the NAM was sending out over 12,000 copies a year. This biweekly magazine had become, according to the NAM's secretary in his 1911 report, "the official organ of a group of manufacturers seeking to improve trade relations between the manufacturers of the United States and the various buyers in the world's markets who have little means of access and limited sources for information concerning the products produced here which are of interest to the foreign buyer, as many such articles cannot be purchased elsewhere in the world; and the great lack of personal representation of our manufacturers in foreign markets makes them singularly dependent upon such a medium." In addition, the NAM began a special export edition of this magazine in 1909. The editors produced special editions to appeal to importers in English-speaking countries and a Spanish edition designed to meet the needs of buyers in Latin America. The foreign department also frequently published special studies devoted to conditions in markets as different as Mexico, Morocco, and the Near East. These publications also discussed foreign business practices and foreign regulation and apprised members of U.S. government publications of interest to market-seeking producers.[30]

The association also published *Confidential Bulletins*, which summarized foreign inquiries about American goods. By the early part of the century foreign buyers began to contact the NAM about purchases here. Publication of these inquiries was made confidential to insure that only members of the association received the benefits from their group's growing reputation abroad. In 1911, for example, the association's foreign department issued 24 of these bulletins summarizing foreign inquiries about American goods. It also continued to publish in four languages the *American Trade Index*, a list of NAM members and their products.[31]

The NAM, in addition, generated information through special task forces sent to investigate foreign conditions. Thus, the executive committee sponsored a trip by the former superintendent of the Eleventh Census who visited Japan to report on its industries and trade practices. In 1912, two former presidents of the association traveled to New Zealand and Australia to investigate labor-management relations there, but also to take note of trade conditions and sales possibilities.[32]

In providing information about foreign trade, however, the NAM did not limit itself to publications alone. At the New York headquarters, the staff sponsored talks by foreign businessmen visiting the United States. The staff itself, many of them expert in trade-related matters, gave speeches and organized meetings about exporting in New York and in other cities. And closer to home, the staff at times organized tours for businessmen of the New York terminal, shipping, and dock facilities as part of a campaign to help American producers improve their packing techniques. The department also set up a school, made up of staff members, to train businessmen in export practices.[33]

Information, in short, was an indispensable aid to many of those inexperienced in foreign trade. But once interest was stimulated, the services of the foreign department of the NAM, and some of the association's other divisions, provided the most assistance to members. The department provided the direct services on a day-to-day basis that facilitated the making of sales abroad. The NAM provided the most comprehensive services to businessmen seeking trade outside of the major corporations' export sales branches.

One of the most important tasks of the foreign department was in translating business correspondence. The association employed a staff of translators who, according to the secretary of the association in 1912, were able to translate from thirty different languages. The NAM's linguists were, for a small charge, available to translate business letters, catalogs, technical literature, and, of great significance, legal documents. In 1911, the bureau provided services to exactly a thousand manufacturers. The department also answered direct questions about foreign trade conditions, laws governing commerce, tariffs, port practices, and the like. Some of this information was generated by a growing government bureaucracy, but the NAM's executive offices made it more accessible by providing direct answers to specific individual questions. Whenever it could, the department provided manufacturers with samples of manufactured foreign products on request.[34]

Of equal importance, the department provided credit reports on foreign manufacturing firms and commercial houses. It investigated the character and financial standing of foreign businesses. By 1912, according to the assistant secretary, the NAM maintained a file of tens of thousands of such reports. While many of these reports were generated by contacting a firm and asking for a statement and references, others were the results of special inquiries. The NAM contacted bankers and merchants in the merchant's city and in addition made inquiries to firms in the United States known to have done business with the foreign concerns. The result was invaluable information that was not, at least regularly and systematically, generated by a government agency. And, if despite the efforts of the credit bureau, there was trouble in collecting, the association maintained a collection bureau. The foreign department kept a current list of foreign attorneys to represent members if necessary. The work of the credit bureau stimulated and then was closely allied with a bureau of foreign buyers. The bureau assembled and kept up-to-date lists of business names and classifications of business firms in many countries. Producers who did not generate a regular foreign business did not keep abreast of such changes and found the work of the bureau of great use.[35]

The NAM also established a bureau of trademarks and patents within the foreign department. This bureau assisted members in registering trademarks abroad, an important requirement for proving ownership in many foreign countries. Some members had not registered their marks at home, since the common law generally protected a trademark's rightful owner, even if the symbol had not been registered. If necessary, the association could refer members to foreign attorneys who specialized in patents and trademark cases.[36]

Efforts begun before the century to help in freight and shipping continued after 1900. The NAM's international freight bureau sought to ease shipping problems by assuring that goods arrived abroad in good shape. This bureau was to assist in making shipping contracts at home and abroad for direct and transshipment of goods. It was also to gather shipment data on bills of lading used by different shippers, their connecting lines, cost of shipping, and custom house procedures abroad. The bureau arranged at times for lower rates because it could combine members' cargoes. The group also tried, unsuccessfully, to effect changes in the practices of shippers. They wanted to alter the standard shipper's contract that reserved the right for shippers to deposit their goods at other than a designated port. Also, they tried to get shippers to do away with charges to deliver from rail to dock those goods shipped in less than carload lots. This bureau eliminated the need for freight forwarders. The NAM's own group was more attentive to smaller producers' needs and provided better service than private shippers, but the bureau did not prosper. The bureau either made arrangements for or handled directly the shipments of 1000 NAM members in 1905. The difficulties of managing so much business prompted the NAM to sell the bureau to a freight-fowarding firm. The economically troubled times of 1907 caused the firm to default on its debts to the NAM, and the bureau was sold in 1908.[37]

The key to the NAM's success with market-seeking manufacturers, however, was its ability to help them make sales. The association furnished current information about customs, tariffs, and custom house procedures, and data about foreign currencies, exchange rates, and the practices of foreign banks. Some of this information came from staff and members who went abroad, and other information was garnered from government publications. Much of this information was gained through the extensive correspondence carried on by the foreign department staff and those in other bureaus and departments who dealt with foreign trade. One of the association's most important sources of information, however, depended on what it referred to as its "foreign correspondents." These 1400 individuals, foreigners or Americans living abroad, provided much information to the NAM's foreign department. The correspondents furnished information about special needs and particular demand in their localities. This information was provided for a small fee, but it was at times information unavailable elsewhere. The 1400 correspondents in 1912 were double the number of the Department of State's consulars, and many were located in cities without American consulates.[38]

All of this general information was to help producers get sales in out-of-the-way places and to encourage manufacturers to take advantage of opportunities abroad. To be sure, many of the sales were not in the major markets garnered by the largest producers. But information about a particular need in a special market might make possible a sale in an area that otherwise might not have seemed propitious for American producers of undifferentiated or highly specialized goods.

The foreign department also cultivated relations with the government. By 1911 the department aided both the Department of State and the Department of Commerce and Labor in disseminating information they had gathered about opportunities for foreign investment and, of more relevance to members of the NAM, for contracts to sell goods to both foreign private enterprises and governments.[39]

In 1914 the NAM further specialized its services by creating two new geographical divisions within the foreign department. They were to study and foster trade with Russia and Latin America. The executive committee appointed a man of wide experience in international banking and finance to run these new departments. In dealing with Russia, as some of the giant firms like International Harvester, Westinghouse, and Singer learned on their own, it was necessary to work closely with the czarist government. The division head developed close relations with the Russian commercial attaché in the United States who acted then as a liaison with officials and merchants in Russia.[40]

The NAM, in short, provided direct services to its members that, as we shall see, were not fully provided by the government. Despite the efforts of the Department of Commerce in later years to improve its direct assistance to businessmen, the association's foreign department was more accessible and indeed more reliable, since the Department of Commerce's efforts were interrupted by Congress' penchant to cut appropriations. By 1914 the work of the foreign department had become one of the most important activities of the association, not only in terms of expenditures, but also in terms of the membership it generated. By 1911 the treasurer reported that the foreign department alone spent almost as much as the general offices of the association, and if the costs of publishing and distributing the foreign editions of *American Industries* were included, then the foreign department accounted for more expenditures than all activities of the association combined. In the years to follow, the foreign department continued to grow in numbers of employees and in the resources that the association spent on it.[41]

By World War I, the NAM had developed a wide variety of services to aid its members in seeking foreign trade. These efforts never fully matched the direct information and sales promotion that the major manufacturers could get from their own employees abroad in sales branches. But the association's efforts provided the information and the services that smaller producers could not provide profitably for themselves. The foreign department, according to a *Saturday Evening Post* journalist, represented the "highest development" in the effort of a private association to expand trade.[42] Its services also satisfied the interests of those in NAM who looked upon export trade as a sometime venture. Those who sold only occasionally did not keep up with government publications, nor did they employ their own foreign sales agents. When they wanted to sell or when they received orders from abroad, they turned to the association to provide a full range of services and information about foreign conditions.

But collective private activity was not exclusively the province of those producers with the smallest stakes in overseas markets. In 1909 some producers who had generated regular foreign sales, usually because their products were distinguished by style or technology, created an association, the American Manufacturers' Export Association. The AMEA and the NAM, to be sure, were not the only groups concerned with foreign trade expansion. Many local merchants' groups, chambers of commerce, boards of trade, citywide trade groups, for example, had committees to study the problems of foreign trade expansion. Industrywide associations of machine tool makers and cotton textile manufacturers also showed concern. But before 1914 the only other cross-industry group devoted to collective activity to promote exports was the AMEA. This association was important as a forerunner to the National Foreign Trade Council, which, as we shall see, was one of the most significant associations to deal with trade expansion, a group that sought to bring together the many diverse elements in the movement for trade expansion.

The AMEA had two clear purposes. First, it was concerned with resolving problems with middlemen and government officials through cooperative efforts. And, second, it sought to press Congress for changes in commercial policy that its members believed were necessary to protect their foreign business.

The AMEA did not model itself on the NAM. It was not so ambitious an organization, since its interests were more circumscribed and its membership more limited. In fact, the AMEA disdained what it saw as the frenetic evangelical fervor of some of the NAM's attempts to convince producers of the need for trade expansion. In a scarcely veiled reference to the NAM, the new association asserted in a statement of principle that the AMEA was "to gather together men of *thorough knowledge regarding export, men of practical experience, men who know,* not to provide a bureau of information, translation facilities or a school for beginners in the field, but to accomplish...larger objects."[43]

The AMEA differed from the NAM in other important ways. It was an association made up for the most part of the port managers of firms that had already established foreign markets. The group never attracted the number of members and public attention, indeed notoriety, of the NAM. The firms its members represented were not for the most part the largest manufacturing enterprises selling in foreign markets, although there were a few like Westinghouse represented. About 90 percent of American manufactured exports in 1911 were shipped by a few major corporations which, the American consul-general in Hamburg observed in a speech to the AMEA, had "properly equipped branches abroad." AMEA members generally were *not* within this group of manufacturers with overseas branch operations, although they were producers who made products with some competitive advantages. Their goods were recognized because of quality, brand name, or technological superiority. They were, in short, the makers of differentiated, unhomogeneous products. Indeed, the president of the American Exporters and Importers Association observed that about 80–85 percent of the orders he received from abroad, and he thought himself typical, were specific requests for the products of a particular manufacturer, a special brand name. Some members dealt with exporters who either purchased their goods outright or sold their products for a commission; other members sold to foreign importers outright or to foreign commission agents.[44]

The group started haltingly, with a membership of only thirty and, at the end of the first year, a financial deficit. Despite its limited size and shaky finances, the AMEA had a full-time, if small, staff. There was at first some confusion about the purposes of the organization. Some members, as the secretary reported in 1911, apparently thought its major function was to be social. By the second year, however, the group's focus was clearly more serious. Indeed the secretary, with the hubris typical of executives of many trade associations, believed that the AMEA's work was of national significance.[45]

The staff believed that the AMEA's major purpose was the preservation of the overseas markets its members had gained for themselves. Furthermore, AMEA members found the practices of the American and foreign governments at times inimical to their interests. They sought to deal directly with the American government to get what they wanted from it and to get the American government to press other governments for changes in their policies and laws, although the AMEA at times tried to work directly with foreign governments and foreign business groups.[46]

The AMEA sought from government, as we shall see more fully in the next chapter, what other business groups wanted. It advocated simplified customs regulations, "scientific" tariff adjustment, reciprocity with other countries, improvement of the American merchant marine, an international parcel post, the placement of commercial attachés in embassies and legations abroad, and the continued professionalization of the consular and diplomatic corps. From foreign governments the AMEA would have liked abolition of discriminatory practices which it believed worked against American interests. Particularly rankling to the AMEA were what they thought were unclear and unfair classification of American goods by foreign customs officials, discrimination against Americans registering trademarks, and taxes on traveling salesmen (a problem mainly in Latin America). To get what it wanted, the AMEA planned to put pressure on the U.S. government. It also planned to have its representatives meet with foreign chambers of commerce to clarify and standardize commercial practices.[47]

Despite the ambitious goals for the organization, the AMEA dealt with practical, somewhat mundane questions at first. The most important work of the early years, according to the secretary, was the improvement of relations between U.S. commission houses and manufacturers engaged in export trade. An AMEA committee met with representatives of the Importers and Exporters Association (composed of commission houses) to discuss common problems and difficulties. The smaller, generally unintegrated manufacturers like those in the AMEA depended upon these commission agents. Since the agent often offered credit to foreign buyers, the smaller manufacturer was paid rather quickly. The source of difficulty between commission agents and manufacturers was the discretion as to prices that the commission agents demanded of manufacturers. Producers simply believed that commission agents too readily lowered prices to make a sale. Then, too, there was little agreement on the length of time that agents should extend credit to foreign buyers. Producers feared that reducing the length of credit would make American firms less competitive with foreign. To resolve this problem they sought information about foreign practices from the Department of Commerce and Labor. Also, manufacturers were unhappy when agents "pushed" the goods of competing manufacturers in the absence of an exclusive agreement with a particular manufacturer.[48]

The AMEA also tried to deal directly with other problems. Particularly troublesome were complaints about damage during shipment. Merchants in the interior complained about the way in which their goods were handled in New York. The AMEA investigated complaints and implored merchants' warehousemen in New York and other seaports to take greater care with shipments. The AMEA developed what it called an employment service to help place those who wanted to work in foreign trade. This service also acted as a clearinghouse of information about those seeking employment. Members needed trustworthy and knowledgeable representatives when they hired someone to represent them abroad. Like the NAM the group also established a credit bureau. The AMEA acquired and disseminated information about the credit-worthiness of individuals and firms with whom members were likely to deal.[49]

The AMEA also served as an intermediary for its members in Washington. The association employed an agent (it is not clear whether he was a full-time employee or simply a Washington-based attorney) to assist members in getting "drawbacks of duties on materials entered into the manufacture of goods exported to foreign countries." The association's Washington official also proved useful to members who lodged complaints with the Department of State about unfair classifications of American products abroad. These services of the AMEA reduced costs for its members, since they could not keep close contact with Washington themselves. "We are in particularly close touch with the departments in Washington," the secretary pointed out, "where their work has a direct bearing on foreign trade extension, from whom we may expect every assistance and to whom we may ourselves be a help."[50]

The contacts that the AMEA developed in Washington proved useful when war broke out in Europe in 1914. The association's executive committee devoted much time to dealing with government officials over questions of neutral rights violations. Indeed the vice-chairman of the association's committee on foreign relations established an office in Washington.[51]

The work of the AMEA, then, was to provide service for its members and lobbying and representation in Washington. Its contacts there were to help those who were already selling in foreign markets. Dealing with government bureaucracy to get drawbacks, the AMEA saved individual members legal and agent's fees. The AMEA sent representatives to testify at congressional hearings, as did other groups like the NAM, although the AMEA's work focused primarily on defending members' interests with other business groups. The European war in 1914 compelled the group to demand that the executive and Congress study the implications of foreign dumping after the war, a conflict that the AMEA, like many others, thought would not last long. Like many in the NAM the president of the AMEA thought that American production would outstrip domestic demand. This association was less agitated by this overproduction analysis than the NAM, however, because members were exploiting advantages and responding to foreign demand. Many members, the president asserted, had developed foreign sales after responding to foreign inquiries.[52]

Thus, the AMEA, like the NAM, was both a service and a lobbying association. As we shall see in the next chapter, the AMEA joined with other groups in efforts to lobby for changes in policy that businessmen believed hindered or threatened their efforts to sell abroad. But the AMEA was in large part a service organization devoted to resolving problems through collective activity. The group gave strength to individual members concerned about the practices of middlemen and the way in which railroads and warehousemen handled their products. The association also provided information about potential employees and about the credit standing of business houses at home and abroad. It provided the private collective activity that the NAM had delivered for its own members.

The attitude of the AMEA toward its collective activities can best be summed up by reference to a retrospective review of business and government delivered at the AMEA's annual convention of 1919. H.C. Lewis, an active member of the association and an official of National Paper and Type Company, noted that government can only provide information and encouragement to those seeking foreign markets. "In a broad way, however, the ultimate permanence and satisfactory development of our foreign commerce must be left to the individual initiative and enterprise of American concerns."[53]

By 1914 American business had established an important stake in sales in world markets, particularly in Europe. American exports were dominated by the major American manufacturers, who through economies of scale, marketing skill, or technological advantages had secured for themselves markets in major industrial countries, and who had begun to make significant sales in other parts of the world, especially Latin America. These efforts were fundamentally the result of private initiative, as were most of the attempts to protect markets once they were established abroad. But, as we have seen, it was not only the largest concerns that made substantial gains through private efforts. Smaller producers turned to trade associations to foster trade in the case of the NAM and to protect what had already been gained in the case of the AMEA.

This is not to say that government was unimportant in these efforts, nor that businessmen did not look to government for assistance. As we shall see in the next two chapters, Congress and the growing federal bureaucracy felt the impact of business lobbying in these years before World War I. And through federal agencies and departments interested in trade expansion, businessmen were able to create mutually beneficial working relationships.

Four

Congress and Trade Expansion: The Tariff, 1897–1917

Interest in the expansion of markets prompted manufacturers to turn their attention to government in order to change federal policies that producers thought limited foreign trade. At about the same time businessmen began to advocate direct government assistance in providing information about foreign conditions and opportunities. By 1900 the National Association of Manufacturers had become the leading business spokesman for trade expansion. The association formulated a full program of proposals for government aid that producers thought were necessary to the promotion of their interests. Many other business associations, for example, chambers of commerce and industry-based groups, supported the NAM. Equally supportive of the NAM were groups devoted to a single issue such as reciprocity or reform of the Department of State's consular service.

Ultimately, some of the proposals were adopted, although the manufacturers did not get everything they had originally hoped for. They succeeded in influencing policy on a number of important issues: the tariff, the antitrust laws, the consular service, foreign branch banking, and the merchant marine. Action was achieved, however, only after long and often bruising battles in Congress. On almost every issue of importance, market-seeking producers faced strong resistance from other business interest groups.

The difficulties of getting Congress to act on issues of concern to market-seeking manufacturers forced them to seek allies in the growing federal bureaucracy. Many producers had concluded that on such issues as the tariff the federal bureaucracy would better serve their interests than a Congress divided at times as its members sought partisan advantage.

Leaders in the Department of Commerce and Labor and the Department of State, as we shall see in the next chapters, welcomed the opportunity to cooperate with businessmen seeking to expand. The bureaucrats, often in competition with each other for funds, often had been frustrated in the Congress, too.

An issue of genuine importance to market-seeking producers was the tariff. The attempts to alter tariff policy illustrate well the difficulties of influencing Congress, the limits of support for trade expansion, and the degree to which many businessmen looked upon government with distrust. To expansionist businessmen, part of the frustration of dealing with Congress, the bureaucracy, and other businessmen was that few people openly opposed the goal of trade expansion.[1] In an economy and society that sanctioned growth and expansion, and which called them progress, increasing markets was a positive objective. No one opposed growth in principle. Difficulties arose, however, when market-seeking producers sought support for policies that challenged established business and political interests. Then, too, reliance on government assistance could be troublesome in other ways. Some of the changes Congress proposed in the tariff, as we shall see, required federal intrusion into what many businessmen thought should remain private.

Manufacturers approached Congress with some reluctance and even distaste. The NAM and like business associations were designed to shield their members from the necessity of engaging in direct partisan activity. Some of the NAM leadership disdained as a sordid activity the rough and tumble of congressional interest politics. This attitude was the result of a perhaps exalted view of their own place in American life. Businessmen thought of their interests as superior to those of other groups in society. Manufacturers harnessed resources, provided jobs, and created wealth. When thwarted, producers believed that larger public interests were frustrated, and often they blamed partisan politics for their inability to gain their objectives. A partisan politician, they thought, put his and his party's advancement above those of the producing classes.

But there was much else to the manufacturers' feelings about the political process. There was a growing fear of governmental interference in business. Indeed one wing of the NAM intensely fought organized labor, trying to protect producers from government "interference" in relations between capital and labor. They objected to federal and state legislation that, businessmen thought, gave unfair advantage to labor in its dealings with managers. Not surprisingly, market-seeking producers approached government warily.

Despite apprehension about partisan politics and the interference of government in business affairs, market-seeking associations tried to influence government. The NAM was the most important of the market-expansionist groups, and by 1900 the association had a large professional staff. The leadership committed itself, especially after the turn of the century, to having its views heard in Washington. As early as 1901 the NAM had set up an office in the capital. During sessions of Congress, the assistant secretary of the NAM, the man responsible for the foreign department, resided in Washington. As important as his lobbying were the NAM's attempts to rally business support for programs and policies advocated by the association. The NAM leadership devoted much time to organizing special issue-oriented associations to focus on the tariff, the merchant marine, consular reform, and the like. When they did not organize such groups themselves, they worked closely on efforts initiated by others, although on the tariff the NAM leadership came to dominate the National Tariff Commission Association organized by others.

In the years before World War I, however, the NAM was far from alone in its lobbying efforts. The American Manufacturers' Export Association retained a lawyer to represent the group regularly before the federal executive departments and the Congress. Even the leaders of groups that did not maintain full-time representatives or lobbyists in Washington came to know the city and its workings well. For it was from among the leaders of chambers of commerce, boards of trade, and industry-based associations that the NAM's directors recruited lieutenants for key campaigns to change the tariff.

The tariff was one of the first political issues to which market-seeking industrialists turned. Indeed the NAM had been founded in large part to correct what businessmen in 1894 felt had been Congress' grievous error of doing away with provisions for reciprocity reductions in tariff rates.[2] Manufacturers' attempts to change the tariff law, that is, to get reciprocity reinstated, illustrate well three important points about the nature of business-congressional relations. First, the struggles over the tariff suggest how difficult it was for producers to influence the leaders at the inner decision-making core of the Congress. In the debates over the 1897 Dingley tariff, the Kasson treaties of 1900, the 1909 Payne-Aldrich tariff, and Wilson's tariff commission, industrialists found themselves deeply enmeshed in congressional and presidential politics. At times, as in the 1897 tariff and in the creation of Wilson's tariff commission, producers got what they wanted. But even then, they were far from controlling or indeed significantly influencing the situation. Businessmen's interests were often lost sight of in political jockeying. Not surprisingly, smaller businessmen found the bureaucracy more sympathetic than Congress to their views and interests, while the largest firms with the greatest stakes abroad turned to internal corporate solutions to the problems of trade expansion.

Second, the political struggle over the tariff commission in 1909 revealed strikingly the extent to which producers feared that government would intrude in their affairs and reveal trade secrets to competitors. Thus, in addition to the conflicting interests among producers on the issue of the tariff, there was also the apprehension of government meddling in their affairs. Businessmen feared government because they could not control or predict what Congress might do.

And third, this fear led to the desire to get agencies divorced from the partisanship of Congress. The movement for an independent tariff commission revealed well the business community's desire to transcend the hurly-burly of the legislative process. Ultimately, businessmen found it easier to work with executive agencies of the federal government than an unpredictable Congress.

The difficulties that the smaller producers were to face in their dealings with Congress were foreshadowed in the successful efforts to reinstate reciprocity in the McKinley administration. The Dingley tariff of 1897, like others before it, was a highly divisive political issue. Yet it was the first major success of the new McKinley administration. On the face of it, the legislation also appeared to be a success for those manufacturers who had advocated reciprocity and government assistance in foreign market-seeking. To be sure, the smaller producers' and manufacturers' associations approved the Dingley legislation in the course of its consideration.[3]

Yet the Dingley tariff and its reciprocity provisions did not satisfy the needs of businessmen seeking wider foreign markets. The tariff was the product more of the political needs of the Republican party, as well as concern for the help that the French might give to the American government's attempt to secure an international agreement on a bimetallic international monetary standard.[4]

Many Republicans interpreted victory in 1896 as a mandate to change the Wilson-Gorman tariff of 1894. Not only did many protectionists object to its lower rates, but many market-seeking producers disliked the abandonment of clauses for reciprocal reductions in tariff schedules between the United States and other countries. Soon after McKinley took office, new legislation on the tariff emerged from the House Ways and Means Committee. Faced with a national deficit and needing revenue, the Republicans in Congress turned to higher tariff rates for luxury goods, calculated thereby to cause a minimum of popular discontent.

The French were apprehensive about the legislation because the majority of their exports to the United States were luxury items: works of art, wines, silks, china, gloves, and woolen dress goods. The American market was important to France, which had exported $66 million worth of manufactures to the United States in 1896, making France fourth after Britain, Germany, and Brazil in exports to the United States. The French were also concerned with two other aspects of the proposed tariff. Aside from the fact that the new law called for specific, that is, higher, duties on goods imported from France, there was also concern about new limits on duty-free imports. Since after traveling to France, Americans often brought French goods into the United States as personal possessions, there was a $100 restriction put on duty-free imports. And, second, to stop an influx of goods that would come in before the tariff went into effect, the bill provided for a retroactive imposition of its rates to 1 April 1897.[5]

French lobbying and international concern about a bimetallic monetary standard also played a part in the making of the Dingley tariff. French diplomats in Washington lobbied the Congress to effect a change in the bill that quickly emerged from the House Ways and Means Committee following the special congressional session McKinley called after his inauguration. Unlike the Germans, Italians, and Austro-Hungarians, who protested to the Department of State, the French preferred to work through the Congress, as domestic lobbyists did. Such efforts had been successful in 1894, when the Democratic Congress sponsored a lowered tariff rate.[6]

Foreign government lobbying, however, was a dangerous tactic, if done too openly. Protectionist members of the Congress used such lobbying as evidence of the effectiveness of proposed increased tariff rates. The French would have failed with the American Congress, had it not been for the potency of the currency issue. Republican interest in the question of bimetallism gave the French an opportunity. The Republicans had tried to soften their strong advocacy of the gold standard by pledging in the 1896 platform to support an international agreement on bimetallism. This sentiment won for McKinley some support among "silver Republicans" from the Rocky Mountain West. A successful agreement on bimetallism depended on the British, the leading commercial power at the time. The United States, however, did not want to approach the British without the support of some of the other European powers and so looked to the French to support a conference on bimetallism. Although the French were interested in the international use of silver, they were really interested in using American desire for their cooperation on the conference as a way to gain tariff concessions from the American government.[7]

In short, the French and some of the Republican Senate leadership had common interests. Republican leader Senator Nelson Aldrich (R.I.) wanted (along with other Republicans) quick action on the tariff in order to restore business confidence, raise revenue, and meet Republican pledges of a return to protection. Senator Edward O. Wolcott, a leading "silver Republican," wanted an agreement on bimetallism. Coming from silver-producing Colorado, he had lost influence at home for supporting McKinley. Wolcott believed that silver could be protected by an international agreement on bimetallism. Aldrich needed Wolcott, strategically placed as a member of the Senate Finance Committee to which the bill would be referred, because the Republicans did not have a working majority in the Senate. Aldrich feared that the bill would linger for months, as had Wilson-Gorman in 1894, thus unsettling a business community that strongly disliked the uncertainty associated with the making of the tariff. Aldrich needed Wolcott's support, and Wolcott needed the support of the French.[8]

Wolcott was strategically placed to meet French interests. Aside from serving as a member of the Senate Finance Committee to which the Dingley bill would be referred, he would sit on the subcommittee that was to draft the Senate's version of the Dingley bill. Aldrich opposed excessive rates, as did the other members of the subcommittee, Orville Platt and William B. Allison. There were, however, strong pressures within the party for higher rates on numerous articles. The French in the meantime supplied the subcommittee, which was meeting out of public view, with detailed memoranda about the effect of the tariff on French products.[9]

The French efforts succeeded, and they had good reason to be satisfied with the bill that came out of the Senate Finance Committee. Wolcott had been able to effect important changes. Retroactivity and the $100 limit had been dropped; art works had been put on the free list; and there had been concessions toward a number of French products. The Finance Committee, however, postponed the question of reciprocity.[10]

Ever since reciprocity had become a part of the 1890 McKinley tariff, market-seeking business groups supported the idea. They protested the Wilson-Gorman tariff of 1894 as a threat to their interests, since reciprocity was dropped. In addition, a small number of Republicans looked upon reciprocity as a way to ward off attacks on protection. The Dingley tariff that emerged from the House Ways and Means Committee had included basically a reiteration of the reciprocity clause of 1890. In another section of the tariff, however, the committee provided language that would have expanded the scope of reciprocity to cover nations in Europe as well as the Latin American nations to which the original 1890 reciprocity clauses had been directed. The committee authorized the president to make agreements for reductions with countries exporting such goods as wines, silks, paintings, and sugar. Lower rates on these products would come into effect if American imports received lower rates.[11]

The French, and more significantly Senator Aldrich, found the language on reciprocity too limited. Aldrich invited the French consul general to confer with him on revising the text of the reciprocity language in the Dingley bill. Aldrich wanted to give the president the power to conclude reciprocal agreements, subject of course to Senate approval. Uncooperative nations, in Aldrich's formulation, risked the retaliation of higher rates or the removal of their products from the free list. The French wanted the benefits of reciprocity immediately, for they had accorded the United States France's minimum tariff since 1893. Discussions continued without result so that the committee postponed issuing a reciprocity statement until a later date.[12]

In the meantime McKinley appointed Wolcott to a bimetallism commission that left for France a few days after the Finance Committee produced its version of the tariff. Wolcott was well received by the French, who were pleased with the changes in the bill. Bimetallism discussions, however, took a long time.

In the Senate, and in a later conference committee, protectionists fought the Finance Committee's version of the bill. When, because of illness, Aldrich had to leave the Senate for several weeks, reciprocity was imperiled. Protectionists within the party attacked the bill; the conference committee was dominated by members from the House, who at the time were more protectionist than those from the Senate. Late in June, when the Senate finally considered the bill paragraph by paragraph, most of the concessions that Wolcott had made to the French were eliminated. It is in this context that reciprocity reappeared. As finally passed, the reciprocity section allowed the president to make treaties that could specify a reduction of up to 20 percent of the duties in the Dingley tariff. The Senate, however, would have to ratify the treaties. Some senators hoped that reciprocity would compensate the French for the abandonment of the Wolcott concessions.[13]

Acceding to the wishes of Senator William E. Chandler (N.H.) and President McKinley the conference committee compromised on reciprocity to make it more appealing to the French. The bill specified the products on which the president might lower duties in return for reciprocal concessions abroad. It enlarged the numbers of alcoholic beverages included, obviously benefitting the wines of France. It also granted the president authority for two years to make tariff agreements following passage of the legislation. The president could reduce rates up to 20 percent and put or keep products on the free list. Such agreements would last for five years. The House had to approve them, since they involved revenue, and the Senate, since they were to be treaties. Senator Chandler thought that reciprocity would "afford an immediate opportunity to gratify the French government." The French consul general did not agree, however. Indeed, he concluded that since the procedure was complicated, reciprocity would lead to nothing. Bimetallism failed ultimately because the British were opposed and because the French did not want to cooperate on bimetallism without British support.[14]

The views and interests of market-seeking producers played a comparatively minor role in the final form of the Dingley bill.[15] The concerns of silver Republicans and the party's need to deliver on campaign pledges were at the heart of the new bill. Protectionists, furthermore, were the real winners in this legislation, as rates were pushed up on a number of articles. Indeed, while approving the return of reciprocity, the NAM's leadership worried that the higher rates of the Dingley tariff would invite foreign retaliation, limiting rather than extending markets.[16]

If, nevertheless, expansionist business interests might be able to think of the Dingley legislation as a superficial success, there was no way to mask the disappointment over the fate of the reciprocity treaties negotiated under the terms of the Dingley legislation. McKinley himself became increasingly committed to the need for foreign trade expansion. That concern, coupled with a desire to accommodate the French in hopes for further cooperation on bimetallism, prompted McKinley to go ahead with negotiations of reciprocal trade treaties with France.[17]

The Dingley tariff provided for reciprocity in three ways. In return, first, for some similar reductions, Congress empowered the executive to reduce duties on products (aimed mainly at France) such as brandies, wines, vermouth, paintings, and statuary. The president, second, could reimpose duties on coffee, tea, vanilla, and tonka beans, if he concluded that the countries exporting such products retaliated against American products. The McKinley administration negotiated a number of understandings in regard to these products. For the most part they were insignificant, with perhaps the exception of the rates on coffee and tea.[18]

Of more significance was, third, the administration's attempt to negotiate sweeping understandings under Section 4 of the Dingley tariff. In return for equivalent reductions by foreign countries, the United States promised to reduce some of its duties as much as 20 percent. But these understandings, aimed mainly at pleasing the French, were highly qualified. They required the approval of the Senate and the House, had to be negotiated within two years after the law went into effect, and were to remain in force for only five years.[19]

McKinley, nevertheless, acted swiftly, appointing the Reciprocity Commission in October 1897. He did not rely on the State Department to negotiate these treaties because it was more and more preoccupied with problems in China and with relations with Spain over worsening conditions in Cuba. The president appointed an able and experienced politician to head the three-man commission, a six-term Iowa congressman, John A. Kasson. Besides distinguished service in the House, Kasson had diplomatic experience, as the American minister in Austria-Hungary and in Germany. He had also served as an American representative at international conferences on West Africa in 1884 and on Samoa in 1889. One of the two other commissioners assisting Kasson had linguistic skills and a serious interest in economics.[20]

The Reciprocity Commission negotiated a total of seventeen treaties, reporting most of them to Congress in December 1899. Four of the treaties did not, according to the Dingley law, require congressional approval, and ten of the remaining treaties drew little public or congressional attention. But four treaties generated strong opposition from protectionist members of the Congress and from among organized business groups committed to high tariffs. The treaties with France, Ecuador, Argentina, and Jamaica (negotiated with Great Britain) incensed protectionist groups already alert to the dangers of imports from the newly acquired territories of Puerto Rico and the Philippines, as well as newly dependent Cuba. Thus, for example, fruit growers in California protested competition from Jamaican imports, and wool growers objected to the 20 percent reduction on wool in the Argentine treaty.[21]

The greatest opposition, however, centered on the French treaty. Kasson had succeeded in getting most American products put under the minimum French scale. This represented a reduction of about 26 percent. In return the United States was to lower tariff rates on French goods about 10 percent. Some products were excluded: boots, shoes, and machine tools. Kasson obviously felt that he had struck a good bargain. The treaty had the support of producers who had already gained foreign markets, such as those refining petroleum and those making agricultural machinery, farm implements, locomotives, and wagons. The French treaty also had the support of the NAM, that group most clearly the spokesman for those seeking to increase foreign trade.[22]

But opposition was strong from predictable business groups. Those who feared foreign competition because of the treaty, for example, makers of paper, brushes, optical instruments, and knitted goods, vigorously opposed it. Groups long identified with protection on principle mounted a public campaign against the treaties. Leaders in this effort were the Boston Home Market Club, the American Protective Tariff League, and the American Iron and Steel Association.[23]

Of more importance was the opposition of influential Republicans in the Senate like Aldrich, Platt, Hanna, and Allison. Kasson made an impassioned defense of the French treaty, arguing that high rates in America would invite foreign retaliation. But the Kasson treaties, as they became known, were a departure from earlier ideas of reciprocity. Originally, the McKinley tariff had given attention to lower duties on goods not produced in the United States in return for reductions abroad (in Latin America especially) on American products shipped there. Despite Kasson's emphasis on the growing industrial markets for American products that the French treaty seemed to leave open, Senate leaders feared disturbing an improving economic situation by troublesome agitation over the tariff.[24]

Indeed, the NAM's lobbying tended to confirm the Senate Republican leaders' worst fears about tariff debates. The NAM called the National Reciprocity Convention to coincide with the Senate's consideration of the Kasson treaties. Held in mid-November 1901 the convention soon fell to public wrangling. Trouble could have been predicted, because the NAM president in 1900 noted that the treaty being negotiated excluded from the reductions such important products as machine tools, pig iron, boots and shoes, leather belting, dynamoes, and arc lamps. He objected to the idea that reciprocity should sacrifice the interests of one industry to those of another.[25]

The convention, discussing by that time the fairly well-set arguments on the need for reciprocity to expand markets, ended up in angry recriminations. The knitted goods and jewelry producers, for example, accused the agricultural implement makers of sacrificing others for their own benefit. The jewelry and knit producers objected to tariff bargaining (and presumably wanted high rates maintained), whereas agricultural machinery manufacturers were indifferent to the issue, since there was foreign demand for their products. Producers with an advantage abroad generally favored lower rates overall, since they believed that high rates in America invited retaliation abroad. In any event, many producers favored reciprocity instead of general tariff reconsideration, which invariably led, they thought, to unstable economic conditions.[26]

The convention hammered out an inoccuous statement on reciprocity, accepting it so long as it did not harm manufacturing, commerce, or farming. To safeguard the interests of all industries, the manufacturers wanted the Congress to establish a reciprocity commission to investigate domestic industrial conditions, preparing reports that would enable the Congress and the president to determine the effects likely to result from reciprocity agreements. They suggested that the commission be given permanent status as part of a new executive department, a Department of Commerce and Industries.[27]

McKinley did not want to divide his party in an election year over what had so often proved to be a truly divisive issue. The president promised Kasson that he would continue the fight for reciprocity after the elections. McKinley continued to support reciprocity, urging in his December 1900 annual message to Congress favorable action on the agreements before it. Kasson thought McKinley's support weak, and he resigned in disgust from the commission in March 1901. The president, however, repeated his support of reciprocity in his second inaugural address in March 1901, and in the following month he took up the theme in a cross-country trip. McKinley referred to it in the speech at Buffalo the day he was shot in September 1901. The president believed in protection, but he thought that that policy had been firmly established and that the United States, within the protectionist system, had to find ways to expand markets.[28]

McKinley's successor was less committed to reciprocity. Like many other politicians of the time, Theodore Roosevelt fell into easy rhetoric about expansion. But the young president did not have the power of a McKinley in his first years in office, and he was less inclined than his predecessor to risk party divisions over an issue that he did not think so important. The public disputes and the patent inability of the National Reciprocity Convention to agree on anything more than the most watered down statements convinced Roosevelt that he should not press for the Kasson treaties. Indeed, in his message of 1902, he advised the Congress that it could ignore them.[29]

The unhappy fate of the French treaties discouraged market-seeking manufacturers. The NAM's president, David M. Parry, summed up the views of many of his membership when he concluded that the tariff needed flexibility in its application and a nonpartisan determination of what rates should be. Support began to develop for the notion of a minimum and maximum tariff. Foreign countries would receive the minimum rate schedule if they did not discriminate against American goods coming into their markets. Such flexible rates were most needed to deal with populous industrial countries like France, since the French wanted access to the American market as much as American producers wanted to increase foreign markets. Support also began to develop for ways in which to take the tariff out of politics. The 1903 NAM convention passed a resolution urging Congress to give the new Department of Commerce and Labor the power to investigate and make recommendations on what tariff rates should be.[30]

Market-seeking producers' interests in lowering tariffs, however, continued early in the twentieth century, weakening protectionist sentiment within the Republican party. Smaller manufacturers also believed that the tariff raised prices and helped trusts make high profits. Larger producers criticized an excessively high tariff because it hurt producers who wanted to export; high American rates invited foreign retaliation. And many businessmen who believed that tariff agitation was an evil in itself, since it tended to destabilize the business economy, wanted some resolution to the debate about tariffs. Instability in an economy attuned to private decisions was much more serious than it is today, when government policy can be used to affect investment decisions.

Those who were discontented with the tariff rates and the process of arriving at those schedules began to seek a "scientific" and nonpartisan way in which to formulate tariff policy. By 1907 the NAM and other business associations interested in protection and expansion fully supported the idea of a tariff commission that would consider the issues involved in making tariff rates outside of the partisan atmosphere in Congress. A commission, the NAM believed, would help keep protection for those who still wanted it, yet allow sufficient reciprocal reductions in rates to foster foreign expansion. An impartial body would also prevent the jolting political battles that unnerved the business community and disrupted private investment decisions.

Opposition to a commission came from predictable sources. The American Protective Tariff League and American Iron and Steel Association (which represented the ultra-protectionist wing of the Republican Party) opposed tampering with what they thought had brought about American industrialization. Many Democrats thought that the commission would only be a means to delay further the final and necessary reduction in the tariff that by 1907 had become the standard Democratic position on the issue.[31]

Nevertheless, by the time a new tariff was taken up in 1907, the NAM had had more experience in politics, and of more importance the association had a leadership willing to fight directly for what it wanted in the Congress. Indeed, the NAM's president, James Van Cleave, had political ambitions and welcomed opportunities to improve his contacts in Washington. In February 1908, Van Cleave led a delegation to Speaker of the House Joseph G. Cannon and Chairman Sereno B. Payne of the House Ways and Means Committee, where tariff legislation would originate. They pressed the two congressional leaders with arguments in favor of a tariff commission. A member of the visiting group, Alvin H. Saunders, president of the American Reciprocal Tariff League, stressed that a "scientific" study of the tariff would be better than a whirlwind campaign to revise the tariff just as the nation pulled out of a serious depression. Despite the efforts of the NAM and the American Reciprocal Tariff League, Cannon thought a commission would not be anything more than a debating society.[32]

But others in Congress, especially midwestern Republicans, tended to support these efforts. Indeed, at the beginning of the December 1907 session two bills were offered in each house to establish a commission. The NAM lobbied in Congress in favor of all of these bills; in March 1908 Robert La Follete of Wisconsin offered the most comprehensive proposal for a commission. The leadership ignored his and the earlier bills. The 1908 Republican party platform called for some reconsideration of the tariff, but not a commission. There matters stood until the House Ways and Means Committee began to consider new legislation on the tariff the day after Taft's election in November 1908. Although Payne opposed in the House a new tariff, as did Aldrich in the Senate, Taft nevertheless supported the idea.[33]

The evolution in 1909 of the Payne-Aldrich tariff illustrates nicely the importance of the congressional leadership and the difficulties business had in convincing the leadership to adopt policies that might threaten their own or their party's interests. Despite business sentiments and lobbying, what mattered ultimately were the attitudes of the relatively small group of Senate and House leaders. Their perceptions and understandings of the needs of the times were crucial, and they determined a tariff that fit their political needs and not those of the well-organized and vocal NAM and its other business supporters.[34]

Business support for an independent tariff commission was to be focused in a major convention held in the capital. Organizers scheduled the meeting for a few days before the Congress assembled for a special session on the tariff, the session which was to produce the Payne-Aldrich legislation. A group of Indiana businessmen initiated plans for the convention to demonstrate the general agricultural, commercial, and industrial interests supporting a "permanent, non-partisan, semi-judicial tariff commission." The NAM became involved in organizing the convention, lending its increasing prestige to the effort.[35]

Like previous attempts to rally and unify a diverse group of businessmen, this meeting revealed the divisions among the groups attending more than any consensus on the issue. The first divergence of views centered on whether the commission should be a creature of the legislature or be in the Department of Commerce and Labor. A second question that generated heated interest was what the duties of the new agency should be. Should it have authority to fix rates or should it be simply a fact-finding agency? All agreed that the then current methods of making the tariff were crude and "unscientific" and that a commission was necessary to provide a study of the "facts." Ultimately, however, the convention went further than the NAM had wanted. Strong sentiment favoring lower raw material prices influenced a majority of delegates to support a commission that would have the power to revise rates through reciprocal agreements, although the rates were to be adjusted within maximum and minimum levels set by Congress. But any "revision" of rates outside of Congress, as NAM leaders knew, would meet stiff congressional resistance in view of the tenacious concern Congress showed about its own powers.[36]

Since the delegates could not stay in session throughout the deliberation on the tariff, the convention founded an association to lobby the Congress. The leadership of the new National Tariff Commission Association (NTCA) overlapped with that of the NAM, giving the latter group the opportunity to modify some of the more unrealistic positions of the convention. One positive result of the convention, and of the NAM's identification with the new lobbying organization, was to win over the support of some protectionist members of the Congress. A commission seemed to them to be a more modest and less offensive way of drafting tariff legislation. It would also give the appearance of nonpartisanship, and in that sense really help save protection.[37]

Despite the efforts of the organizers of the tariff commission convention and of the new NCTA, the legislation that first emerged from the Congress proved disappointing. The Payne bill, pushed through the House by limiting debate and amendments, did not provide for a commission. In an effort to gain something, business proponents turned to Senator Beveridge, who had supported the idea of a strong commission. He reintroduced a bill first proposed in 1908, which as it turned out contained provisions that profoundly upset the leadership of the NAM. Like other proposals, Beveridge's provided for a seven-man commission of businessmen and experts in tariff law, customs administration, foreign commerce, and statistics. What disturbed NAM leaders, and small businessmen in general, was the authority the bill granted the commission to examine industrialists under oath and to study the books of their firms. These powers were necessary, Beveridge thought, to assist Congress in establishing a tariff system based on differences between foreign and domestic production costs. The bill was politically more astute than some others, and thus dangerous to the NAM leadership, because it provided that Congress would have kept exclusive control over setting prices.[38]

Senator Aldrich, in his central position of power as chairman of the Senate Finance Committee, took advantage of the apprehensions of the NAM leadership. Although Aldrich was opposed to a commission, he sought a compromise with small producers when he realized that NAM lobbyists were opposed to the government auditing a firm's books and interrogating its officers. After a series of conferences among President Van Cleave, Senator Aldrich, and Senator Beveridge, Beveridge drafted a compromise. A commission was to assist the president in discharging the duties of the executive spelled out in the legislation, especially in regard to imposing maximum and minimum rate schedules and in administering customs laws. Advisers would assist Congress by studying costs and prices in American and foreign industries. In these discussions over the compromise, Aldrich and Van Cleave opposed granting tariff assistants the power to subpoena witnesses and business records. Beveridge finally relented and agreed to eliminate subpoena powers. With these concessions from Beveridge, Aldrich then included provisions for advisers as an amendment to one tariff bill. The amendment, as described by the president of the National Trade Commission Association, was a vague addition to the tariff law. The board, he said, grew out of the "insertion into the Payne tariff bill, with the utmost difficulty, of a single ill-defined sentence authorizing the President to employ such persons as he thought best to investigate the provisions of the bill. Under this indefinite authority, the President . . . created the . . . Tariff Board."[39]

Two concerns prompted the NAM's support for Payne-Aldrich and a weak commission, or Tariff Board as Taft interpreted the legislation. In the first place, many of the NAM's leadership vigorously opposed giving the government power to look into business records. In addition, the NAM was becoming sensitive to the criticism that the group was less than sound on protection. NAM membership had grown significantly because of its opposition to unions and its support of trade expansion, but still many members were concerned about the need for protection. At the 1909 convention of the NAM, the leadership reaffirmed the group's strong commitment to the protectionist principle.[40]

Debate on the nature of a commission suggests that, while the NAM was willing to seek federal help, the association was unwilling to sanction a great increase in the power of the government to look into businessmen's activities. Never in the United States had there been the support found, for example, in Germany for close state-business relations. Indeed, there remained in the United

States a strong small entrepreneurial and individualistic ideology. Moreover, this was a period when government had prosecuted many of the largest manufacturing corporations under the antitrust laws. While smaller businessmen could approve government applying the antitrust laws, many feared giving government too much power, especially when many of these businessmen contemplated the Congress or executive providing support to the demands of labor unions. Opposition, however, was more than the result simply of an ideological hostility to government intrusion into private business affairs. Businessmen feared that government officials might give cost data or trade secrets to competitors.[41]

Yet not everyone agreed with the leadership. A few within the NAM continued to fight for a stronger commission. They were spurred on when the congressional conference committee on the bill further weakened the idea of a commission. The legislation provided that Congress would not be bound by the president's tariff advisers and that the president would not be able to use their advice to reopen the question of tariff rates once set by the Congress.

Thus, a scientific commission to study the tariff was the victim of the power structure of the Congress, especially within the Senate, responding to its own concerns. A strong board also did not develop because the NAM, which had taken charge of the movement, balked at further government intrusion into private business matters. The smaller producers in the NAM were not willing to pay the price for a fully "scientific" and impartial commission that would have had the power to look at their books. The tariff board was a step beyond the horse-trading of traditional tariff making, but it did not replace the old system, and it clearly did not reduce the power of members of Congress for whom the tariff often proved to be a crucial issue in their districts. The board also did not do enough to convince opponents of the political tariff-making process that it was an improvement. They saw it as an innocuous political compromise. When the Republicans lost ground in the next congressional election, however, many within the party attributed the loss of seats to public dissatisfaction over the making of the Payne-Aldrich tariff, further souring leaders on tariff revision.

Whatever modest contributions the tariff board could make were further reduced by President Taft's political ineptitude. The board, a group supposedly impartial and above politics, became itself a sharply partisan issue in Congress. This was not Taft's intention, for he sought to appoint a distinguished panel and a well-qualified professional staff. The president appointed as chairman of the board, Henry C. Emery, Yale professor of political economy; the members were James B. Reynolds, assistant secretary of treasury and Alvin H. Saunders, chairman of the American Reciprocity Tariff League. Congress appropriated $75,000 for the year ending 30 June 1910, with which the board appointed a staff made up of an executive secretary, a statistician, a reporter, and four clerks.[42]

The board's first assignment was to help Taft administer the maximum and minimum rate provisions of the Payne-Aldrich tariff. Section 2 of the act provided for an additional 25 percent ad valorem duty on all dutiable articles. Constituting the general or maximum tariff, these maximum rates were to counteract possible foreign discrimination against American products. Taft could authorize minimum rates if he found no evidence of discrimination against U.S. products.[43]

Between October 1909 and April 1910, the board investigated discrimination by surveying foreign regulations, laws, and tariffs. The United States had been receiving minimum rates in some countries, although not in the important Canadian, German, and French markets. Similar studies of foreign practices had been made in the Department of State's Bureau of Trade Relations and, of course, the State Department was in charge of negotiations with foreign governments in efforts to reduce rates placed on American products. Tariff board members took part in conferences with German and French representatives, and Emery was a member of the commission that dealt with the Canadians over ill-fated attempts to develop a broad reciprocity treaty with Canada. Although negotiations did not result in removal of all discriminations, the board reported to Taft that the penalty rate was *not* warranted.[44]

Taft, after negotiations on maximum and minimum rates, requested and received an appropriation of $250,000 in order for the board to take on a larger study of the tariff and its effects on commerce and industry. Many protectionists wanted no more meddling with the tariff. But Republican leaders in Congress supported Taft's request, largely to placate the insurgents in the party. Democrats generally opposed continued support of Republican tariff policy. Some were pleased, however, that Taft tried to expand the board's activities. This was especially true among Democratic legislators who thought there was little chance of creating a tariff commission whose recommendations on rates would be binding.

But many businessmen assumed that the study would lead to better rates, equalizing costs of production with foreign competition. The board itself, however, was not so sanguine. Indeed, Chairman Emery became increasingly skeptical about the goals being set by proponents of a tariff commission. Emery came to look upon tariff making as primarily a political process. His discussions with businessmen revealed that many of them had begun to question the idea of the tariff commission, too. Although the board could gain a general idea of one factory's operating costs over a long period, it was hard to calculate unit costs. In Emery's opinion politicians talked glibly about the "scientific" determination of tariffs and too many failed to consider problems of varying costs or how the board could determine the standard or average costs of about 4000 items covered by the tariff. To be successful, a "scientific" policy would have needed constant adjustments because of shifts in foreign and domestic costs and alterations in foreign rates. Average costs would have not protected the least efficient and would have been too much for the most efficient producers. Who was to be protected was a profoundly political question. Emery knew that there would always be a difference of opinion on the tariff, since it was not simply a pure business proposition.[45]

Business advocates of a stronger commission, however, continued their lobbying. Business' well-organized efforts to get a commission bill passed in 1912 were defeated in Congress. Skilled parliamentarians interested in other issues defeated the commission proposal at the very time that the National Tariff Commission Association worked hard to display business support. The NTCA supported a bill that provided for a commission with power to investigate the effect of foreign tariffs on American exports, make reports to both the Congress and the president, and appear before the House Ways and Means Committee. As before, however, there was division in the business ranks over whether or not producers were to be compelled to provide information. Some businessmen continued to believe that such compulsion was a threat to private property. President Kirby, of NAM, argued that there would be better cooperation from business if information was voluntarily provided. The convention meeting in Washington, D.C., however, disagreed with him and voted finally to support compulsion. This meeting of the NTCA (11-12 January 1911) represented a movement that in three years had gained momentum and had bypassed the NAM leadership on the question of the power of the executive to investigate private business. By 1912 the NTCA represented over 100 business organizations in 42 states, although the NAM was still the largest and most influential single group in the association.[46]

The NTCA's discussions were somewhat beside the point, however, when Congress failed to take up the bill proposing a stronger commission. Supporters of the concept of a "scientific" commission turned in defeat to what they already had, Taft's tariff board. While they hoped that the board would be adequate to provide a nonpartisan method to tariff legislation, it became in fact even a less effective instrument to serve their interests when, in part because of Taft's inept handling of the issue, the board became the focus of a bitter partisan battle which eventually led to the board's demise.

The board's most serious political trouble began over Canadian reciprocity. Taft called a special session of Congress early in April 1911 to consider Canadian reciprocity treaties. The Democrats did not object, and indeed liked the idea of reciprocal reductions in tariff rates. They continued, however, to disapprove of the Payne-Aldrich schedule of rates and attempted to change particularly unsatisfactory sections of the legislation through "pop-gun" bills. The tariff board was injected full force into the controversy over prevailing tariff schedules because Taft vetoed a "pop-gun" bill lowering comparatively high rates on woolens. The president urged the Congress to postpone changes in rates until a full report appeared from the board on wool and the woolens industry. Meanwhile, Taft vetoed other reductionist bills such as the "farmers free list," which affected products consumed by farmers. These lower rates were to compensate farmers for changes in reciprocity legislation with Canada. Taft accompanied his veto with a plea to Congress to wait for the board's report on reciprocity before making changes in existing rates.[47]

Taft's position only made enemies for the board in these years. Insurgent Republicans and many Democrats came to view it as a device to keep tariff rates up. Taft created this impression himself because he vetoed the "pop-gun" bills, cautioning Congress to await the reports of the board, but approved Canadian reciprocity without receiving the board's report on it. His critics accused him of using the board only to forestall legislation that he did not like.

The reports of the tariff board itself also exacerbated the partisan situation. Different factions within Congress sought to sustain their positions on the tariff by reference to the reports of the board. On 17 May 1911 Taft transmitted to Congress the board's first full report on the pulp and newsprint industry. Begun in October 1910, this study compared the costs of production between the Canadian and the American industries. Some protectionists saw in this analysis evidence only of the need to protect those American firms with an unfavorable comparison of costs. But not everyone, even among protectionists, accepted such an extreme point of view. And those who favored reduction, such as Robert M. La Follette, drew an entirely different conclusion. Further protection, he argued, would only serve to preserve those manufacturers with outmoded machinery, enterprises which did not deserve to survive. The more efficient firms, in contrast, did not need protection and to give it to them would allow them to achieve excessive profits.[48]

Partisan struggle over the tariff became more pronounced when Taft submitted the board's report on the wool industry. The thorough woolen study was ready for Congress when it convened in December 1911. Taft recommended a reduction in rates in order to equalize the differences in costs. Optimistically, he envisioned that the report would convince the skeptics of the real usefulness of the board. Instead, protectionists denounced Taft for failure to maintain protection. The Democrats thought that the reductions were not adequate and reintroduced earlier legislation on woolens that the president had vetoed. In addition, the Democrats charged that the delay brought about by Taft's earlier veto had simply allowed the industry to continue for a little longer to make excessive profits. Democrats on the Senate Finance Committee questioned the reliability of the data included in the report, as well as the honesty of the businessmen who testified. Taft ended up vetoing a measure to lower woolen rates that was supported by Democrats and some of the insurgents in the Republican party. The wool schedule, as a result, remained unchanged and a stalemate developed over the tariff.[49]

The board in these struggles became a hated symbol to both protectionists and reductionists and died when appropriation bills for fiscal 1913 omitted its funds. To be sure, the board had been expected to do the impossible. The fact was that the tariff was a political question and not, as the NAM and many other businessmen so often repeated, a business proposition. Manufacturers' conflicting interests in the tariff were subordinate to the interests of blocs within the Congress which had their own factions to foster, individual members who had to protect the interests of their constituents, and the most powerful members of the congressional leadership who had their own positions to secure.

In frustrating businessmen, the tariff issue revealed the limits of organized business influence with the Congress. Businessmen and their associations, to be sure, had access to the Congress. Not only at hearings, but also in private meetings the leaders of the NAM and the important special issue groups were able to argue their positions to the most powerful members of Congress. Despite their efforts, however, the fact remained that too many members of Congress saw in nonpartisan tariff-making a threat to their own political interests. As we shall see, such political problems also faced the smaller market-seeking manufacturers when they confronted other issues central to policies for expanding trade. (Larger producers were generally aloof from these struggles, although they did become involved with merchant marine policy.)

Smaller manufacturers still remained interested in the tariff board and its work. At first they made little headway with the Wilson administration, which came to office in March 1913. But as Wilson approached reelection in 1916 he sought support from the business community, and some of his political advisers persuaded him to create a tariff commission to win business support.[50]

Woodrow Wilson entered office intending to change the tariff. He dramatized the new Underwood tariff of 1913, portraying a special session of Congress called to consider the legislation as a struggle of the people against the lobbyists. The new president denounced the pressures put on the government by "special interests."

The success in passing the tariff in 1913 disinclined Wilson and the Democrats from revising the tariff board, which had expired at the end of fiscal 1912. Some of the board's functions were transferred to a new bureau in the Department of Commerce and Labor, the Bureau of Foreign and Domestic Commerce (BFDC). Congress authorized this bureau to conduct the cost-of-production studies that had been made between 1888 and 1891 by the Bureau of Labor and between 1910 and 1912 by the tariff board.[51]

War in Europe hindered the work of the BFDC, making studies abroad impossible. At home, the inability to compel producers' cooperation created difficulties for the cost of production division similar to those faced by the tariff board. American industrialists at times refused agents access to their records, fearing that information on costs might be made available to competitors. Business support for a commission nevertheless remained, even though the NTCA collapsed in 1914. The NAM kept up its campaign for such a nonpartisan method of determining the tariff, and the newly organized (and politically self-conscious) Chamber of Commerce overwhelmingly supported the idea, as a 1913 referendum of the membership indicated. Aside from limiting retaliation against American goods abroad, many businessmen saw a commission as a way in which to avoid the instability and uncertainty that tariff revision invariably caused in the business economy.[52]

When war broke out in Europe many businessmen were concerned about the conflict's disruption of international commerce, fearing especially the further instability to come after the war as foreign countries adopted new trade policies. More than ever before, there would be a need for careful policy-making to respond to foreign governments' perhaps inimical policies. These fears kept alive support for a commission.[53]

Wilson had hoped that the 1913 legislation had taken care of the tariff issue for awhile. But Democratic losses in the 1914 congressional elections, which saw the tariff as an important issue, showed well that it still exercised a lively impact on politics. Some Democrats, as a result, came around to the view that the creation of a commission would disarm some Republican critics of the administration's tariff policies.[54]

Wilson remained unconvinced of the need for a commission until late in 1915, when vocal business support helped change his mind. In 1916, on the eve of an election in which the president had made efforts to broaden his base of support both with Republican progressives and with the business community, Wilson came out in favor of a tariff commission. Originally, he opposed the idea since, as Secretary David Houston, of the Department of Agriculture, recorded, Wilson maintained that it had been tried and had failed. And Wilson thought that the Federal Trade Commission and the Department of Commerce had the full powers of a tariff commission already. Houston, however, continued to try to change Wilson's mind. Although Houston doubted that the tariff could ever be entirely taken out of politics, a commission would counter the claims of the extremists on both sides of the issue, helping the administration politically.[55]

As Wilson's thinking about a commission began to change, he had to face the sharp dissent of Secretary of Commerce William C. Redfield, a skillful advertiser of his department and a resourceful bureaucratic infighter who vehemently objected to a commission. Although Redfield was never part of the inner circle of the administration, and indeed was looked upon by some of Wilson's intimates as a foolish blusterer, he enjoyed a good reputation in the New York business community. And, as we shall see in chapter 6, he had carefully cultivated members of the Congress. Houston and Secretary of the Interior Franklin K. Lane tried to convince Redfield of the political importance of an independent commission. Finally, Redfield admitted grudgingly the political expediency of the commission idea. Yet he continued to defend the work of his department and its cost of production division, maintaining that its work was done efficiently and at low cost.[56]

Houston's arguments and the persistent advocacy of a commission by the NAM and the Chamber of Commerce convinced Wilson that he must support the necessary legislation. Wilson justified this turnabout by arguing that the

European war would lead to a need to study new conditions. A commission would also provide invaluable information on the actual operation and impact of the tariff laws. He also noted that such a body would provide the Department of State with information about foreign conditions and help the treasury administer the tariff laws.[57]

Wilson maintained that he had not changed his attitude toward protection to assure Democrats in Congress that the party's point of view on the tariff would be represented on the commission. While he, gave such assurances, his attitude had in fact changed. He was now willing to admit the possible need for protection, especially in view of the fear that after the war foreign manufacturers might dump their goods here. To businessmen Wilson described his commission idea as a "common sense" solution to the problem of the tariff which abandoned the partisanship that had characterized the tariff before. In an address to the National Grain Dealers Convention in Baltimore in September 1916 the president said he abandoned partisan tariff theories in favor of a commission which would "see the facts and state them, no matter whose opinions those facts contradict."[58]

The administration confounded the Republicans with the plan, although the strictest protectionists in the party had always been skeptical of a commission and were deeply suspicious of one supported by someone with ideas on the tariff as suspect as those of Woodrow Wilson. Of more concern to the administration was opposition in the Democratic party. Influential southern Democratic committee chairmen were opposed to the idea, believing that it betrayed party principles. Southern Democrats considered the commission a way to save the protectionist system, noting that prominent protectionists had always led the movement for a nonpartisan body to make the tariff. Other Democrats, however, took a more moderate view of the issue and helped push it through. The opposition forced Wilson to have his commission attached as an amendment to a revenue bill, a way to avoid a direct confrontation with Democratic opponents. It was two months before the 1916 election.[59]

The amendment provided for a commission of six members appointed by the president with the consent of the Senate. It was to study the administrative and fiscal effects of the tariff laws, the competitive conditions between American and foreign producers, and the comparative costs of production in the United States and abroad. The commission was also to investigate accusations of foreign dumping of goods, a provision popular with businessmen. On all its findings it was to make an annual report to Congress and the president. The bill took the cost of production division from the Bureau of Foreign and Domestic Commerce and put it in the new agency. The commission could compel witnesses to give testimony under oath and, although members and employees of the commission were to keep trade secrets, this power of compulsion continued to disturb some businessmen.[60]

A commission was not appointed for nine months. Not only was Wilson's time increasingly consumed by the diplomatic problems preceding the United

States' entry into World War I, but also there were difficulties in finding politically qualified appointees. Finally, tariff expert Frank W. Taussig, of Harvard, was made chairman; Secretary of the Treasury William G. McAdoo suggested the rest of the committee, trying to get a geographical balance, as well as an appropriate number of party representatives. The original six were neither doctrinaire protectionists nor free traders, although as a group they tended to favor a liberal trade policy. Nothing suddenly changed, however, since the commission needed time for study and the gathering of information. There was a more common attitude, though, among these six than among later groups of commissioners. Republican victories after World War I led to a reversal of tariff policy in 1922. The Republicans appointed commissioners more to their liking. In the 1920s, protectionist ideas won out again in debates on the tariff, even though the 1922 Fordney-McCumber tariff provided for a more flexible tariff system. That legislation authorized the president, on the basis of the commission's findings, to adjust tariff rates to equalize American and foreign costs of production.[61]

Thus the tariff continued to be an intensely partisan issue. Despite the work of the commission during and after the war, the Congress continued to make tariff policy along well-established lines. Overall, then, market-seeking producers did not find a ready reception of their tariff ideas in the Congress. The House jealously guarded its own powers in the making of the tariff. A commission that "took the tariff out of politics" would threaten the power of a number of members of Congress in their own districts, if locally important industries were hurt. The leadership of the Republican party had other reasons for skepticism, at first toward reciprocity and then toward a tariff made by experts. Leaders like Aldrich firmly believed that too much tampering with the tariff caused economic instability. This concern, however, was tempered with practical political problems. The leadership had to placate two wings of the party. The largest number remained protectionists, but significant members of the party favored some "scientific" adjustments of the tariff.

Another reason for difficulty was the fact that there was no unanimity in the business community. Many feared letting down protectionist barriers. In contrast, businessmen who were concerned with lower costs of raw materials were willing to accept government intervention in the affairs of producers. The Kasson treaties and the agitation for a board and a commission all divided businessmen. Canadian reciprocity failed because of Taft's political ineptitude, but also because American agricultural interests vigorously opposed many of the concessions.

All in all, then, the Congress proved a frustrating place for market-seeking manufacturers. Producers (especially the smaller ones who dominated the movement for reciprocity and the tariff commission) had access to members of Congress and to some of its leaders. But when these producers' interests conflicted with other business interests and, more importantly, when they conflicted with those of the leadership of the party in power, businessmen had little chance of getting what they wanted.

Market-seeking manufacturers, as a result, did not in these years confine themselves entirely to trying to influence Congress. They also attempted to work with the bureaucracy. They found there that producers' interests were better served, since the bureaucracy looked for business allies in its own dealings with Congress.

Five

Congress, Business, and Bureaucracy: The Department of State and Consular Reorganization

Businessmen did not rely entirely on the Congress to make the changes that were necessary to expand business abroad. In turning to the Department of State and later to the Department of Commerce and Labor, market-seeking producers gained significant allies. Both departments provided important services and helped advocate changes in commercial policy. But businessmen gained more than assistants and advocates. Government bureaucrats provided sustained attention to issues related to market expansion. The smaller and medium-sized businessmen's interests in expansion shifted with changes in the domestic economy. As economic conditions improved at the end of the 1890s and in 1910-11, businessmen turned their attention back to the glut of domestic orders. The pressures of rapid domestic expansion deflected attention from the difficulties of selling abroad. The bureaucracy, however, continued its interest in businessmen's expansion and its battle for the policies that served business interests.

Bureaucrats were far from cynical in these efforts, even though there were strong motives of self-interest behind attention to market expansion. Within the Department of State there were those who believed foreign markets were necessary to relieve overproduction. A more professional department, they thought, would better serve manufacturers interested in expansion. Businessmen interested in expansion, moreover, would create a constituency to support other changes within the State Department. In the 1890s, and especially after the Spanish-American War, many diplomatists concluded that the department was not equipped for the enhanced world role thrust upon the United States. Then, too, a larger and more active department would also give greater scope to many of the ambitious younger men who entered public service in the 1890s. They sought careers that would use their talents and energies and contribute something lasting to the public interest. Public service seemed more noble than business, because most wanted more out of life than simply to make money.

The Department of State's consular service was the first of the federal agencies to receive the attention of market-seeking smaller producers. The consular service remained the most significant ally smaller businessmen selling abroad had until World War I. American consular officials were the most obvious government

91

employees to provide information about foreign conditions and assistance when difficulties arose with foreign officials. Yet those who turned to consuls found much to criticize in the consular service's performance. Early efforts to make changes during the 1890s were unsuccessful, but businessmen and bureaucrats gained experience in dealing with each other that proved significant in later years. Businessmen concluded that the source of the service's inadequacies was the patronage system of appointment.

By 1900, the consular branch of the Department of State employed more than a thousand men in over 700 foreign cities and towns. Consular officials were assigned to an office abroad, the rank of the chief official supposedly related to the importance of the post. The service was divided into several classes of officials. All of the following were loosely referred to as consuls: consul-general, vice consul-general, deputy consul general, consul, vice-consul, deputy consul, commercial agent, and vice commercial agent. There were lesser employees at consulates, too: consular clerk, interpreter, marshall, and clerk.[1]

The consular service was as old as the Republic. Secretary of State Thomas Jefferson required in 1790 that consuls assist Americans engaged in maritime commerce and make reports on American ships entering and leaving their districts, on foreign military preparations, and on general political and commercial conditions abroad. As time passed, other duties were added. Consular officials were to act as notaries, aid American seamen, issue visas, report on foreign health conditions, and try to keep out undesirable emigrants. With the decline of the American merchant marine after the Civil War, the consuls became more and more important in the government's revenue-collecting activities. They had to verify the value of goods shipped to the United States, assuring customs officials at American ports of entry that cargo was not undervalued. Until the mid-1890s, certifying invoices was the consuls' most important task both in the view of Washington officials and of the consuls themselves.[2]

Interest in selling manufactured goods abroad increased during the depression of the 1870s, and the department began to respond to the needs of producers selling overseas. A departmental circular in 1877 ordered consuls to report on exports needed in their foreign districts. In Washington, the department began in the 1870s to issue consular reports monthly, as well as annually. By the 1880s there were those like Secretary Frederick Frelinghuysen who believed that reorganization was necessary to make the service more useful to businessmen.[3]

The first business group, however, to advocate sweeping changes in the department was the Boston Merchants Association. Members were prompted by the prospect of another turnover in the consular service following the election of Grover Cleveland in 1892. Association members had tried to encourage Boston businessmen to sell abroad. To protect the foreign trade of those already selling overseas, the group had also focused attention on the issues that were to occupy small market-seeking producers, for example, an isthmian canal, reciprocal tariff treaties, and a federal department devoted to manufacturers. As was to be expected, the Democratic Cleveland administration began a wholesale removal of Republican-appointed consuls. The patronage-inspired purge began at the same time as the serious depression of 1893, which focused more business attention than ever before on foreign markets. The Boston Merchants Association sought the support of like-minded business groups to bring about a change in the system of patronage appointments to the consular service.[4]

The merchants in Boston brought the issue to businessmen in many different cities by cooperating with the National Board of Trade (NBT). Making the case for a service of permanency and professionalism, the NBT was able to stimulate the interest of numerous local boards of trade and chambers of commerce. By the end of 1894, these groups besieged Congress with letters, resolutions, and petitions urging reform of the consular service. The issue appeared urgent to smaller businessmen who could never hope to match the large numbers of employees and resources the major corporations devoted to foreign trade.[5] By 1895 the National Civil Service League joined in support of the small businessmen seeking change in the Department of State. The league was more disinterested than its business allies. It fervently supported reform of the consular service, since officials stationed abroad far from public scrutiny had a greater opportunity for mischief. The league, which had long opposed the patronage system, was not popular among professional politicians. But it had among its membership Theodore Roosevelt, who was in later years as president to play an important role in altering the consular service, an issue he first became concerned about in the 1890s.[6]

Business critics believed that the patronage system produced consular officials who were slack in their attention to duties and who had little commitment to the service. The result was low morale. The system of appointment, they thought, primarily rewarded political partisanship. As one commentator put it, perhaps too harshly, politicians "too notorious to make it safe to name them for a domestic berth ... have been pitch-forked into the foreign service." Whether or not the business interpretation was close to the mark, rapid turnover when a new party entered the White House led to breaks in personal relations, trade talks, and long-term expertise.[7]

Flowing from the patronage were other "evils" which businessmen attacked. Promotion was not based on merit, and there was no security of a tenure system. Good people would not apply, critics charged, if political connections were more important than a job well done. Salary schedules were haphazard, at times depending on the solicitous consideration of a friendly member of Congress. Insufficient funds for housing forced consuls to locate far from the center of the cities to which they were assigned.[8]

The uncertain amount of payment made consuls rely on the fees that they received for supplemental income. Indeed lower-ranked officials like commercial agents had no payment other than fees. Businessmen charged, however, that the services they needed did not always bring the most remunerative fees to the consul, and so businessmen questioned whether their interests were adequately attended to.[9] The Treasury Department had no way to check the accuracy of the consuls' reports on fees, nor on the honesty of the officials turning in the reports. Moreover, some businessmen accused consuls of overcharging for their services.[10]

The commercial agents became a particular object of criticism. They were often aliens, appointed by a consular official with the approval of the Secretary of State. These agents usually resided in areas where American commerce was so small that it did not warrant a consulate. As foreigners, agents were not entirely concerned with fostering American interests. Indeed, rather than spreading American commerce abroad, commercial agents used their connections with the United States to promote their own trade interests in the American market, since most agents continued to engage in their own businesses. The agents, however, were a significant part of the consular service, making up 395 of the 713 officials in the service in 1900.[11]

Market-seeking producers were not the only ones critical of the consular service. Businessmen and congressmen concerned with the tariff as a source of revenue also complained about the consuls' performance. One of the consuls' primary responsibilities was to establish the value of exports coming to the United States from their districts. In the best of circumstances, this was a difficult task. But understaffed offices with inexperienced employees apparently did not do a very good job. It is difficult, if not impossible, to estimate losses in revenue because of underevaluation, but in 1897 the NBT guessed that the loss was as high as $20,000,000 a year.[12]

But it was businessmen desiring trade expansion and worried about British and German competition who were the consular service's most outspoken critics. These smaller manufacturers dominated the business organizations that advocated reform of the consular service. They believed that better information and better representation were required to gain and keep foreign markets. In the late 1890s the Boston Merchants Association was still one of the most active supporters of change, although it was joined by other energetic groups: National Association of Manufacturers, the Cleveland Chamber of Commerce, and the Boston Chamber of Commerce. And support was genuine if less energetic in commercial associations all across the country. Congress received memorials and petitions supporting change from groups in Saint Paul, San Francisco, Cincinnati, Baltimore, Indianapolis, New York, Cleveland, and other cities.[13]

Businessmen advocated a few fundamental alterations in the consular system. The simplest was regular inspection of consulates already in operation. Inspections were held in 1897 and again between 1903 and 1904. These resulted in a few changes in the system, although some consuls lost their jobs. Of more substance, the business reformers wanted specially trained and more professional consuls, men who were, in short, more "businesslike." They were to understand the problems and interests of American manufacturers, while at the same time knowing the languages, customs, and ways of doing business in areas to which they were assigned. Some businessmen thought that the fastest way to achieve such results was by the establishment of a special school, perhaps on the model of the military service academies.[14]

Businessmen encouraged and then supported legislation introduced by sympathetic members of the Congress. The first in what turned out to be a series of such bills was introduced in 1894 when Senator John T. Morgan (Alabama) and Representative Bellamy Storer (Ohio) proposed a reorganization of the service. At the heart of the proposal was a series of examinations upon which promotions and appointments were to be made. The Senate defeated the Morgan bill after it had been favorably reported from committee in 1895. Henry Cabot Lodge adopted Morgan's proposals and reintroduced them to the Senate in 1896, with no more success. Representative Robert Adams introduced a bill for a study commission in 1897. Although between the late 1890s and 1906 these and similar bills were again introduced, they received little attention on the floor, indeed rarely being debated.[15]

Business advocates of such legislation found the Congress opposed to changes in the consular service. Members saw the changes as another threat to the patronage system. In many ways, President McKinley provided an excellent example of the conflict over acceptance of what business wanted and the needs of political leaders. As congressmen from Ohio and later governor, McKinley had voiced the sentiments of businessmen interested in the expansion of trade. Indeed, he had spoken of the need to improve the consular service. Yet, as leader of his party, he was one of the chief dispensers and beneficiaries of the patronage. The previous Cleveland administration had reduced the number of patronage slots by 30,000 places when it expanded the rolls of the civil service. With the party faithful clamoring for jobs, McKinley could not remove the consular service from the patronage system. Although he and his political advisers sought to appoint only competent men, candidates for consul were nevertheless to be drawn from among the ranks of deserving party workers.[16]

Businessmen interested in change were not disheartened, and by the turn of the century they had stepped up their efforts. In December 1901 leaders of several business groups formed a national organization to lobby for the changes they wanted, with Harry Garfield of the Cleveland Chamber of Commerce as chairman. The group hired a lobbyist in Washington to keep its views before Congress, and it also held national meetings in the capital to demonstrate support for legislation to change the consular service.[17]

Finally, in 1906 a bill proposed by Senator Lodge passed. It included a number of provisions that were acceptable to business advocates of reform. The legislation divided the service into specific classes, with salaries dependent on the rank at which one served. The highly unpopular commercial agent was abolished. To improve supervision, the legislation established an inspection corps and required that most fees be accounted for and sent to the Treasury. State Department stamps were to be used in order to assure that documents were properly executed. Consular officers were to be transferred from post-to-post only within the same class; only Americans were to be hired for clerical positions that paid more than $1,000.00. On the critical issue of appointment, Lodge provided examinations which would base appointment and promotion on merit. But these provisions, central to business' efforts to overcome the patronage system, were deleted when the Senate considered the bill.[18]

With requirements for examination omitted, the bill passed the Senate in January 1906. The patronage safe, there was little serious discussion, other than on the question of salaries. The bill passed the House in March, and after consideration by conference committee, the Lodge Act went to the president, who signed it on 5 April.[19]

Roosevelt, however, did what the Congress had been unwilling to do. In an executive order in June 1906 he ordered that examinations determine promotions from the lower grades of the service and that tests be required for those who were to be appointed by the president to the consular service. Roosevelt expressed a commitment to nonpartisanship, for he declared that the political affiliation of a candidate would have nothing to do with either those chosen to take the examinations or those who were eventually appointed. That part of the business community interested in consular reform applauded the president's initiative. But the legislation and the executive order did not fully satisfy some of the business groups, since they feared that a future president might reverse Roosevelt's order. Even though Taft continued to abide by his predecessor's initiative, efforts for permanent legislative changes were renewed when Wilson was elected. Some businessmen feared that the Democrats would return the service to the "spoilsmen." The Stone-Flood Act of 1915, and ultimately the Rogers Act of 1924, set the consular agency securely within a merit system.[20]

From this brief history it is clear that Congress had not simply responded to the needs and pressures of the business community. Legislators at every opportunity had rejected efforts to place the consuls in the civil service system. Crucial to the final success of consular reform were President Roosevelt and Secretary of State Elihu Root, both of whom had long been identified with civil service reform. But of equal significance, upper-level more or less permanent members of the bureaucracy had played key roles, at first in encouraging businessmen seeking change and then later in working out the details of legislative alterations. The effort to bring about change in the consular service has another significance, too. It taught key members of the State Department bureaucracy the importance of business support in the department's dealings with Congress. Lessons learned in the consular reform movement were put to good use, as the department identified itself as an advocate of and assistant in efforts to expand trade. In years to come, efforts to enlarge the service further, reorganize the department, and make it more "professional" were tied in part to business' interest in trade expansion. And professionalization was to some of its advocates in the department a very personal matter indeed. A professional service would allow promotion on the basis of initiative, talent, and hard work.

Of those assisting Secretary Root, the most important in reorganizing the consular service was Wilbur Carr. He had become chief of the Consular Bureau in 1902, chief clerk of the department in 1907, and director of the consular service in 1909. Carr was a major figure in the effort to use business' concern about trade expansion to further the interests of the department in the Congress. Carr was not alone, for other men such as Gaillard Hunt, Francois S. Jones, and Frederick Emory had worked assiduously to improve the department's relations with the business community. All of these men provided their superiors with the detailed knowledge of day-to-day operations, the continuity of interest, and the professional bureaucrat's perspective on organizational structure.

The motives of these men, like those of most people, were complex. There was in what they advocated a fortuitous mixture of self-interest (they wanted careers of meaning and usefulness) with the broader needs of their institution and the business community. To secure satisfying careers, they required a bureaucratic setting in which achievement and efficiency were rewarded. To make the department more professional, and less the plaything of patronage and politics, they needed the support of the business community. But this is not to say that their support of trade expansion was less than genuine. Nor is it to suggest that their concern for business interests was completely selfish. Indeed many in the department believed that trade expansion was essential to the United States' well-being and its ability to deal with the problems of an increasingly complex industrial economy. And some saw their task as convincing a less than fully committed business community to take more interest in expansion and more care when it tried to sell overseas.[21]

Yet the bureaucrats' concern for trade expansion was clearly part of the State Department's effort to promote and protect the department's interests in the Congress. The department came to identify with trade expansion because it did not have a "natural" constituency. Foreign policy was of little concern to the public, and the Congress, especially the House, tended to reflect popular indifference to foreign affairs. Before businessmen developed a significant interest in trade expansion in the late 1890s, the State Department had identified itself with the important task of collecting revenue generated by the tariff. Consuls played a key part in this work, certifying the value of foreign imports. These valuations determined the revenues received from the tariff, the major source of public funds in the late nineteenth century. After 1900, increasing demands on the department because of foreign travel, trade, and immigration all were used to justify the importance of the department before an indifferent and at times hostile Congress. And World War I provided another opportunity, as the State Department helped persons stranded abroad and aided in the disposition of American holdings in foreign stocks and property.[22]

The movement for changes in the consular service schooled department bureaucrats in mobilizing business support. Consular reform, as we have seen, was an increasingly important issue to market-seeking businessmen as, at the same time, critics in the department found the service inadequate. One of the most effective opponents of the patronage system in the department was Gaillard Hunt. He had joined the department in 1887, quickly becoming disillusioned with the effects of the spoils system through firsthand experience. He was passed over for a promotion for which, of all the applicants, he was the most qualified. The man who got the job he had wanted was ill-suited, although deserving politically. Such personal setbacks threatened Hunt's desire for a useful career, and he translated his personal disappointments into a wider criticism of the way the Department of State worked.[23]

Eventually Hunt was able to garner significant business support for change in the department. His first effort, however, at departmental reform was to help Francois S. Jones draw up the foreign service bill of 1894, which was to reorganize the entire service. In order to get this bill passed, Hunt began to cultivate the support of a few congressmen interested in altering the consular service. Hunt realized that the department needed business allies, as did Frederick Emory, of the Bureau of Statistics, who in the 1890s tried to make the department's data about foreign economic conditions more useful to businessmen interested in expansion. Although at times frustrated by manufacturers' inconstant attention to the issue, Hunt was able eventually to draw into the movement for change a man of energy and of great standing in the business community. Harry Garfield, a friend of Hunt's, was the eldest son of the late president. Garfield was a prominent Cleveland lawyer, active in the city's business circles, who had devoted much time to promoting efficiency in municipal government. Hunt outlined for his friend the need for change in the dpartment, after Garfield's interest in the world increased with America's victory in the Spanish-American war. Garfield became an enthusiastic supporter of Hunt's proposals for changes in the department. Garfield cultivated support among business groups outside of Cleveland, saw the president in Washington, testified before committees of the Congress, and visited important members of the legislative branch.[24]

At first, Garfield met with both congressional and business indifference, although the Lodge bill of 1900 was reported out of the appropriate House and Senate committees. Garfield continued his organizational efforts among businessmen, eventually hiring a man in Washington to devote full time to increasing business and congressional support for consular reform. Efforts to stimulate interest in the business community gained some ground in the first years of the twentieth century.[25]

By 1905 Elihu Root had become Secretary of State and leadership of the consular reform effort passed to him. He came to the Department of State after reorganizing the War Department, and he was willing to work actively for consular reorganization. The diligent but busy Root relied on members of the department for detailed information and guidance in his reorganizational efforts. Wilbur Carr was the most notable of those within the department helping him, for he had thought systematically about organizational problems. Carr sought to apply to the Department of State a machinelike efficiency in order to get a cohesive department with a unified purpose (the elimination of waste) seeking coordinated objectives.[26]

Carr in 1892 had started in a lowly position as a departmental clerk. From the first he exhibited ambition and the attention to detail that eventually brought him promotions in a department populated with men of good birth, leisurely habits, and fashionable education. By 1896 he was drafting consular instructions and letters and looking into the finances and accounts of the Consular Bureau. In August 1896 he was designated acting chief clerk. His experiences in what was the chief administrative agency of the department convinced Carr of the need to bring the State Department more fully into the civil service system. In March 1897 Carr transferred to the Consular Bureau, a move that was to have a profound impact on his career.[27]

Carr's work in the consular service, as in his first post, focused on basic administrative questions. As he became familiar with his new responsibilities, his interest in civil service reform increased. At the same time, Carr began to learn about politics, especially the protective tariff and the silver questions, through discussions with friendly colleagues.[28] He also applied himself to systematic studies of Latin, French, political science, and political economy. His interest in international law led him to take a law degree at Georgetown; he was admitted to the bar in 1901.[29]

As he advanced rapidly in the department, Carr became increasingly critical of the unsystematic way it operated. "No one in all the one hundred years of the Department's existence," Carr remarked in his diary, "has seen fit to compile even the most used of its laws, and rulings." Carr's views of the department's amateurism were most influenced by the death of President McKinley. As a Republican, Carr was saddened by the president's death, but what troubled him more was the unprofessional way in which the Department of State had to deal with the chief executive's passing. In informing foreign governments of the change in power, the department relied on a few veteran bureaucrats to draft notes which these men virtually had to send themselves. Carr concluded that the department was not organized to handle affairs of an increasingly important international power. "The lack of organization," he noted in recounting the department's response to McKinley's death, "was painfully evident."[30]

Carr was given the opportunity to do something about this when in November 1901 he succeeded the retiring head of the Consular Bureau. Almost immediately he became involved in the legislative efforts to change the consular service. The Senate Committee on Foreign Relations considering Lodge's bill introduced in 1900 wanted a classification of the different ranks proposed in a reorganized consular service. Carr substantially prepared it himself and sent it to Lodge. In the course of the deliberations on the bill, Carr and a few others in the department interested in the legislation met with representatives of some of the business groups gathered in Washington to lobby in Congress. The meetings of representatives of boards of trade and chambers of commerce supporting the legislation were, according to Carr, "without practical result."[31]

Carr disapproved of the way in which the consular reorganization legislation was handled. The changes in the consular service, he thought, had been left too much in the hands of business groups and important members of Congress like Senator Lodge. "The Lodge Bill," Carr noted in his diary, "is much better than no bill, but not half so good a bill as might be drawn by the Department and be open to no greater objection." In the future Carr saw to it that the State Department played a more active role in matters affecting its interests. As director of the consular service he assiduously presented the department's views to businessmen, the Congress, and the press. Making the department's case was one thing, but building support was not an easy matter. He had little regard generally for congressional politicians, although he himself learned to play the political game well.[32]

Carr got an opportunity to engage in congressional politics firsthand after Roosevelt appointed Elihu Root secretary of state on 1 July 1905. Root was a distinguished New York attorney who came to the State Department after a successful tenure as secretary in the War Department. Unlike his predecessor, John Hay, whose distinction lay in other fields, Root had excellent ties to business, especially in Wall Street. And as Secretary of War he had cultivated influential members of Congress. Of greatest utility to the department, however, was the secretary's close, almost fatherly, ties to the younger President Roosevelt.[33]

The new secretary of state, like the president, was interested in organizational efficiency, a goal that Roosevelt had long championed through his support of an independent civil service system. Like others at the Department of State, Root believed that its organization was not capable of meeting the growing needs of an increasingly important world power. Writing to Lodge a few months after assuming office, Root stated bluntly that "the organization is defective. We must get the defect cured.... It is going to take money and it is going to take affirmative legislation." His attention quickly focused on the need for change in the consular service. "The great trouble ... with the consular service ... [is] that it is used as a place of refuge for a great number of men who have lost their chance in life, and whose friends get them in here because they have to be supported in some way. A service composed of men who have used up all their enthusiasm and energy and ambition upon something else, cannot be very effective at best, and the men whom we get on such a basis are apt to be men who have always been weak and inefficient."[34]

As Root looked into the system's administration, he became more and more scornful. He particularly disdained the irregularly administered examinations for consul instituted under McKinley and administered to the party faithful. On a scale of ten, Root wrote, "a man who rates seven is passed. It has evidently come to be regarded as cruel and inhuman treatment not to pass a man. In view of the character of the examination a rejection would practically be an imputation of idiocy."[35]

Soon after entering the department, Root began a study of how to improve the consular service. In calling for information about the service's operation, he came into contact with Carr who, as chief of the Consular Bureau, knew as much as anybody about its operations. In consultation with Lodge, Root examined previous legislation and with the help of his subordinates drafted another bill which Lodge introduced.[36]

Carr became closely involved in getting the bill through the House. He argued the department's case for the changes requested before a subcommittee of the House Committee on Foreign Affairs to which it was referred. The subcommittee chairman, Edwin Denby, worked closely with Root and others like Carr in planning strategy to get the bill passed. Carr spent four days testifying. He had briefed Denby, the chief supporter in the House, and indeed had drafted the committee's report. He had prepared for Denby what he called a "prompt" book, or what we might call a briefing book today. Carr found the required parliamentary tactics frustrating. Despite well-prepared arguments and ample supporting evidence, some members remained opposed to changes that threatened their interests. The Speaker of the House, for example, saw a threat to congressional prerogatives in giving the president authority to assign the posts of consular offices. But the chief difficulty, according to Congressman Denby, was that the House was hardly interested in the bill, despite years of agitation by business.[37]

Despite the lack of general congressional interest in sweeping changes, Root put business support for change to good use. As he had reported to the Senate Foreign Relations Committee in December 1905, "There has been a great mass of complaints from the business people of the country regarding our Consular Service. There have been for years discussions and resolutions by various commercial and business bodies on the subject—chambers of commerce and boards of trade and all kinds of business associations by the hundred."[38] The secretary sent a copy of the draft Lodge bill to commercial organizations all over the country along with a personal note requesting support. Although the Senate, according to some newspaper accounts, did not like being pressed by business groups encouraged by Root, he continued to encourage active business cooperation. Root and Lodge also encouraged a consular reform convention to meet in Washington at the time the bill was being considered, if they did not themselves organize and orchestrate the convention.[39]

Root also sought the cooperation of influential members of the Congress who supported the Lodge bill. The secretary of state had had experience with Congress in trying to change the War Department and took pride in his ability to deal with the Congress. "One has to get into direct personal touch with the members of the committees having the matter in charge," he wrote describing his methods. One then had to "convince them of the fact that he has more knowledge of the subject than they have, and that he is sincere." Root believed that members of Congress wanted to do the right thing. Problems arose only when local interests were strong, the members of Congress were faced with an election, and the prerogatives of the Congress were perceived to be threatened.[40]

The legislation for which the Department of State had worked so assiduously passed, but not before, as we have seen, Congress struck out details that threatened its power over patronage. Nevertheless key members in the department learned important lessons from the long effort to change the consular service, although the department had to wait for Roosevelt's June 1906 executive order to take the consular appointments out of politics. Carr and others in the bureaucracy gained experience in how to approach the press, business organizations, and Congress. What was learned was put to good use in gaining support for further desired changes within the State Department. And Carr, despite frequent references to his revulsion at the ugliness of political tactics, became a master at congressional politics. He applied what he learned early. Representative Denby, with whom Carr worked closely on consular reorganization, wanted to have a consul's salary raised. The man stationed at Windsor, Ontario, was a protégé of the congressman. Since Denby "is a member of the Sub-Committee of the House in charge of the bill," Carr admitted frankly to his diary, "I thought the increase desirable from a tactical point of view," although apparently to comfort his conscience he added that the increase was "quite justifiable on other grounds."[41]

Less than a year after Roosevelt's executive orders, Root made Carr chief clerk of the Department of State. The position was important administratively, giving Carr the equivalence of an executive directorship. Once in office Carr took the opportunity to bring in new accounting procedures, allowing for a better understanding of where appropriations stood at any one time. He also established guidelines for internal promotions, combined the cipher and telegraph offices, and supervised the compiling of the laws relating to the department and the foreign service.[42]

Despite his demanding new duties, Carr did not lose interest in the consular service. Indeed, he continued efforts to increase its services, scope, and professionalism. Much of Carr's own pride was involved in the service, but there were other reasons for his interest. Businessmen who needed the assistance of the consular service were an important constituency for the department. As chief clerk, Carr was more likely than the secretary to deal with Congress over appropriations for the department. Carr sought out representatives of business associations to remind them of the usefulness of the department, and he provided direct assistance to businessmen who requested it. Similarly, he tried to build a good image of the work of the consular service in the public and business press. For the use of businessmen, he had consuls prepare surveys of needs and opportunities abroad. Although he realized that the consul should not replace the businessman in making a sale, it would not hurt the department if the consular service helped conspicuously. Carr cultivated important members of congressional committees with whom he had to deal, making a point of visiting their offices and seeing them socially at receptions and dinners. And he directed subordinates to prepare materials for congressmen's speeches.[43]

As part of his effort to improve efficiency and professionalism within the department, Carr tried assiduously to get Congress to pass legislation codifying the changes in the consular service that Roosevelt had extended by executive order. In 1912 the chairman of the House Committee on Foreign Affairs introduced legislation to make into law Roosevelt's executive orders. The changes did not get through a Congress unsettled by the political jockeying of the election year. There were, however, improvements to Carr's liking in the 1915 Stone-Flood Act, which essentially gave congressional approval to the idea of appointment and promotion on the basis of merit. The constitutional question of Congress limiting the power of appointment from the president was neatly compromised. The secretary of state was required to report only the names of those qualified for appointment or promotion as determined by examination or efficiency reports. The legislation, however, did not require the president to make appointments or promotions from those on the list.[44]

Carr and other members of the department continued their efforts to bring the further changes that they thought were necessary. Indeed the significant 1924 Rogers Act was in large part drafted under Carr's direction. This legislation merged the diplomatic and consular services, increased salaries significantly, and required examinations for appointment.[45]

Carr's experience with and contacts in Congress were put to good use when Taft became president in 1909. He worked closely with Secretary Root's successor, Philander Knox, to increase the department's appropriations. Increased budgets were in fact justified, for the demands on the department expanded as the United States assumed an enlarged role in international affairs, American citizens traveled more frequently, and businesses had a larger number of foreign customers. The department had grown from only 75 officers and clerks in 1887 to 152 in 1909. It needed a larger staff and better accommodations abroad. In justifying an increase in appropriations in 1910 Carr and Knox made much of the consular service's assistance in helping business find opportunities for capital investment and the sale of manufactured products. All of this was done, they argued, in spite of the fact that other countries had provided more money to aid commerce. They justified a larger staff in order to allow for specialization, since few employees spent enough time on any one subject to become experts who could do their work professionally.[46]

By the end of Knox's tenure, Carr had developed a low opinion of Congress, but he had devised a strategy necessary to deal with legislators. The House Committee on Foreign Affairs was made up of members who, Carr thought, could not for the most part see foreign affairs as a whole. Party advantage was the foremost consideration, although the chairman also feared going before the House and being challenged on his committee's recommendations. He concluded, therefore, that departmental proposals and supporting evidence should be short, clear, and convincing. Estimates of need should be carefully related to some popular notion or theme, or upon a policy of the government or of the Congress.[47]

Trade expansion was a theme that Carr seized upon time and again. Market-seeking businessmen had been organized for a long time, and they were an important source of pressure in Congress. Like Carr and other members of the bureaucracy, business groups had developed close contacts with members of Congress (especially from their own districts) and with leaders of important committees. As early as 1910, Carr tried to make clear the connection between the needs of business and those of the diplomatic service. In a speech delivered to a Saint Louis business group in 1910, Carr stated that "we look to you to hold up the hands of the Administration in continuing the good work of placing and keeping the diplomatic and consular service upon a basis of efficiency and not of politics." Efficient and good men, he argued, were important for expansion and the protection of foreign trade. He wanted to dispel prevalent misconceptions about diplomacy, for, as he said, "diplomacy and trade go hand in hand." He reminded the businessmen that diplomats negotiate commercial treaties, help to protect patents and trademarks, and keep up the fight for equal opportunity; they work to maintain the conditions under which trade was possible.[48]

Carr's concern for trade expansion was not always matched by that of businessmen. Smaller producers' interest in foreign trade was not constant, and Carr and, as we shall see, members of the Commerce Department worked hard to encourage businessmen to expand abroad. It was a frustrating task at times. Indeed, after years as director of the consular service, the department's chief clerk, and chief of the Consular Bureau, he admitted he knew little of what business really wanted. He noted that while the audience for a speech to the Foreign Trade Convention of 28 May 1914 was friendly, some seemed bored or even bemused by his remarks. As he had before at such business gatherings, however, Carr took the opportunity to ask the assembled businessmen to support the department's efforts to attain higher salaries, government-owned buildings abroad, better clerical allowances, and greater "elasticity," that is, greater freedom for the professionals within the department to do their work.[49]

The Department of State's interest in trade expansion was more focused and sustained than that of the smaller businessmen who were most in need of government assistance. Smaller producers' attention to trade expansion waxed and waned with changes in the domestic economy. Carr was not the only one in the Department of State to become frustrated at business' inconstant interest. The consuls who more and more saw their careers tied to the successful expansion of American trade were often frustrated and discouraged by the business community's behavior. They complained of carelessness in packing and of inattention to foreign tastes. One consular report bluntly told "The Old Story: Obstinacy and Blundering by Our Manufacturers." Carr and others within the department wanted businessmen to see trade expansion as a long-term proposition and to be more systematic in cultivating overseas sales.[50]

Manufacturers, however, appeared satisfied with the changes that had come about. By World War I they were served abroad by professional consuls who provided information and service to producers seeking to export. Under Carr's direction consuls increased the number of reports they contributed to government publications. Carr instituted a confidential service to provide information to businessmen about foreign trade conditions, since he did not want foreign governments or businessmen taking advantage of information gathered by American consular officials. In one year (1910), 199 confidential bulletins were issued, and a daily publication of foreign opportunities for American businessmen listed a total of 1500 items. The consular service encouraged manufacturers and independent export firms to file their catalogs with American consulates abroad where they could be made available to foreign importers. In 1910, American consuls forwarded 14,000 letters to the department, so information important to business was abstracted and published. And Carr required officials from the most commercially active areas to return home to provide American manufacturers with firsthand information about foreign commercial practices and needs in their districts. Consuls also provided the department with information for negotiations.[51]

The work of the consuls was for the most part directed at the interests of the smaller producers, who were more numerous if not economically as significant as the larger producers. But the larger firms at times relied on the Department of State's consular service too. In making direct investments in assembly plants and factories, the largest firms occasionally needed the assistance of American consular officials. International Harvester, for example, turned to the department in building a factory in Russia. The czarist government exercised strict control over economic activity, and it was difficult for private firms to deal directly with the Russian government. More generally, even firms with extensive marketing networks at times used information gathered by consuls and made available by the department.[52]

Overall, however, the department was of less significance to larger producers than to the smaller. Most large producers were able to arrange for the construction of their own foreign facilities. Then, too, some firms preferred to mask their American ownership in at times hostile foreign environments. Officials of Singer in France, for example, bypassed the local American consul in disputes over substantial payments of back taxes. Singer's representatives hired French lawyers to deal directly with French officials.[53]

The department for its part was ambivalent about the foreign operations of some of the largest American corporations. Building factories abroad, some

State Department officials thought, did not benefit the American economy, since foreign facilities took jobs from American workers. The department resolved to be courteous to requests for assistance in building manufacturing plants overseas, but not overly helpful. Moreover, too much assistance to the largest American companies could create problems with Congress, where hostility to big business remained strong. The department's lack of sympathy for direct investment in branch factories lasted well into the 1920s.[54]

In return for the aid the department did provide, especially to the numerous smaller firms, it wanted business support in its struggles with Congress over appropriations. To bureaucrats interested in rationality, order, predictability, and planning, the ways of Congress epitomized inefficiency. At best Congress appeared to be a throwback to a slower era which made few demands on the services of the federal government. The difficulty for the State Department was that the businessmen who most needed government assistance in promoting trade, and those who could most benefit from the work of the consuls, were those whose interest in foreign markets were tied to swings in the domestic business cycle. When domestic demand was good, they tended to neglect foreign trade. Similarly, their interest in the problems of the Department of State were far from constant. Carr and consular officials encouraged businessmen to keep up foreign trade contacts, even when sales were good at home. Carr and many of his colleagues understood that the consular service, and in many ways the Department of State itself, would prosper so long as American manufacturers maintained an interest in expanding foreign trade.

An improved consular service was not the only way the Department of State assisted manufacturers. As commercial matters became more important the department required expert information to negotiate commercial treaties and assess foreign tariffs. These specific tasks of economic diplomacy were to be handled by the Bureau of Trade Relations, created in 1903. That bureau succeeded the Bureau of Foreign Commerce, which was moved to the Department of Commerce and Labor created in 1903. The Department of State's Bureau of Foreign Commerce was the name given to the department's Bureau of Statistics in 1897. The latter had been responsible for compiling and preparing the department's publications on commerce. Under the energetic leadership of Frederick Emory in the 1890s the Bureau of Statistics published better edited yearly volumes of *Commercial Relations of the United States with Foreign Countries*, as well as the monthly *Consular Reports*. It also sponsored and published *Special Consular Reports* on particular topics, especially on foreign industries and markets for American goods. And from time-to-time the bureau prepared memoranda on special issues of commercial interest to the secretary or members of Congress.[55]

Changing the name of the Bureau of Statistics in 1897 was part of the department's initial effort to appeal to market-seeking businessmen. Officially the new name was to avoid confusion with similar offices in other executive departments. Privately, however, the head of the bureau, Frederick Emory, thought that the change would make a favorable impression on the business community. Emory used increased appropriations to enlarge the Bureau of Foreign Commerce's services to businessmen. One of its first efforts was the publication of daily "advance sheets" from consular reports. These were to provide information quickly about overseas sales opportunities and changing foreign conditions. Members of the bureau, especially its chief, increased contacts with business in less official ways. Emory addressed numerous business organizations and wrote articles for the public press on trade-related matters.[56]

Congress undercut the work of the Bureau of Foreign Commerce (BFC) by creating the Department of Commerce and Labor in 1903. Legislation establishing the new department provided for the transfer of the Bureau of Foreign Commerce to the Department of Commerce and Labor, although the State Department was able to get congressional authority to create a successor to the BFC. Not to confuse matters with the new department, the State Department dropped all reference to "commerce" in its new agency, which it called the Bureau of Trade Relations (BTR). The new bureau had the responsibility of scrutinizing incoming consular reports to edit out sensitive political and diplomatic information. Once edited the reports were sent to the Commerce and Labor Department for further editing and eventual publication. The bureau was to be the State Department's channel for requests to the new Department of Commerce and Labor for commercial data and for special studies on commercial questions. In effect, the BTR had been stripped of its most important trade-related functions. The bureau, however, continued to answer businessmen's questions about foreign tariffs and economic conditions, and independently it compiled data for the department's internal use. The BTR prepared the annual reports on changing foreign commercial conditions which the secretary transmitted to Congress, something which the department was well aware would keep it prominently in view of Congress.[57]

Secretary Root wanted to make the bureau the State Department's expert on questions related to foreign commerce and investment. Root believed that the lack of specialized attention to trade and investment weakened the department's effectiveness. Tariff negotiations with the Germans in 1906 pointed up American diplomacy's disadvantages, as an ad hoc three-man American team met nine German negotiators whose full-time duties were to study Germany's commercial interests and defend them in negotiations with foreign governments. The German negotiations also pointed up to the department what businessmen already knew, that foreign discriminatory tariffs posed a threat to America's substantial trade with Europe. The secretary regularly requested increased appropriations in order, among other things, to improve the BTR. Root left the department before the changes he wanted were effected. But the increasing public and congressional discussion of 1908 of a change in the tariff gave force to Root's requests for more money.[58]

The tariff legislation of 1909, the department argued, made imperative the expansion of the State Department that Root had advocated. The Payne-Aldrich tariff established a minimum and maximum schedule of rates. To get the lower tariff rate, 25 percent below the maximum, a foreign country had to demonstrate that it did not unduly discriminate against American goods. The United States government had to satisfy itself that a foreign government was not discriminating excessively. Secretary Knox, echoing Root, requested enlarged appropriations so that the department could make judgments about foreign discriminations against American goods as required in the new tariff laws. (Taft, as we have seen, assigned the task ultimately to the tariff board.) Knox also justified more money by reference to the department's by then standard arguments that growing foreign trade brought more work and that the department needed to expand to help business develop the great potential of the Latin American and Far Eastern markets. Knox used an ingenious argument about these new areas. Although trade in those two parts of the world was miniscule compared with that in Canada and Europe, the smallness only showed the potential for growth.[59]

The department received an extra appropriation at the end of the congressional session, as members hastened to adjourn. The Department of State then went ahead and made changes in its organization, adding staff and creating new offices. But the 1909 tariff in fact did not increase the work of the department. President Taft, relying on advice from the tariff board, announced in April 1910 that all foreign countries had met the government's requirements and deserved the minimum schedule. Nevertheless, the department had been successful in tying its own interests to one of the major domestic and congressional issues, the tariff.[60]

One of the most important organizational changes Knox brought about with the extra appropriation was the creation of a counselor's office. The counselor was to be an international lawyer in charge of negotiations on all issues, including commercial and trade matters. In the past the department had hired international lawyers as the need arose to conduct negotiations over fisheries, boundaries, and the like. The new counselor was to be on a par with an assistant secretary, since his appointment required the Senate's consent. The funds that Knox received also allowed him to establish firmly newly created geographic divisions, which were to help increase the department's specialization.[61]

What funds were left went to expand the staff of the BTR. Knox appointed two men to the bureau who had worked for the Department of Commerce and Labor. Both were committed to the expansion of American trade. They thought that exports could be expanded by careful attention to changes in the commercial treaties and foreign tariffs they reviewed. The bureau also studied foreign tariffs, compiled statistics for the use of the department, and initiated special counselor reports on commercial issues. Quite often these special studies, a large number as time went on, were directed at the particular interest of one industry or group of businesses. The BTR occasionally published its own statistical reports. Members of the bureau, like men in the consular service, made frequent visits to meetings of business groups to encourage greater and more systematic efforts at trade expansion. And they tried, too, to make their offices a welcome stop for businessmen visiting Washington.[62]

The BTR, in short, provided another source of information for market-seeking manufacturers. Of more significance probably, the bureau was another agency of the government vitally concerned with the promotion of American trade, in part because of the department's own self-interest. Attention to the details of commercial negotiations and the trade policies of foreign governments served the interests of market-seeking producers, especially during those times when smaller manufacturers turned full attention to the domestic market. The bureau, like the consular service, provided continuity of interest in trade promotion.

The BTR, however, became a casualty of a growing rivalry between the Department of State and the Department of Commerce and Labor. The rivalry persisted throughout the Wilson administration and centered on the question of which department was the more appropriate place for the government to promote the interests of American business abroad. Not until after Herbert Hoover had been secretary of commerce for several years was the dispute settled in favor of his department. Before then the two departments jockeyed in Congress for sole authority to help business promote foreign commerce. Both departments sought to enlist business support for their positions, diffusing the energies of a business community not fully attentive to the possibilities of trade expansion.

The State Department lost the first congressional battle over which department should help promote trade. President Taft, formerly secretary of war, believed that the executive departments needed to be reorganized to promote efficiency. And so Taft acceded to congressional requests for an examination of the growing bureaucracy, appointing in 1911 the President's Commission on Economy and Efficiency. One of the many subjects it took up was duplication in the government's efforts to promote trade. Secretary Knox and his closest advisers saw in the commission's investigation an opportunity to gain full responsibility for the government's efforts at trade promotion. But the State Department's effort was thwarted in the House of Representatives. Some influential members, including the Speaker, had been angered by what they considered the department's deception over the 1909 Payne-Aldrich tariff. They maintained that the appropriations provided to conduct trade negotiations proved unnecessary since the minimum tariff schedule quickly came into effect. To make matters worse, however, congressional critics charged that the State Department had used the appropriation to create within the department new offices that the Congress had rejected in previous years. Congress had specifically refused to create an undersecretary to act as the department's chief executive officer, and some members of the House saw the counselor's office as another name for something the Congress had forbidden. The Department of State's congressional opponents received further support for their opposition in a report of the president's efficiency commission, which concluded that the BTR had exceeded its original responsibilities. A House subcommittee on appropriations recommended dropping the BTR and other new departmental positions. The agency was omitted from the House's 1912 Legislative, Executive and Judicial Appropriations bill.[63]

The department quickly mobilized some of its most faithful business supporters to help defend the bureau in the Senate. A conference committee on the legislation restored some of the new posts taken away by the House bill, but the committee failed to appropriate money for the BTR. Congress authorized the Department of Commerce and Labor to create a Bureau of Foreign and Domestic Commerce to take on the tasks performed at the Department of State. The department, however, was able to salvage something of this legislative debacle. Through an oversight, Congress required that the new agency of the Commerce Department had to continue to have consular reports edited by the State Department.[64]

A month after Congress had done away with the BTR, the secretary issued the departmental order that created the Office of Foreign Trade Advisers to continue the work of the defunct bureau. The department saw the September 1912 order as necessary to keep its efforts on behalf of businessmen before that part of the commercial and industrial community interested in trade expansion. "It seems very important," one of the two new trade advisers observed about his work, that it "shall not be confined to current matters ... (reciprocity or commercial treaties) which develop of themselves, but that there should be a free field for initiative and constructive work such as may suggest itself from time to time. In this way, the larger aspect of the commercial functions of the Department can be kept well to the front and can be impressed both on the general public and on the business interests of the country." It took some time for the new office to get functioning, and there appears to have been over a year of confusion on its work getting underway. But by 1913, the trade advisers were again controlling much of the government's information on trade promotion, as they edited incoming consular reports before forwarding them to the Department of Commerce and Labor.[65]

The office, however, suffered from an inability to keep a permanent staff, although one of the original advisers stayed on for several years. At the end of January 1916 the office was changed again, becoming the Office of the Foreign Trade Adviser. Although at first the staff was reduced, during the war it was again increased, as specialists were added to deal with questions relating to strategic commodities, financial issues, and reparations. Two others concerned themselves with tariffs, commercial treaties, and industrial property.[66]

The departmental order creating the Office of Foreign Trade Adviser gave it broad responsibility for coordinating economic matters within the department, for example, giving advice to the geographic divisions and the secretary on economic issues, reviewing correspondence in other offices relating to economic questions, studying legislation as it might affect American trade, assuring that businessmen visiting the department were sent to the appropriate officials helping to draft correspondence where technical expertise on economic matters might be necessary, and drafting memoranda on general economic questions not handled in the geographic divisions.[67]

Nevertheless, this new office, like the one before it, was plagued with a rapid turnover in personnel. In part this was a result of the war, as staff was shifted around to deal with increasingly complicated issues arising from the conflict. It was in part, also, a reflection of employee frustration over the fact that the office's work was not so grand as its original organizational order would have suggested. The office was no longer to work explicitly toward trade expansion because of the hostility engendered in the Department of Commerce, which under Secretary of Commerce William C. Redfield was to take center stage in the Wilson administration's efforts to promote trade. Then, too, other agencies within the Department of State handled economic questions; the geographic divisions dealt directly with economic issues as they related to policy in their areas.[68]

The Office of Foreign Adviser, however, was the nucleus of a greater and better-coordinated effort on the part of the State Department to deal with foreign economic problems, eventually becoming in 1921 the Office of Economic Adviser. Although the office continued to provide information to the department and to the business community, and although Wilbur Carr and the consular service maintained the department's positive image in the eyes of the public and Congress, during the peacetime Wilson years the Department of Commerce became the locus of the government's effort to build ties between market-seeking producers and the bureaucracy. The war, as we shall see, changed matters dramatically, for Wilson created a War Trade Board, which tended at times to subordinate American producers' interests to larger wartime considerations. And in Wilson's handling of negotiations in the peace treaty, he relied heavily on the reports of the experts he took with him to Paris. But as with the consular service, the department's Bureau of Trade Relations and its Office of Foreign Trade Advisers represented a genuine concern over providing a needed service, that is, trade expansion in order to help the American economy, with the obvious self-interest of serving a constituency that would support the department before congressional committees. Playing bureaucratic politics in Congress could be a dangerous business, as the demise of the Bureau of Trade Relations demonstrated in 1912. But the Department of State's fortunes would improve in 1918, and the Commerce Department, which did so well in 1912, would have tougher times with Congress after the war, as we shall see.

The Department of State thus provided assistance to American businessmen in more than one way, and through more than one agency. The department provided much information through its publications. Consuls represented

Americans abroad, and, when necessary, they interceded with foreign officials on behalf of American interests. The department more generally sought to negotiate advantageous commercial treaties and sought to protect American trademarks and patents when used overseas. At the same time, the State Department believed that it needed to cultivate support in the business community. Except for the largest manufacturers, American producers' interest in foreign trade was irregular. The largest producers often built factories abroad, a policy department officials could not support enthusiastically. In any event, the goodwill of market-seeking businessmen was essential to a department that had no other "natural" constituency. Congress remained essentially indifferent to foreign affairs, as did the American public, before World War I. In a society where business interests and values were strong, the support of market-seeking businessmen was essential to a department that could see America's foreign interests and responsibilities expanding faster than the Congress or the American people could. And so businessmen interested in trade expansion gained encouragement and support from more than one branch of the Department of State.

Complicating the State Department's efforts to cultivate the interested business community, however, was the growing bureaucratic struggle with the Department of Commerce and Labor over who in the government should be responsible for the promotion of commerce abroad. The Commerce Department tried to build business support for its own efforts at trade expansion. Such competitive efforts were often counterproductive, wasting time and resources. Bureaucratic competition could be dangerous, too, in a Congress that was less than fully attentive to the arguments about who should get what in trade promotion. The struggle, however, did heighten interest of the bureaucracy in "educating" businessmen to the benefits of trade expansion.

Congress had created the Department of Commerce and Labor in 1903 in part to help promote foreign and domestic commerce. The overlapping jurisdictions with the State Department created a fundamental confusion in America's foreign trade policy, and it fueled a bureaucratic struggle between these two departments that continued well into the 1920s. Businessmen interested in trade expansion were drawn into this struggle simply because each of the two departments sought business support for its own requests before Congress.

Six

Coordinating Foreign Trade Expansion: The Department of Commerce, 1913–17

Perhaps ironically, it was the Wilson administration's commerce secretary, William Cox Redfield, who induced the largest manufacturers to cooperate with the government to foster foreign trade. Before 1913, congressional and bureaucratic exponents of trade expansion had concerned themselves almost exclusively with helping smaller manufacturers, most of whom did not have significant economic advantages in selling abroad. Redfield's efforts were similarly directed toward improving the Department of Commerce's services to these businessmen. But he was much less hostile to the interests of big business abroad than his two predecessors had been. Secretaries Oscar S. Straus and Charles Nagel had conceived the promotional work of the department as a way to assist smaller businessmen in competing against the larger producers who so easily dominated export trade. Redfield, in contrast, believed that larger and smaller producers had greater common interests than many in business and government had realized, and he tried to use the department to bring these business interests together. Greater unity among producers interested in foreign trade would strengthen the alliance between businessmen and the Department of Commerce in the effort to bring about congressional changes in maritime, banking, and antitrust policy. At the same time, the secretary saw greater business solidarity as necessary to help the department build general public, congressional, and labor support for the notion that an expanded foreign trade was important to the national interest.

Redfield's positive attitude toward big business was a break with the past, but concern for providing assistance to businessmen was not. The leaders had seen the department as a service bureaucracy, thinking of it as providing assistance to business much as the Department of Agriculture aided farmers. Serving its business constituency well became important politically, especially in dealing with Congress. Legislators proved to be parsimonious, and the early years of the Department of Commerce's history were marked as much by disappointed hopes as by the achievement of goals. Congress did not provide the appropriations necessary for the department to fulfill perhaps exaggerated hopes of business-men who wanted a bureaucracy to promote actively domestic and foreign commerce. Further weakening the effectiveness of the Department of Commerce and Labor was the struggle with the Department of State. Bureaucratic energy was spent in disputes over which of the two should help in the expansion of foreign commerce.

To achieve their goals and hold their own in bureaucratic struggles Commerce Department officials, like those in the Department of State, tried to gain business support for their department. Secretaries Straus and Nagel began this effort by developing close working relationships with business trade associations. The department focused on the smaller businessmen, since Straus and Nagel believed that the department's role was to encourage an interest among smaller producers in selling abroad. Both saw foreign trade as another arena in which trusts thwarted the interests of smaller businessmen, as big business moved swiftly to dominate the exports of industrial goods before World War I.

Motives varied for supporting a Department of Commerce and Labor in 1903. Small manufacturers' desire for trade expansion, to be sure, was one of the reasons for the formation of the department. Many of those who were hired for the new department sympathized with these businessmen. President Roosevelt, however, supported a Department of Commerce and Labor because it was to contain a Bureau of Corporations. The bureau was to be an agency responsible to the president which he could use to investigate big business. Roosevelt sympathized with supporters of trade expansion, but he recognized that it was the larger firms that were going to be the most successful. Indeed one reason for his caution in dealing with the antitrust issue was his understanding that big business led the way in exports. "The same business conditions which have produced the great aggregations of corporate and individual wealth have made them very potent factors in commercial competition" in export markets.[1] Greater efficiency was a persuasive argument with some members of Congress who thought that the Treasury Department had become too large. The duties some of its divisions performed were more logically concerned with commerce than with finance and revenues. Proponents of the new department suggested that such agencies as the Lighthouse Board, the Bureau of Steamboat Inspection, the Bureau of Navigation, and the Bureau of Statistics be moved to the Department of Commerce and Labor.[2]

Initial support for a department devoted to manufacturers developed after the United States government departed from tradition and established the Department of Agriculture in 1862. Congress charged that new federal agency with the responsibility to promote the interest of one group. As America industrialized, producers thought that their interests were as significant as those of farmers. Beginning in the 1880s, and increasing in the 1890s, when more and more producers sought foreign markets, small business groups advocated a department devoted to manufacturers. Responsibility for the interests of labor was tacked onto the new department because of a supposed common interest between labor and capital, although union leaders preferred a separate cabinet-level agency. In 1913 the Department of Commerce and Labor was finally divided into two separate departments, a logical step in view of the fact that the department had devoted more resources and attention to business than to labor.[3]

Despite the many different reasons for supporting a new department, there was some consensus on its tasks among those who worked there. Bureaus were moved from the Department of State, as well as from the Treasury. The Department of State's Bureau of Foreign Commerce combined with Treasury's Bureau of Statistics to become the Commerce Department's new Bureau of Statistics. The combination brought together two agencies that had worked to create support for trade expansion within the State Department and the Treasury.[4]

Consensus on goals turned to conflict, however, when decisions had to be made on which part of the new bureaucracy was to do what. According to the 1902 bill creating the Department of Commerce and Labor, it was "to foster, promote and develop the various manufacturing industries of the United States, and markets for the same at home and abroad, domestic and foreign, by gathering, compiling, publishing, and supplying all available and useful information concerning such industries and such markets." Disputes over the assignment of tasks in the new department hindered work substantially for two years. The Bureau of Manufacturers finally emerged as the agency in the Department of Commerce that was to serve the interests of market-seeking producers, but only after much disagreement with the Bureau of Corporations. Another bureaucratic war was fought within and outside the Commerce and Labor Department over which agencies were to be responsible for collecting data about overseas trade. The Department of Commerce's Statistics Office wanted to be the chief collector of such data, something which the Department of State resisted. The Bureau of Statistics also ran into opposition in the department, for the Bureau of Labor refused to relinquish some of its own data-collecting activities.[5]

Changes at the top level of the department prolonged the perhaps inevitable organizational problems of a new bureaucracy. Roosevelt appointed Victor H. Metcalf secretary in mid-1904 to succeed the first secretary, George B. Cortelyou, who had resigned to manage Roosevelt's reelection campaign. Metcalf appointed a new head of the Bureau of Manufacturers late in 1904. The secretary's choice, J. Hampton Moore, began the task of building a bureau that would serve the interests of manufacturers, especially those engaged in trade expansion. But Moore resigned the following June, and it was his successor who in fact started to build an effective bureau. John M. Carson, a journalist well connected to Republican leaders, was the new head. Carson, like Moore, wanted to expand trade and planned to find and publicize trade opportunities at home and abroad. Both hoped to promote commercial education and disseminate information about foreign conditions. Essential to Moore's effort, as he saw it, was the need to develop closer ties to market-seeking businessmen. The bureau corresponded with commercial and industrial associations nationwide. Form letters requested information about the sales, experiences, and problems of those already engaged in the export trade, as well as about the needs of those who would like to begin to sell abroad. Carson, as a result, focused the bureau's attention on smaller and medium-sized firms in order to provide the assistance needed by enterprises, unlike the major corporations, without great experience in selling overseas.[6]

The department's efforts to help market-seeking firms, however, were not confined entirely to the Bureau of Manufacturers. Responding to requests by the secretary in 1905, Congress funded a corps of special commercial agents who were to investigate trade opportunities. They were not conceived of, the secretary maintained, as a replacement for the Department of State's consuls. Unlike consular officials they were not confined to a limited geographical area. The department hired four men with the $30,000 appropriation it received; two were to go to the Far East, one to Canada and Mexico and the last to South America. Secretary Metcalf instructed the agents to study foreign business conditions: what foreign goods business merchants purchased, what if anything was imported from the United States, the tastes and special needs of foreign buyers, and whatever else the agents thought might help expand foreign trade.[7]

The repayment of political debts rather than entirely commercial considerations dictated the early work of the agents. Metcalf had received vital assistance for the agents from southern congressmen. Southern support for the agents was amply rewarded, as they were instructed to give great attention to the export of cotton products. From China the commercial agents sent back extensive reports on the prices of foreign cotton products imported there, local tastes, and marketing practices necessary for successful trade. Because of the trips of these employees, the department was able to make available some eight thousand samples of cotton goods imported into China. In the next few years, the agents became specialists in several lines of goods, especially in cotton fabrics, cotton seed oil, leather products, agricultural machinery, and machine tools. As the agents proved themselves useful, businessmen from other industries requested thorough studies of possible foreign opportunities for them. By 1912 the bureau employed thirteen special agents who clearly felt overworked. Although some members of Congress criticized active government support of a few classes of manufacturers, the department argued that such service was part of its congressional mandate.[8]

The department and the Bureau of Manufacturers helped market-seeking firms in other ways. Aside from providing information about selling particular lines of goods abroad, the Commerce and Labor Department tried to develop contacts between U.S. businessmen wanting to sell and foreign importers wanting to purchase American goods. In 1905, the Bureau of Manufacturers began compiling lists of American firms interested in developing or already engaged in export markets. The bureau in 1908 requested from the State Department the names of foreign purchasers who made inquiries to our consuls about American products. The Department of Commerce also directly contacted consuls about foreign importers whose names could be supplied to American merchants interested in selling abroad. The department enlisted the aid of business groups in distributing the assembled lists of foreign buyers. Abroad the Commerce Department made available the names of American producers interested in expanding their export trade.[9]

To assist American manufacturers further, the Commerce and Labor Department asked the consuls to comment on the reputation and reliability of foreign merchants whose names the consuls supplied to the department. This request raised a difficult question of policy for the Department of State. On the one hand, the department would compete with commercial reporting firms like Dun and Company that already provided such information for a fee. On the other hand, and of greater concern, the department worried that such information implied endorsement of certain foreign businesses. The department's policy on this and direct business requests for consuls' opinions varied over the years, although by 1911 the State Department had relaxed considerably its earlier prohibitions against officials' expressing their opinions. Generally, the department advised inquiring American businessmen to check on the consuls' information with a reliable American firm that supplied commercial ratings of foreign houses. Like the British, the U.S. State Department disclaimed responsibility for information supplied by government officials.[10]

As another service to businessmen, the Commerce and Labor Department sought congressional support in 1910 for the publication of a directory of world trade. A favorable business response to advance announcements of a directory convinced congressmen of its value, and the Congress appropriated funds for publication. In 1911 the department tried to publish only the names of those foreign firms actively engaged in importing and known to be reliable in their communities. Although there were inevitable errors, and although the State Department derided the project, the *World Trade Directory* was a success, earning indeed a handsome profit for the government.[11]

An equally popular service of the new department and its Bureau of Manufacturers was the publication of *Foreign Trade Opportunities*. In 1905 the Bureau of Manufacturers had assumed the Bureau of Statistics' responsibility for publishing consular reports. The department published the consular data in a variety of forms; there was a major report yearly, shorter monthly editions and excerpts on a daily basis. *Foreign Trade Opportunities*, first published in 1906, was simply another way to call attention to the information in the consular reports. The publication provided businessmen with detailed information about what was sought abroad, as well as the name of the consul who had originally suggested the opportunity. The department believed that such efforts increased the Bureau of Manufacturers' effectiveness, and it clearly strengthened the ties between the department and those smaller and medium-sized enterprises seeking to sell overseas.[12]

Fears that this information was too widely distributed and too easy for foreign rivals to make use of made the department more secretive. The bureau began to send out "confidential circulars" to interested businessmen. The circulars provided the specifications for the sale of such things as drainage pipe, supplies for foreign armies, rails and cars for street railway projects, and the like. The most confidential pieces of information were sent out in the mail, usually as a single-sheet, although confidential "tips" continued to be published in *Foreign*

Trade Opportunities, requiring that interested businessmen write for further information. In 1912 the department sent out 136 confidential circulars and had over 2000 listings in *Foreign Trade Opportunities*.[13]

Thus, by the time Roosevelt's third secretary of commerce, Oscar Straus, left office in 1909, the Commerce and Labor Department provided a greater number and variety of services to firms seeking to sell abroad, and the contacts between the department and the smaller and medium-sized market-seeking firms had increased. But Straus had done more than continue the work of his predecessors. He had begun an effort to establish closer, more formal ties between his department and the business community. He had used the general interest in trade expansion, and the fact that few in principle were opposed to such a goal, in order to build a closer formal relationship between his department and smaller businessmen. Straus's efforts came to little during his own tenure as secretary, but they were the first steps to the closer ties forged by his successor among smaller businessmen and later by Wilson's commerce secretary among larger manufacturers.

Theodore Roosevelt had appointed Oscar Straus commerce secretary in 1906. His family owned Macy's, and he had long been an advocate of free trade. Straus did not join the Republican party until 1896, when his own Democratic party was captured by "Bryanism." Like many others, he welcomed increasing interest in expanding foreign commerce. Making peace in a new political home required him to change his views on several issues. When he concluded that a free trade policy was not a likely prospect, Straus became a staunch supporter of reciprocity. More generally, he believed that businessmen and government should be less antagonistic. Straus had been active in a number of business associations, and he had been president of the prestigious New York Board of Trade and Transportation. His associational work had convinced him of the "importance of establishing a closer relationship between the commercial bodies of the country and the Government."[14]

As secretary, Straus combined his interests in lower tariffs and trade expansion with his desire to foster closer contacts between business and government. His most important effort was sponsorship of a National Council of Commerce. Straus's ideas developed in conjunction with those of Gustav Schwab, the head of an importing house in New York, who had been active in local New York merchant groups and such national associations as the American Reciprocal Tariff League. Initially, Straus approached Schwab to get his association's general support for the department's requests for larger congressional appropriations, especially in ways designed to encourage foreign trade. The two concluded, however, that closer, more regular ties between government and business were necessary to promote foreign commerce and the interests of the department.[15]

Straus and Schwab envisioned an advisory body of representatives from the principal urban commercial associations. The group would meet to discuss measures referred to them by the secretary of the Commerce and Labor Department. The secretary wanted his department, on the one hand, to be responsive to the needs of the business community, since he believed that businessmen seeking foreign trade needed more governmental assistance than others. Straus, on the other hand, knew that he would need strong business support for the Commerce and Labor Department to defend its budget and program in Congress.[16]

In October 1907 Straus invited representatives of leading commercial organizations to establish a National Council of Commerce. Eighty-nine delegates from 29 chambers of commerce and boards of trade, representing a total of 21 different cities, attended the organizational meeting. Besides representatives from local commercial associations, 21 national groups sent delegates. The NAM was prominently represented with seven representatives. The meeting adopted a proposal which called for annual meetings in Washington of the entire council. The work of the council, however, was to be performed by an advisory committee of fifteen members. This committee was to meet at least four times a year, serving as an intermediary between the Commerce Department and the major commercial and industrial associations.[17]

Straus conceived of the council as an unofficial group with close ties to the government. He rejected those formal arrangements that were common in European countries, especially Germany, where businessmen were compelled by law to join chambers of commerce and pay dues. Members of the department were to be ex officio members of the advisory committee of the council, although they were to have no vote. To give some permanence to the council, the advisory committee established a Washington office and hired a full-time staff to work for the committee's executive secretary. The Washington office was to maintain close ties to the departments of Commerce and Labor and of State, as well as others like the Interior and Agriculture, whose work at times touched on foreign commerce and domestic trade.[18]

Straus, then, envisioned the council as directly involved with the executive branch, but he also thought that the group would take part in the congressional policy-making process. Speaking to a Boston group of merchants in February 1908, he said that the council was to act as an agent of business, cooperating with both Congress and the executive departments "in formulating policies and legislation affecting our domestic and foreign commerce."[19]

Early in 1908 Straus began to pose questions and assign tasks to the advisory committee. He wanted assistance in the department's plans to study foreign markets with special agents. The council, he thought, was "in a position to suggest the order of their relative importance, taking into consideration the ability of a given industry to take advantage of any foreign markets that may be developed as a result of such investigations." The council's recommendations would "serve as a guide to the work of the special agents" of the department. In fact, in many cases, agents were appointed on the recommendation of the council.[20]

Straus also saw the National Council as keeping the department in touch with a wide spectrum of business opinion. Like many others at the time, small businessmen as well as the general public, the secretary feared that concentrated private corporate power exercised too much influence on American political life. Straus thus found the representative character of the council essential, so that in matters of foreign trade where big business was dominant he would be able to get the views of a large sample of businessmen.[21]

Straus had a grand vision of the National Council of Commerce as a broad-based organization presenting ultimately a national perspective on business interests. Its most useful work, however, was in trade expansion, in large part because Straus seized on expansion as a concrete and demonstrably important business concern. The secretary thought that businessmen had the best insight, through practical experience, into what they needed to further sales. He believed that making known their interests would help the department develop useful programs, but also allow it to fulfill its legislative mandate to promote domestic and foreign commerce.[22]

Straus's successor in the Taft administration, Charles Nagel, shared many of his views about the need of small business support for the department. But Nagel was more hostile to big business and trusts than his predecessor, and when first in office he wanted to keep a proper distance between government and private interests. Indeed the Taft administration became estranged from America's largest enterprises when the Justice Department vigorously prosecuted trusts. Nagel and Taft eventually came to support a national chamber of commerce to represent a broad business constituency and find support within business for the administration. Nagel supported the National Council of Commerce (NCC), although unlike Straus he had no intention of considering the council a quasi-official body. Considering the council as nothing more than another private commercial body undermined its efforts. And when a New York *Journal of Commerce* article attributed to Nagel critical views of the council's inactivity, the NCC began to fold. A month after the article appeared its chief officers resigned.[23]

A NAM study of whether or not to revive the NCC concluded that Nagel's failure to support it had hurt, especially his refusal to consider it quasi-official. Lack of administration support had made the council no more important than many other commercial bodies, and it never had much more than an opportunity, as the NAM concluded, to distribute "information gathered by the Department of Commerce, already available for anyone who might apply for it."[24]

In fact the group probably failed because its leadership was too narrowly based. Gustav Schwab, whose free trade views were not typical, had put Straus in touch with men who believed strongly in reciprocity. The majority of American businessmen remained protectionists, and many of them thought that tampering with the tariff, even for reciprocity treaties, was dangerous. To many businessmen, tariff revisions meant economic dislocation and "political" agitation. Although support for trade expansion was probably broader than for reciprocity, the National Council of Commerce was too closely identified with the movement for reciprocity. Schwab had drawn up the list for the initial invitations to attend the organizing meeting in Washington. Prominent and taking an influential role at the first meeting was William R. Corwine, secretary of the American Reciprocal Tariff League. Indeed, Corwine became the executive secretary of the National Council of Commerce.[25]

After being in office a few years, Nagel came to appreciate Straus's efforts to create a broad-based business group to advise the department. And so the administration supported the creation of the U.S. Chamber of Commerce in 1911. Taft announced publicly in his message to Congress in December 1911 that he supported a "central organization" of businessmen which would represent "different phases of commercial affairs." The administration was unpopular among larger businessmen, and the business community generally was unnerved by the Supreme Court's decisions the previous spring breaking up Standard Oil and American Tobacco. Since then, the administration had also begun proceedings against U.S. Steel. Taft advocated the new group in the part of his message dealing with foreign policy, probably because he saw the expansion of trade as one of the most obvious areas of common interest in the business community.[26]

Nagel and the department were directly involved in forming the Chamber of Commerce. Indeed the initial letter proposing such a national body was drafted by A.H. Baldwin, head of the Bureau of Manufacturers. The secretary sent Baldwin to commercial associations across the country, especially to those made up of smaller manufacturers and merchants who exhibited the greatest interest in a national group. The largest industrial concerns were not interested at first, and indeed were somewhat skeptical about the prospects for success of such a group. Nagel and Taft wanted the new chamber to provide the government with information and advice about policies affecting business. They hoped to make it possible for businessmen to understand whether planned ventures were legal before they were undertaken, rather than awaiting the decisions of the courts.[27]

On 22 April 1912 a large meeting was held in Washington to form the Chamber of Commerce. Nagel envisioned a group that would "touch elbows with the government" but not work hand in hand with it. The secretary did want, however, to give the group greater standing abroad, and so proposed that the chamber get a national charter from Congress. But Congress ignored Nagel's suggestion, and the Chamber of Commerce was then incorporated in the District of Columbia.[28]

The chamber quickly established itself as a more authoritative representative of business opinion than many other trade associations, in large part because of its referendum procedure. Generally, the chamber submitted major national policy questions to a referendum of member groups. This allowed the membership to keep greater control of the organization's policies and kept the leadership in step with the members. The chamber envisioned that the referendums would give the group greater influence before the Congress.[29]

But the group also tried to improve relations with the executive departments. Taft and Nagel both welcomed such efforts. They planned to solicit the new chamber for recommendations on pending legislation. One of Nagel's major concerns was how to control monopoly and he wanted the opinion of chamber members. Like his predecessors he planned to use the chamber and other associations to champion the department's interests before the Congress.[30]

Despite the department's role in forming the Chamber of Commerce, Nagel turned his attention to helping smaller businessmen in other ways. In the last years of Taft's term, Nagel devoted himself to reorganizing the Bureau of Manufacturers in order to make it more efficient in providing services to market-seeking producers. Nagel attempted to join together the Bureau of Statistics with the Bureau of Manufacturers to form a new Bureau of Domestic and Foreign Commerce (BFDC). It took several years to get these changes through a lethargic Congress, which seemed satisfied that changes in the consular laws and the creation of the department met the needs of businessmen seeking foreign markets.[31]

Nagel's efforts in behalf of smaller manufacturers were closely tied to his concern over the trusts. He believed that the larger corporations were the most interested in export trade because they could secure foreign orders on their own. To counter the domination of foreign trade by the largest corporations, Nagel wanted to create a more efficient agency within the department to assist smaller businessmen. Nagel's first step was to bring younger men into the Bureau of Manufacturers. During the Taft years the work of the bureau increased. Between 1911 and 1912 the rejuvenated bureau doubled the number of inquiries processed about market information provided in *Foreign Trade Opportunities*. The department attributed this increase to the bureau's improved efforts. While in part this was perhaps the case, it was also a reflection of a weakening demand in the domestic economy. The secretary attacked problems with the department's corps of special agents. Nagel successfully put through a name change: "special agents" became "commercial agents," a recommendation made by the agents themselves because as special agents foreign governments looked on them with suspicion. The new commercial agents were also allowed after 1911 to make regular trips to visit with interested American businessmen, and Congress appropriated funds for such travel. Nagel increased direct mail contacts between business and the department. When Taft left office in 1913, the bureau had a mailing list of over 18,000 manufacturers, classified according to the 400 different kinds of goods that they sought to sell in foreign markets.[32]

Thus, when a Democratic administration took office in March 1913, the Department of Commerce and Labor was firmly established as one of the two government departments providing significant services to small and medium-sized firms seeking to expand sales abroad. Secretary Nagel had carried through some of his predecessor's ideas about the need for closer business-government contacts and improved services to market-seeking producers. But like Straus, Nagel looked upon the department's aid as a service to smaller and medium-sized producers.

Nagel clearly shared the hostility to big business found in the Taft administration's Justice Department. He viewed helping smaller businessmen gain foreign markets as a way for the government to assist them in protecting themselves against some of the largest, most "predatory" firms. William C. Redfield, secretary of commerce under Wilson, shared his predecessor's desire to expand foreign trade. But his analysis of the importance of foreign trade to the American economy was more sophisticated than that of Nagel and Straus, and, more important, Redfield was considerably less hostile to big business than his two predecessors. In fact, he believed that big business should cooperate with the government in trade expansion.

Secretary Redfield had practical experience in trade expansion. He had been a successful manufacturer of printing machinery, some of which he had sold in foreign markets. By 1900, however, Redfield had turned his considerable energy beyond his own business. He attended the Democratic National Convention in 1896 as one of the Gold Democrats. Thereafter, he took a more active role in politics. He served for more than a year as the commissioner of public works in Brooklyn, and he was elected to· Congress in 1910. Instead of standing for reelection in 1912, he helped organize and lead the Wilson campaign in New York, for which he was rewarded the post of secretary of commerce. Redfield had first come to Woodrow Wilson's attention through his writings on the tariff; indeed, Wilson said that he had "primed" himself on the issue by studying Redfield's published speeches.

Redfield planned to gain big business' cooperation in trade expansion through the creation of a national council on foreign trade. The secretary's leadership in establishing the council won him the support of some of the largest manufacturers engaged in foreign sales. Yet Redfield did not neglect the interests of smaller producers. Central to his efforts to promote trade expansion was improvement in the services that the Department of Commerce (newly separated from the Labor Department in 1913) provided smaller producers interested in overseas markets. Redfield was a "booster" of trade expansion because he saw American efficiency leading to increased production which in turn, he thought, meant that the United States needed foreign markets.

Redfield's business experiences and growing interest in public life prompted him to write on changes in the American economy. In 1912 he published a well-received book, *The New Industrial Day*. As labor became more efficient, Redfield thought the United States would need more markets abroad, markets increasingly dominated by the better organized British and Germans. Hence, he saw the need for better organization at home. Once the business community and the general public realized the importance of foreign markets, he was confident that support for changes in policy would be forthcoming. But he feared that such support might not come soon enough, and so Redfield set himself the task of "educating" opinion.[33]

123

Once in office Redfield concentrated on implementing the services of the Department of Commerce's newly created Bureau of Foreign and Domestic Commerce and on building support for expansion within the business community. The new secretary moved on several fronts. After a complete review of procedures within the BFDC, Redfield went to Congress for increased appropriations to expand the bureau's activities. Some of the money he received helped him to establish district offices in cities far from Washington. These offices were charged with the responsibility of bringing the department's services closer to manufacturers. In a move that stirred controversy, Redfield requested Congress to establish a service of permanent commercial attachés assigned to the countries with which the United States traded most heavily. He also wanted an increased number of commercial agents to seek out trade opportunities. And finally in a request that particularly disturbed the Department of State, he wanted consular officials to report to the Commerce Department any information that bore directly on commercial matters. Although some of Redfield's proposals met with vigorous opposition from the Department of State, he ultimately succeeded in getting the commercial attachés. Congress did not, however, require the State Department's consulars to report directly to the Department of Commerce.[34]

Redfield defined clearly the role he wanted the BFDC to play. He thought that the work of the BFDC was "necessarily of a missionary character. It partakes of the nature of a commercial reconnaissance." He increased the size of the bureau's staff, so that by 1915 it had grown to 171 employees. Redfield's concern for efficiency in business was reflected in his operation of the department. Although publicly he extolled the Department of Commerce's efficiency, privately he continued to complain about the difficulties of improving operations. Early in 1915, for example, he scolded the BFDC for taking three weeks to answer a very simple letter from a businessman.[35]

Redfield's first year in office was marked by great activity. By 1914 the BFDC had established branch offices in New York, Boston, Chicago, Saint Louis, Atlanta, New Orleans, San Francisco, and Seattle. These offices were equipped to answer inquiries that businessmen had formerly directed to the main offices in Washington. Redfield envisioned that the branches would serve as intermediaries between businessmen and the commercial and consular officials of the U.S. government abroad. The branches kept lists of U.S. and foreign dealers at home and abroad who handled various lines of merchandise. Often information requested by a manufacturer who wrote to consuls in a foreign city had already been gathered by the department and reported in publications or kept in the files of the bureau. The branch offices maintained libraries of the department's publications and could forward to Washington inquiries about trademarks, foreign tariffs, foreign revenue laws, and regulations on traveling salesmen that could not be routinely answered in the field. Consuls on trips home used the branch offices to meet with manufacturers and exporters. The branch offices distributed as much information as they could to encourage and stimulate interest in foreign trade. And when Congress failed to authorize the opening of branches in certain cities, the department worked out agreements with a number of local business groups who acted as conduits to local businessmen for department information.[36]

Equally important to the work of the bureau and its branches were the increased number of publications sponsored by the department. The BFDC took responsibility for publishing "Foreign Trade Opportunities," which were published in the department's *Daily Consular and Trade Reports*. The branches made it easier for producers who wanted to follow up one of these rather general pieces of information, since manufacturers had only to apply to the branch for more specific information. The Commerce Department also continued and expanded its "Confidential Bulletins and Circulars," which primarily contained information about commercial prospects abroad and were sent only to a list of those producers who had registered with the department. The department also updated the *Trade Directory of South America*, which provided the names of commercial houses that handled various lines of goods.[37]

If the publications and the branch offices were to do the department's "missionary" work of stimulating interest in trade expansion, the commercial attachés were to do the "reconnaissance" that Redfield had spoken about. As it turned out, they were a primary source of information about business opportunities overseas, but they did more than gather information.

The secretary set tough standards for the work of the commercial attachés. An attaché's work, he wrote, "must be tested by its practical value and cannot be called promoting commerce unless actual orders result. While, therefore, it would be a mistake to measure the work wholly by the volume of orders known to have been taken by American manufacturers in a given time as a result of its work, this, nevertheless, is the standard of success toward which we must work and by which, in some measure at least, that work must be tested."[38]

Soon after taking office, Redfield requested appropriations to send out ten special agents to study markets in Central and South America. The $50,000 appropriation allowed for an updating of earlier studies. The investigation provided important information, Redfield believed, for producers of cotton sacks, lumber, flour, hardware, machinery and machine tools, electrical appliances, wearing apparel, and furniture. The special agents also collected information on banking and finance, transportation, and commercial law. As with the department's commercial agents who had done the earlier studies, many of the special agents returned to the United States to meet with American producers of the products they investigated.[39]

Despite the value of information culled from these reports. Redfield continuously pressed his subordinates to make the results of the BFDC's efforts of practical use to American producers. To serve their needs better, Redfield sent out a series of letters requesting information about the foreign trade activities of manufacturers prominent in the midwest. He wanted their suggestions for new services, as well as their criticisms of the department's current efforts. Generally, the response to this letter, as to others, was disappointing. E.E. Pratt, director of BFDC, commented that "while some of them [the letters] are very interesting, the majority seem to be rather barren of suggestions." But the secretary was undeterred, convinced only that the department needed to do more "missionary" work.[40]

Redfield's energetic style led to some administrative problems. He took a personal interest in the department's day-to-day efforts to expand trade, but his concern appeared to some of his subordinates to be meddling. In one instance his interference provoked an unpleasant public controversy with one of the directors of the Bureau of Foreign and Domestic Commerce, E.E. Pratt. There were other difficulties. The department suffered from a high turnover in these years, something not entirely attributable to Redfield. More his responsibility, however, was the fact that he wasted his energies in an uninformed "boosterism." In the face of unfavorable economic conditions, for instance, Redfield tried to get wool manufacturers to sell abroad. His persistence led to an extraordinary correspondence with wool manufacturers who exasperatedly tried to provide Redfield with the economic "facts of life" in the industry. Similarly, he took a great interest in developing the Russian market. "We think in the Department of Commerce," Redfield wrote to the new U.S. ambassador to Russia, "that Russia offers the greatest single field in the world for the development of American trade." Obviously events were to prove Redfield wrong, but he had not looked very closely at the obstacles to trade with Russia. The department's attaché in Petrograd reported a much less promising atmosphere there because "American merchants and American bankers do not understand Russia."[41]

In spite of his failings, Redfield brought about changes that met with approval in the business community. Foreign businessmen and consular agents generally thought the American system of aiding foreign trade efforts was good. A report of the Cincinnati Chamber of Commerce noted that although some American foreign agents did not know foreign languages, which made it difficult to get well acquainted with foreign officials and businessmen, the United States had an efficient bureaucracy. The Germans especially were hampered by bureaucrats who at times restricted distribution to businessmen of some of the reports from their consuls in the field.[42]

Redfield in his 1915 report quoted from laudatory letters about the department's services and the work and assistance given either directly or through "Trade Opportunities" by the bureau's attachés abroad. A manufacturer of machinery wrote of the courtesy of the branch office in New York. An attaché in Chile was commended for assisting an American firm selling cast iron pipe, grading equipment, and railroad supplies. The attaché intervened with local companies and authorities in the Ministry of Public Works in order to get specifications modified in proposed contracts. But the commercial attachés were more than troubleshooters. Many of them made a point of cultivating local officials. The bureau's attaché in Australia, for example, developed cordial relations with a new minister of Home Affairs, through whose office contracts were let for the federal railways and other public works.[43]

Besides improving services and publications, Redfield tried to build greater public and private support for trade expansion. To convince producers of the need for overseas trade was, he thought, an important part of his task as secretary. Redfield knew that a lack of sustained interest in trade expansion, especially among smaller producers, was one of the primary difficulties in promoting it. At the same time, Redfield saw business support for foreign trade as essential to the department's efforts to get Congress to systematize and rationalize American commercial policy. Increasing business interest in foreign trade, in short, would help him build a department that would help develop that trade. As time went on, Redfield identified personally more and more with the bureaucratic goals of the department. Hence, the secretary took a very close hand both in encouraging business to export and in dealing with Congress. His success with Congress was quite notable in the years before the war in Europe began to disrupt international commerce and the department's attempt to increase America's share of it.

Redfield did more to establish close ties with the press than any of his predecessors. He agreed with the American Manufacturers' Export Association when it resolved in 1917 that "National security in foreign trade can arise substantially only from a broad public appreciation of its value as a national asset; hence extensive publicity by the Press, with the aid of Governmental Departments and trade associations, is essential to affect the public generally and Labor particularly with a sense of their dependency on our foreign trade so that united and intelligent action may inspire domestic legislation and a foreign policy." The director of the BFDC worked out an agreement with representatives of the Trade Press Association to publicize information about foreign trade in special interest business publications. Redfield made himself available to reporters, handed out frequent statements, and saw to it that the publications of his department were distributed broadly.[44]

Even though Redfield worked hard on press relations, his main missionary effort was directed at business associations and, whenever possible, at making direct contacts with businessmen. Toward these ends, the Commerce Department distributed questionnaires to individual businessmen on how best to promote trade. To encourage interest in trade expansion, Redfield sent representatives of the department to business conventions. Through its branch offices, the department sponsored meetings with commercial and special agents who reported their findings about foreign conditions directly to businessmen. Commercial agents who had studied hardware production and sales abroad, for example, traveled to American producers in a number of cities to show them

127

samples of the work of European competitors, as well as to provide information and answer questions about European markets. Likewise, agents informed American textile machinery manufacturers of Chinese interest in American products and provided information about trade and sales conditions in Latin America to producers of machine tools.[45]

But this information was not only directed at increasing business interest in trade expansion. Business support, according to Redfield's way of thinking, was essential for his other goals: coordinating foreign commercial policy, getting legislation to "rationalize" it, and gaining support for the Department of Commerce as the coordinator of commercial policy. One of the central problems of Redfield's Department of Commerce, as it had been with that of his predecessors, was the relationship with Congress. Redfield worked assiduously to build close ties with members of Congress. The secretary provided data, reports, and studies to members of Congress. To gain the goodwill of Claude Kitchin, an influential House committee chairman, Redfield made the department's cost of production studies available to the House Ways and Means Committee so that if statistical studies were necessary in regard to the tariff, the department's "scientific" data would be used. Redfield responded quickly to congressional requests, giving them personal attention. In answering an inquiry from an Alabama senator about what the department had done for the South, Redfield responded with a detailed report on how studies of Central and South American markets were useful to southern industries.[46]

The secretary did not confine himself entirely to building up goodwill, however. At times, he asked for support in return for the services his department rendered. In response to a request for information about the tariff, Redfield directly asked Senator F.M. Simmons (N.C.), who was fending off a Republican attack on the Democratic tariff, to help his department. In sending the requested information, Redfield asked the senator, who was a member of the Finance Committee, to support the department's appropriations. Redfield argued that the department did important work supporting policies of the administration and that it merited support. Redfield made it clear to legislators at every opportunity the importance of the department's work to Congress and to their business constituents.[47]

Redfield, more than his predecessors, used the growing support he had from expansionist business organizations to press Congress to adopt policies and approve appropriations the department wanted. Complaints, for example, that Pittsburgh had not been included among the cities that received a branch of the BFDC gave Redfield an opportunity to lecture businessmen on the importance of loyalty to the department.[48] Similarly, Redfield used business interest in trade expansion in his congressional battles to increase the number of commercial attachés. Willys-Overland's Export Department complained to the department that the lack of a commercial attaché in India limited sales because there was no local American official to deal with Indian officials over a local embargo. Other groups like the Philadelphia Chamber of Commerce had written to the department about the need for a commercial attaché in India, and the department promptly sent copies of these letters to members of the appropriations committees in Congress.[49]

Redfield saw the Department of Commerce as the most appropriate government agency to assist in promoting foreign trade, and, as the years went by, he tried harder to enlist the support of the business community for the expansion of his department. For example, he organized a major meeting of businessmen in 1916. A delegation of thirty secretaries of chambers of commerce, boards of trade and commercial organizations met at the Department of Commerce. After they were received by the presdient at the White House, Redfield made a strong case to these influential men to support efforts in Congress to increase appropriations for the department. The meetings in Washington also included tours of the department and lectures on its services.[50]

The theme of helping the department was taken up outside of Washington too. When departmental employees spoke at business gatherings, they regularly made a plea for support of increased appropriations. Attendance at such meetings, however, became an issue on which Redfield needed business assistance. Congress refused to pay for such travel, since in the past government officials were paid to attend political conventions. Redfield enlisted the aid of business associations in getting this troublesome rule removed. "Meanwhile I wonder," he wrote the executive secretary of one prominent business group, "if it would not be possible for a body like yours to address a communication to the Speaker of the House of Representatives and to the President of the Senate pointing out the mistaken character of this [refusal] .... If you think well of the matter I would give you the precise details with suggestions concerning what should be written."[51]

On the whole, the secretary was quite successful in his dealings with Congress. He warded off State Department attacks on the attaché system with the help of the business community, and he had sympathetic businessmen put pressure on the congressional committees overseeing the work of the department. His success disconcerted leaders in other federal departments, but so long as he had business support and the cooperation of the president, he could best his rivals. The war, however, undermined Redfield's efforts at coordinating business and governmental promotion of foreign trade. As Congress and the president turned their energies toward war, Redfield encountered growing difficulties in keeping the support he had built up within Congress and among businessmen.

Overall, however, Redfield had created a greater coherence in the relations between business and government in the years before World War I. The Department of Commerce and the Department of State, too, provided greater numbers of services to market-seeking businessmen than ever before. Efforts were being coordinated in Redfield's department, as we shall see in the next chapter, to improve the merchant marine and remove the restrictions of the antitrust laws on foreign commerce.

While the Wilson administration built upon the work of its predecessors, Redfield did not confine himself to assistance to small and medium-sized firms. He had a broad view of the national importance of foreign trade expansion, and the secretary realized that general support for expansion could be stimulated only if all those interested in foreign trade were involved. And so Redfield tried to draw the larger firms into an alliance with the Commerce Department and the smaller firms. Unlike his Republican predecessors, Redfield did not look upon helping smaller firms as his only task, and he clearly did not see such assistance as a way to thwart the largest firms, as had Straus and Nagel.

The alliance Redfield worked out between large and small producers helped him bring about major changes in antitrust, merchant marine, and foreign banking policy. Redfield gained the support of almost all those businessmen interested in promoting foreign trade. With the coming of war in Europe Redfield and his business allies were able to get changes in federal policy through Congress. America's entry into the war, however, shattered his control of the forces working to expand foreign trade. Following the war, Redfield was unable to pull together again the alliance among the Commerce Department and large and small manufacturers. Other agencies of government became more involved in trade expansion. Moreover, the largest business firms began to see the expansion of commerce in a new light after the war, and they had less need to cooperate with the Department of Commerce.

Seven

World War and Foreign Trade

The Department of Commerce and Labor's small-business orientation changed, as we have seen, when Woodrow Wilson took office. Secretary Redfield had close ties to the medium-sized and larger, more advantaged producers selling in foreign markets. As we saw in the last chapter, Redfield was far from unsympathetic to the smaller producers selling abroad, but he wanted his department to lead in forming an alliance among those in business and government interested in foreign trade rather than to support exclusively the smaller manufacturers against the larger, as had Straus and Nagel.

Redfield recognized an important distinction within the business community interested in enlarging foreign trade. Many of the larger and medium-sized producers were selling abroad because of economic advantage. They saw threats to their exports from foreign competitors but more importantly from inconsistent and at times hostile policies of their own government. At the same time, smaller producers who wanted to develop trade had interests in common with the larger ones who sought to protect what they had already gained. Redfield tried to get these two groups to work together.

Redfield's perception of what needed to be done was formed in part as a result of his own study of the situation, but also because of his experience in the American Manufacturers' Export Association. As we saw in chapter 3, the AMEA was made up of manufacturers who generally sold abroad because of genuine economic advantages. While the AMEA tended to disdain the amateurish promotional efforts of groups like the NAM, Redfield recognized that the two groups had common interests. Like the novices, the AMEA believed that several governmental policies had to be changed. It advocated continued improvements in the consular service, government assistance to the American merchant marine, and greater flexibility in tariff policy. But the AMEA was a step beyond business groups which sought to introduce their members to foreign sales for the first time. Redfield's business colleagues took a larger view and saw that a fundamental difficulty in the expansion of foreign trade was the government's lack of consistency and coordination in policy. The AMEA favored, according to a resolution at its seventh annual meeting, "a definite and vigorous commercial policy of a permanent nature, one that will be carried out regardless of changes occurring in the administration of our domestic affairs."[1]

131

After his term as president of the AMEA, Redfield took over a bureaucracy newly streamlined, as the Department of Commerce and Labor became two separate-departments in 1913. He was determined to make the department the leader in coordinating the government's efforts at trade promotion. Of more significance was the new secretary's view of the major firms as potential allies of his department and of those smaller manufacturers inexperienced in selling overseas. Redfield believed that the only way to get Congress to change policies harmful to those engaged in foreign trade was through the cooperation of large and small manufacturers in lobbying.

To make the Commerce Department the governmental and business leader in trade expansion, Redfield moved on several fronts. One major effort was to coordinate the federal bureaucracy's efforts at trade promotion. Promotional activities had been spread over a number of governmental agencies and departments. Since the Department of Agriculture employed agents to travel overseas gathering information about prospective sales, Redfield proposed that the Department of Commerce and Agriculture exchange the information that each acquired that might be useful to the other. Similarly, the Commerce Department worked with the Interior Department in order to help the lumber industry develop foreign sales.[2] To limit duplication in the collection of data, Redfield established interdepartmental committees to insure that each department knew what the others were doing. The Department of Commerce's Bureau of the Census, for example, collected almost identical data for its Census of Manufacturers to that collected by the Department of Agriculture's Bureau of Statistics.[3]

Commerce's major rival in promoting trade was the Department of State, and Redfield early in his tenure at the Commerce Department tried to improve relations between the two. Secretary of State William Jennings Bryan approved of Redfield's efforts and encouraged his subordinates to cooperate with the Department of Commerce. Bryan, unfamiliar with or indifferent to the previous rivalry between the two departments, ordered his employees not to infringe on work properly belonging to the Commerce Department. The secretary of state promised to provide the Commerce Department with information on economic conditions and changes in foreign legislation. Bryan also had consuls forward letters to the Department of Commerce from businessmen who had made inquiries about trade matters. The two departments also scheduled joint meetings with the Foreign Trade Advisers and the director of the BFDC to discuss common problems.[4]

These efforts eventually proved fruitless. In the early years of the Wilson presidency, to be sure, relations between the two departments seemed to improve, but they worsened again later in Wilson's administration. Misunderstandings, suspicion, and duplication of effort were problems that Redfield continually had to concern himself with. By the time he resigned in November 1919, the two departments were bitterly accusing each other of trying to take over the

132

other's responsibilities. Redfield's successor, J. W. Alexander, made it his policy bluntly to inform the Department of State of "instances of direct infringement on the part of the Foreign Trade Adviser's Office" on his department's duties.[5]

Redfield's strategy of coordination was more successful with the other bureaucracies engaged in promoting foreign trade. The secretary tried to involve other agencies like the Department of Agriculture in cooperative efforts without seeming to threaten to remove functions from them. Ultimately, however, this was impossible with the State Department because the mission to promote and protect foreign trade was essential to that department's growth and success. It resisted the Commerce Department once Redfield clearly threatened the Department of State's role in trade promotion.[6]

The bureaucratic rivalry with the State Department consumed the energy and time of many of Redfield's departmental associates. But Redfield's primary efforts were directed at building an alliance between the Commerce Department and major business groups interested in trade expansion, and at getting these groups to work together.

In establishing ties with the business community, Redfield decided to work through one group instead of acting as the mediator among a number of business associations. The key coordinating business association was to be the National Foreign Trade Council. Like the National Council of Commerce, Straus's earlier effort to create a key association, the NFTC was to speak for manufacturers interested in foreign trade, although it was not to be a body made up of representatives of all the different conflicting business interests. The secretary's objectives were twofold. On the one hand, he hoped to use the support and influence of leading businssmen and bankers to impress leaders in Congress and the president with the broad support he had from the business community. On the other hand, he hoped to have the NFTC convince other businessmen, labor leaders, and the public generally of the benefits of foreign trade expansion.[7]

These were not to be easy tasks. Many small businessmen were hostile to the role of the "trusts" in foreign trade, believing that it was monopolistic control that gave the large firms advantages. The Justice Department reflected some of these views. It investigated and prosecuted some large businesses in these years. For their part, the leaders of big business distrusted government, especially the Department of Justice and the Supreme Court. Big business was still a popular target of hostility, and it had been so in the 1912 presidential campaign. The Supreme Court in major cases had broken up Standard Oil in 1911, and lower courts had ruled against some American firms' sales agreements with foreign cartels.[8]

Despite these hostilities, there was sentiment for more cooperation among businessmen themselves and between them and government. In 1910, the leaders of the NAM appointed a special committee to explore the possibilities of improving relations with like-minded trade organizations and with the secretary of Commerce and Labor. Discussions with representatives of other associations were held at monthly meetings in New York at NAM headquarters. The NAM modelled its ideas of cooperation on German trade associations that brought businessmen and government officials together to expand trade. Little came of the NAM efforts, but the need for greater cooperation among business associations continued to be discussed widely. Businessmen who had been active in the National Council of Commerce proposed that the National Chamber of Commerce, founded in 1912, work hand-in-hand with the Department of Commerce, which would then "lead business into foreign markets." Although the Chamber of Commerce's leadership rejected formal ties, business sentiment had evolved to the point where closer informal ties among a larger range of businessmen became possible.[9]

Redfield knew of the increased sense of need for cooperation, but he was determined not to dilute his efforts by trying to work directly with all of the groups interested in promoting foreign trade. He thought it best to deal with one small group. To avoid offending the leaders of established organizations, he helped to form a new association: the National Foreign Trade Council. It became the essential business group in Redfield's strategy to bring about closer business-government relations and greater cooperation among businessmen. To found the new association, Redfield approached three groups interested in foreign trade issues, the Pan American Society of the United States, the American Manufacturers' Export Association and the American Asiatic Association, to convene the National Foreign Trade Convention in Washington. Meeting in May 1914, the convention sought to draw attention to the national importance of foreign trade, the broad business interest in its promotion, and the need for a new business group devoted to the issues of trade expansion.[10]

Indeed, the convention was more than a forum for a reassertion of already well-known support for trade expansion. Out of its deliberations emerged the permanent Foreign Trade Council with James A. Farrell, the president of U.S. Steel, as its leader. The council was limited to thirty-five members, many of whom were leaders of some of America's largest banks and corporations. Besides Farrell, other prominent members were A. C. Bedford, president of Standard Oil of New Jersey; Alba B. Johnson, president of Baldwin Locomotive Works; Fred I. Kent, vice-president of the Bankers Trust Company; and Cyrus H. McCormick, president of International Harvester. Some of the major corporations represented were General Electric, Westinghouse, Ingersoll-Rand, Willys-Overland, United States Rubber, Lackawanna Steel, American Shipbuilding, Seattle Car and Foundry, and Anaconda Copper Mining; among the banks were National City Bank of New York, First National Bank of Chicago, Security Trust and Savings Bank of Los Angeles, Bankers Trust Company of New York, and the Irving National Bank of New York.[11]

Secretary Redfield insured public attention to the meetings. Both he and Secretary of State Bryan addressed the convention and President Wilson personally greeted the delegates at a White House reception. Bryan spoke generally, assuring the delegates that the government could be counted on to protect the legitimate interests of Americans engaged in business abroad. Redfield spoke more directly to the concerns of the assembled delegates. He assured them that his department would work "to remove any barriers that may stand in the way of our foreign trade, whether they be at home or abroad." Redfield's reference to the domestic scene appealed to the larger producers who believed that the executive and Congress, as much as foreign competitors, worked against their interests.[12]

The giant firms represented on the council did not need government to help them learn of market opportunities or to provide them with general commercial data. Most had their own foreign departments to gather such information. Broadly speaking, they sought to cooperate with government to make more secure the markets they already had. They wanted not so much assistance to promote trade as consistency in policy. They were primarily concerned that major issues affecting their vital interests not be the product, as they saw it, of partisan politics.[13]

Government policy toward foreign trade had developed haphazardly, with no apparent plan, and at times contradictorily. The lack of coordination among departments and between Congress and the executive departments, and the lack of cooperation between government and business, worried the larger producers as they began to confront problems that they could not entirely solve alone. Smaller and intermediate-sized producers of goods for export were from the 1890s on keenly aware of the need for government assistance, and so they were prominent in the earlier efforts to bring about consular reform and changes in the tariff.[14]

The largest corporations, which had been content to go it alone before about 1910, turned to government because of concern over specific issues. Alone, the largest producers would have been unable to convince Congress of the need for changes in the policies toward foreign branch banking, the merchant marine, and the antitrust laws as they affected export combinations. They needed to unite with other businessmen concerned for their own reasons about these issues. Then, too, big businessmen selling overseas thought it advantageous to educate both the public and Congress to the importance of foreign trade, and they welcomed the opportunity to tie their interests in overseas markets to the broader goals propounded by the Department of Commerce.

The leaders of the NFTC gladly acknowledged the importance of Secretary Redfield's efforts in forming the council, referring to him as the father of their efforts. But the group was not by any means simply to be a creature of the Department of Commerce. The NFTC struck out on its own in a campaign to educate public and congressional opinion about the national economic importance of foreign trade. The council began a campaign to create friendly relations with the Chamber of Commerce and other business associations. At the same time, the once aloof heads of major corporations and leading banks cultivated the congressional leadership. They were trying to reduce hostility and resistance to the changes in policy that they saw in their interests.[15]

The success of the NFTC and through it of Redfield's efforts depended fundamentally on whether smaller and larger producers could work together where they had common interests. Both the larger and the smaller producers interested themselves in the Latin American market. As a result, both were in need of American branch banking facilities and services. Likewise, an improved American merchant marine was needed for sales there. The larger producers were concerned also about the dependence of American producers on foreign ships for shipments to Europe. Both the larger and the smaller had an interest in seeing the antitrust laws relaxed in regard to combinations selling overseas. The smaller producers needed these combinations to reduce the costs of selling and shipping, to break into Latin American markets especially. The larger producers needed to be able to form combinations in order to confront the competition of foreign cartels more effectively.

Redfield saw clearly that these mutual interests could provide the common ground of cooperation between what heretofore had been a diverse group of business interests at times hostile to each other. The secretary approached his role as leader and coordinator with great anticipation. The United States, he thought, had achieved much without business and government cooperation, and he optimistically felt that much more could be done with manufacturers and the Department of Commerce working together.[16]

Redfield began his work of bringing businessmen together at a propitious time. The Wilson administration at an early stage had addressed itself to the need for foreign branch banks in the Federal Reserve legislation passed in 1913. Indeed, initial nervousness among businessmen about Wilson was calmed by the administration's support for the foreign banking provisions of the Federal Reserve Act. By 1913, there was a fairly widespread belief among businessmen selling overseas that the United States was at a disadvantage in international trade because it did not have branch banks overseas. Moreover, the United States did not have the ability to discount bills drawn on foreign trade, relying instead on British financial markets. Although Congress passed the Federal Reserve legislation in December 1913, the system was not set up until November 1914. American foreign traders' concerns about the form the system took provided an instructive lesson to both large and small producers about their common interests. The NFTC took great pains to point up advantages to all producers in the years that followed passage of the Federal Reserve legislation, as changes and alterations clearly became necessary in the initial system.

The 1913 Federal Reserve Act authorized American banks to establish facilities abroad, independent of the Europeans. Bankers were empowered to establish foreign branch facilities in three different ways. Large national banks with a capital or surplus of more than $1,000,000 could establish branches in foreign countries or American dependencies. The national banks were also allowed to form banking corporations which could then establish branches abroad, so long as these operations did not provide banking services in the domestic market. Finally, national banks could create subsidiary banks which could then establish operations abroad.

The bill also created a discount market in the United States. In section 13, the legislation authorized American national banks to accept drafts drawn against foreign trade, and Federal Reserve Banks were permitted to buy and sell bankers' acceptances and bills of exchange. National banks could rediscount short-term foreign bank acceptances, allowing American exporters to finance their trade with American banks without having bank acceptances rediscounted in London.[17]

While these changes in banking law were generally acceptable to bankers and manufacturers, the act still needed to be implemented when the NFTC was organized in May 1914. And, as time went on, the NFTC and smaller producers concluded that additional legislation was needed to increase the numbers of branches and improve the workings of the discount market set up in 1914. Smaller manufacturers supported additions to the original Federal Reserve legislation, which would have loosened the restrictions limiting participation in foreign banking. In part, these changes were prompted by the fact that the larger banks like the National City Bank of New York and the First National Bank of Boston dominated American branch banking abroad. In an amendment to the section authorizing branch banking in the original Federal Reserve Act, Congress permitted national banks to invest in banks or corporations chartered to engage in foreign banking. The president signed the legislation in September 1916. These banks and corporations became known as "agreement corporations" because the legislation made no provision for federal chartering. Agreement corporations were chartered by the states, but before the Federal Reserve allowed national banks to participate in these corporations, the Federal Reserve required the new corporations to come to agreements about the ways in which they would operate. Capital and surplus requirements were still so high that most smaller banks continued to be unable to participate. As a result, in September 1919 Congress significantly reduced the requirements of capital and surplus necessary before investing in a bank or corporation chartered to do business abroad. Any bank could become involved, so long as it did not invest more than 5 percent of its capital and surplus in the venture.[18]

Banking nevertheless remained an issue that concerned NFTC members and smaller producers too. The changes brought about in 1913 and 1916, while welcome, did not satisfy manufacturers. Until 1919 the smaller manufacturers felt that the legislation benefited the larger banks and manufacturing corporations. For their part, the largest banks and corporations still found American financing of foreign trade inadequate. To improve the availability of short-term financing of foreign trade, Congress passed the Edge Act in December 1919.

137

The Edge legislation was primarily part of the U.S. effort to help Europe reconstruct after the war. It was designed to provide long-term postwar financing of major projects, since capital requirements abroad were vast and the periods of time for repayment long. The bill nevertheless allowed for corporative financing of American foreign trade. And as opposed to the agreement corporations, Edge corporations were to be federally chartered. Congressional supporters believed that such federal charters suggested the urgency the government put on financing trade, especially of agricultural goods. Unlike the banks authorized in the 1916 amendment to the original Federal Reserve legislation, the Edge corporations were to carry on both short- and long-term financing. In fact, the Federal Reserve limited Edge corporations to only one or the other, primarily that of long-term financing.[19]

As interested as small and large producers were in the fate of banking policy, market-seeking manufacturers were far from the key elements in the changes that occurred. The need for additions to banking legislation clearly showed, however, an area in which both small and larger producers had complementary interests.[20]

It was the European war, however, that provided Redfield the opportunity to take the initiative in changing two other sets of policy of major concern to businessmen engaged in foreign trade. Apprehension that the Allies would adopt exclusionary trade policies toward the United States created the political atmosphere to continue to overcome hostilities between large and small businessmen and to convince the president and Congress of the need for changes in the antitrust laws and merchant marine policies. The alliance that Redfield put together was not long-lived, nor was it very strong. But in the context of the war, Redfield was able to get his large and small business supporters to cooperate.

Indeed restrictions in antitrust legislation were the most compelling reason for the leaders of the largest corporations to cooperate with the Department of Commerce. As troublesome as were foreign tax laws, tariff rates, patent restrictions, and trademark infringements, the rise of European cartels provided sharp competition to major producers. Similarly, the smaller manufacturers were stymied when competing with foreign cartels, which often joined producers, bankers, and shippers to promote exports.

Apprehension about foreign cartels convinced both small and large producers of the need for an exemption from the Clayton Antitrust Act, as it was applied to foreign trade. The Clayton Act, passed in 1914, made no allowance for combinations among those exporting. This injured the smaller producers who in certain lines of products could only meet foreign competition by joining together to lower shipping and selling costs. Larger producers were at a similar disadvantage, although what disturbed them most was a prohibition against lowering foreign prices without a similar reduction in the domestic market. Not only could they not lower prices abroad to meet foreign competition, but they also could not lower prices in return for exclusive selling contracts with foreign merchants.[21]

In response to complaints from both large and small manufacturers, Congress instructed the newly created Federal Trade Commission (FTC) to conduct a thorough study of the problem of combination in export trade. The FTC study was wide-ranging. The commission solicited information from 10,000 manufacturers interested in foreign trade, as well as about 5,000 merchants, and several hundred officials of business associations. The FTC concluded that "in seeking business abroad, American manufacturers and producers must meet aggressive competition from powerful foreign combinations, often international in character. In Germany, England, France, Italy, Austria-Hungary, Switzerland, Holland, Sweden, Belgium, Japan, and other countries business men are much freer to cooperate and combine than in the United States. They have developed numerous comprehensive combinations, often aided by their governments, which effectually unite their activities both in domestic and foreign trade." The report focused on Germany and its system of cartels as the primary example of government-business cooperation detrimental to American interests. Six hundred cartels covered almost every major industry in the German empire, and many of them carried on vigorous campaigns to expand their export trade.[22]

In fact, German firms in two industries crucial to important members of the NFTC were among the most effective of the German combinations. German electrical manufacturers' exports accounted for a significant percentage of the country's exports of manufactures. The two great firms of the industry, as well as subsidiaries in the domestic and foreign markets, worked harmoniously to expand their foreign trade. The Allgemeine Electricitäts Gesellschaft and Siemens-Schuckert were significant competitors of the American giants, General Electric and Westinghouse. Iron and steel industry exports were handled through one selling agency of the Stahlwerks Verband. The union of iron and steel makers had stimulated foreign sales, too, by bounties and special prices. Syndicates of steel, coal, and glass producers were important in France and Belgium. At times, some of these sales efforts were multinational, as when silk-ribbon producers in France and Germany agreed to market their products jointly. Highly centralized organizations conducted business in a number of other countries: Italy, Russia, Austria-Hungary, Switzerland, and Sweden. Many of these associations competed with American efforts in foreign trade. Coordinated activities abroad existed, in addition to the industries already mentioned, in agricultural machinery, oil, sulphur, superphosphates, cement, matches, chocolate, embroidery, silk goods, watches, cotton goods, condensed milk, canned fish, currants, iodine, cocoa, and dyes.[23]

In Asia's great industrial power, Japan, there was also extensive cooperation. A few major trading firms combined manufacturing, mining, shipping, and sales. Producers of textiles worked through an effective export organization to market goods in North China. In all of these efforts, Japanese businessmen received the encouragement and assistance of their government, especially in Far Eastern markets.[24]

Britain allowed combinations, too. Coal was exported through the cooperation of mine operators, shipping lines, and domestic and foreign distributors. Likewise, British producers of cement cooperated with each other. Most ominous to U.S. machinery manufacturers was the formation of the Representation for British Manufacturers, Ltd. This group represented some of the largest British manufacturers of machinery, and its goal was to solidify sales in traditional markets and to increase and extend sales elsewhere. American machinery producers had made real progress in selling overseas and looked with concern at Britain's attempts to stop the American advance. The FTC was equally alarmed, since it anticipated the formation of similar groups in order to extend the foreign trade of British producers of electrical equipment, cotton textiles, tobacco, pottery, steel, and wallpaper.[25]

While smaller manufacturers were most vulnerable to the competition of these large foreign combinations, a point emphasized by the commission's report (p. 4), larger producers' interests were threatened, too. The NFTC believed that the antitrust laws needed to be relaxed in order to place American exporters on "an equal footing with combinations of foreign rivals organized to resist American competition and combinations of foreign buyers equipped to depress the price of American products." Leaders of the AMEA expressed similar views in the final resolutions of the Eighth Annual Convention in 1917 where they registered their support for allowing cooperation in export trade. "The Association... directs the attention of the government, Congress, the public generally and labor especially, to the self-evident fact that American manufacturers cannot compete with foreign manufactures produced, vended, and delivered under state aid."[26]

Redfield, drawing on his own experience as a producer of printing presses, anticipated serious damage to the interests of medium-sized manufacturers if the antitrust laws were not changed. Foreign combinations were most harmful to the efforts of "a large number of concerns of moderate size making specialties of many kinds which found no opportunity to enter foreign markets" because of foreign combinations. Such American firms were at times the largest producers "in their own particular lines but these lines were sometimes not of such widespread use as to warrant the expenditure of money and effort to secure foreign trade." These moderate-sized firms were not able to compete with German producers because of that government's policy of assistance to cartels. "Only the very largest, the so-called trusts," Redfield went on, "were able to enter the field in competition, and by no means all of these were able to do so."[27]

The largest manufacturers had wanted changes in the antitrust laws before passage of the Clayton Act. That legislation only made private efforts to counter foreign cartels more uncertain. As in most cases when the largest corporations faced a problem abroad, leading firms among the manufacturers of steel, agricultural machinery, and electrical equipment first had sought private solutions to their foreign problems. Indeed NFTC President James A. Farrell had attempted to form a joint selling venture abroad among major American steel producers. The proposed export group would have had common sales agents, as well as common price-setting agreements. Nothing came of these efforts because of apprehension of prosecution under the antitrust laws. Similar fears aborted efforts to make agreements with foreign organizations of steelmen. The ostensibly social visit of the British Steel Association in 1913 in fact included general discussions of common policies on prices and the divisions of markets. Nothing came of these discussions for fear of violating the antitrust laws. Some manufacturers, to be sure, were prosecuted for cooperating with foreign industrialists. In the production of the primary product, aluminum, the courts ruled against foreign agreements. G.E. nervously made overtures and agreements with foreign concerns, never knowing whether they were to bring prosecution. Interest in cooperating with or even joining foreign combinations was an alternative discussed by members of NFTC. At the very least, however, most wanted freedom to do what they thought was necessary to meet the competition of foreign and domestic firms selling abroad. At the second national convention of the NFTC, the leadership devoted an entire session to the need for legislation which permitted combination in export trade. The consensus was that such combinations were probably legal if they were not in restraint of domestic trade, but there was uncertainty about how the Justice Department would interpret the antitrust laws. As one speaker concluded, "it seems to be a moot question and probably had best be clarified by legislative action."[28]

Discussions about altering the antitrust laws encountered public and congressional hostility and suspicion before Congress passed the Clayton Act. But the failure of the legislation to exempt export combinations aroused the opposition of smaller producers whose assistance was clearly necessary in order for Congress to make major changes in antitrust legislation.[29]

Redfield became the leader of efforts to change the antitrust laws. For the secretary of commerce, President Wilson was the major problem. He was not sympathetic to the statist arrangements that allowed cartels to flourish in Germany. At first he resisted what he thought were efforts to alter the antitrust laws. Wilson steadfastly supported the Clayton Antitrust Act, even though it encountered stiff opposition from the export-oriented part of the business community. Wilson and other supporters of the Clayton legislation wanted to strengthen the antitrust laws by making more explicit what were to be considered monopolistic business practices. Opponents maintained, however, that the bill failed to recognize that conditions differed in the domestic and foreign markets. These arguments failed to persuade Wilson, at least at first.[30]

Redfield was not deterred. Ultimately, he was able to use the FTC, which Wilson had supported, to loosen some of the restraints on combinations in foreign trade. Redfield first tried to convince Wilson to allow export combinations under the supervision of the new FTC. The secretary made two arguments to the president. First, appealing to Wilson's concern about smaller businesses' decreasing opportunities in the economy, Redfield maintained that to prohibit export combinations played into the hands of the largest corporations which had advantages in selling abroad. Second, he maintained that the integration brought about by combinations, whether of large or small interests, promoted efficiency in foreign trade and would help mark out a larger foreign field for American business. In 1914 Wilson was not fully convinced by Redfield's arguments, although he supported an amendment to the FTC legislation which gave the new commission the power to study the impact of foreign combinations on American business. The men appointed to head the FTC did not need to be convinced of the importance of foreign trade, and they looked upon the authorization to investigate the impact of foreign combinations as a great opportunity to assist market-seeking manufacturers. They held hearings in a number of cities and circulated questionnaires to ascertain business opinion on the question. The need to change the antitrust laws had widespread support in the business community, reflected in the report published in 1916.[31]

In the face of such obvious business support for relaxations in the antitrust laws, Wilson by 1916 had changed his mind about export combinations. And he supported the legislation submitted by North Carolina Congressman E. Y. Webb which accepted the recommendations of the FTC report. Although first introduced in 1916, the Webb bill was not finally passed until 1918. Some smaller businessmen remained skeptical of big businesses' enthusiastic support for the proposed legislation. They did not believe the altruistic motives of larger producers supporting smaller manufacturers in the latter's efforts to gain foreign markets. Larger producers, some of the opponents argued, had more to gain by the legislation than smaller businessmen did. In fact by strengthening the already powerful big businesses engaged abroad, critics maintained, the Webb legislation would make competition even more difficult for their smaller competitors. Nevertheless, the House of Representatives passed the legislation overwhelmingly in 1916. Support was also strong in the Senate, but the Webb-Pomerene Bill met the determined opposition of a small number of senators who were able to delay passage for two years. This small group, largely of Midwest Republicans, continued to see the legislation as the first assault in a campaign of big business to do away with the antitrust laws. The senators thought that smaller producers would lose, not gain, overseas sales and that at home they would be further hurt by large corporations grown more powerful with assured sales abroad. Some critics, carried away by the fervor of the war in Europe, went so far as to accuse the legislation's proponents of wanting to adopt policies followed in Germany, activities that some Americans believed had contributed to the war itself.[32]

Supporters of the Webb Act countered that the FTC, which would supervise the combinations, would assure that the antitrust laws were not violated. Redfield marshalled his alliance of smaller and larger producers to put pressure on Congress. These manufacturers argued that the war made the legislation more necessary than ever before. American manufacturers sold more and more in Latin America in markets lost by the warring European countries. The Webb legislation would help meet the inevitable and vigorous postwar European competition to regain lost markets. President Wilson echoed most of the arguments of the bill's supporters. Finally, the overwhelming support from small, as well as large producers, overcame objections in the Senate and the legislation was passed, coming to Wilson for his signature in April 1918.[33]

The Webb-Pomerene Act primarily exempted export trade associations from those provisions of the Sherman Anti-Trust Act that forbid combinations in restraint of trade; it also relaxed the Clayton Act's strictures on acquiring part or all of the stock of another corporation. Relaxed antitrust restrictions were only for those combinations engaged in the export trade and for so long as the combinations did not adversely affect domestic trade. Associations had to register with the FTC, which gained authority to prosecute unfair competitive practices abroad by American firms.[34]

Redfield and the NFTC felt a sense of accomplishment in having worked together with smaller businessmen to pass the Webb legislation. The Webb Act, as it turned out, proved less significant than almost all of its advocates thought it would be. The war dramatically changed conditions abroad, making postwar foreign competition much less severe than American producers had feared. Instead of regaining markets lost in Latin America and Asia, the Europeans were consumed in the early postwar years by the problems of reconstruction.

Despite success in passing the Webb legislation, and despite the Department of Commerce's efforts to focus attention on Latin American opportunities opened up because of the war, Redfield's centralization of market-expansion efforts in his own hands was far from complete, and the alliance that he had forged between business and the executive branch was fragile. An issue of central importance to the NFTC was the merchant marine, and it was from this issue that eventually the limits of the new alliance became quite clear.

The quality of the American merchant marine was at first, however, the one issue that most easily drew together those engaged in foreign trade. Producers of all sizes depended on shippers to get their products delivered abroad. Some firms like U.S. Steel and Swift and Company, to be sure, purchased their own fleets of ships. But these vessels only carried a part of the total company sales abroad. James A. Farrell, president of U.S. Steel and of the NFTC, noted that one of the primary purposes of his council was "to arouse public interest in the creation of a mercantile marine which in our foreign trade was chiefly conspicuous by its absence."[35]

American manufacturers became increasingly concerned about the merchant marine as European naval races increased and the diplomatic crises over Morocco and the Balkans periodically threatened war. In the years before 1914 there was great apprehension that American trade would be hampered by a major European conflict. But whether there was war or not, American producers believed that foreign shipowners gave preference to foreign merchants and manufacturers, or that a combination of foreign shippers could increase rates to hurt American trade.[36]

The shipping problems that concerned prominent businessmen in 1914 were by no means new. Whereas in 1860 over 70 percent of all goods carried from overseas arrived in American ships, by 1900 American merchantmen carried less than 10 percent. To be sure, percentages do not tell the whole story, because there was a marked increase in American trade in these years. Nevertheless, many engaged in the export trade were concerned that American ships played a lesser and lesser role in shipping goods to America's overseas markets.

The Civil War played havoc with the American merchant fleet, for ships were either destroyed or, to protect themselves, they changed registry to foreign flags. After the war, the Congress retaliated against those who had registered their ships abroad and forbade them to reregister. This was not a hardship to all, since many probably would not have reregistered their ships had they been given the opportunity. Underlying Civil War changes was the fact that American shipbuilding and maintenance costs, compared with those of European rivals, had begun to increase. America's wooden ships might cost less to build than the iron vessels of Britain and Germany, but the value of the American ships decreased rapidly, and repair costs were almost double those for iron ships. Some foreign critics also charged that American shipbuilding companies expected profits well in excess of what was expected abroad. High profits, however, were necessary in order to attract capital in a burgeoning economy that provided many attractive alternatives for investment.

U.S. shipbuilders, on the one hand, and shipowners and operators, on the other, came into sharper and sharper conflict as the century drew to a close. The differing views on policy created a stalemate in congressional policy making that further contributed to the decline of the American merchant marine. Builders supported a bounty to American vessels. The shipbuilding industry's attempts to obtain subsidies as a way to help the American merchant marine were unsuccessful, because congressional opponents did not want what they thought was an already overly protected industry to get further advantages. Congress instead imposed tariff barriers on materials necessary for shipbuilding, such as cable, anchors, copper, zinc, rope, canvas, and the like. It also excluded foreign-made ships from American registration. Shipowners and operators unsuccessfully opposed protectionist rates on shipbuilding materials and on prohibitions against foreign-made ships. American shipping companies, as a result, had to pay more for ships, becoming less competitive against foreign operators, and American manufacturers turned to foreign ships.[37]

The debate remained stalemated until World War I. The European War, however, helped refocus the attention of government and the manufacturers on the merchant marine, as the conflict disrupted shipping and producers perceived new trade opportunities, especially in Latin America. The Wilson administration's handling of the merchant marine question was not to the liking of many manufacturers and ship operators, some of whom were prominent and influential members of the NFTC. The disapproval of the administration's policy exposed the fragility of the alliance that Redfield worked out with big business. Although government policy proved to be less detrimental than many businessmen first thought it would be, there remained a deep skepticism about the government's ability to solve important problems.[38]

As in the campaign to alter the antitrust laws, Redfield tried to lead the effort to change merchant marine policy. He failed to become the coordinator of efforts to change shipping policy because of William Gibbs McAdoo, secretary of the treasury. McAdoo was closer to Wilson personally than Redfield; the treasury secretary married the president's youngest daughter in May 1914. Redfield opposed McAdoo's early suggestions about shipping policy, an opposition that gained for the commerce secretary the enmity of the influential secretary of the treasury. Redfield's doubts about McAdoo's policy reflected the views of many in the foreign trade community, presaging some of the problems that the administration was going to have with business and the Congress over its approach to the merchant marine.[39]

McAdoo took the lead in trying to change merchant marine policy once war broke out in Europe in 1914. The secretary, a southerner in an administration concerned with the interests of southern agriculture and beholden to southern politicians, quickly understood the serious problems cotton farmers had because of the shipping crisis in the fall of 1914. McAdoo tried to make his policies palatable to other interests such as market-seeking manufacturers and shipowners. But his suggestions for improving the American merchant marine only raised fears among manufacturers and shippers of an excessive involvement of government in the private sector.[40]

Officially, McAdoo became involved in shipping policy because the Bureau of War Risk Insurance was established in his department. Once he became aware of the importance of shipping, McAdoo deliberately undercut Redfield's effort to take the lead in shipping policy. Although merchant marine issues logically fell to the Department of Commerce, McAdoo lacked confidence in Redfield's ability. He thought the commerce secretary "a slow-witted person with very little initiative or energy." This was patently unfair to Redfield, whose hesitation about shipping policy was a reflection of an awareness of the complexities of the problem, as well as of the political dangers involved. Redfield, involved with shipping issues for twenty years, urged restraint to McAdoo whose interest in the merchant marine issue had only developed in 1914.[41]

The president moved as quickly as possible to deal with the shipping crisis created by the European war. When war broke out, it brought about the chaotic shipping conditions that so many in the export trade had feared. The initial impact of foreign conflict was to bring the American export trade to a virtual halt, since in 1914 over half of American exports and imports were shipped in

British carriers. The Department of Commerce and the Department of the Treasury cooperated in getting legislation passed to ease the crisis in shipping, as Congress quickly approved a Ship Registry Bill. The new law allowed the registration of foreign ships more than five years old, revoking thereby a law that had made foreign registration difficult in the United States. The act also empowered the president to suspend regulations about the size of crews and the inspection of vessels. The results were swift, and by the end of 1914 over 100 ships had changed registry.[42]

As the Wilson administration took other measures to ease the shipping problem, McAdoo emerged as the chief spokesman on the merchant marine. The need for war-risk insurance gave the Department of the Treasury the major role in shipping policy. Foreign companies had written over two-thirds of the war-risk insurance for American ships. The British predominated in this business, but British law prevented coverage of the losses occurring if ships were captured by the British Navy. Since the British soon controlled the North Atlantic, this was a serious risk to shippers. United States companies found themselves beseiged to write policies, and rates rose accordingly. As a result, the Wilson administration proposed that the government issue coverage at rates comparable to what shippers might have gotten abroad. Secretary Redfield was far from unaware of the problems, but it was Secretary of the Treasury McAdoo who seized the initiative, calling meetings in his department among government officials, financiers, and interested businessmen from the shipping industry.[43]

A bill creating the Bureau of War Risk Insurance moved easily through Congress, and the president signed it in early September. The rates that the government set for its insurance remained steady at about 5 percent of the value of the cargo, whereas in the dangerous North Sea, private companies were charging almost 30 percent; for shipments to Germany it was impossible to get insurance. The bureau was busiest in the early months of the war, after which private commercial underwriters were able to organize themselves to provide coverage.[44]

McAdoo's involvement in the drafting, passage, and implementation of the Ship Registry legislation, and the creation of the Bureau of War Risk Insurance turned his attention to longer-term changes to deal with the problems of America's foreign trade. McAdoo had no illusions about the ships newly registered in the American trade. Once the war ended and comparative costs again proved unfavorable to the United States, he was sure that those ships would reregister abroad. As a result, he turned his attention to what became one of the Wilson administration's most ambitious schemes to rejuvenate the American merchant marine. The secretary proposed that Congress establish a shipping corporation with the government as the primary or, if necessary, the only stockholder. The corporation was to buy or lease a large fleet of ships to supplement shipping to Europe and to create routes to Central and South America.[45]

Shipowners were the most vocal opponents of McAdoo's proposal. They were making handsome profits, and they resisted as strongly as they could. Once the initial crisis passed, the war revived American trade and the merchant marine. The severe shortage of tonnage and the increased demand for available shipping caused a marked rise in the earnings of merchant vessels. Shipping rates rose dramatically. By the fall of 1915 some cargoes to European ports were paying rates 1600 percent higher than before the war! The Chamber of Commerce conducted a poll in the spring of 1915 that indicated strong opposition to the plan in Atlantic and Pacific seaboard areas. In the south and west, where agricultural exports were important, there was less hostility, although some found it hard to accept the idea of the government leasing ships from private owners. Such leases appeared as special treatment for shipowners, a group that many small businessmen and farmers had believed were too privileged anyway.[46]

As time passed, the bill picked up more opposition because American shipyards literally sprang into action at the prospect of the large profits to be made by building ships for an American merchant marine operating virtually without competition. As the legislation dragged through Congress, the press turned more and more against it. Eastern, especially New York, newspapers were savage in their criticism. The New York *Times* referred to the scheme as "preposterous," while the New York *Journal of Commerce* simply called it "crazy."[47]

McAdoo nevertheless pressed ahead. He opposed the subsidies that the shipowners suggested were necessary on a long-term basis to offset the higher costs of running American ships. The secretary was in step with the Democratic party platform that had rejected subsidies in 1912. Equally unacceptable as a device to help ship operators were proposals to repeal or weaken legislation that protected American seamen. The requirements for size of crews and working conditions, shipowners maintained, raised their costs. Stalemate developed each of the times Congress considered McAdoo's Ship Purchase Bill. The bill did not receive much of a hearing the first time. Congressional Democrats, especially in the Senate, were themselves apprehensive about the diplomatic and military implications of the bill. They feared the consequences if a government-owned ship were attacked or captured. Wilson nevertheless had a practically identical bill reintroduced when the Congress reconvened in December 1914. This fared no better in the Senate, as skeptical Democrats were joined by Republicans opposed to such a "socialistic" measure. Although the legislation passed the House, the administration could not keep Democratic senators in line, and Congress adjourned without Wilson's shipping bill.[48]

Redfield was drawn into the fight for McAdoo's plan. He overcame some of his earlier reluctance to support the legislation, especially in view of Wilson's and McAdoo's concern about party loyalty after the defection of senatorial Democrats. McAdoo involved Redfield in the process by utilizing Department of

147

Commerce data in the legislative battles. And Redfield had something to gain, since the secretary of commerce would serve on the board of the government's shipping corporation should it be approved. But businessmen in associations like the NFTC remained opposed to McAdoo's plans for ideological reasons, as well as for reasons of self-interest. Even though the NFTC and other business-men were very much interested in increasing trade with Latin America after the war, they drew the line at such a dramatic increase of governmental power in the private sector.[49]

Business opposition and legislative inaction induced McAdoo to change his tactics. He wedded the need for ships to the growing concern for preparedness, which was especially strong in the ranks of the Republican party. By the summer of 1915 new private merchant vessels were in short supply, so that new sources of ships had to be found. McAdoo proposed that the government build ships as part of a preparedness program and use them to carry cargo abroad. The summer and fall of 1915 seemed a better time to make such a radical proposal, since the first half of 1915 had seen extraordinary growth in America's trade with foreign nations. The difficulties of finding adequate, reasonably priced shipping had convinced many farmers and manufacturers that perhaps the government had a greater role to play than heretofore thought. The Chamber of Commerce in the summer of 1915, for example, conducted another of its referendums. This one showed that more than half of the businessmen polled favored government ownership of a private company through purchase of stock to build ships; a more substantial 80 percent approved government attempts to control rates.[50]

Redfield and others in the administration, however, continued to urge cau-tion. Colonel House did not want to raise a politically divisive issue before the 1916 elections. Secretary of Agriculture Houston and Redfield wanted the full cabinet to approve the proposal before the administration took a stand on such a potentially controversial program. But McAdoo, with Wilson's approval, went ahead. If anything, the treasury secretary was proposing a more daring and comprehensive program than the one the year before. He wanted a permanent policy toward maritime issues, to be administered by a shipping board, which would be made up of the secretaries of the navy and commerce, ex officio, and three presidential appointees. The board was to be empowered to lease or charter cargo vessels. If such leases were unavailable, the board could itself have ships built. Ships constructed and to be leased by the board were to be produced privately, although if necessary in navy yards. The ships were to be built accord-ing to standards set by the navy and manned by American seamen. But the board was to do more. Like the Interstate Commerce Commission, it was to regulate rates, services, and routes provided by the merchant marine. McAdoo wanted a legislative mandate for cooperation with the Interstate Commerce Commission in order to assure cooperation between shipping and railroad interests. The board was also to be empowered to retaliate against foreign discriminatory practices.[51]

After lengthy discussions with members of Congress, the navy, and officials of the Seamen's Union of America, the administration presented a bill in January 1916 incorporating McAdoo's ideas. What came out of Congress, however, was legislation much modified from what he had originally designed. The House required that the shipping board terminate five years after the end of the war. In the Senate, the bill was further revised. It prevented the government from purchasing foreign ships from belligerents or vessels already engaged in American trade. And the government could not operate ships until every effort had been made to lease or sell ships to private owners on terms suitable to the government. The bill Wilson signed in early September 1916 provided $50 million to the board to purchase and construct merchant ships, which could then be sold or leased to private citizens, although the government retained the right to repossess them whenever necessary. The board had to arrange for bidding on ships to insure private owners an opportunity to operate these government ships. The board was far from what McAdoo originally envisioned, and members of the Senate tended to emphasize its regulatory rather than its promotional aspects. The Congress made clear that it did not want the government to operate vessels, unless there was an emergency. McAdoo looked upon the board, however, as a beginning of an effort to achieve a long-term maritime policy that would help the United States expand into new markets.[52]

The modified bill and board it created nevertheless caused alarm among businessmen, especially among the influential manufacturers whom Redfield had tried to recruit into a business-government alliance. In principle, the NFTC supported continued government-business cooperation in promoting and protecting foreign trade. But the council's chief spokesman on maritime policy, Charles Dollar, was an influential owner of a Pacific shipping line. He scoffed at the notion of the government purchasing ships. Dollar thought that the government would buy vessels at a time when they were extremely expensive. He adhered to a long-standing proposal that the government make a payment to shipowners to make up the difference between salaries paid to American crews and lower foreign salaries. In that way, the ships would be competitive and yet remain in private hands. His harsh words in January 1917 about the government's policy, according to the *Proceedings of the Fourth National Foreign Trade Convention*, received loud applause.[53]

Despite business qualms, the chairman of the Shipping Board, Edward Hurley, moved energetically. "We are building ships," he said in 1918, "not alone for the war, but for the future of world trade." Before becoming chairman in 1917, Hurley had been interested in promoting trade. A prominent Illinois businessman, he had served as vice-president of the Illinois Manufacturers Association and had been one of the leading planners of the NFTC. One of his first contacts with government was to assist in the preparation of a report for the BFDC on banking conditions in Argentina, Brazil, and Chile. In late 1914, he became the first vice-chairman of the FTC and along with its chairman, Joseph Davies, proceeded to encourage American manufacturers to increase their foreign commerce.[54]

As chairman of the Shipping Board, Hurley saw a great opportunity to aid American commerce by providing a merchant fleet for expansion after the war. Like many others Hurley thought of Latin America as a "natural field" for American exports. Hurley amassed great powers. When the United States joined the war, Wilson extended the authority of the Shipping Board to include the requisition of American vessels so that it could acquire those still under construction in American yards and enemy ships interned in American harbors. The Shipping Board set up the Emergency Fleet Corporation in April 1917. The corporation was to be the administrative body that in fact had the responsibility, under the board, to provide ships. Between 1917 and 1919 Hurley and the corporation began to assemble an enormous fleet by taking ships and also by spending over $2 billion to construct new ships.[55]

Hurley, singlemindedly determined to have ready for the postwar years a merchant fleet that would meet the needs of a burgeoning American commerce, so unnerved the British with his enthusiasm that they became involved in bitter disputes with him over merchant shipping after the war. President Wilson had to instruct Hurley not to talk about his postwar plans for the American fleet so as not to upset the British during the war. Nevertheless, Wilson agreed with Hurley's opposition to putting the American fleet under inter-Allied control as the British desired.[56]

Hurley's achievement, however, was significant, and in fact became more obvious after the war ended. The peak in deliveries of new ships did not come until 1919, and the program of building did not end until 1921. By 1918 the United States built ships three times as fast as Great Britain. As a result, the distribution of world shipping had been altered by the wartime policy of the Shipping Board.[57]

Poor health forced Hurley to resign in 1919. Although he had been directly responsible for the building of the merchant fleet, he had little lasting linfluence over how it was to operate in the future. The Congress late in that same year decided to dispose of the huge number of ships provided by the war emergency. Congress favored turning the ships back to private enterprise. Emergency provisions that had stimulated rapid construction were repealed at the end of 1919, and in January 1920 hearings were held to explore new policies. Under the direction of Senator Wesley Jones of Washington, the Senate Commerce Committee drew up shipping legislation, which became the Merchant Marine (Jones) Act of 1920. Wilson signed the new bill in early June 1920.[58]

The act authorized a procedure by which the Shipping Board could dispose of its fleet, but it also provided for the continuance of the Shipping Board to help promote the interests of the merchant marine. The board received authorization, for example, to provide money for the future construction of ships when necessary. And the act guaranteed shipping routes to areas that had long interested those in the development of foreign trade. If necessary, the government would keep open "essential trade routes," something that appealed especially to smaller market-seeking producers. The legislation also authorized American insurance companies to combine their efforts to provide marine insurance, exempting them from the antitrust laws.[59]

The new shipping program, however, got underway during a short but sharp depression. Indeed, an enormous surplus of ships was part of the economic problem. The board nevertheless went ahead with plans to sell ships, not the best time given the worldwide slump, and to keep essential trade routes to Latin America, the Mediterranean, Africa, and the Orient operating until private capital would invest in these routes. The board in 1921 continued to operate vessels over 41 separate routes.[60]

As helpful and encouraging as the board's activities were, they were not sufficient to provide the United States with the kind of merchant marine that many of the most enthusiastic market-seeking businessmen and government officials had wanted. Part of the problem had to do with the quality of the ships that were for sale. While some had been built with the most advanced techniques of the maritime builder, many others were little better than the slow and ineffi-cient tramp steamers common to European builders before World War I. Most serious was the board's inability to provide easily for the replacement of tonnage purchased. Without significant government support, the costs of building in the United States were prohibitive, and purchasing ships abroad led to such discrim-ination that American buyers were equally at a cost disadvantage with foreign competitors. Price was a problem too. Some of the efforts in the 1920s were more simply to sell government surplus at the best price than to sell ships for purposes of developing trade. And the government attached strings to some sales, requiring that ships be used only in specified sea lanes. Finally, purchasers of ships were not so financially secure as chief competitors in Britain. The American buyers were comparatively small operators, heavily in debt to the U.S. government for their initial capital investment and to private lenders for their working capital. By the 1930s, the United States had a greater percentage of shipping tonnage than she had in 1914 but still maintained less than half the tonnage of Great Britain, and American ships were generally regarded as inferior in terms of architecture and engineering.[61]

Aside from these long-term effects, the Wilson administration's policy toward shipping revealed sharply the limits of the cooperation between the administra-tion and big businessmen, and many smaller businessmen as well. Collaboration between the two seemed to go well so long as Redfield was the center of activity. Throughout the war Redfield had urged the president to follow a coordinated and consistent policy toward foreign trade expansion,[62] but when others, especially McAdoo, intruded into foreign trade issues, other perspectives invariably came to the fore. McAdoo and the president were most solicitous of the needs of agriculture, especially of that in the South. Such an orientation was for them simply prudent politics, but their attachment to agricultural interests inevitably helped to erode the business-government cooperation that Redfield had worked so assiduously to cultivate. Many members of the NFTC saw subsidies as the only answer to offset the comparatively higher costs of operating American ships. But the Democratic administration remained adamantly opposed to subsidies, a position strongly supported by farmers.

Attempts to improve the merchant marine after 1914, as we have seen, proved as divisive as they had before the war. Redfield lost the initiative to McAdoo and later Hurley. McAdoo's proposals provoked hostile reactions among members of the NFTC, which made hollow the rhetoric of cooperation between business and government. Although the American merchant marine emerged from World War I in a better position than it had been for decades, Redfield's vision of the Department of Commerce as the chief coordinator of business-government efforts at promoting trade was blurred by the experience of the merchant marine issue. When Europe went to war in 1914, Redfield thought that the conflict would give him the opportunity to make changes in several policies that he and many businessmen thought necessary to promote American trade. American involvement in the war, however, created a momentum of its own that overtook Redfield's efforts. The merchant marine was not the first nor the most serious instance of the war eroding the alliance that Redfield built and his position as the leader of efforts to get business and government to work together.

The European war, which had given Redfield such opportunities to draw businessmen and his department together, ultimately destroyed his efforts at leading the market-expansion effort when the United States entered World War I. Wilson created the War Trade Board, which effectively took control of American trade and ruined Redfield's chances to control market-seeking, to say nothing of his pretensions to be the chief administration spokesman for market expansion. The WTB was not hostile to market expansion, but clearly its primary concern was to win the war. And the head of the WTB, Vance McCormick, was much less single-minded in using the war to advance the interests of American trade than was Edward Hurley at the Shipping Board or Redfield at the Department of Commerce.[63]

President Wilson at first gave the Commerce Department full responsibility over the war export trade. The Urgent Deficiencies and Espionage Acts of June 1917 had conferred on Wilson the authority to license exports. He gave that responsibility to the Department of Commerce's Bureau of Foreign and Domestic Commerce (BFDC), which established the special Export License Division to deal with its new tasks.[64]

The issue of the control of exports, however, inflamed old bureaucratic rivalries between the Department of Commerce and the Department of State, although it was no longer only a matter of which agency would best promote trade. Because of the war, other agencies interested themselves in exports. Thus in August, by executive order, Wilson transferred the licensing powers of the BFDC to the Export Administrative Board, made up of representatives from the three departments (State, Agriculture, and Commerce) and from the Food Administration and Shipping Board. Redfield objected bitterly to the president about these changes. Wilson explained, however, that "the convinction has grown upon me that we began wrong in our arrangements for the administration of the control of exports . . . and I believe that the only solution is to entrust the whole action and detail of administration in that matter to one instrumentality, . . . the Exports Board." Redfield took this loss personally, and in a plaintive letter to Wilson on August 22 said that "I cannot conceal from you . . . that quite apart from the thing done, the manner of its doing had deeply hurt me." Wilson in following correspondence took no note of Redfield's personal complaints and concerned himself with getting Redfield to assign Commerce Department personnel to help out until the new agency was fully functioning.[65]

Wilson further strengthened the handling of foreign commerce with the creation in October 1917 of the War Trade Board and War Trade Council. The WTB became the administrative agency responsible for foreign trade, replacing the Export Administrative Board. Organizationally, the new board included the same members as the old, adding only a representative from the Treasury Department and the War Industries Board. The WTB had substantial powers over American commerce, since it controlled imports and licensed exports.[66]

The shift of power to the WTB weakened the Department of Commerce's key agency in trade expansion, the BFDC. The bureau's director wrote to Redfield a few weeks after the creation of the WTB to discuss what his division could do to continue efforts to expand trade. B. S. Cutler, one of the major supporters of trade expansion within the department, regretted that the effort to promote foreign trade would not be possible during the war. Aside from the restrictive legislation, he observed that the public might think businessmen unpatriotic if they seemed too concerned publicly about gaining new business. He thought, however, that the BFDC could continue to give practical information to businessmen interested in trade expansion, although the government's own restrictions and the disrupted conditions in foreign markets made the advice somewhat beside the point. Cutler concluded that the Department of Commerce's interests would be best served by collecting and disseminating information to other government agencies about foreign trade and commerce. Betraying a great concern with the future bureaucratic role of the department, he thought that a monopoly on gathering trade data and the expertise in interpreting them would make the Commerce Department the center of postwar reconstruction efforts.[67]

Redfield agreed with Cutler and encouraged his proposals, but he concentrated on other ways to maintain the role of the Department of Commerce as the coordinator of business-government efforts to promote trade. The WTB's handling of export licenses provided Redfield with an opportunity to keep his department as the agency most useful to businessmen interested in trade expansion. Redfield defended and helped both small and large firms that saw themselves unnecessarily restricted by the WTB. Generally, the WTB's responsibilities were to assure the United States essential supplies, to use available shipping as efficiently as possible, and to make sure that enemy powers did not receive American goods. The WTB worked through several bureaus to achieve these goals. Perhaps inevitably the WTB came into dispute with businessmen. Troublesome to market-seeking producers were the efforts to assure adequate supplies of commodities that were needed for the war effort at home. The WTB's attempt to restrict imports of what were defined as nonessential products caused disagreements with businessmen. The board also made up blacklists of companies that traded with the enemy, prohibiting licenses for them. Equally troubling were the sharp restrictions on what could be sent to neutrals.[68]

Businessmen bitterly complained about the WTB. Business complaints that did not go directly to the WTB came to the Department of Commerce. Redfield and his department were perceived as sympathetic. BFDC's short-lived handling of export licensing at the beginning of America's wartime involvement had reassured many who had feared that the government would issue an embargo against almost all foreign trade. Businessmen found the WTB's centralized procedures confusing at best, its personnel inaccessible, and its decisions arbitrary. Any dispute with the board complicated business for producers. Tinplate manufacturers, for example, appealed to Redfield to help secure the release of a shipment contracted for abroad before the creation of the WTB, but subsequently held up because of priorities given to other shipping. Redfield interceded successfully for these producers with both his subordinates and the WTB.[69]

Redfield defended more general manufacturers' interests in other disagreements with the WTB. The board's orders restricting commerce to the neutral countries near Germany in northern Europe caused much opposition. The problem was that the WTB restrictions and decisions on these matters were not quickly and widely publicized. Writing to the secretary of the treasury, Redfield observed that "hundreds of establishments did not know whether they may safely finish up articles in process for which they have materials, and hundreds also have no certainty as to the existence of any such definite policy in relation to neutral countries." Redfield's attitude toward the board's regulations and procedures was in close accord with that of the NFTC. Although Redfield was successful in simplifying matters a bit, there was still much to be done, in the opinion of the NFTC and other business groups.[70]

To complicate Redfield's task of keeping business sympathetic to his goals, small businessmen believed that the WTB favored larger businessmen, although the larger producers in the NFTC were as critical of the WTB as the smaller ones were. Relations between the Department of Commerce and the WTB, not surprisingly, became at times unpleasant. Perhaps resentful of the WTB's accusations that the department was not cooperating fully with its efforts, Redfield finally blasted the WTB in July 1918. Relations boiled over in a dispute between the WTB and the exporters and importers of furs from Russia. Redfield and his high-ranking associates resented bitterly that low-level members of the WTB often rejected or ignored their suggestions. In an angry letter to Chairman Vance McCormick, the secretary said that "the matter of any one license is relatively trivial—a sympathetic helpful attitude to our commerce is vital. There is no room in America for a government autocracy. It is against that spirit in your board that I protest.... Does the War Trade Board intend to use its vast powers in helping or hindering American industry? I care little what your regulations may be but it is vital to the country to have it clear in what spirit they are to be enforced." Redfield went on in the communication to compare the WTB's approach to that of the Germans. "There has," he said, "crept into your work what one of your Board calls 'strong arm methods.' They may be efficient. German methods are efficient but we abhor them, and efficiency does not excuse injustice."[71]

Redfield's rhetorical question was not answered. The WTB's chairman supported the goals of an expanded American commerce. War priorities simply got in the way of the interests of particular firms and individuals. Redfield championed these businessmen, for his own purposes, but also because he believed injustices were done. As a matter of policy, however, the WTB tried to allow as much to be exported as possible, and there were market-seeking businessmen who praised the work of the board.[72]

But the disputes were not to be the only irritant to Redfield. The secretary's consternation increased when the president assigned the WTB to the Department of State for dismantling after the war. Redfield, as we shall see in the next chapter, concluded that he needed to make one last effort to regain the momentum he had at the beginning of the Wilson years to build a coordinated business-government alliance in the promotion of foreign commerce.

The war, thus, severely damaged Redfield's efforts to make the Department of Commerce the coordinator of trade policy, as well as the peacemaker between large and small manufacturers. There were successes, to be sure. The war had created the atmosphere that allowed the passage of the Webb legislation, which permitted export combinations. Wartime conditions also forced a consideration of the politically touchy merchant marine problem, although the merchant marine issue revealed that Redfield's coalition was a shaky one within the business community interested in trade expansion. The NFTC would try to present a unified front on the importance of trade to the entire economy. But other, perhaps narrower, interests within the NFTC still held sway on critical issues like the merchant marine. Redfield's inability to coordinate shipping policy revealed the limits of his alliance. Before and especially during the war, many other groups became concerned with the issues that Redfield defined as essential to the promotion of trade. As such the war weakened the secretary's claim that the Department of Commerce was the appropriate place to centralize the government's effort to expand foreign commerce.

Redfield's frustration during the war was revealed in the increasingly angry assessment that the WTB hindered the expansion of American commerce. The secretary determined that after the war he would regain for the Commerce Department the role of coordinator of trade expansion. His effort failed, as we shall see, and he left government at the end of 1919.

With Redfield gone, the effort to present a coherent and coordinated approach to the promotion of foreign trade, weak and ineffectual as it had been, dissipated entirely, as the government was caught in the cross-currents of demobilization, and as big business reassessed its role in the world market.

Eight

The Failure of Industry-Government Coordination: The Postwar Years

World War I profoundly enhanced the United States' influence in the international economy. The U.S. had become a major creditor nation, holding a large percentage of the world's gold supplies. These changes had an impact on efforts to expand foreign trade as American manufacturers had to adjust to new conditions in the world economy. At the same time, the war undermined business-government relations in promoting trade expansion. High-ranking members of the Wilson administration, prominent bankers, leading manufacturers, and some members of Congress realized that the United States' new creditor status implied larger responsibilities for the stability of the international economy. As a creditor the United States needed to import heavily from abroad, especially since the U.S. had virtually captured the world's gold supplies. Imports would provide the dollars abroad to pay for American exports. Foreign trade became an important official consideration since it touched on a number of the other major postwar international economic issues: repayment of loans, reconstruction aid, fluctuating exchange rates, and reparations. American manufacturers were caught up in the debates on many of these issues. Both the more and the less advantaged producers wanted to hold on to or further develop foreign markets. But smaller producers, as in the years before, gave little attention to foreign markets during 1919, when domestic demand increased rapidly. Confused conditions in a slowly recovering Europe made sales there unlikely in any case for smaller producers. Interest remained strong in Latin American markets, although demand at home was the first consideration. In contrast, the larger firms, at least those with established marketing structures, assembly plants, and factories in Europe, rebuilt or expanded their facilities in Allied and former enemy countries alike.[1]

The war destroyed Redfield's efforts to bring coherence and coordination to foreign trade policy. During the war, as we saw in chapter 7, the War Trade Board coordinated export and import policy. To complicate matters further for the Department of Commerce, Congress and the executive authorized other wartime agencies to involve themselves with bankers and manufacturers doing business overseas. As soon as the war ended Redfield tried to regain control over foreign trade policy. His attempt to get Congress to centralize foreign trade promotion in the Department of Commerce failed. Soon after, Redfield left government in late 1919, and his successor was unable to pull together the Department of Commerce's unraveled efforts to coordinate American trade expansion. Coordination was given to an Economic Liaison Committee in the Department of State, which assembled mid-level bureaucratic experts on trade policy from many different departments. But the committee did little more than provide a forum for an exchange of views. And the Central Foreign Trade Committee, established in 1919, met only once, even though it was supposed to bring together high-ranking officials regularly.

Officials in the Departments of State and Commerce realized the importance of a coordinated policy toward foreign trade, and indeed toward other economic issues. The failure to develop coherent foreign trade policies was but a small part of the larger problem of bureaucratic disintegration in the last years of the Wilson administration. The president directed his energies to the Treaty of Versailles and domestic political problems. He had little time to formulate and implement coordinated policies toward major international economic issues. His views were general and what policies emerged were ill-formed, although he knew what he did not want. Wilson rejected British and French proposals for restrictive trade agreements, since they conflicted with his larger international goals. And he spurned efforts to extend far into the postwar period inter-Allied wartime commissions. On the domestic side, the president desired to return economic issues to the private sector, preferring to leave trade and finance to manufacturers and bankers. As a result, government attempts to promote trade floundered. There were many in business and government who saw a need for continued government encouragement to foreign trade, but the Wilson administration was incapable of the necessary coordination and leadership. The ties between business and government weakened as the larger, advantaged firms made their own arrangements abroad and the smaller, less advantaged firms turned to the domestic market.[2]

World War I significantly altered the United States' place in the world economy, for the U.S. became the leading international creditor. When Europe went to war in 1914 the U.S. owed $3.7 billion more to foreign creditors than foreign debtors owed in America. At the end of 1919, the first full year after the war, the situation had reversed itself. The U.S. had become a creditor for intergovernmental debts (something she had not been before the war) of $9.6 billion. The total foreign indebtedness on private and governmental acounts was $12.6 billion. American foreign trade had increased immensely, too. In its own way, the increase in foreign trade represented as important, if not so long-lived, a change in the international economic position of the United States. American industrial output doubled in less than seven years between 1914 and 1921. In dollar terms, adjusted for inflation, American foreign trade in manufactures increased from $655 million (1910-14) to $1,272 million (1913-25).[3]

These financial and commercial changes transformed the circumstances in which American manufacturers sold in the world. The Wilson administration did not fully develop a coordinated policy to deal with all of the changes. The new conditions, along with economic dislocations in Europe following the war, altered the ways in which the largest American producers perceived the foreign market, while limiting for a short time the ability of smaller producers to sell abroad. Less directly, the war contributed to the breakdown of some of the relationships between business and government in promoting foreign trade.

After the war New York became the international financial capital, replacing London. The American dollar remained strong when compared with the weakening currencies of the European powers, bringing about sharp fluctuations in exchange ratios, with European currencies depreciating vis-à-vis the dollar. These fluctuations inevitably affected trade in manufactures, although in the immediate years after the war American manufactured trade continued at a high level. By 1921, many European industries had not revived, making American producers very important to European reconstruction. Manufacturing had not fully recovered in any of the major European countries. With 1913 as an index of 100, manufacturing production in Russia in 1921 stood at only 23, Great Britain 55, France 61, and Germany 75.[4]

Buoyant as trade seemed to be in 1919–20, profound alterations had occurred in the United States' trade posture. Depreciating foreign currencies made foreign goods relatively cheap in the American market while the lack of foreign exchange made it difficult to buy American products abroad. The scarcity of dollars added a premium to the price of American products, which, had it not been for the disruption of European economies, would have significantly reduced American sales.[5] Complicating the situation, principal and interest obligations on public and private debt put more foreign currency into American hands. Unbalanced trade between the United States and Europe and Canada could not be settled by transfers of gold. The United States held gold stocks in excess of all other nations, and foreign holdings were not large enough to balance the deficits on trade accounts.

The United States, thus, had to buy foreign products in order to put dollars in foreign hands. In the sixty years' domination of international economic transactions Britain had often had an unfavorable trade balance on the visible accounts since imports exceeded exports. In this way, however, Britain kept sterling in circulation and made possible foreign purchases at home. In addition, she solidified her international economic position by providing services in shipping, insurance, and bank credits which earned her foreign exchange.[6]

The United States was hard pressed in only a few years to make the adjustments in policy and institutions to match what Britain had built up over several decades. Moreover, protectionist sentiment remained strong in the United States. Indeed there was a real antipathy among smaller businessmen and farmers to lowering the barriers to the world's greatest market. Congress reflected protectionist sentiment in 1921 by passing a measure that significantly raised rates on farm products and provided antidumping clauses that pleased smaller businessmen. Wilson vetoed the emergency tariff bill that would have raised agricultural duties, and Congress sustained Wilson's veto, although soon after it sent President Harding similar legislation which he signed into law in May 1921. Many larger manufacturers, bankers, and officials of the State Department, the Commerce Department, and the Department of the Treasury opposed such legislation to no avail. They saw clearly the need to increase imports.[7]

Another way to meet America's new responsibilities would have been to postpone or cancel the intergovernmental war debts contracted by foreign governments during the war. Theoretically, this would have been in the interests of exporters, since it would have allowed vast foreign sums to be diverted for European reconstruction, thereby stimulating purchases in the United States, the world's only fully functioning industrial economy. But theory flew in the face of a fairly widespread sentiment, even among those who might benefit the most, that foreign debts had to be paid. The Congress and much of the public looked upon the debts as a business proposition, pure and simple. Congress and the administration opposed proposals to forgive the debts, to reduce the principal or interest, and to extend the period for repayment. President Wilson and his closest advisers thought that failure to have them paid would disturb the domestic economy. The budget would not have a chance of being balanced and taxes would have to be raised. Wilson and Secretary of the Treasury Carter Glass wanted very much to return to a prudent balanced budget. Such an example from Washington, they thought, would help restore confidence and stimulate economic expansion.[8]

Reparations were a thorny issue which also affected trade. If reparations were too high, the German economy would not recover quickly. Left out of the world's trade, she would become a burden, hurting the United States and other countries that had traditionally traded with her. The United States, however, had little impact on the final designation of reparations. American representatives did not participate in the crucial discussions on German payments. The president withdrew America's unofficial observers to teach his critics a lesson when the U.S. Senate refused to accept the peace treaty.[9]

Reparations were closely tied to other issues, especially long-term credits or reconstruction loans for the European economies. These loans were important to the United States since they would help revive economically the country's major trading partners in Europe. But most Wilson administration officials, as well as many bankers and manufacturers, did not want government involved in more public lending. Wilson and Secretary Glass feared politicizing aid to Europe. The onset of World War I, they thought, had shown the dangers of pursuing political goals with economic tactics. As it turned out, however, the private sector could not provide enough of the required long-term loans. Short-term credits became available through the Edge Banks. Short-term credits did help commerce to a degree, while not satisfying the underlying requirements of credits for substantial reconstruction in Europe.[10]

Trade with Latin America posed fewer problems than that with Europe. As the prewar European suppliers of Latin American markets (Britain and Germany) declined in importance, United States producers increased their sales. Latin

American trade balances were favorable with the United States. The United States imported large quantities of raw and semifinished materials, making South American purchases easier in the U.S. economy than European purchases. Europe imported a smaller proportion of America's manufactured goods in 1925 (32 percent) than she had in 1914 (37 percent). Latin America's share increased slightly from 13 percent in 1914 to 16 percent in 1925.[11]

The U.S. failed to respond to the new requirements of its world role for a number of reasons. Ideology, personality clashes, and bureaucratic gamesmanship all contributed to the failure. Ultimately, at the highest level, the president had higher priorities than the direct promotion of American foreign trade. President Wilson, Secretary of State Lansing, Secretary of the Treasury Glass, and Secretary of Commerce Redfield all appreciated the implications of America's new creditor position, as did others of the president's advisers and associates. They understood that in order to sell abroad the United States had to buy abroad.

But Wilson did little to flesh out in policy what his perception of America's new economic position required. The president increasingly devoted his attention to the Paris Peace Conference. He believed firmly that a settlement of the war on his terms would bring about the political settlement that would lead to economic stability and then recovery. The Wilson administration's postwar approach to trade policy confined itself to indirect assistance and for the most part to half-hearted support of measures adopted earlier. The president thought that strengthening the basic avenues of commerce was enough to promote foreign trade. And so, what changes came were mostly refinements of earlier policies toward the merchant marine, antitrust laws, and foreign branch banks. The private Edge corporations, institutions designed to provide long-term credits, were the major innovation. Through 1919 the official policy of the Wilson administration gave a very low priority to the direct promotion of American foreign trade and investment.[12]

Other members of the Wilson administration failed to take the lead and address the issues that would have allowed the U.S. to assume greater responsibility for its new role in the international economy. Secretary Lansing gradually lost influence with the president. By the summer of 1919 Lansing had returned from France to the department in Washington, there to nurture his resentments at Wilson's shabby treatment at the Peace Conference. Only a sense of duty made him keep his post after the president suffered a stroke at the beginning of October 1919. He had few opportunities to present to the president his mature views of America's new position in the world economy and of the importance of American foreign commerce in manufactured goods. Mrs. Wilson and Joseph Tumulty, those closest to the bedridden Wilson, kept Lansing away. And the secretary himself was fatigued by the years of making policy during the futile search for neutrality and then during war.[13]

Secretary Glass, who enjoyed a closer relationship with the president, nevertheless, was unable to act upon his own perception of the changed nature of America's role in the world. He opposed direct governmental loans to bring about

European reconstruction. Glass thought that private capital would be adequate to meet reconstruction needs, believing like so many others that the European states would recover more quickly than in fact they did. The secretary, moreover, thought that too much government interference in trade and investment had helped precipitate World War I. He wanted the private sector to take a greater role in financing postwar reconstruction in hopes of keeping the process apolitical.[14]

Redfield undercut what influence he had left at the end of the war by devoting himself to reviving his prewar plans to combine all of the government's trade promotion programs in the Department of Commerce. His efforts, as we shall see, failed in a fruitless struggle in Congress.

While high-ranking officials were preoccupied with the peace treaty and bureaucratic politics, lower-level officials continued to provide day-to-day assistance to American businessmen. Employees at both the departments of commerce and state saw great opportunities for American business in the altered postwar international economy. These officials wanted to take advantage of the weakened position of European industrial powers to allow American producers to solidify markets cultivated during the war, especially in Latin America. Members of the BFDC at the Commerce Department and of the Latin American Division in the Department of State spent much time helping individual businessmen.[15]

The departments of state and commerce helped American private interests in several ways in Latin America. Assistant Secretary of State Breckinridge Long, for example, interceded for Bethlehem Steel in negotiations to get a contract for an arsenal in Brazil in 1919. This was part of a strategy to keep foreign influence at a minimum in Latin America and to foster close economic relations which, officials thought, would reduce the need for the kind of direct intervention in South America that had occurred in the Caribbean. The department gladly cooperated when business tried to weaken or dislodge German interests. In the Department of Commerce, middle-level officials in the BFDC tried to provide direct assistance to businessmen, especially in Latin America. There, goals were less ambitious than at the State Department. The Commerce Department wanted to solidify its position by expanding upon the assistance and information that it had provided before the war.[16]

Indeed, the provision of trade information had become more and more important to the Department of Commerce's efforts. As Redfield lost control over trade promotion during the war, he stepped up the department's efforts at collecting information about foreign, especially Latin American, markets. The secretary planned to make his department useful again by providing information to businessmen with whom contacts were generally good. But the Commerce Department never had a monopoly on the collection of such information, and providing such data to businessmen became a source of bureaucratic rivalry after the war. The State Department had increased its own collection of information, and other agencies had generated much information of use to businessmen, too.

To make decisions about export licenses, the WTB had amassed large files about foreign needs and American suppliers. The WTB was assigned to the Department of State for phasing out. Moreover, the Inquiry, which provided Wilson with expert information about the postwar situation, amassed great quantities of data about economic conditions and issues. The Department of State analyzed neutral trade and the plans of neutral nations for postwar trade and also made studies during the war of possible areas for the expansion of American trade after the war.[17]

The efforts of the Department of State and the Department of Commerce, however, were hindered by the unsystematic way in which the Wilson administration went about the transition from war to peace. The State Department was disorganized enough by the need of many top officials to accompany President Wilson to Paris for the Peace Conference. Equally serious was the Congress' cut in the department's appropriations, a reduction which occurred even though the president gave the State Department the responsibility for phasing out several wartime agencies. Furthermore, some bureaucracies like the War Trade Board had lost key personnel by the time of the transfer, thus putting further burden on the understaffed Department of State.[18]

With increased responsibilities and insufficient personnel, the Department of State created an Economic Liaison Committee to study the implications of the United States' new economic role in the world and to make policy recommendations. The committee was to provide from several departments the expert opinion of specialists on tariff, exchange rates, shipping, and the like. The committee met regularly in 1919 and 1920 and then with less frequency in the 1920s. Ultimately the group had little influence on policymakers, although it served as a useful forum for discussion. The committee's chairman, Wesley Frost, set out to centralize foreign economic policymaking in the Department of State. While not successful in the last analysis, he succeeded in wresting from the Commerce Department the initiative on foreign trade issues in 1918 and 1919.[19]

Postwar economic and political dislocations thus had the most serious consequences for the Department of Commerce. The Congress' failure to appropriate funds adequate for the department to resume its prewar trade promotion efforts, as well as the president's lack of attention to trade issues, weakened and then ruined Secretary Redfield's plan to have his department coordinate government assistance to American business in developing foreign markets. Redfield's failure and his departure from government left the Department of State with the lead in efforts to coordinate foreign trade and foreign economic policy. But under a weakened Lansing and then under a man of no independent stature, Bainbridge Colby, the department did not have the leadership at the top to follow with any vigor the desires of the middle-level officials who wanted the State Department to take the lead in formulating and coordinating economic policy and trade promotion.[20] It was not until the early 1920s that Herbert Hoover clearly won out over the Republican successor at the Department of

State, Charles Evans Hughes, and made the Commerce Department again the focus of the government's efforts to promote foreign trade.

When the war ended, Redfield decided that he was going to regain for his department its role as coordinator of the government's trade promotion efforts. His attempts to regain lost ground in 1918 were made at a time when Congress cut appropriations or refused the department authority to spend funds already appropriated. The problems of the immediate postwar period further deflected congressional attention and made it more difficult for Redfield to get what he wanted. The Congress had failed to appropriate enough money to support the work of the department's district offices. The secretary had been unable to convince the legislature that personnel increases and a large workload justified more money. Even more galling were legislative restrictions on spending money appropriated for the promotion of foreign commerce. The secretary despaired when he failed to get the Commerce Department's salary system rationalized, to say nothing of raises. Dejected, he turned for help to business allies. Redfield concluded in a letter to the secretary of the NFTC that "in fact, I am coming to the point of believing that intelligent distribution of material is the most important function that we have." He went on in the letter to say that the NFTC had to help in view of "the particular disabilities under which the Bureau of Foreign and Domestic Commerce is now laboring."[21]

The NFTC tried to assist Redfield. The council's secretary wrote to NFTC members asking them to "take the trouble to have a personal interview with your Congressman and at least one of your Senators, and urge upon them the importance of Congressional action" to restore funds cut from the Department of Commerce.[22] In early 1920, Congress authorized the expenditure of previously appropriated money, but by then Redfield had left the government.

Budgetary problems were nothing compared to the setbacks Redfield suffered when he tried to regain the Department of Commerce's role as the coordinator of the government's trade promotion campaign. Redfield's prewar plans to coordinate the government's trade expansion forces were jeopardized during the war, when a number of agencies, bureaus, and other departments gained some responsibility over trade-related issues. Following the war, Redfield asserted that the Commerce Department was the "rightful" leader of the government's promotion efforts. He wanted to gain responsibility for coordinating the other agencies involved in trade promotion. When these attempts failed, Redfield left government. His successor, J. W. Alexander, scarcely had time or the ability to join the disparate groups that Redfield had tried to weld together.

It became obvious to Redfield that he had to fight to reestablish the Commerce Department as the leader in trade promotion when Congress turned over the WTB to the Department of State for phasing out at the end of the war. The failure to gain authority over the WTB was only a symptom of the more serious unraveling of the department's program to coordinate trade promotion. By the fall of 1919 Redfield was deeply troubled by the fact that the responsibility for trade promotion was scattered among a number of departments and agencies. Redfield, for example, saw the War Finance Corporation's authority to spend one billion dollars to promote commerce as a notable infringement on his department's responsibilities. Although those in charge of the corporation were courteous to the Department of Commerce, the secretary wrote that "there is no close cooperation."[23]

The lack of mandatory cooperation was a problem in the Commerce Department's relations with other parts of the bureaucracy, too. The Federal Reserve Board and the Interstate Commerce Commission took decisions that ultimately had an effect on the work of trade expansion. Neither routinely consulted with the Department of Commerce. The Shipping Board, as a matter of courtesy, consulted with the Commerce Department at times, but not mandatorily. The Shipping Board's overseas officers, moreover, collected information about foreign trade and shipping conditions, but were not required to make them available to the Department of Commerce. The Federal Trade Commission, like the Shipping Board, Redfield felt, had a direct impact on foreign trade promotion, but there was no "obligation for that Commission to function in close relation with the Department of Commerce." Of more concern to Redfield was the fact that "the Federal Trade Commission is given the supervision over the combinations permitted by law for developing foreign trade. This is a function which falls directly within the organic law of the Department of Commerce."[24]

The behavior of other agencies disturbed the secretary, too. The Inter-American High Commission had distinctive commercial functions. A body designed to draw together representatives from Latin America and the United States, it had as its nominal American representative, as ex officio chairman, the secretary of the treasury. It infringed on the Department of Commerce's work, Redfield thought, in a number of ways: providing uniform regulations for commercial travelers, promoting the standard classification of merchandise, simplifying customs relations. Most disturbing to Redfield, however, was the special attention the commission gave to the protection of patents and trademarks, tasks which duplicated the work of his department's special section dealing with protecting American trademarks abroad. Its desire to arbitrate commercial disputes abroad seemed to foreclose another area in which the Commerce Department should represent the U.S. Similarly, the Railroad Administration, Redfield feared, would have a negative effect on the work of his department in that the administration had the right to embargo freight.[25] None of these commissions, agencies, and boards were required to work closely with the Department of Commerce. Redfield saw in the proliferation of governmental bodies a threat to the goal which, he maintained, all agreed upon: the extension of American commerce. "The question," he said, "is not one of individuals but one of organization. There can be no clear-cut commercial policy carried out by separate bodies that do not interfunction. Any industrial organization composed as is the commercial organi-

165

zation of the government would fail, for the seeds of decay are planted in the very separateness of the component parts. It is not urged that these bodies should cease to be or that their functions should be altered. There are separate duties belonging to each, although many of those duties lie in a common field with the Department of Commerce." What Redfield wanted was the authority to put these bodies under the supervision of the Department of Commerce. "It should be recognized," Redfield wrote, that the Department of Commerce "is the focus of commercial organization on the part of the government and as such these various independent bodies should be so headed up into it that the world of commerce at home and abroad may know there is one center for commerce... and not a congeries of unrelated parts which operate indeed in personal harmony and peace but without those effective results which can come along from systematic and unified effort."[26]

To rein in these agencies, Redfield turned to friends in the Senate, particularly Senator William J. Harris (Ga.). The senator introduced, at the secretary's prompting, a resolution requesting information from the various agencies engaged in trade promotion in order to formulate legislation leading to greater cooperation among agencies interested in foreign trade. The resolution, which eventually passed, had been drafted in the Commerce Department's solicitor's office. Although the agencies dutifully responded to the senator's request, nothing came of Harris's resolution. Neither congressional leaders nor administration officials were inclined to take on the political battle necessary to insure what Redfield wanted, and so he left office in December 1919.[27]

Redfield's successor, J. W. Alexander, faced congressional attacks on the department. Alexander found the other agencies less cooperative than had Redfield. In March 1920, the new secretary complained to the sympathetic Senator Harris that "the broad powers of the Department of Commerce were being so infringed upon by other governmental agencies that the Secretary of Commerce was becoming powerless to control and perform the important duties intended in the creation of this Department."[28]

House members looking to eliminate waste and duplication questioned the need for the department's commercial attachés, arguing that their work could be done by the State Department's consular service. These critics thought that the BFDC should do nothing more than disseminate domestically the trade information collected by the Department of State's officials abroad. As a result, in 1920, the House Appropriations Committee eliminated the commercial attachés and substantially reduced funds for the BFDC to spend on the promotion of commerce. The subcommittee in charge of the Department of Commerce's budget request justified the drastic reductions as a way to minimize duplicating efforts with the Department of State. Although the funds cut were restored on the House floor, the Department of Commerce's leadership was alarmed at the growing opinion that its work in the promotion of foreign trade only mirrored that of the Department of State. Redfield's successor made clear to the department's congressional friends the reasons for keeping the two separate, that is, the need to assure that a strictly economic view be taken abroad by the commercial attachés. Matters became so serious that Secretary Alexander feared that the constant state of uncertainty about the status of the various parts of the department reduced morale and led to a turnover of experienced personnel who quite easily found well-paying jobs with private industry engaged in foreign sales.[29]

The department was spared the removal of its commercial attachés and the strangulation of the work of the BFDC. But in the waning days of the second Wilson administration Secretary Alexander was able to achieve nothing of what Redfield had hoped to accomplish. By the time the administration came to an end, the government's efforts to promote foreign commerce were spread widely among a variety of agencies, boards, and commissions.

Moreover, the contacts between the department and the private business constituency that Redfield worked so hard to develop eroded. The Commerce Department, for example, took little part in important attempts to bring the United States into line with foreign export practice and terminology. The NFTC and the Chamber of Commerce led these efforts at uniformity with the cooperation of the American Manufacturers' Export Association, Philadelphia Commercial Museum, American Exporters and Importers Association, Chamber of Commerce of the State of New York, New York Produce Exchange, and New York Merchants Association.[30]

The war's end had created a bureaucratic morass, as the government tried to readjust to peace. The conflicts over Wilson's peace treaty further deflected attention from concern over trade expansion. Businessmen themselves began to respond to a new world situation, drawing away from government.

The NFTC and some of the other export groups of manufacturers did not need so close contacts with the Department of Commerce any longer. The NFTC had achieved what it had set out to do. The government had changed the antitrust laws and had begun to address some of the problems of the American merchant marine. The group continued to talk about keeping contacts with the two departments and maintaining a cooperative attitude toward them. In the future these contacts allowed the NFTC, the Chamber of Commerce, and the NAM to make their point of view known to the government as other issues arose in the 1920s. But by the end of the war, the ties between the Commerce Department and the business community of market-seeking manufacturers were looser than at the beginning. Indeed, as we shall see, the business contacts with wartime bureaucracies had raised questions among big businessmen about the soundness of relying too heavily on government cooperation.

The war and its aftermath forced the larger manufacturers to reassess their relationship to the world market. The enormous increase in production during the war and the emergence of the U.S. as a major creditor nation made such rethinking necessary. Smaller producers, for example, those most commonly in the NAM, responded to the swings in the international and the domestic economies as they had before the war, although some of the leaders of the association quickly understood the implications of America's new world economic role and the need to increase imports. Many members nevertheless deferred sales abroad to take care of the burgeoning postwar demand at home, although the interest in foreign trade remained. The association's continued interest in trade expansion was perhaps manifested best in increasing appropriations for the NAM's foreign department.[31]

But it was the largest manufacturers with established markets abroad, those who had dominated the American manufactured export market in the years before the war, who displayed the most sophisticated understanding of the problems and implications of the United States' new international economic role. The NFTC soon after the war explored the ways in which the United States and manufacturers were to deal with new foreign conditions. They advocated expanded imports as a way to ease European balance of payments problems, advocating again, as they had for many years, flexibility in adjusting tariff rates. They supported efforts to finance foreign trade through private long-term credits, to establish American corporations to purchase foreign securities, and to improve American acceptance banking to help finance trade. These issues made them acutely aware again of the importance of government in creating an atmosphere conducive to carrying out their business. But their view of government was mixed, and there was less enthusiasm for the close contacts advocated by some leaders of the NFTC before the war. The war had shown them the inefficiency of government. More than that, the leaders learned, they thought, a historical lesson: involving politics too much in commerce leads to military conflicts. Having had much business in Europe before the war, they were sensitive to Europe's problems. Of more importance, they understood America's larger responsibilities as the world's major creditor nation. Some members of the NFTC and the NAM, to be sure, continued to fear aggressive selling by European producers. But such attitudes softened in the years after World War I, for Europe failed to recover as quickly as expected and American producers were able to continue to make sales in Latin American markets that had grown during the war.

Postwar conditions, furthermore, contributed to a strengthening of the position of the largest firms abroad. Uncertain exchange rates encouraged American firms to reinvest foreign profits abroad. Too much would be lost by repatriation. Rebuilding factories and assembly plants was necessary, as was the reestablishment of sales branches in Europe.[32]

With the European economies in disarray at the end of the war, American manufacturers knew that there would be increased demand for the steel and machinery which had made up so much of American manufactured exports. Similarly, the larger producers saw that they would be able to increase sales in Latin America, a market in which they had begun to make inroads before the war. As one speaker at the National Foreign Trade Convention put it in 1915, "it is safe to say that 75% of our principal exports to Latin-America are the products of large organizations. To the River Plate, we ship agricultural machinery, steel products, oil products...; to Brazil, Chile and Peru, steel and oil products, locomotives and electrical machinery. A further analysis would show that our exports are largely natural monopolies; the products of highly specialized industry—such as automobiles and typewriters, and patented and advertised specialties."[33] Smaller producers, however, were the ones who stood the most to gain from the war in sales to Latin America. Traditional American suppliers of the simpler products of industrial manufacture, the standard homogeneous goods, benefitted from the disruption of British and the destruction of German industrial contacts with Latin America. John E. Gardin, described by colleagues in the American Bankers' Association as the "dean" of American banking, thought Latin American trade would offset some problems created by the war. Increased sales to Latin America and Asia, of both specialized and homogeneous products, Gardin thought, would repair some of the injurious effects of disrupted European trade and confused exchange markets.[34]

Leaders of the NFTC, nevertheless, realized that the extraordinary increase in American exports was only temporary and that Europe would someday again become a major producer. Americans wanted to continue to sell in world markets, but the largest producers understood clearly the implications of the United States' new status as a creditor nation: the U.S. had to import as well as export. The United States could not expect to export to Europe on a regular basis again until the European economies improved their own export sectors.

The war had other effects on big business attitudes. It brought about a fuller and, in its way, more limiting view of the role of government. As before the war, the leaders of big business believed that the level of manufactured exports would be determined by those who had significant advantages because of superior technology, marketing skills, and mass production capabilities. The experience of many producers during the conflict, however, dampened somewhat prewar willingness to work closely with government. The war tended to reinforce older suspicions about government and stimulate new fears about politicizing international economic relations. Wartime measures on the merchant marine in particular did not satisfy many of the businessmen who had advocated a new policy, creating some general disappointment about government.

Producers with substantial advantages faced the postwar period, however, with greater contacts with the government than ever before. During the war they had had to deal with several bureaucracies charged with supervising war trade and shipping. With the demise of these boards after the war, the producers' primary contacts were the Department of State and the Department of Commerce. These two departments had gathered much data during the war about foreign economic conditions, and they were eager to assist businessmen. The NFTC was willing to support the efforts of these bureaucracies, but their services were not essential to the continued sales abroad of the major manufacturers.

In addition, the war had given some (though by no means all) of the business-men in the NFTC a much wider perspective on international trade. Some thought inaccurate the rhetoric of American expansionism in a finite world. The world's markets had grown greatly in the past, and there was no reason they could not do so again. Trade was not a matter of participating in a fixed-size economy for a reallocation of shares, but of participating in a growing world economy. To be sure, not everyone took these views, even in the NFTC. Personal perspective seemed to have much to do with it. Those who did business in highly competitive industries making homogeneous products tended to look at the world in highly competitive terms. The larger firms did not, and more significantly, neither did those bankers from the largest banks who had to function consciously as members of a larger international economic system.

The NFTC, and the leading manufacturing firms represented there, had by 1920 concluded that the United States' increased role in the international economy had fundamentally changed the interests and the problems of American producers selling in world markets. At their first meeting after the war, to be sure, prewar views of the needs of American manufacturers were heard. The theme of the April 1919 convention was "American Foreign Trade Essential to American Industry." The organizers of the convention, as President Farrell of U.S. Steel said, believed that the abrupt end of the war created special problems for American producers. Curtailed orders from Europe, the traditional great market for American manufactured products, as well as "keener competition" in other markets, made necessary compensating outlets for American foreign trade.[35]

But after another year of chaos in European finances, difficulties in foreign demobilization, and revolution in Germany and Hungary, the NFTC began to appreciate that important changes had come about indeed, and that for the larger manufacturers the problem of seeking new trade had become somewhat irrelevant. The European economies, recovering more slowly than many American manufacturers had anticipated, created a large demand for American products. Former chief industrial rivals in Germany and Britain were finding it difficult to meet demand in their home markets and were not reviving their trade with Latin America as quickly as many Americans had feared they would. And, more important for domestic policy, leaders in the NFTC realized the implications of America's new creditor status. The convention of 1919 found this to be an important issue, especially as it affected foreign trade. The 1919 convention's final declaration recognized clearly that America's problem was no longer simply to find foreign markets for itself, but how to help create foreign markets for others. "Nations which are our debtors are confronted with economic problems," the 1919 final declaration stated, "and will endeavor to curtail their purchases of finished products from us, and to enlarge their sales to us. They must meet their obligations by finding a market for their products." The convention in the same statement recognized the reasons that foreign governments might try to keep American commerce from Europe. "The restrictions now imposed on American imports into the markets of our European associates in the war seriously impede the free flow of our commerce; but insofar as they are the outgrowth of a policy of safeguarding home industry and conservation of financial resources depleted by the heavy load of war liabilities, adverse criticism would seem unwarranted so long as such restrictions are not discriminatory."[36]

Not everyone within the NFTC accepted or perhaps understood the implications of the United States' new world role. Reflecting the views of the seemingly more competitive commercial world of the prewar years, the president of the convention, Alba B. Johnson, argued that the United States had not planned as well as Europe had for the postwar years. But other NFTC leaders had drawn other conclusions from wartime experience. Farrell, while urging Americans to look for new markets and to seek "the discovery of new opportunities in old markets," reminded the delegates to the opening session that "we must not forget that foreign trade is not one-sided...expansion of our exports is not attainable without corresponding expansion of our imports. The invisible balance that prior to the war was against us, and that offset the habitual favorable balance of our exports of goods, has been transformed into a huge invisible balance in our favor, which our debtors will now seek to offset by a visible balance of exports to us." Imports were not the only answer to these problems. Fred I. Kent, of Bankers Trust Company, noted in a major speech that the United States must increase some services purchased abroad, but most importantly had to increase foreign investment. Only in this way would the United States be able to keep up its foreign trade.[37]

NFTC members who had seen the far-reaching economic and foreign implications of the war made suggestions that, although clearly not representative, mirrored the sentiments of some of the government's own experts in the Department of State. Those who had been on the scene in Europe came back with a more sober view of the problems of reconstruction than those like Alba B. Johnson who had viewed things only from this side of the ocean. Maurice Coster, the vice-president of Westinghouse Electric International Company, had some stern advice for his colleagues after returning from a business visit to Europe. Referring to private talks with leaders of European industry, Coster said that Americans had to realize that the war had left the Allied countries "practically bankrupt." Worse still, there was a dire lack of manpower for industry. The transition to peacetime was much more chaotic there than in the United States because foreign industries had been much more fully converted to producing munitions and other war materiel. Europe depended on the United States for peacetime necessities. The war, Coster maintained, put American manufacturers in an unparalleled position "to undersell the allied industries in their own markets." If we were permitted to go freely into these markets and compete without restriction, it would mean the temporary, if not the permanent, destruction of Europe's industries.[38]

Coster's views were not reflected by all those at the convention. Some urged vigorous efforts in Europe, and others thought that the U.S. should face up to the possibilities of renewed competition in neutral markets by former European competitors.[39] R. R. Fox, a representative of a company which made mechanics' tools, reflected the older views. Great Britain, he maintained, had already sent hundreds of experts to South America, Australia, and the Orient to regain old business. He thought that the Europeans in general would again be formidable foes because of the war. "They have learned the great value of cooperation and concentration of effort during the war, and from their years of experience in handling foreign trade it will be no experiment for them to make a more aggressive campaign in this direction than ever before."[40]

But another year of drift and confusion in Europe caused a greater awareness of the changes that had come about. The council's leadership saw clearly that some permanent changes had occurred. The issues that concerned the NFTC were no longer so prominently the domestic questions of policy that helped rather than hindered the business of the larger producers. The major issue became how to deal with the full implications of the United States' new creditor role, especially in Europe, where exchange rates were only the most obvious example of the serious dislocations in the European economies.

The theme of the NFTC convention in 1920 was "The Effect of Being a Creditor Nation." The NFTC met in five general sessions and fifteen special group meetings to explore the implications of the momentous changes that had overtaken the United States during and after World War I. The supremacy and strength of the United States' position in the world economy had become clearer, as Europe failed to recover as quickly as expected. The United States itself faced problems, but the inflation and disorganization in the transition to peace, and then the short but sharp depression of late 1920–21, were nothing compared with the serious problems encountered in Europe.[41]

Businessmen's views were, however, divided on what the new situation meant. Some continued to adhere to older views of the surplus. James A. Farrell, president of the council and of U.S. Steel, saw the importance of imports if the United States was to have outstanding foreign debts paid. He saw great opportunities in new markets and in what he called "the economic rebirth of the civilized world." But the great expansion of American productive capacity during the war disturbed him, because it would lead to further surpluses that would have to be exported. And although he spoke generally, he believed that American trade abroad would be facilitated by helping Europe to recover and by our purchase of foreign goods, preferably raw materials. The war, he thought, would make foreign markets imperative for the businessman. According to Farrell, U.S. Exports of manufactures for most firms before 1914 were "fortuitous and casual." Until the war "direct interest or participation in foreign trade was still very far from general among American producers." Some, to be sure, missed entirely the war's impact on the United States' role in the international economy. Frederick J. Koster, president of California Barrel Company, in a pedestrian speech on the future of exports, reminded his listeners of the usefulness of foreign trade during a depression. He urged vigilance, too, in a rough and competitive world.[42]

But some analysts had entirely broken out of conventional thinking about trade and saw in the war even greater implications for the United States. George E. Roberts, vice-president of National City Bank of New York, sketched a broad vision of the United States' role in the international market for manufacturers. For many years a contributor to the monthly circular of the National City Bank, Roberts was accustomed to studying the "big picture." Roberts's speech, "The Function of Imports in Our Foreign Trade," ranged widely as he developed his analysis of America's importance in the world economy. Although he did not challenge Farrell by name, his remarks directly contradicted many basic premises of the president of U.S. Steel. "It is a mistake," Roberts said, "for us to advocate foreign trade, as is sometimes done, on the ground that we have so greatly increased our general productive capacity that we cannot consume the output of our industries. That is not true in a general sense, including all the industries of America. The people of the United States could easily consume a volume of production equivalent to twice the present industrial capacity of the country, provided production was adjusted and balanced to their wants." But the demand was not there and it was easier to export to countries with demands like the United States', especially since the U.S. needed the products of foreign countries. Roberts saw the need, as did many others in the NFTC with more conventional views, for increased imports. "No well-supported argument can be made in favor of trying to expand our exports without increasing our imports. That is a waste of energy; it simply cannot be done." Like others, too, he saw the need for Americans to buy foreign securities and invest abroad in order to help foreign governments meet their financial commitments to the United States.[43]

But Roberts came to question the entire outlook of leaders like Farrell and many of the smaller manufacturers who tended to view the world narrowly from the perspective of their own experience in one particular industry. Adopting a broad perspective, like that of Westinghouse's Coster the year before, Roberts noted that "in the eagerness of individuals to sell and amid the apprehensions which arise from rigorous competition, the people of every country are prone to overestimate the dangers which threatened them from the competition of other countries." One country, because of advantages or extraordinary effort, might create a dominant position in one industry. "But the same reasons which prevent a great one-sided trade in favor of the United States likewise forbid such a trade in favor of any other country. It is impossible for any country to monopolize the trade of the world." Great Britain, he went on, always imported more than she exported, and Germany in the five years before the beginning of the war, also imported more than she exported. Fears of Great Britain, Germany, or Japan were misplaced. "None of them in the long run will sell any more than it buys, or make in the aggregate any more commodities than it consumes. None of them will make goods for other countries without wanting something in return."[44]

Roberts concluded with an attack on the static view of the world's demand. He thought that such views were "fundamentally wrong." "There is," he asserted perhaps hyperbolically, "no limit to the amount of work to be done or the amount of business to be had, because there is no limit to the amount of wealth that may be created from the natural resources or to the consumptive demands of the world's population."[45]

Roberts's views were not extreme, nor did he hold them exclusively. Eugene P. Thomas, president of United States Steel Products Company, the subsidiary operation that handled the exports of U.S. Steel, agreed with Roberts. Implicit in Thomas's remarks was a repudiation of some of Farrell's fundamental assumptions about foreign trade. Thomas's views were in their own way more significant than Roberts's, because he was directly engaged in selling manufactured goods on the world market. Discussing the increase in American exports, Thomas questioned the fundamental view of many of those who had most actively advocated the development of foreign trade. "Foreign trade is necessarily reciprocal. We have long been accustomed to speak of competition for foreign trade in terms of commercial warfare. The result has been a deplorable confusion of ideas with regard to the true conception of commerce among nations, which is mutual exchange to mutual benefit. The time has come when it is of vital importance to us, not only to recognize that fact, but to adopt it as the guide of our commercial policy."[46]

The editor of *Bankers' Magazine*, Elmer H. Youngman, also challenged those who viewed international commerce as a war for static shares of the world market. Youngman concluded a speech devoted to financing overseas sales by a discussion of what he called a "higher conception of foreign trade." "I wish to enter a protest against the too widely accepted belief," he said, "that foreign trade is something to be contended for and fought over as hungry dogs fight over a bone." He thought it wrong for a nation to "proceed on the theory that the earth is a very small place, where only a limited amount of trade can be done.... The earth is a very large place, and the business to be done practically without limit. The more trade one nation has the more there will be for others and for all." The needs for better clothing, food, and shelter were not only great in China, Mexico, and Latin America, but also in Europe and the United States. His higher conception of trade was to supply this demand. This was "the stupendous problem to which the nations of the world may wisely address themselves without danger of exhausting its remunerative possibilities." Youngman, perhaps mildly overenthusiastic, nevertheless expressed well a different conception of foreign trade when he concluded that "the share which any one nation may get does not depend upon keeping some other nation from participating, but rather in doing its best by maximum production to add to the common stock, and by the greater abundance and consequently diminished cost to multiply the number of consumers and to stimulate consumption—the Aladdin's lamp of commerce, domestic and foreign."[47]

Youngman's remarks, like those of the others who questioned the rhetoric of commercial warfare, were a logical conclusion when one examined the advantages of the United States' major firms. The large-scale mass production, mass distribution operations lowered unit costs and eventually prices, making possible wider sales. Although Youngman's views were not those of all the leaders of the NFTC, most of the council had long agreed that they gained foreign markets because of their firm's advantages. As James A. Farrell said, "Any study of our international commerce will disclose the fact that in the last analysis it is our industrial development, our productive capacity, which determines the degree of our continuous participation in the competition for foreign markets. As this industrial development went on, there inevitably came into being an element in it which deliberately devoted itself to foreign trade because of the benefits and advantages which it yielded and not merely as a means of supplementing domestic production."[48]

If grappling with the implications of the United States' new financial role in the world undermined the static view of the world economy, the war experience also profoundly affected NFTC members' views of the role of government in international trade. Whether members saw the international market as static or expanding, almost all agreed that the government's place in the conduct of the foreign trade of American manufactures should be minimal. The NFTC supported better appropriations for the Department of Commerce and the Department of State to provide information and more professional representation abroad. They wanted protection from discrimination, but they did not want politicization of trade. On most other matters they desired the role of government to be limited; as, for example, in the case of dealing with the merchant marine, the financing of foreign trade, and the provision of long-term capital to reconstruct Europe.[49]

Attitudes toward government were not a matter simply of a fairly traditional anti-statist ideology, but were more the result of the experience of the war. Government appeared costly and inefficient, and, more significant, a politicized foreign commercial policy seemed to have been a major cause of World War I. Then, too, the position in world markets of the largest manufacturers had improved. They dominated sales to Europe; in Latin America sales increased because of the weakness of former commercial rivals. Finally, the largest producers had achieved many of their political goals. Despite the NFTC's unhappiness over the way in which the government went about improving U.S. shipping, the American merchant marine was stronger than it had ever been. With the Webb Act of 1918, antitrust restrictions were relaxed on foreign trade ventures.

Although the war brought about changes that the largest producers had wanted, it created new issues that needed remedying. Members of the NFTC raised anew the charges that the government hindered their efforts in selling abroad. Wartime allies sensitized some NFTC members to the unfairness of paying taxes abroad and at home. The NFTC's outspoken Robert Dollar wanted Congress to look into the question, and he advocated as a solution incorporation abroad. "We want," he said, "the privilege of forming corporations in foreign countries

175

so that we will not be compelled to pay taxes twice. By the American law we pay taxes in foreign countries to the foreign countries. That is right, we are doing business there, but it is not right that we should pay especially the excess profits taxes in this country which deprive us of the privilege of extending and developing our foreign commerce. . . . We have regulations innumerable to hold us down and prevent our doing things, and mighty few regulations to help us to develop foreign commerce. All that is wrong." Dollar had overlooked provisions in the 1918 income tax law which allowed for foreign tax credits. But the issue of taxes reminded Dollar, and others at the convention, of earlier themes about governmental hindrance of foreign trade. The American government, many in the NFTC thought, again hindered the development of American trade through ill-advised and uncoordinated policies. Dollar concluded the welcoming address of the 1920 convention with reference to a long-held attitude toward Congress. "Now if Congress will only say, 'We are not going to help you but we are going to put no obstructions in your way,' I want to tell you we'll come pretty near developing foreign trade." Others echoed Dollar's views. "The laws which have been placed on our statute books," the president of the Bank of California said, "were framed by men who understood the problems of their own localities but who had no broad outside view. . . . Many of our laws tend to assure our competitors' success rather than our own, and ignorance and prejudice stand in the way of change."[50]

The fate of Redfield's efforts at coordination prompted these negative views of government. Speakers attacked the Congress for destroying the efforts of officials like the former secretary of the Department of Commerce who had endeavored to bring about a great coordination of trade policy. W. W. Nichols, of Allis-Chalmers, read a speech which presented an indictment of the government's failures to bring about order and consistency in trade policy, leaving instead a "serious absence of team-work in the operations of the governmental departments concerned." All the departments (State, Commerce, Agriculture, Labor and Treasury), he said, weaken and undermine the work of the others in transacting business related to foreign markets and world trade. "Independent action leads only to confusion, and multiplication of effort is wasteful and ineffective. Businessmen would decide that this can be due to but one cause, the absence of wise and centralized administration."[51]

This is not to imply that the NFTC forgot the importance of government, especially American diplomats. Government continued to be important to foreign trade because, as Dollar had said, diplomats had to intercede to limit foreign interference with our trade. "Without a strong foreign service to forestall misunderstandings, adjust differences, extend trade and other peaceful relations, and above all to exert our high influence in the preservation of international peace, our future becomes indeed mysterious and uncertain. . . . Time and again, as we fully know, well laid plans of foreign traders are unexpectedly checked by some legal restriction abroad, which is nothing other than governmental interference that can only be countered by governmental action."[52]

The involvement of government in private business and American life, however, made businessmen reluctant to rely on the government more than appeared absolutely necessary. In 1919 Alba B. Johnson, the president of the NFTC convention, stated bluntly that "our adventures in government operation of railroads, telegraphs, telephones, etc. have emphasized the truth that was already perfectly well-known, that no business operation can be conducted as efficiently and successfully by government as by private management." In 1920, Fred I. Kent made the same point even more bluntly: "one of the great lessons taught by the war is the fact that government cannot operate economically and with efficiency, and that the value of government and its only duty during times of peace lies in the regulation of the activities of its people in such manner as to leave the greatest amount of freedom to individuals, and at the same time protect the interests of all its people."[53]

What the NFTC wanted of government, then, was a removal of what the group thought to be hindrances to the private furtherance of trade and the more efficient and coordinated use of those agencies of the government to provide information and to represent American interests abroad when necessary.

Nine

The Limits of Industry-Government Relations and Export Trade Expansion, 1893–1921

There were by 1921 several patterns of relationships between government and manufacturers exporting goods. These patterns altered occasionally later, as world trade declined in the 1930s and took a different turn in the period after 1945. But by 1921 some fundamental relationships had been established, and these arrangements were the result of both the bureaucratic needs of governmental departments and the continuing development of economic institutions and structures.

By the time Woodrow Wilson left office, the largest American manufacturers had resolved that private initiative was, as it had been before, the preferred way to extend export markets. Ties to the government had eroded during the war, and the most prominent government official seeking a close working relationship between government and the export community, William C. Redfield, had resigned in 1919. Postwar issues such as foreign debts, reconstruction loans, and tariffs were all influenced by domestic considerations that were sometimes at variance with the foreign trade interests of the largest producers. As before, however, what determined the behavior of the largest corporations abroad was their own technological and marketing advantages. In a confused and at times inauspicious economic environment, then, the largest producers invested in restoring and expanding foreign factories, assembly plants, and marketing organizations. In part this was a result of unfavorable exchange conditions and in Europe the need to recover from the war. But it signalled, as before, the continuing strength and dominance of the largest producers in foreign markets, a strength gained by economic advantage based on technology and organizational efficiencies. The smaller producers behaved as they had in the years before the war. As demand increased in 1919 and early 1920, sales abroad became less important. Troubled conditions in foreign markets played a part in the short-run decline of interest in foreign sales. When overseas markets again looked promising, the smaller producers initially turned to their own cooperative agencies to assist in fostering sales. The budget for the NAM's foreign department increased markedly in the depressed years of 1920 and 1921, and the NAM took on the task of organizing a Webb corporation (NAMUSA) for its members.[1]

Manufacturers both large and small realized the importance of government in creating an atmosphere at home conducive to the development of foreign trade through policies relating to the tariff, antitrust, foreign branch banking, and the merchant marine. Abroad, the U.S. government had to protect the interests of its citizens by limiting foreign discrimination against its products. Ultimately, however, sales were determined by market conditions abroad and the advantages, or the lack of them, of U.S. producers. Relations between the manufacturers and government were more distant in 1919 and 1920 than they were in 1916-17 before the United States entered the war. Contacts were to improve and increase again in the 1920s, as Herbert Hoover reorganized and expanded the work of the Department of Commerce. Hoover and his colleagues, however, were less sympathetic than Secretary Redfield to U.S. exporters who built assembly plants and factories abroad. The commerce secretary, and especially some of his subordinates in the BFDC, did little to assist the largest producers build plants abroad, since they looked upon these efforts as taking jobs away from Americans. The Commerce Department did encourage the establishment of marketing facilities, especially in Latin America, where Hoover thought that U.S. firms could help build and supply public utilities. And the department assiduously looked after the interests of smaller manufacturers, again especially in Latin America. But the ties made with the smaller manufacturers in the 1920s loosened again in the 1930s, as international trade declined drastically in the worldwide depression. Relations changed again in the years after World War II, when the United States assumed global responsibilities and government was better organized to make use of America's private economic power, especially to achieve strategic and political objectives.[2]

The important conclusions of this study have to do with the dynamics of business-government relations and trade expansion before 1921. When Woodrow Wilson left office, the U.S. government provided many more services to American businessmen interested in increasing their foreign trade than ever before. Key officials in the departments of Commerce, State, Treasury, and Agriculture, as well as in the Shipping Board and the FTC supported the search for foreign trade. But efforts to coordinate the government's activities were thwarted by partisan congressional politics, nationalistic economic policies, and the simple inability of the government's departmental bureaucracies to work closely together.

In the face of this inability of government to coordinate its effort, and in part because of traditional business fears and hostility about government, what became most significant in the development of overseas trade after the war, as before, was the private effort of the largest corporations. They had to earn sufficient returns to cover their large capital investments, and they needed a high degree of coordination to assure a rapid and regular distribution of their goods through numerous sales branches. These large firms required a degree of control over their markets that stimulated continued efforts to improve marketing structures, to build branch factories, and to assure supplies of raw materials. The economic dislocation in European production after the war, and especially the problems of fluctuating exchange rates, made direct efforts mandatory. Indeed government could not satisfy the needs of the largest corporations. Congress, especially the House, was driven by a perhaps excessive concern for local interests, whereas the federal bureaucracy was marked by overlapping jurisdictions and internecine conflict.

Smaller manufacturing firms were more likely to depend on what federal aid and assistance the government could provide. Small producers combined to sell abroad, taking advantage of the Webb-Pomerene Act's exemptions from the antitrust laws. The act proved a disappointment to its supporters, and many of the corporations formed after the war disbanded during the depression of late 1920-21. Similarly, the Edge Act ultimately failed to provide the stimulus to exports and European reconstruction that its supporters hoped it would have. The 1919 act amended the Federal Reserve legislation to provide federal charters to corporations which would undertake foreign banking and investment. The European economies took longer to recover than American officials expected, and the capital provided by Edge Corporations (only two were formed by 1921) was clearly insufficient for reconstruction abroad.[3]

It is more appropriate to talk of the limits of business-government relations in the export expansion of American manufacturers before 1921 than of the cooperation and coordination of producers and government. This is not to overlook for a moment, however, that governmental policies affected markedly the environment in which manufacturers expanded their foreign business. The degree to which the antitrust laws were enforced, the level of support provided the merchant marine, the strength of encouragement given to branch banking abroad, and the flexibility of tariff rates all affected the way in which foreign business was conducted. After the war, governmental policy toward European reconstruction and war debts likewise influenced the environment for business. How these many issues affected the larger as opposed to the smaller producers in large part determined the dynamics of the relationship between business and government in expanding American foreign trade. The largest producers were able at times to meet problems created by governmental policy through private initiative. Purchasing their own fleets of ships somewhat lessened the dependence on foreign vessels and a weak American merchant marine; building branch factories abroad overcame the tariffs often enacted by foreign governments in retaliation for high American rates. To get branch banks to help conduct foreign business and American financiers to provide the long-term capital necessary to help Europe rebuild after the war were essentially tasks that required close cooperation with Congress and sympathetic federal bureaucracies, although the private sector was to continue to dominate efforts to expand export markets.

Since commercial and trade issues were settled more or less to the satisfaction of the largest manufacturers by the end of the war, they returned to the cultivation of foreign markets, an enterprise they conceived to be an essentially private effort. Indeed, because of the confusions of the wartime bureaucracy and the political paralysis of the last years of the Wilson presidency, the largest manufacturers became increasingly skeptical about the necessity of government assistance for their efforts. And one of the "lessons" taken from the World War I experience was clearly that of the dangers of politicizing international economic relations by business using government for its own purposes, or vice versa.

To the extent, then, that the largest producers depended on government, it was a result of the need to change policy which affected the general environment of conducting foreign business. With the smaller producer, however, government's provision of market information and representation abroad were more directly relevant to making sales overseas. For the most part, the larger producers had their own sources of market information and their own business employees to represent them abroad. The smaller manufacturers generally did not have a volume of sales that would justify hiring foreign employees to look after their interests and to gather market information. The government's services were more critical economically to smaller producers, although private collective efforts of trade associations, especially those of the NAM, were significant too.

On a more theoretical level, this study has been in many ways a comparative analysis of the relative rates of development of private economic bureaucracies, as opposed to those of government bureaucracies. The functions, specialization, and constituencies of these business and government institutions were obviously different, but this is an essential point to keep in mind when studying the interaction of business and government. Big business did not rely on the American government to further its interests in foreign markets. Anti-statist ideology and sentiments played a part, but fundamentally the independence of big business was a result of market conditions. The largest corporations sold abroad because of mass production, mass distribution processes based in many cases on technological and organizational advantages. Critical to making the most profitable use of technological and marketing advantages was the production of a continuing flow of products with low unit costs. As important to the largest firms as the speedy distribution of their products was frequent and accurate information about changes in the market for their goods. Governmental agencies did not contribute fundamentally to this economic process, although they could be of assistance at times.

Attention to bureaucracies' attainment of goals and the compatibility of institutions raises some questions about the work of others who have studied the interaction of business and government in the development of foreign markets and more generally in the consideration of the nature of the relationship between the U.S. government and business. Burton I. Kaufman's study of the relationship between business and government in the expansion of foreign trade overestimates the reliance of manufacturers, especially the largest, on the government. In his analysis coordination between business and government is too close. Joan Hoff Wilson portrays a relationship of considerably less coordination, but her study does not fully consider the question of the degree of business reliance on government or the significance of one institution for another. Ellis Hawley's much more subtle analyses of the general nature of the political economy of U.S. business-government relations do not apply well to those businessmen and bureaucrats considered here, although Hawley's ideas have proved useful in Michael Hogan's work on U.S. foreign policy toward resource management, communications, petroleum, and investment. Hawley's studies, like that of political scientist Grant McConnell, portray the development of a symbiotic relationship between parts of the federal bureaucracy and business, where both sides gain from the contacts. While there are elements of this kind of relationship in commercial policy and in the promotion of foreign trade, the relationship was more tenuous than that described by Hawley and McConnell. Big business especially was much less dependent on the governmental bureaucracies than the bureaucracies were on business support. Moreover, the relationship between business and government was not ongoing and growing. Contacts and cooperation were greater before U.S. entry into the war than after. It is clear, however, that the smaller producers were more dependent on the government than the larger for market information and representation abroad, services that could make the difference between whether or not a firm was able to complete a sale. The larger producers were more dependent on the government in the sense that it influenced the general environment in which they conducted business, although they were able to adjust by private means to hostile or inauspicious foreign and U.S. governmental policies toward their efforts.[4]

Why was it that closer relations did not develop between big businesses selling abroad and the government? The answer, I believe, is the result of both different institutional goals and rates of managerial "maturity." In the three decades before World War I there had been a managerial revolution in U.S. business. Mass distribution and mass production created a manufacturing sector of enormous productive power, concentration, and complexity. Low-cost production and distribution, along with a high degree of industrial concentration, gave industries producing oil, steel, machinery, processed food, and electrical equipment important advantages in developing foreign markets. The key to the advantages of mass production was the speed at which a high volume of output was produced and distributed. To create and then administer large mass-production, mass-distribution firms required the development of large private bureaucracies. While there were variations in the rates at which these bureaucracies grew and the degree of control they achieved, these firms developed methods of planning, administration, and fiscal control unmatched by organizations anywhere else in American society.

In comparative terms of the development of managerial structures, the large-scale corporation was more highly developed bureaucratically than the executive departments of the federal government. The specialization, the division of labor, and the economic rationality of the largest corporations made them fundamentally more advanced managerially than the government bureaucracies that came into contact with the larger firms in the development of foreign trade. By World

War I, major American corporations employed many thousands of employees worldwide. The levels of bureaucratic control were greater and the scale of operations more complex than anything undertaken by the U.S. government at the time. Then, too, most of the major corporations had a longer history as major bureaucratic institutions than the federal bureaucracies. The State Department was as old as the government, but it had not begun to modernize as a bureaucracy until the turn of the century. The Department of Commerce was not established until 1903, and it did not take on the size and significance of the State Department until the 1920s. As we have seen, the federal bureaucracies depended on the goodwill and cooperation of business when members of the executive agencies had to deal with the Congress. Both the departments of State and Commerce needed business support in disputes over budgets and "turf."

For many of the industries dominated by the large-scale firms, foreign markets represented an important part of their total sales. When foreign governments challenged them abroad, and it was fairly common after 1900, many of these firms responded not primarily by turning to government for assistance, but by employing foreign nationals to conduct their sales overseas, by building assembly plants to get around high tariffs, and by working patents in markets where they had to be worked. These solutions were managerially more consistent than turning to government. The largest firms needed, as much as possible, control of and predictability in their markets in order to keep a high volume of products flowing. The larger producers turned to government only when absolutely necessary, especially on the questions of the merchant marine and the right to combine to sell abroad. They built through the NFTC a group that would have access to the government over issues of policy that concerned them. But the economic strengths of those firms that first garnered significant sales abroad were the primary means for protecting overseas markets. To the largest producers government was important but not by any means the first step or the only step in developing and protecting foreign markets.

Finally, this study throws into high relief another important point about the relationship between business and government. The corporations, both the large and the small, had simple and more measurable goals to achieve than the governmental bureaucracies. Profit was an explicit goal for business. The governmental bureaucracies, especially at the Department of State, had much more diffuse goals than the business community. Equally important, they had fewer resources than the larger firms to achieve their objectives.

In short, the big business bureaucracies were clearly attuned to the goals that were to be achieved, and they had the bureaucratic apparatus and experience, as well as the resources, to begin to realize their goals. The dynamics of the relationship between business and government were determined by the dissimilarity of bureaucratic development and mission. The largest corporations especially responded to the forces of the market at home and abroad, and these forces were more important in determining their behavior and ultimately their attitudes than what Congress and the federal bureaucracy did or did not do. But government, to be sure, affected the behavior of business. In important ways, the Congress was of greater significance than the bureaucracies for the behavior of the manufacturers, for it determined the nature of the business environment in which foreign trade was to be conducted.

The federal bureaucracy itself, as we have seen, had its own reasons for supporting the expansion of American foreign trade. The departments of State and Commerce both sought the support of an interested business constituency. Manufacturers well served by these departments were inclined to support them before Congress as the bureaucracies tried to increase their responsibilities and appropriations. These efforts for returned favors were not by any means an entirely cynical ploy. The Department of State firmly believed that it needed to grow to handle the United States' increased role in the world more professionally. And the Department of Commerce defined its mission in terms of assisting the American business community. Because trade expansion was the interest of two major bureaucracies, the departments of Commerce and State, parts of the executive branch (especially at the middle levels where employees tended to serve for longer periods than in the top positions) made the expansion of foreign trade an almost constant concern. In many ways, then, the bureaucracy kept interest in trade expansion alive for the smaller producers whose desire to sell abroad fluctuated with demand in the domestic economy.

Thus there were important limits to business-government relations in the promotion of American exports of manufactured products. Contacts varied between the largest and smallest producers, between businessmen and different federal departments, and between Congress and the manufacturing community. Moreover, the relationships that developed were fluid. At times, firms and business associations worked closely with members of Congress or the bureaucracy, only to pull back as issues or personnel changed. It was the fluidity, or the tenuousness of the contacts, that characterized the structural relationship between business and government, and not the fact that the numbers of contacts increased between the early 1890s and 1921.

Appendixes

Appendix A
Industries in Major Industrial Groups
(According to Bureau of Labor Statistics Classes)

Manufactured Food
Meat packing and wholesale poultry
Processed dairy products
Canning, preserving, and freezing
Grain mill products
Bakery products
Miscellaneous food products
Sugar

Textiles
Spinning, weaving, and dyeing
Special textile products
Jute, linen, cordage, and twine
Canvas products
Apparel
House furnishing and other nonapparel

Chemicals
Industrial inorganic chemicals
Industrial organic chemicals
Plastic materials
Synthetic rubber
Synthetic fiber
Explosives and fireworks
Drugs and medicines
Soap and related products
Paints and allied products
Gum and wood chemicals
Fertilizers
Vegetable oils
Animal oils
Miscellaneous chemical industries

Petroleum and Coal
Petroleum products
Coke and products
Paving and roofing materials

185

Appendix A

Iron and Steel

Metal furniture
Blast furnaces
Steel works and rolling mills
Iron foundries
Steel foundries
Iron and steel forgings
Tin cans and tin ware
Cutlery
Tools and general hardware
Other hardware
Metal plumbing and vitreous fixtures
Heating equipment
Structural metal products
Boiler shop products and pipe bending
Metal stampings
Metal coating and engraving
Lighting fixtures
Fabricated wire products
Metal barrels, drums, etc.
Tubes and foils
Miscellaneous fabricated metal products
Steel springs
Nuts, bolts, screw machine products

Machinery

Steam engines and turbines
Internal combustion engines
Farm and industrial tractors
Farm equipment
Construction and mining machinery
Oil field machinery and tools
Machine tools and metalworking machinery
Cutting tools, jigs, and fixtures
Special industrial machinery
Pumps and compressors
Elevators and conveyors
Blowers and fans
Power transmission equipment
Other industrial machinery
Other commercial machinery and equipment
Refrigeration equipment
Valves and fittings
Ball and roller bearings
Machine shops
Wiring devices and graphite products
Electrical measuring instruments
Motors and generators
Transformers
Electrical control apparatus
Electrical welding apparatus
Electrical appliances
Industrial wire and cable

186

Engine electrical equipment
Electrical lamps
Radio and related products
Tubes
Communication equipment
Storage batteries
Primary batteries
X-ray apparatus

Transportation	Motor vehicles
	Truck trailers
	Automobile trailers
	Aircraft and parts
	Ships and boats
	Locomotives
	Railroad equipment
	Motorcycles and bicycles

Source: Mary Locke Eysenbach, *American Manufactured Exports, 1879–1914: A Study of Growth and Comparative Advantage* (New York, 1976), pp. 265–68.

Appendix B
The 100 Largest Industrial Corporations by Assets in 1909 and 1919

Rank in 1909	Company
1	United States Steel Corp.
2	Standard Oil Co. (New Jersey)
3	American Tobacco Co.
4	International Mercantile Marine Co.
5	Anaconda Co.
6	International Harvester Co.
7	Central Leather Co.
8	Pullman Co.
9	Armour & Co.
10	American Sugar Co.
11	United States Rubber Co.
12	American Smelting & Refining Co.
13	Singer Manufacturing Co.
14	Swift and Co.
15	Pittsburgh Consolidation Coal Co.
16	General Electric Co.
17	A.C.F. Industries, Inc.
18	Colorado Fuel and Iron Corp.
19	Corn Products Co.
20	New England Navigation Co.
21	American Can Co.
22	American Woolen Co.

Appendix B

Rank in 1909	Company
23	Lackawanna Steel Co.
24	Jones & Laughlin Steel Corp.
25	Westinghouse Electric Corp.
26	B.F. Goodrich Co.
27	Atlantic Gulf & West Indies S.S. Lines
28	Deere and Co.
29	Union Oil Co. of California
30	E.I. duPont de Nemours & Co.
31	Consolidation Coal Co.
32	Republic Steel Corp.
33	Virginia-Carolina Chemical Corp.
34	International Paper Co.
35	American Locomotive & Equipment Corp.
36	Bethlehem Steel Corp.
37	National Biscuit Co.
38	Cambria Steel Co.
39	Associated Oil Co.
40	National Distillers & Chemical Corp.
41	Calumet & Heels, Inc.
42	American Agricultural Chemical Co.
43	Crucible Steel Co. of America
44	Lake Superior Corp.
45	Allis-Chalmers Manufacturing Co.
46	Sears, Roebuck & Co.
47	U.S. Smelting, Refining & Mining Co.
48	United Copper Co.
49	National Lead Co.
50	Phelps Dodge Corp.
51	Lehigh Coal & Navigation Co.
52	International Steam Pump Co.
53	American Express Co.
54	Morris and Co.
55	Western Electric Co., Inc.
56	American Writing Paper Co.
57	Baldwin Locomotive Works
58	Copper Range Co.
59	United Fruit Co.
60	General Asphalt Co.
61	United Shoe Machinery Corp.
62	Borden Co.
63	Mexican Petroleum Co.
64	Goldfield Corp.
65	American Cotton Oil Co.
66	Wells Fargo & Co.
67	American Hide & Leather Co.
68	Lehigh Valley Coal Co.
69	Houston Oil of Texas
70	Guggenheim Exploration Co.

Appendix B

Rank in 1909	Company
71	Lehigh and Wilkes-Barre Coal Co.
72	Eastman Kodak Co.
73	Pressed Steel Car Co.
74	Railway Steel Spring Co.
75	Harbison-Walker Refractories Co.
76	Development Corp. of America
77	American Malting Co.
78	Greenwater Copper Mines & Smelter Co.
79	American Linseed Co.
80	Intercontinental Rubber Co.
81	Union Bag–Camp Paper Corp.
82	New Riber Co.
83	International Nickel Co. of Canada, Ltd.
84	U.S. Cast Iron Pipe & Foundry Co.
85	Chicago Junction Railways & Union Stock Yards Co.
86	American Ice Co.
87	U.S. Realty & Improvement Co.
88	New York Dock Railway
89	National Enameling & Stamping Co.
90	Pittsburgh Plate Glass Co.
91	Schwarzchild and Sulzberger Co.
92	Pennsylvania Steel Co.
93	Tide Water Oil Co.
94	International Salt Co.
95	Texaco, Inc.
96	General Cigar Co., Inc.
97	Cudahy Packing Co.
98	Union Typewriter Co.
99	Allied Chemical & Dye Corp.
100	American Steel Foundries, Inc.

Rank in 1909	Rank in 1919	Company
1	1	United States Steel Corp.
2	2	Standard Oil Co. (New Jersey)
9	3	Armour & Co.
14	4	Swift & Co.
–	5	General Motors Corp.
36	6	Bethlehem Steel Corp.
–	7	Ford Motor Co.
11	8	United States Rubber Co.
–	9	Socony Mobil Oil Co., Inc.
–	10	Midvale Steel and Ordnance
16	11	General Electric Co.
4	12	International Mercantile Marine Co.
6	13	International Harvester Co.
5	14	Anaconda Co.

Rank in 1909	Rank in 1919	Company
–	15	Sinclair Oil Corp.
95	16	Texaco, Inc.
12	17	American Smelting & Refining Co.
30	18	E.I. duPont de Nemours & Co.
3	19	American Tobacco Co.
–	20	Union Carbide Corp.
50	21	Phelps Dodge Corp.
–	22	Magnolia Petroleum Co.
26	23	B.F. Goodrich Co.
–	24	Standard Oil Co. of California
24	25	Jones & Laughlin Steel Corp.
8	26	Pullman Co.
15	27	Pittsburgh Consolidation Coal Co.
25	28	Westinghouse Electric Corp.
49	29	Sears, Roebuck & Co.
–	30	Standard Oil Co. (Indiana)
–	31	Liggett and Myers Tobacco Co.
–	32	Chile Copper Co.
59	33	United Fruit Co.
10	34	American Sugar Co.
7	35	Central Leather Co.
–	36	Gulf Oil Corp.
13	37	Singer Manufacturing Co.
17	38	A.C.F. Industries, Inc.
19	39	Corn Products Co.
–	40	Kennecott Copper Corp.
21	41	American Can Co.
31	42	Consolidation Coal Co.
–	43	Aluminum Co. of America
22	44	American Woolen Co.
–	45	Pure Oil Co.
–	46	Prairie Oil and Gas Co.
43	47	Crucible Steel Co. of America
–	48	Wilson and Co., Inc.
32	49	Republic Steel Corp.
33	50	Virginia-Carolina Chemical Corp.
–	51	Goodyear Tire & Rubber Co.
42	52	American Agricultural Chemical Co.
–	53	Cuba Cane Sugar Corp.
–	54	Youngstown Sheet and Tube Co.
55	55	Western Electric Co., Inc.
54	56	Morris and Co.
–	57	R.J. Reynolds Tobacco Co.
41	58	Calumet & Heels, Inc.
27	59	Atlantic Gulf & West Indies S.S. Lines
–	60	Great Northern Iron Ore Properties
23	61	Lackawanna Steel Co.
–	62	Atlantic Refining Co.
–	63	Procter & Gamble Co.

Appendix B

Rank in 1909	Rank in 1919	Company
35	64	American Locomotive & Equipment Corp.
97	65	Cudahy Packing Co.
–	66	Steel and Tube Co. of America
29	67	Union Oil Co. of California
–	68	F.W. Woolworth & Co.
72	69	Eastman Kodak Co.
–	70	P. Lorillard Co.
–	71	Studebaker Corp.
49	72	National Lead Co.
34	73	International Paper Co.
51	74	Lehigh Coal & Navigation Co.
28	75	Deere and Co.
18	76	Colorado Fuel and Iron Corp.
–	77	Ohio Oil Co.
47	78	U.S. Smelting, Refining & Mining Co.
–	79	Vacuum Oil Co.
–	80	Utah Cooper Co.
61	81	United Shoe Machinery Corp.
37	82	National Biscuit Co.
63	83	Mexican Petroleum Co.
57	84	Baldwin Locomotive Works
–	85	Firestone Tire & Rubber Co.
–	86	Midwest Refining Co.
–	87	Montgomery Ward & Co., Inc.
39	88	Associated Oil Co.
–	89	Libby, McNeill & Libby
–	90	Maxwell Motor Co., Inc.
–	91	Crane Co.
83	92	International Nickel Co. of Canada, Ltd.
–	93	Packard Motor Car Co.
65	94	American Cotton Oil Co.
–	95	Greene Cananea Copper Co.
45	96	Allis-Chalmers Manufacturing Co.
–	97	Pierce Oil Corp.
93	98	Tide Water Oil Co.
–	99	Inland Steel Co.
99	100	Allied Chemical & Dye Corp.

Source: A. D. H. Kaplan, *Big Enterprise in a Competitive System* (rev. ed.; Washington, D.C., 1964), pp. 140–43.

Notes

Preface

1. For the statistics on export trade, see U.S. Department of Commerce, Bureau of the Census, *Historical Statistics of the United States, Colonial Times to 1957* (Washington, D.C., 1961), p. 544; William Appleman Williams, *The Tragedy of American Diplomacy* (rev. ed.; New York, 1962); idem, *The Roots of the Modern American Empire: A Study of the Growth and Shaping of Social Consciousness in a Marketplace Economy* (New York, 1969); Walter LaFeber, *The New Empire: An Interpretation of American Expansion, 1860-1898* (Ithaca, N.Y., 1963); Carl P. Parrini, *Heir to Empire: United States Economic Diplomacy, 1916-1923* (Pittsburgh, 1969); Burton I. Kaufman, *Efficiency and Expansion: Foreign Trade Organization in the Wilson Administration, 1913-1921* (Westport, Conn., 1974); Jeffrey J. Safford, *Wilsonian Maritime Diplomacy, 1913-1921* (New Brunswick, N.J., 1978). Also see doctoral dissertations by Paul Philip Abrahams, "The Foreign Expansion of American Finance and Its Relationship to the Foreign Economic Policies of the United States, 1907-1921" (Ph.D. diss., University of Wisconsin, 1967) and Robert H. Van Meter, "The United States and European Recovery, 1918-1923: A Study of Public Policy and Private Finance" (Ph.D. diss., University of Wisconsin, 1971). Revisionist studies prompted a lively scholarly debate. Two penetrating critics are Paul S. Holbo and the English scholar J. A. Thompson. See Paul S. Holbo, "Economics, Emotion, and Expansion: An Emerging Foreign Policy," in H. Wayne Morgan, ed., *The Gilded Age* (Syracuse, 1970), pp. 199–221, and J. A. Thompson, "William Appleman Williams and the 'American Empire,'" *Journal of American Studies* 7 (April 1973): 91–104.

2. Kaufman, *Efficiency and Expansion*, p. xvi.

3. I am not alone in my view of Kaufman's analysis. Michael J. Hogan criticizes Kaufman for his "uncomplicated emphasis" on government's role in trade expansion and for ignoring attempts to limit government's intrusion into private affairs. See Michael J. Hogan, *Informal Entente: The Private Structure of Cooperation in Anglo-American Economic Diplomacy, 1918-1928* (Columbia, Mo., 1977), pp. 8–9.

4. Richard H. K. Vietor, "Businessmen and the Political Economy: The Railroad Rate Controversy of 1905," *Journal of American History* 64 (June 1977): 47–66. Vietor emphasizes the importance of changes in the market economy to businessmen's political activity.

5. Thomas J. McCormick, "State of American Diplomatic History," in Herbert J. Bass, ed., *State of American History* (Chicago, 1970), pp. 119–41. McCormick takes note of the importance of studying the role and influence of private groups on American foreign relations.

6. For a full discussion of the applicability of Parsonian sociological analysis to political economy, see William H. Becker, "The Political Economy of American Expansionism, 1898-1920: A Parsonian Perspective," *Proceedings of the Program of the American Historical Association Meetings*, December 1977 (Ann Arbor, Mich., 1978). Parsons's theory has devel-

oped over a long period of time, although there are several questions that recur. Of most use for this study was Talcott Parsons and Neil Smelser, *Economy and Society* (Glencoe, Ill., 1957). Other important theoretical works include Parsons's *Toward a General Theory of Action* (Cambridge, Mass., 1951), *The Social System* (Glencoe, Ill., 1951), *Essays in Sociological Theory* (rev. ed.; Glencoe, Ill., 1954), and *Structure and Process in Modern Societies* (Glencoe, Ill., 1960). Parsons's early work *The Structure of Social Action* (New York, 1937) is an extended analysis and criticism of other major social theorists. Parsons himself dealt with applying his analysis to organizations in two pieces, "A Sociological Approach to the Theory of Organizations," *Administrative Science Quarterly* 1 (June–September 1956): 63–85 and 225–39. A useful guide to the theoretical work of Parsons is Max Black, ed., *The Social Theories of Talcott Parsons: A Critical Examination* (Englewood Cliffs, N.J., 1961). Max Weber's classic analysis of bureaucracy is to be found in *From Max Weber: Essays in Bureaucracy,* ed. and trans. H. H. Gerth and C. Wright Mills (New York, 1958), pp. 196–264.

The argument and initial analyses of the product life cycle theorists of international trade can be found in Raymond Vernon, "International Investment and International Trade in the Product Life Cycle," *Quarterly Journal of Economics* 80 (May 1966): 190–207. Louis T. Wells, Jr., ed., *The Product Life Cycle and International Trade* (Boston, 1972) is a highly useful volume which applies Vernon's ideas; the volume also provides a guide to other literature on the subject. Raymond Vernon, ed., *The Technology Factor in International Trade* (New York, 1970), explores in detail one of the major reasons for changing patterns of international trade. See also Staffan Burenstam Linder, *An Essay on Trade and Transformation* (New York, 1961), pp. 82–123.

One

1. Mary Locke Eysenbach, *American Manufactured Exports, 1879–1914: A Study of Growth and Comparative Advantage* (New York, 1976), p. 8; William Arthur Lewis, "International Competition in Manufactures," *American Economic Review* 47 (May 1957): 579.

2. W. S. Woytinsky and E. S. Woytinsky, *World Commerce and Government: Trends and Outlook* (New York, 1955), pp. 40–41.

3. Eysenbach, *American Manufactured Exports*, pp. 2–5; Alex F. McCalla, "Protectionism in International Agricultural Trade, 1850–1968," *Agricultural History* 43 (July 1969): 329–43; J. H. Richter, "The Place of Agriculture in International Trade Policy," *Canadian Journal of Agricultural Economics* 12 (January 1964): 1–9.

4. William Ashworth, *A Short History of the International Economy Since 1850* (3d ed.; London, 1975), pp. 191–93; three other useful studies of international economic life are A. G. Kenwood and Alan L. Lougheed, *The Growth of the International Economy, 1820–1960* (London, 1971); John B. Condliffe, *The Commerce of Nations* (London, 1951); Alfred Maizels, *Industrial Growth and World Trade* (Cambridge, 1963). A masterful economic history of Western Europe is David S. Landes, *The Unbound Prometheus: Technological Change and Industrial Development in Western Europe from 1750 to the Present* (London, 1969).

5. Ashworth, *Short History*, pp. 204–7; Rondo E. Cameron, *France and the Economic Development of Europe, 1800–1914* (Princeton, N.J., 1961), pp. 485–510; Arthur R. Conan, *Capital Imports into Sterling Countries* (London, 1960), pp. 82–83; Herbert Feis, *Europe the World's Banker, 1870–1914* (New Haven, Conn., 1930), pp. 3–32; John H. Dunning, *Studies in International Investment* (London, 1970), pp. 143–89.

6. Ashworth, *Short History*, pp. 207–10; Werner Schlöte, *British Overseas Trade from 1700 to the 1930's,* trans. W. O. Henderson and W. H. Chaloner (Oxford, 1952), pp. 79–105; Albert H. Imlah, *Economic Elements in the Pax Britannica* (Cambridge, Mass., 1958), pp. 42–81; S. B. Saul, *Studies in British Overseas Trade, 1870–1914* (Liverpool, 1960), pp. 17–64; D. C. M. Platt, *Latin America and British Trade, 1806–1914* (London, 1972),

pp. 274–313; idem, *Finance, Trade, and Politics in British Foreign Policy, 1815–1914* (Oxford, 1968), pp. 85–101.

7. Ashworth, *Short History*, pp. 210–11; Imlah, *Economic Elements*, pp. 156–98; Saul, *Studies in British Overseas Trade*, pp. 65–89; William M. Scammell, *The London Discount Market* (London, 1968), pp. 159–91; Arthur I. Bloomfield, *Monetary Policy under the International Gold Standard, 1880–1914* (New York, 1958), pp. 29 ff.

8. Ashworth, *Short History*, pp. 212–15; Imlah, *Economic Elements*, pp. 156–98; Scammell, *Discount Market*, pp. 159–91; Platt, *Finance, Trade and Politics*, pp. 7–53.

9. Ashworth, *Short History*, pp. 215–16; Eysenbach, *American Manufactured Exports*, pp. 2–5; Woytinsky and Woytinsky, *World Commerce*, pp. 10–12, 33–52; Maizels, *Industrial Growth and World Trade*, pp. 79–84.

10. Ashworth, *Short History*, pp. 226–28; Woytinsky and Woytinsky, *World Commerce*, pp. 32–52; Schlote, *British Overseas Trade*, pp. 79–105; Platt, *Latin America and British Trade*, pp. 305–13.

11. Ashworth, *Short History*, pp. 228–31; Woytinsky and Woytinsky, *World Commerce*, pp. 12, 40–44, 199–200, 743–50.

12. Ashworth, *Short History*, pp. 228–31.

13. Eysenbach, *American Manufactured Exports*, p. 40.

14. U.S. Department of Commerce, Bureau of the Census, *Historical Statistics of the United States, Colonial Times to 1957* (Washington, D.C., 1961), p. 544; hereafter cited as *Historical Statistics*.

15. Tom Kemp, *Industrialization in Nineteenth-Century Europe* (London, 1969), pp. 81–118, 179–203; Lewis, "International Competition," pp. 578–87; William Arthur Lewis and P. J. O'Leary, "Secular Swings in Production and Trade, 1870–1913," *Manchester School of Economics and Social Studies* 23 (May 1955): 113–52; Paul Gordon Lauren, *Diplomats and Bureaucrats: The First Institutional Responses to Twentieth-Century Diplomacy in France and Germany* (Stanford, Calif., 1976), pp. 154–77; Saul, *Studies in British Overseas Trade*, pp. 105–33.

16. Eysenbach, *American Manufactured Exports*, p. 6, note 2, pp. 126–27.

17. Eysenbach, *American Manufactured Exports*, pp. 40–42.

18. *Historical Statistics*, pp. 544–45; Eysenbach, *American Manufactured Exports*, pp. 2–3, 40. Robert E. Lipsey, *Price and Quantity Trends in the Foreign Trade of the United States* (Princeton, N.J., 1963), p. 142; the Fisher price indexes for all exports were 102 for 1879–81 and 100 for 1912–14. See Lipsey for a full discussion of price and quantity indexes of export trade; also see his Appendix A.

19. Jeffrey G. Williamson, *Late Nineteenth-Century American Development: A General Equilibrium History* (New York, 1974), pp. 202–20.

20. Eysenbach, *American Manufactured Exports*, pp. 40–42.

21. Ibid., pp. 5–6; League of Nations, Economic Intelligence Service, *Industrialization and Foreign Trade* (New York, 1945), p. 13; Lipsey, *Price and Quantity Trends*, pp. 40–44; Lewis, "International Competition," p. 579.

22. Eysenbach, *American Manufactured Exports*, p. 6, note 2, pp. 126–27.

23. U.S. Department of Commerce, Bureau of the Census, *Statistical Abstract of the United States, 1925* (Washington, D.C., 1926), p. 449.

24. Alfred D. Chandler, Jr., "The Structure of American Industry in the Twentieth Century: A Historical Overview," *Business History Review* 43 (Autumn 1969): 290–93, and A. D. H. Kaplan, *Big Enterprise in a Competitive System* (rev. ed.; Washington, D.C., 1964), pp. 140–42.

25. Chandler, "The Structure of American Industry," pp. 291–93.

26. *Historical Statistics*, p. 544; Lipsey, *Price and Quantity Trends*, pp. 62–78; Ilse Mintz, *American Exports during Business Cycles, 1879–1958*, National Bureau of Economic Research, Occasional Paper 76 (New York, 1961), pp. 13–19, 67; William Appleman Williams,

The Tragedy of American Diplomacy (rev. ed.: New York, 1962), pp. 22–23; Walter LaFeber, *The New Empire: An Interpretation of American Expansion, 1860-1898* (Ithaca, N.Y., 1963), pp. 60, 150–54, 176, 412.

27. Williamson, *General Equilibrium History*, pp. 202–20.

28. Staffan Burenstam Linder, *An Essay on Trade and Transformation* (New York, 1961), pp. 82–109; Louis T. Wells, Jr., ed., *The Product Life Cycle and International Trade* (Boston, 1972), pp. 11–15; E. H. Phelps Brown and M. H. Browne, *A Century of Pay* (London, 1968), pp. 41–66.

29. Lewis, "International Competition," p. 579.

30. Eysenbach, (*American Manufactured Exports*, pp. 92–138) sees the supply side as the most important aspect of the development of exports, although she attributes great importance to demand too. Much depends on whether one takes a long-term or a short-term perspective. Over the long run, supply seems to be a major factor, but over the short term, demand seems more important in determining prices and quantities exported. See Lipsey, *Price and Quantity Trends* pp. 62–78.

31. Department of State, *Review of the World's Commerce: Introductory to Commercial Relations of the United States with Foreign Countries during the Year 1900* (Washington, D.C., 1901), pp. 21–49; New England Cotton Manufacturers Association, *Transactions*, 1896, pp. 260–63; 1897, pp. 268–69, 271–78, 284 ff., 322–25; 1898, pp. 227–32; 1899, pp. 96; 1900, pp. 181–82; 1902, pp. 216–17, 228–230, 358, 373–74; 1903, pp. 422–37; Matthew Simon and David E. Novack, "Some Dimensions of the American Commercial Invasion of Europe, 1871–1914," *Journal of Economic History* 24 (December 1964): 591–605.

Two

1. Alfred D. Chandler, Jr. *The Visible Hand: The Managerial Revolution in American Business* (Cambridge, Mass., 1977), pp. 240–84; Duncan McDougall, "Machine Tool Output, 1861–1900," in *Output, Employment, and Productivity in the United States after 1800*, National Bureau of Economic Research, Studies in Income and Wealth, no. 30 (New York, 1966), pp. 497–98, 500–512; Ross Robertson, "Changing Patterns of Metalworking Machinery, 1860–1920," in *Output, Employment and Productivity*, pp. 479–96; Nathan Rosenberg, "Technological Change in the Machine Tool Industry, 1840–1910," *Journal of Economic History* 23 (December, 1963): 414–43.

2. Chandler, pp. 240–44, 285–86.

3. Chandler, pp. 249–50, 290–92; Richard B. Tennant, *The American Cigarette Industry* (New Haven, Conn., 1950), pp. 17–63; Glenn Porter and Harold Livesay, *Merchants and Manufacturers: Studies in the Changing Structure of Nineteenth Century Marketing* (Baltimore, 1973), pp. 197–227; Patrick G. Porter, "Origins of the American Tobacco Company," *Business History Review* 43 (Spring 1969): 59–76; Nannie May Tilley, *The Bright-Tobacco Industry, 1860-1929* (Chapel Hill, N.C., 1948), pp. 573–76.

4. Chandler, pp. 250, 292–93; Herbert Manchester, *The History of the Diamond Match Company* (New York, 1935), pp. 60–64; Ohio Columbus Barber, "The Match Industry," in Chauncey Depew, ed., *1795-1895: One Hundred Years of American Commerce* (New York, 1895), pp. 460–65; Mira Wilkins, *The Emergence of Multinational Enterprise: American Business Abroad from the Colonial Era to 1914* (Cambridge, Mass., 1970), pp. 91–93, 101, 177, 194.

5. Reese W. Jenkins, *Images and Enterprise: Technology and the American Photographic Industry, 1839-1925* (Baltimore, 1975), pp. 96–179; Reese W. Jenkins, "Technology in the Market: George Eastman and the Origin of Amateur Photography," *Technology and Culture* 16 (January 1975): 1–19; Wilkins, *Emergence*, pp. 61, 66, 212.

6. Chandler, pp. 252–53; Charles B. Kuhlman, "Processing Agricultural Products after 1860," in Harold F. Williamson, ed., *The Growth of the American Economy* (2d ed.; New York, 1951), pp. 437–40; Arthur E. Marquette, *Brands, Trademarks and Good Will* (New York, 1967), pp. 18–19, 30–33, 40–77; Harrison J. Thornton, *The History of the Quaker Oats Company* (Chicago, 1933), pp. 45–71; John Stork and Walter D. Teague, *Flour for Man's Bread* (Minneapolis, 1952), pp. 255–74.

7. Alfred D. Chandler, Jr., "The Beginnings of 'Big Business' in American Industry," *Business History Review* 33 (Spring, 1959): 1–10; Chandler, *Visible Hand*, pp. 299-301; Mary Yeager Kujovich, "The Dynamics of Oligopoly in the Meat Packing Industry: An Historical Analysis," (Ph.D. diss., Johns Hopkins University, 1973), pp. 1270–52; Mary Yeager Kujovich, "The Refrigerator Car and the Growth of the American Dressed Beef Industry," *Business History Review* 44 (Winter 1970): 460–82; U.S. Department of Commerce and Labor, Bureau of Corporations, *Beef Industry. Report of the Commissioner of Corporations on the Beef Industry, March 3, 1905* (Washington, D.C., 1905), pp. 15–70; "Armour and Company, 1867-1938," in N. S. B. Gras and Henrietta Larson, *Case Book in American Business History* (New York, 1939), pp. 623-43.

8. Bureau of Corporations, *Beef Industry*, pp. xix, 15–70, 270–71, 277–78; Kujovich, "Dynamics of Oligopoly," pp. 308–17; Wilkins, *Emergence*, pp. 189–90; Chandler, *Visible Hand*, pp. 391–401.

9. Harold F. Williamson and Arnold R. Daum, *The American Petroleum Industry: The Age of Illumination, 1859-1899* (Evanston, Ill., 1959), pp. 202–31, 252–86, 463–87; Ralph W. Hidy and Muriel E. Hidy, *Pioneering in Big Business, 1882-1911* (New York, 1955), pp. 71-73, 100-107.

10. Depew, *American Commerce*, pp. 438–40, 451–53; Alfred S. Eichner, *The Emergence of Oligopoly: Sugar Refining as a Case Study* (Baltimore, 1969), pp. 32–39; Thomas C. Cochran, *The Pabst Brewing Company* (New York, 1948), pp. 54, 73–74, 95. Chandler noted (*Visible Hand*, p. 320) that he could find only eight trusts that operated in the national market. Six of the eight, however, dominated their industries for many decades. These successful trusts were in industries devoted to the refining of petroleum, cottonseed oil, linseed oil, sugar, whiskey, and lead.

11. Chandler, *Visible Hand*, pp. 326–27; Victor S. Clark, *History of Manufactures in the United States, 1869-1893* 3 vols.; (New York, 1929), 2:519–23; R. Chaney, "The Cotton Seed Oil Industry," in Depew, *American Commerce* pp. 452–55; Alfred Lief, *"It Floats": The Story of Procter and Gamble* (New York, 1958), pp. 80–112.

12. William P. Thompson, "The Lead Industry," in Depew, *American Commerce*, p. 440; Wilkins, *Emergence*, p. 185; Chandler, *Visible Hand*, p. 327.

13. Charles H. Fitch, "Report on Manufacture of Hardware, Cutlery and Edge Tools, also Saws and Files," in U.S. Department of Interior, U.S. Census Office, *Report on the Manufactures of the United States at the Tenth Census* (Washington, D.C., 1883), pp. 705–27; *Hardware Dealer, A Magazine of Ideas and Information for Hardwaremen*, October 1896, p. 551, and July 1895, p. 66; *American Artisan*, 1 November 1884, p. 17; *Hardware, Review of the American Hardware Market*, 10 May 1891, p. 19, and 10 January 1892, p. 21.

14. Charles H. Fitch, "Report on the Manufacture of Interchangeable Mechanisms," in *Report on the Manufactures of the United States at the Tenth Census*, pp. 611–704; Chandler, *Visible Hand*, pp. 272–81.

15. Andrew B. Jack, "The Channels of Distribution for the Innovation: The Sewing Machine Industry in America," *Explorations in Entrepreneurial History* 8 (February 1957): 113–41; Robert B. Davies, "Peacefully Working to Conquer the World: The Singer Manufacturing Company in Foreign Markets, 1854–1889," *Business History Review* 43 (Autumn 1969): 299–346; idem, *Peacefully Working to Conquer the World: Singer Sewing Machine in World Markets, 1854-1920* (New York, 1976), pp. 59–78, 140–41; Wilkins, *Emergence*, pp. 37–45.

16. U.S. Bureau of Corporations, *Report of the Commissioner of Corporations on International Harvester* (Washington, D.C., 1913), pp. 3, 26, 55–56, 71–72, 188–89, 333–40; Cyrus Hall McCormick III, *The Century of the Reaper* (New York, 1933), pp. 45–53, 60, 81–83; William T. Hutchinson, *Cyrus Hall McCormick* (2 vols.; New York, 1935), 2:698–718, 728; Chandler, *Visible Hand*, pp. 305–7.

17. Wilkins, *Emergence*, pp. 213–14; Samuel Crowther, *John H. Patterson, Pioneer in Industrial Welfare* (New York, 1926), pp. 87–119, 264–84; Isaac F. Marcosson, *Wherever Men Trade* (New York, 1945), pp. 33–46; Chandler, *Visible Hand*, pp. 307–8.

18. Crowther, *Industrial Welfare,* pp. 213–14; Marcosson, *Wherever Men Trade,* pp. 33–46; Chandler, *Visible Hand,* pp. 307–9; Davies, *Peacefully Working,* pp. 55–172.

19. L. A. Peterson, *Elisha Graves Otis, 1811–1861* (New York, 1945), pp. 13–16; Michael Massouth, "Technological and Managerial Innovation: The Johnson Company, 1823–1898," *Business History Review* 50 (Spring 1976): 46–68; Wilkins, *Emergence,* pp. 46, 51, 200.

20. Porter and Livesay, *Merchants and Manufacturers*, pp. 182–83; Wilkins, *Emergence*, pp. 212–13; Walter Geist, *Allis-Chalmers: A Brief History of 103 Years of Production* (New York, 1950), pp. 12–14, 17.

21. Chandler, *Visible Hand*, pp. 311–12.

22. Wilkins, *Emergence*, p. 59; Prout, *A Life of George Westinghouse* (New York, 1921), pp. 62, 113, 262–63.

23. Wilkins, *Emergence*, pp. 95–96; Prout, *Westinghouse*, pp. 263–64, 271–72.

24. Wilkins, *Emergence*, pp. 52–59; Frank L. Dyer and Thomas C. Martin, *Edison: His Life and Inventions* (2 vols.; New York, 1929), 2:376; U.S. Department of State, Bureau of Foreign Commerce, *Commercial Relations of the United States with Foreign Countries, 1902* (2 vols; Washington, D.C., 1902), 1:688–89.

25. Wilkins, *Emergence*, pp. 58–59, 66–67; Harold C. Passer, *The Electrical Manufacturers, 1875-1900: A Study in Competition, Entrepreneurship, Technical Change, and Economic Growth* (Cambridge, Mass., 1953), pp. 7–8, 328–29; John W. Hammond, *Men and Volts: The Story of General Electric* (Philadelphia, 1941), pp. 57, 69–70, 91.

26. Chandler, *Visible Hand*, p. 312.

27. Ibid., pp. 312–13; Wilkins, *Emergence*, pp. 155–59, 212; Charles M. Wilson, *Empire in Green and Gold* (New York, 1947), pp. 168–73; Charles H. Candler, *Asa Griggs Candler* (Atlanta, 1950), pp. 95–186.

28. Wilkins, *Emergence*, p. 213; Chandler, *Visible Hand*, pp. 313–14; Porter and Livesay, *Merchants and Manufactures*, pp. 183, 193.

29. Chandler, *Visible Hand*, p. 314; Porter and Livesay, *Merchants and Manufacturers*, pp. 180–96; Mira Wilkins, "An American Enterprise Abroad: American Radiator Company in Europe, 1895–1914," *Business History Review* 43 (Autumn 1969): 326–27.

30. Passer, *Electrical Manufacturers*, pp. 321–34.

31. Wilkins, *Emergence*, p. 29; Herbert N. Casson, *Cyrus Hall McCormick, His Life and Work* (Chicago, 1909), pp. 123–37.

32. Helen M. Kramer, "Harvesters and High Finance: Formation of the International Harvester Company," *Business History Review* 38 (Autumn 1964): 283–86.

33. Ibid., pp. 286–89.

34. Ibid.; Bureau of Corporations, *International Harvester*, pp. 71, 333–40.

35. Kramer, "Harvesters and High Finance," pp. 297–99.

36. Davies, *Peacefully Working*, pp. 114–15.

37. Ibid., pp. 95–96.

38. Ibid., pp. 101–3, 109–13, 124–31.

39. Hidy and Hidy, *Pioneering*, pp. 259–68; Williamson and Daum, *Age of Illumination*, pp. 661–76.

40. U.S. Department of Commerce and Labor, Bureau of Corporations, *Report of the Commissioner of Corporations on the Steel Industry* (Washington, D.C., 1911), 1: 63–85, 407; American Iron and Steel Association, *Bulletin*, 2 January 1895, p. 4, 10 March 1895, p. 59, 20 November 1895, p. 261, 1 October 1895, p. 221, 1 November 1895, p. 245, 10 April 1896, pp. 84, 86, 10 June 1895, p. 133, 1 May 1896, p. 101, 30 January 1895, p. 29, 2 January 1895, p. 15, 9 January 1895, p. 12, 1 June 1895, p. 125, 1 July 1895, p. 150, 20 September 1895, p. 211, 10 March 1895, p. 62, 10 February 1896, p. 37; Charles E. Edgertown, "The Wire Nail Association of 1895–96," *Political Science Quarterly* 12 (1897): 246–72, and *U.S.* v. *U.S. Steel Corporation*, 223 U.S. 55 (1915), both reprinted in William Z. Ripley, ed., *Trusts, Pools and Corporations* (Boston, 1916), pp. 46–72, 164–69; U.S. Industrial Commission, *Reports of the Industrial Commission on Trusts and Industrial Combinations* (19 vols.; Washington, D.C., 1900–1902), 1: 199–207; Victor S. Clark, *History of Manufactures in the United States* (3 vols.; New York, 1929), 17–88; Peter Temin, *Iron and Steel in Nineteenth-Century America: An Economic Inquiry* (Cambridge, Mass., 1964), pp. 175–92; Wallace E. Belcher, "Industrial Pooling Agreements," *Quarterly Journal of Economics* 19 (November 1904): 111–23; Burton J. Hendrick, *The Life of Andrew Carnegie* (2 vols.; New York, 1932), 2: 50–51; Joseph F. Wall, *Andrew Carnegie* (New York, 1970), pp. 767–68.

41. Ralph L. Nelson, *Merger Movements in American Industry, 1895–1956*, National Bureau of Economic Research, General Series, no. 66 (Princeton, N.J., 1959), pp. 37–40; U.S. Industrial Commission, *Reports of the Industrial Commission*, vols. 1 and 13, passim; Eichner, *Emergence of Oligopoly,* pp. 1–25; Alfred D. Chandler, Jr., *Strategy and Structure: Chapters in the History of the American Industrial Enterprise* (Cambridge, Mass., 1962), pp. 22–43.

42. Hendrick, *Andrew Carnegie,* 2:7–20, 24–34; Bureau of Corporations, *Steel Industry*, p. 76; Melvin I. Urofsky, *Big Steel and the Wilson Administration: A Study in Business-Government Relations* (Columbus, Ohio, 1969), pp. xxi–xxii; Andrew Carnegie to John A. Leishman, 7 May 1896, Carnegie Papers, vol. 37, Library of Congress; A. M. Moreland to Charles M. Schwab, 6 December 1897, Carnegie Papers, vol. 46; "Committee Report of the Representatives of...Rail Pool," 15 November 1897, Carnegie Papers, vol. 46; Chandler, "Beginnings of 'Big Business,'" pp. 18–19; Temin, *Iron and Steel,* pp. 157–59, 171–74, 180–85, 190–93.

43. *Iron Age,* 8 March 1895, p. 511, 19 July 1900, p. 47, 18 March 1897, p. 6, 15 July 1897, p. 20, 4 March 1897, p. 8, 19 November 1903, pp. 33–34, 5 July 1900, pp. 42–43; American Iron and Steel Association, *Bulletin,* 20 February 1896, p. 11; U.S. Industrial Commission, *Reports of the Industrial Commission,* 13:728, 731; *U.S.* v. *U.S. Steel Corporation,* pp. 134–35; House Committee on Investigation of the United States Steel Corporation, *Hearings on United States Steel Corporation,* 62d Cong., 1st sess. (1911), pp. 2720–22. (These hearings are often referred to as the Stanley hearings, bearing the name of the chairman of the committee. Hereafter cited as Stanley Hearings.)

44. *Iron Age,* 26 July 1900, p. 37, 4 March 1897, pp. 17–18, 15 October 1903, pp. 22–23.

45. Ibid., 4 January 1900, p. 22, 5 July 1900, pp. 42–43, 2 August 1900, pp. 40–41; U.S. Industrial Commission, *Reports of the Industrial Commission,* 13:725–72; Stanley Hearings, pp. 2725–30, 2747–48.

46. U.S. Industrial Commission, *Reports of the Industrial Commission,* 1:192–99, 955–56, 998–1001; U.S. Department of Commerce, Bureau of Corporations Records, Statement of American Steel Hoop Company, May 6, 1910, Record Group 122, File No. 2604, 41, National Archives; "First Annual Report of Federal Steel Company for Fiscal Year Ended, December 31, 1899," p. 51, Bureau of Corporations Records, File No. 1938.

47. William H. Becker, "Foreign Markets for Iron and Steel, 1893–1913: A New Perspec-

tive on the Williams School of Diplomatic History," *Pacific Historical Review* 44 (May 1975): 233–62; Wall, *Carnegie,* pp. 585–86.

48. Bureau of Corporations, *Steel Industry*, pp. 98–106; Wall, *Carnegie*, pp. 767–73.

49. Urofsky, *Big Steel*, p. xxix; Abraham Berglund, *The United States Steel Corporation: A Study of the Growth and Influence of Combination in the Iron and Steel Industry* (New York, 1907), pp. 78, 95–98; *U.S.* v. *U.S. Steel*, pp. 160–61; U.S. Industrial Commission, *Reports of the Industrial Commission*, 1:173–77; Bureau of Corporations, *Steel Industry*, pp. 63, 79–81; Chandler, "Beginnings of 'Big Business,'" pp. 22–23.

50. Abraham Berglund, "The United States Steel Corporation and Price Stabilization," *Quarterly Journal of Economics* 38 (1923): 5–6, 14–15, 19; idem, "The United States Steel Corporation and Industrial Stabilization," *Quarterly Journal of Economics* 38 (1924): 609–16.

51. Chandler, *Visible Hand*, pp. 33–35; Chandler, "Beginnings of 'Big Business,'" pp. 1–30; Glenn Porter, *The Rise of Big Business, 1860–1910* (New York, 1973), pp. 54–84.

52. Porter, *Rise of Big Business*, pp. 79–84; Shaw Livermore, "The Success of Industrial Mergers," *Quarterly Journal of Economics* 50 (1935): 68–95; Chandler, *Visible Hand*, pp. 336–38.

53. Lightweight machine tools are of two kinds: one type is the metal cutting (grinding and milling) machine and the other is the metal forming machine (a press or hammer). Heavier and more specialized machines were often designed to order for one industry or firm. See Robertson, "Changing Patterns," pp. 479–96.

54. Ibid.; McDougall, "Machine Tool Output," pp. 500–512; Rosenberg, "Technological Change," pp. 414–30; Nathan Rosenberg, *Technology and American Economic Growth* (New York, 1972), pp. 98–107.

55. U.S. Department of Commerce, Bureau of the Census, *Historical Statistics of the United States, Colonial Times to 1957* (Washington, D.C., 1960), pp. 409, 570, 577. The number of manufacturing firms were smaller than the number of factories. In 1916, the first year that data are available about the numbers of manufacturing corporations, there were 80,200. The numbers were probably slightly higher in 1900, since the recorded numbers of mergers among manufacturing corporations averaged about 100 per year between 1900 and 1916.

56. *Iron Age*, 14 October 1903, pp. 22–23.

57. U.S. Industrial Commission, *Reports of the Industrial Commission*, 13:733.

58. See the American Iron and Steel Association *Bulletin* for the years before and after 1900 for a sampling of Swank's thinking. Also see Paul Herbert Tedesco, "Patriotism, Protection, and Prosperity: James Moore Swank, The American Iron and Steel Association, and the Tariff" (Ph.D. diss., Boston University, 1970).

59. Wall, *Carnegie*, pp. 585–86.

60. Ibid., pp. 585–672.

61. U.S. Industrial Commission, *Reports of the Industrial Commission*, 13:725–60.

62. Ibid., p. 731.

63. Ibid., p. 730.

64. Porter, *Rise of Big Business*, pp. 79–84.

65. U.S. Industrial Commission, *Reports of the Industrial Commission*, 13:731; National Association of Manufacturers, *Proceedings of the Twenty-fifth Annual Convention, 1920* (New York, 1921), pp. 28–30; hereafter cited as NAM *Proceedings*.

66. NAM, *Proceedings*, 1895, pp. 10–13.

67. Albert K. Steigerwalt, *The National Association of Manufacturers, 1895–1914: A Study in Business Leadership* (Ann Arbor, Mich., 1964), pp. 39–45.

68. NAM, *Proceedings*, 1898, pp. 3–16; NAM, *Proceedings*, 1895, pp. 33–44, and "Circular of Invitation" reprinted before the *Proceedings*, n.p.; Steigerwalt, *National Association of Manufacturers*, pp. 39–100.

69. NAM, *Proceedings*, 1895, pp. 33–44.

70. NAM, *Proceedings*, 1901, p. 23.

71. NAM, *Proceedings*, 1911, pp. 99–100; Steigerwalt, *National Association of Manufacturers*, pp. 42–43.

72. NAM, *Proceedings*, 1897, pp. 5–9, 11–12.

73. NAM, *Proceedings*, 1900, pp. 25–28, and NAM, *Proceedings*, 1901, pp. 20–21.

74. NAM, *Proceedings*, 1900, pp. 60–74, and NAM, *Proceedings*, 1901, pp. 60–74.

75. NAM, *Proceedings*, 1900, pp. 3–5, and Robert H. Wiebe, *Businessmen and Reform: A Study of the Progressive Movement* (Cambridge, Mass., 1962), pp. 109–14, 170–74; Steigerwalt, *National Association of Manufacturers*, pp. 103–13.

76. Wiebe, *Businessmen and Reform*, pp. 90–94; Samuel P. Hays, "Introduction: The New Organizational Society," in Jerry Israel, ed., *Building the Organizational Society: Essays on Associational Activities in Modern America* (New York, 1972), pp. 1–15.

Three

1. Estimates of the percentage varied, although most observers thought the major corporations' share was substantial, anywhere from 80 to more than 90 percent. See James Howard Gore, "The Relation of Industrial Combinations to Export Trade," *George Washington University Publications, Political Science Series*, 1 (Nov. 1907), in Bureau of Corporation Records, Record Group 122, file no. 5575, National Archives. The annual reports of some corporations estimate their share in their industry's exports; see, for example, United States Steel Corporation, Annual Reports, 1904–14 in Bureau of Corporation Records, R. G. 122, file no. 6136–195. See also American Iron and Steel Association, *Bulletin*, 1 March 1912, p. 17.

2. Alfred D. Chandler, Jr., *The Visible Hand: The Managerial Revolution in American Business* (Cambridge, Mass., 1977), pp. 316–44; Mira Wilkins, *The Emergence of Multinational Enterprise: American Business Abroad from the Colonial Era to 1914* (Cambridge, Mass., 1970), pp. 70–110; David S. Landes, *The Unbound Promotheus: Technological Change and Industrial Development in Western Europe from 1750 to the Present* (London, 1969), pp. 231–359; Patrick G. Porter and Harold C. Livesay, "Oligopoly in Small Manufacturing Industries," *Explorations in Economic History* 7 (Spring 1970): 371–79.

3. Alfred D. Chandler, Jr., "The Structure of American Industry in the Twentieth Century: An Historical Overview," *Business History Review* 43 (Autumn 1969): 255–81; Thomas R. Navin, "The 500 Largest American Industrials in 1917," *Business History Review* 44 (Autumn 1970): 360–86.

4. Wilkins, *Emergence*, pp. 70–110; Abraham Berglund, "The United States Steel Corporation and Price Stabilization," *Quarterly Journal of Economics* 37 (1923): 1–30; Reese W. Jenkins, *Images and Enterprise: Technology and the American Photographic Industry, 1839–1925* (Baltimore, 1975), pp. 185–86, 233–34; Robert B. Davies, *Peacefully Working to Conquer the World: Singer Sewing Machines in Foreign Markets, 1854–1920* (New York, 1976), pp. 92–173; Mary Yeager Kujovich, "The Dynamics of Oligopoly in the Meat Packing Industry, an Historical Analysis" (Ph.D. diss., Johns Hopkins University, 1973), pp. 170–252; Glenn Porter and Harold C. Livesay, *Merchants and Manufacturers: Studies in the Changing Structure of Nineteenth Century Marketing* (Baltimore, 1973), pp. 154–96; Harold F. Williamson and Arnold R. Daum, *The American Petroleum Industry: The Age of Illumination, 1859–1899* (Evanston, Ill., 1959), pp. 475–87.

5. Chandler, *Visible Hand*, p. 38; U.S. Industrial Commission, *Reports of the Industrial Commission on Trusts and Industrial Combinations* (19 vols.; Washington, D.C., 1900–1902) 13: 728–72. Wilkins, *Emergence*, pp. 70–110; National Foreign Trade Council, *European Economic Alliances: A Compilation of Information on International Commercial Policies after the European War and Their Effect upon the Foreign Trade of the United States* (New

York, 1916), pp. 7–36, 69–81; National Foreign Trade Council, *Report of the Committee on Co-operation on Foreign Trade of the National Foreign Trade Council* (New York, 1915), pp. 4–19; George Stocking and Myron W. Watkins, *Cartels in Action* (New York 1946), pp. 320–22.

6. Matthew Simon and David E. Novack, "Some Dimensions of the American Commercial Invasion of Europe, 1871–1914," *Journal of Economic History* 24 (1964): 591–605; Frank A. Vanderlip, *The American "Commercial Invasion" of Europe* (New York, 1902); Jenkins, *Images and Enterprise*, pp. 178–79; Davies, *Peacefully Working*, pp. 95–96.

7. See pp. 38–39 above.

8. House Committee on Investigation of the United States Steel Corporation, *Hearings on United States Steel Corporation*, 62d Cong., 1st sess. (1911), pp. 1297–1344, 2717–50. (These hearings are commonly referred to as the Stanley hearings, named after the chairman of the investigative committee. Hereafter cited as Stanley Hearings). American Iron and Steel Association, *Statistics of the American and Foreign Iron Trades for 1910* (Philadelphia, 1911), p. 43.

9. Stanley Hearings, pp. 1317, 2748–49; Gore, "The Relation of Industrial Combinations," pp. 22–27; U.S. Industrial Commission, *Reports of the Industrial Commission*, 12: xxv–xxvii, 725ff.; United States Steel Corporation, Annual Reports, 1904–14. In investigating the steel industry, the Bureau of Corporations employed special examiners who analyzed the behavior especially of U.S. Steel in European markets. See the examiners' reports nos. 56, 113, and 114 in Bureau of Corporations Records, Record Group 122, file nos. 2635-7, 2635-6-1; 2635-8-1, National Archives.

10. Mira Wilkins, *The Maturing of Multinational Enterprise: American Business Abroad from 1914 to 1970* (Cambridge, Mass., 1974), pp. 151–53; see also Gertrude G. Schroeder, *The Growth of Major Steel Companies, 1900–1950* (Baltimore, 1953).

11. Wilkins, *Emergence*, pp. 95–96; Henry G. Prout, *A Life of George Westinghouse* (New York, 1921), pp. 263–64, 271–72.

12. Wilkins, *Emergence*, pp. 94–95; U.S. Federal Trade Commission, *Electric-Power Industry, Supply of Electrical Equipment and Competitive Conditions* (Washington, D.C., 1928), pp. 142–44; U.S. Federal Trade Commission, *Report on Cooperation in American Export Trade* (Washington, D.C., 1916), part I, 278.

13. Kendall Birr, *Pioneering in Industrial Research: The Story of the General Electric Research Laboratory* (Washington, D.C., 1957), pp. 31–66, 97–103; I found insightful an unpublished paper of Louis Galambos, "The Economic Effects of the Reorganization of the Sources of Knowledge in America, 1870–1920," presented at the Smithsonian Institution, March 1976.

14. Davies, *Peacefully Working*, pp. 95–96. Also see Alfred D. Chandler, Jr., and Stephen Salisbury, *Pierre S. DuPont and the Making of the Modern Corporation* (New York, 1971), pp. 142–43; and Jenkins, *Images and Enterprise*, pp. 185–86, 233–34. Technology and innovation in American industry before the turn of the century resided in the on-the-job kinds of improvements in machines and methods to increase productivity. Nineteenth-century American industrialization, as Nathan Rosenberg has pointed out, "involved the solution of problems which required mechanical skill, ingenuity and versatility, but not, typically, a recourse to scientific knowledge or elaborate experimental methods." See Nathan Rosenberg, *Technology and American Economic Growth* (New York, 1972), p. 54. Ralph W. Hidy and Muriel E. Hidy, *Pioneering in Big Business, 1882–1911* (New York, 1955), pp. 14–75; Alfred D. Chandler, Jr., *Strategy and Structure: Chapters in the History of the American Industrial Enterprise* (Cambridge, Mass., 1962), pp. 383–90; Richard C. Edwards, "Stages in Corporate Stability and the Risks of Corporate Failure," *Journal of Economic History* 35 (June 1975): 428–57; Nestor E. Terleckyj, "Sources of Productivity Advance: A Pilot Study of Manufacturing Industries, 1899–1953" (Ph.D. diss., Columbia University, 1960).

15. U.S. Department of Commerce and Labor, Bureau of Corporations. *Report of the Commissioner of Corporations on International Harvester* (Washington, D.C., 1913), pp. 33–40, 54–55, 188; Elizabeth C. Pickering, "The International Harvester Company in Russia: A Case Study of a Foreign Corporation in Russia from the 1860's to the 1930's" (Ph.D. diss., Princeton University, 1974), pp. 45–103; Helen M. Kramer, "Harvesters and High Finance: Formation of the International Harvester Company," *Business History Review* 38 (Autumn 1964): 297–301.

16. Wilkins, *Emergence*, pp. 102–3; International Harvester, *Annual Report 1911* (1912); Pickering, "International Harvester Company in Russia," pp. 104–46; Robert Hume Werking, *The Master Architects: Building the United States Foreign Service, 1890-1913* (Lexington, Ky., 1977), pp. 229–31. International Harvester's relations with the Russian government are discussed in the records of the U.S. embassy in St. Petersburg, found in Foreign Service Posts Records (Russia–diplomatic), Record Group 84, National Archives. See, for example, M. Schuyler's correspondence with Russian officials, 6–8 January 1910 and W. W. Rockhill to B. A. Kennedy, 5 March 1910, v. 4496; B. A. Kennedy to W. W. Rockhill, 21 January 1910 and B. A. Kennedy, memorandum, 29 December 1909, v. 4475. Other information is included in Huntington Wilson, telegram, to American embassy in St. Petersburg, 14 March 1910, and G. Perkins to P. Knox, 14 February 1910, file 23549; Perkins to Huntington Wilson, 24 February 1910, file 164.21 in 82, State Department Records, Record Group 59, National Archives.

17. Davies, *Peacefully Working*, pp. 115–17; Wilkins, *Emergence*, pp. 101–3; Mira Wilkins, "An American Enterprise Abroad: American Radiator Company in Europe, 1895–1914," *Business History Review* 43 (Winter 1969): 326–46.

18. Wilkins, *Emergence*, pp. 101–3; G. C. Allen and Audrey G. Donnethorne, *Western Enterprise in Far Eastern Economic Development* (New York, 1954), pp. 231–33.

19. Wilkins, *Emergence*, pp. 83, 86–87; U.S. Department of Commerce and Labor, Bureau of Corporations, *Report of the Commissioner of Corporations on the Petroleum Industry*, Part 3, "Foreign Trade" (Washington, D.C., 1909), pp. 89–92, 287–91; Hidy and Hidy, *Pioneering*, pp. 520, 549–53, 563–64.

20. Melvin I. Urofsky, *Big Steel and the Wilson Administration: A Study in Business-Government Relations* (Columbus, Ohio, 1969), pp. 1–36.

21. Wilkins, *Emergence*, pp. 80–82; William B. Gates, *Michigan Copper and Boston Dollars* (Cambridge, Mass., 1951), pp. 61–64, 82–83; Harvey O'Connor, *The Guggenheims* (New York, 1937), pp. 111–12, 118, 123, 281; F. Ernest Richter, "The Amalgamated Copper Company, *Quarterly Journal of Economics* 29 (February 1915): 400–406.

22. Wilkins, *Emergence*, pp. 87–88.

23. Ibid., pp. 88–89.

24. Ibid., pp. 91–93; U.S. Department of Commerce and Labor, Bureau of Corporations, *Report of Commissioner of Corporations on the Tobacco Industry* (Washington, D.C., 1909), Part 1, pp. 69–70, 82–84, 88, 165, 169 ff.; U.S. Industrial Commission, *Reports of the Industrial Commission*, 13:322–27.

25. Wilkins, *Emergence*, p. 96; Thomas J. Watson, *Men–Minutes–Money* (New York, 1934), pp. 257–58; Saul Engelbourg, "International Business Machines: A Business History" (Ph.D. diss., Columbia University, 1954), pp. 281–85.

26. Mira Wilkins and Frank Ernest Hill, *American Business Abroad: Ford on Six Continents* (Detroit, 1964), pp. 11–14, 22–25, 37–39, 434–35.

27. Ibid., pp. 4–14.

28. National Association of Manufacturers, *Proceedings of the Eighteenth Annual Convention, 1912* (New York, 1913), p. 307.

29. NAM, *Proceedings*, 1905, pp. 89–95; NAM, *Proceedings*, 1903, p. 96; NAM, *Proceedings*, 1912, p. 2; NAM, *Proceedings*, 1914, p. 3.

30. NAM, *Proceedings*, 1905, p. 93; NAM, *Proceedings*, 1909, pp. 78–79; NAM, *Proceedings*, 1911, pp. 99–100; NAM, *Proceedings*, 1914, pp. 23–24.

31. NAM, *Proceedings*, 1911, pp. 95–97; NAM, *Proceedings*, 1912, pp. 305–13; NAM, *Proceedings*, 1913, p. 36.

32. NAM, *Proceedings*, 1897, pp. 9–11; NAM, *Proceedings*, 1913, pp. 36–39.

33. NAM, *Proceedings*, 1911, p. 96; NAM, *Proceedings*, 1914, pp. 21–38.

34. NAM, *Proceedings*, 1912, pp. 61–62, 308.

35. Ibid., pp. 303–13.

36. Ibid., pp. 309–10.

37. NAM, *Proceedings*, 1900, pp. 28, 36–49; NAM, *Proceedings*, 1908, p. 125; National Association of Manufacturers, *Circular of Information*, (Philadelphia, 1898), pp. 1–2; Albert K. Steigerwalt, *The National Association of Manufacturers, 1895–1914: A Study in Leadership* (Ann Arbor, Mich., 1964), pp. 48–49.

38. NAM, *Proceedings*, 1912, pp. 305–13; NAM, *Proceedings*, 1913, p. 36.

39. NAM, *Proceedings*, 1911, pp. 95–97.

40. NAM, *Proceedings*, 1914, pp. 21–30.

41. NAM, *Proceedings*, 1911, p. 63; NAM, *Proceedings*, 1918, p. 77; NAM, *Proceedings*, 1919, pp. 143, 189; NAM, *Proceedings*, 1920, pp. 125–26; NAM, *Proceedings*, 1922, pp. 148–50.

42. Forrest Crissey, "Teamwork in Tradebuilding," *Saturday Evening Post*, March 14, 1914, p. 64.

43. Emphasis in the original. American Manufacturers Export Association, *Proceedings of the Second Annual Convention, 1911* (New York, 1912), n.p. Hereafter cited as AMEA, *Proceedings*.

44. AMEA, *Proceedings*, 1911, pp. 17–28, 48–56.

45. Ibid., pp. 48–56, 60–75.

46. AMEA, *Proceedings*, 1915, pp. 32–36, 228–36.

47. AMEA, *Proceedings*, 1911, pp. 48–56, 60–75.

48. Ibid., pp. 17–28, 48–56.

49. Ibid., pp. 48–56.

50. Ibid., p. 55.

51. AMEA, *Proceedings*, 1915, p. 234.

52. Ibid.; AMEA, *Proceedings*, 1911, pp. 60–75.

53. H. C. Lewis, "The Relations of Government to Foreign Commerce, Export Problems of the United States," in AMEA, *Proceedings*, 1919, p. 185.

Four

1. Scholars like William Appleman Williams and others have emphasized the consensus for market expansion. See William Appleman Williams, *The Tragedy of American Diplomacy* (rev. 2d ed.; New York, 1972), pp. 33–57; Walter LaFeber, *The New Empire: An Interpretation of American Expansionism, 1860–1898* (Ithaca, N.Y., 1963), pp. 60, 150–54, 176, 412. For an excellent discussion of the ways in which politicians interpreted the economic significance of the tariff in the nineteenth century, see G. R. Hawke, "The United States Tariff and Industrial Protection in the Late Nineteenth Century," *Economic History Review* 28 (1975): 84–99.

2. National Association of Manufacturers, *Proceedings of the First Annual Convention of the National Association of Manufacturers*, January 22–24, 1895 (Philadelphia, 1896), p. 8.

3. U.S. Congress, *House Report 2263*, 54th Cong., 1st sess. (Washington, D.C., 1895), pp. 296–300.

4. Nathaniel W. Stephenson, *Nelson W. Aldrich: A Leader in American Politics* (New York, 1930), pp. 138–48; Leon B. Richardson, *William E. Chandler: Republican* (New York, 1940), pp. 535–66; H. Wayne Morgan, *William McKinley and His America* (Syracuse, N.Y., 1963), pp. 276–85; Lewis L. Gould, "Diplomats in the Lobby: Franco-American Relations and the Dingley Tariff of 1897," *Historian* 39 (August 1977): 659–80.

5. Gould, "Diplomats in the Lobby," p. 660. Edward Nelson Dingley, *The Life and Times of Nelson Dingley, Jr.* (Kalamazoo, Mich., 1902), p. 423; Edward Stanwood, *American Tariff Controversies in the Nineteenth Century* (2 vols.; Boston, 1903), 2:377–84; Frank W. Taussig, *The Tariff History of the United States* (8th ed.; New York, 1931), pp. 326–27. Gould's is the most useful work on this subject.

6. Gould, "Diplomats in the Lobby," pp. 661–63.

7. Ibid., pp. 662–65.

8. Ibid., pp. 664–65.

9. Ibid., pp. 665–67.

10. Ibid., p. 668.

11. Paul S. Holbo, "Economics, Emotion, and Expansion: An Emerging Foreign Policy," in H. Wayne Morgan, ed., *The Gilded Age* (Syracuse, N.Y., 1970), pp. 199–221; Gould, "Diplomats in the Lobby," p. 667.

12. Gould, "Diplomats in the Lobby," p. 668; Tom E. Terrill, *The Tariff, Politics, and American Foreign Policy* (Westport, Conn., 1973), pp. 200–204.

13. Gould, "Diplomats in the Lobby," pp. 671–76; U.S. Congress, *Congressional Record*, 55th Cong., 1st sess. (March 22, 1897), p. 121 and (May 25, 1897), pp. 1229–32.

14. Gould, "Diplomats in the Lobby," pp. 677–79.

15. As Gould's work demonstrates, reciprocity appears in a different light when seen from the perspective of the committee that wrote the legislation of Section 4, the part dealing with reciprocity treaties. Gould concludes that "a general sweeping search for foreign markets represented at most a residual part of a more significant attempt to use reciprocity as a bargaining counter with France. The exigencies of negotiations with the French, rather than anxieties about overproduction, had more to do with the final language of the two sections. The portions of Section 3 that deal with luxuries like wines, brandies, and paintings were almost exclusively aimed at France as compensation for the lost Wolcott rates and to retain cooperation on bimetallism" (p. 680).

16. NAM, *Proceedings*, 1901, pp. 5–9.

17. Terrill, *Tariff*, p. 202 ff.

18. Ibid., pp. 200–201; Taussig, *Tariff History*, pp. 353–60.

19. Terrill, *Tariff*, pp. 200–203.

20. Ibid., pp. 202–3; Edward Younger, *John A. Kasson, Politics and Diplomacy, from Lincoln to McKinley* (Iowa City, 1955).

21. Terrill, *Tariff*, p. 203; Younger, *Kasson*, pp. 375–76.

22. Terrill, *Tariff*, p. 204.

23. American Iron and Steel Association, *Bulletin*, 25 December 1900, p. 212.

24. Robert H. Wiebe, *Businessmen and Reform: A Study of the Progressive Movement* (Cambridge, Mass., 1962), pp. 104–12.

25. NAM, *Proceedings*, 1900, p. 18.

26. See the views of the manufacturers of hand agricultural tools, pressed gloves, general mining machinery, air compressors, vehicles, ice, etc., in NAM, *Proceedings*, 1901, pp. 62–96.

27. *Proceedings of the National Reciprocity Convention 1901* (Washington, D.C., 1901), pp. 145–50; Joseph Kenkel, "Tariff Commission Movement: The Search for a Non-partisan Solution of the Tariff Question" (Ph.D. diss., University of Maryland, 1962), pp. 2–24.

28. Terrill, *Tariff*, pp. 204–7; U.S. Senate, Committee on Foreign Relations, *Reciprocity Convention with France*, 56th Cong., 1st sess., 1899, Senate Doc. No. 225 (Washington,

D.C., 1900), pp. 63–64, 66–81; New York *Times*, 25 October 1901, p. 8 and 10 March 1901, p. 1; John A. Kasson, "Impressions of President McKinley, with Especial Reference to His Opinions on Reciprocity," *Century* 63 (December 1901): 275; Morgan, *William McKinley*, pp. 462–66; Henry Cabot Lodge to Nelson W. Aldrich, 20 June 1901, Nelson W. Aldrich Papers, Library of Congress; James D. Richardson, ed., *Messages and Papers of the Presidents* (20 vols.; Washington, D.C., 1917), 13:6620–22.

29. Richardson, *Messages and Papers*, 14:6652, 6713–14; Theodore Roosevelt to Nicholas Murray Butler, 12 August 1902; Roosevelt to Joseph B. Bishop, 27 April 1903; Roosevelt to Lodge, 11, 23 May 1904 and 2 June 1904; Roosevelt to Elihu Root, 2, 14 June 1904, in Elting E. Morison et al., eds., *The Letters of Theodore Roosevelt* (8 vols.; Cambridge, Mass. 1951–54), 3:313, 471–72; 4:796, 803, 812–13, 833; Kenkel, "Tariff Commission," pp. 17–24. Roosevelt supported treaties with Cuba and the Philippines because they were necessary to strengthen those islands on account of their strategic location.

30. NAM, *Proceedings*, 1903, pp. 69–73, 255–56.

31. *American Economist*, 24 April 1908, p. 193; 14 February 1908, pp. 73–74, 78, 81–82; Kenkel, "Tariff Commission," pp. 25–29.

32. Kenkel, "Tariff Commission," pp. 25–29.

33. U.S. Congress, House, 60th Cong., 1st sess., 1907–8, H.R. 13098, H.R. 162; U.S. Congress, Senate, 60th Cong., 1st sess., 1907–8, S. 3163, S. 3089.

34. Kenkel, "Tariff Commission," pp. 25–29; see the address of John Barrett, director, International Bureau of American Republics, in NAM, *Proceedings*, 1909, pp. 38–50; NAM, *Proceedings*, 1912, p. 265.

35. Quoted from Indianapolis *Star*, 17 January 1909 in Kenkel, "Tariff Commission," pp. 29–36; Wiebe, *Businessmen and Reform*, pp. 90–92.

36. Kenkel, "Tariff Commission," pp. 29–36.

37. Ibid.

38. Ibid., pp. 37–42.

39. Ibid.; Claude G. Bowers, *Beveridge and the Progressive Era* (Cambridge, 1932), p. 353.

40. NAM, *Proceedings*, 1909, pp. 65, 130–54, 176–77.

41. Kenkel, "Tariff Commission," pp. 37–42; Louis Galambos (with the assistance of Barbara Barrow Spence), *The Public Image of Big Business in America, 1880–1940: A Quantitative Study in Social Change* (Baltimore, 1975), pp. 117–56; Alfred L. Thimm, *Business Ideologies in the Reform-Progressive Era, 1880–1914* (University, Ala., 1976), pp. 40–71; see also Louis Galambos, *Competition and Cooperation: The Emergence of a Modern Trade Association* (Baltimore, 1967).

42. Kenkel, "Tariff Commission," pp. 37–42.

43. U.S. Tariff Commission, *Reciprocity with Canada: A Study of the Arrangements of 1911* (Washington, D.C., 1920), pp. 265–70.

44. Papers of the Tariff Board, Correspondence Relating to Organization of Board, in the Records of the U.S. Tariff Commission, Record Group 81, National Archives, Washington, D.C. Hereafter cited as Tariff Commission Records.

45. H. C. Emery to William Howard Taft, 26 March 1910, in U.S. Congress, Senate, *The Tariff Board*, 61st Cong., 2d sess., 1910 Senate Doc. 463, p. 2; U.S. Congress, House, Committee on Appropriations, *Hearings before Subcommittee of House Committee on Appropriations...in Charge of Sundry Civil Appropriation Bill for 1913*, 62d Cong., 2d sess., 1912, Part 4, pp. 5, 10–11. H. C. Emery to C. Curtis, 7 April 1910; H. E. Miles to A. H. Saunders, 28 June 1910; H. E. Miles to H. C. Emery, 27 September 1910, file 100.03; Henry C. Emery, Speech, Manchester, N.H., 29 September 1911, file 120.2, Tariff Commission Records; Henry C. Emery, *The Tariff Board and Its Work* (Washington, D.C., 1910), pp. 7–13.

46. Kenkel, "Tariff Commission," pp. 66–72; NAM, *Proceedings*, 1912, pp. 265–66; National Tariff Commission Association, *The National Tariff Commission Association Convention* (Washington, D.C., 1911), pp. 23–88. See National Tariff Commission information in file 100.03, Tariff Commission Records.

47. Kenkel, "Tariff Commission," pp. 79–87; L. Ethan Ellis, *Reciprocity, 1911* (New Haven, Conn. 1939), passim; U.S. Tariff Commission, *Reciprocity with Canada: A Study of the Arrangement of 1911* (Washington, D.C., 1920), pp. 40–49; U.S. Congress, House, 62d Cong., 1st sess., 1911, H.R. 11019, H.R. 4413, H.R. 12812.

48. Kenkel, "Tariff Commission," pp. 81–84.

49. Ibid., pp. 84–85; U.S. Congress, House, 62d Cong., 1st sess., 1911, H.R. 11019.

50. John T. Snyder, "Edward P. Costigan and the United States Tariff Commission" (Ph.D. diss., University of Colorado, 1966).

51. In fact, as Wilson's chief biographer Arthur S. Link points out, there was probably no more lobbying in 1913 than before; see Arthur S. Link, *Wilson: The New Freedom* (Princeton, N.J., 1956), pp. 186–90; Kenkel, "Tariff Commission," pp. 98–101.

52. "Work of the Cost of Production Division," 5 June 1916, Cost of Production Division Records, Tariff Commission Records; Chamber of Commerce of the United States of America, *Referendum No. 2: On the Question of a Permanent Tariff Commission* (Washington, D.C., 1913).

53. The Wilson administration's tariff policies caused great consternation among businessmen. See Chamber of Commerce of the United States of America, *A Permanent Tariff Commission* (Washington, D.C., 1915).

54. See the letter of Congressman J. M. Cox to Woodrow Wilson, 24 August 1915, Woodrow Wilson Papers, Library of Congress, for a typical view of the party professionals; hereafter cited as Wilson Papers. Discussions of the political importance of the tariff can be found in P. W. Brown to Wilson, 26 April 1915; M. A. Mathews to Wilson, 11 August 1915; C. C. Miller to Wilson, 24 August 1915, Wilson Papers. Kenkel, "Tariff Commission," pp. 104–6.

55. David F. Houston, *Eight Years with Wilson's Cabinet* (2 vols.; Garden City, 1926), 2:196–97; Wilson to J. M. Cox, 27 August 1915; Wilson to M. A. Mathews, 17 August 1915, Wilson Papers; Kenkel, "Tariff Commission," pp. 106–9.

56. William Cox Redfield to Franklin K. Lane, 6 December 1915; Redfield to P. W. Brown, 7 December 1915, General Records of the Office of the Secretary of Commerce, Record Group 40, National Archives, Washington, D.C. Wilson's associates' views of Redfield can be found in Link, *New Freedom*, p. 139; Kenkel, "Tariff Commission," pp. 108–10.

57. Wilson to Kitchin, 26 January 1916, Wilson papers; Kenkel, "Tariff Commission," p. 113.

58. Washington *Post*, 26 September 1916, quoted in Kenkel, "Tariff Commission," p. 117.

59. Kenkel, "Tariff Commission," pp. 98–117.

60. Ibid.

61. Ibid.; Snyder, "Edward P. Costigan," pp. 3–27; Joan Hoff Wilson, *American Business and Foreign Policy, 1920–1933* (Lexington, Ky., 1971), pp. 67–100.

Five

1. Department of State, *Regulations Prescribed for Use of the Consular Service of the United States* (Washington, D.C., 1896), pp. 3–4, 254; Thomas G. Paterson, "American Businessmen and Consular Service Reform, 1890's to 1906," *Business History Review* 40 (Spring 1966): 80.

2. Graham H. Stuart, *American Diplomatic and Consular Practice* (New York, 1936), pp. 30–36, 360; Warren Ilchman, *Professional Diplomacy in the United States, 1779–1939: A Study in Administrative History* (Chicago, 1961), pp. 1–6; William Barnes and John H. Morgan, *The Foreign Service of the United States: Origins, Development and Functions* (Washington, D.C., 1961), p. 58; Richard Hume Werking, *The Master 'Architects: Building the Foreign Service, 1890–1913* (Lexington, Ky., 1977), pp. 2, 29–31; Chester L. Jones, *Consular Service of the United States* (Philadelphia, 1906), pp. 4–5; Wilbur J. Carr, "The American Consular Service," *American Journal of International Law* 1 (October 1907): 894–907.

3. Jones, *Consular Service*, pp. 46–56, 63–79; Barnes and Morgan, *Foreign Service*, pp. 60, 125–27, 350; Werking, *Master Architects*, p. 29; Department of State, *Regulations* (1896), pp. 142–53; John W. Foster, *The Practice of Diplomacy* (Boston, 1906), pp. 210–20.

4. U.S. Senate, *Reorganization of the Consular and Diplomatic Service*, Rept. 1202, 56th Cong., 1st sess., 1900; Paterson, "American Businessmen," p. 80; Werking, *Master Architects*, pp. 32–33.

5. Werking, *Master Architects*, p. 33.

6. Ibid., pp. 34–35; Theodore Roosevelt, "Six Years of Civil Service Reform," *Scribner's Magazine* 18 (August 1895): 242, 247; William D. Foulke, *Fighting the Spoilsmen* (New York, 1919), pp. 104–5; Ilchman, *Professional Diplomacy*, p. 64; Elting E. Morison, et al., *The Letters of Theodore Roosevelt* (8 vols; Cambridge, Mass., 1951–54), 6:1497; Paul R. Van Riper, *History of the United States Civil Service* (Evanston, Ill., 1958), pp. 169–70; Donald M. Dozer, "Secretary of State Elihu Root and Consular Reorganization," *Mississippi Valley Historical Review* 29 (December 1942): 339–50.

7. Albert H. Washburn, "Some Evils of Our Consular Service," *Atlantic Monthly* 74 (August 1894): 243.

8. Paterson, "American Businessmen," pp. 82–83.

9. All consular officers could retain the notarial fees they received, the so-called unofficial fees. Fees that had to be reported to the Treasury Department were "official fees." After 1868, all fees in excess of $1000 per year had to be turned into the Treasury. Department of State, *Regulations* (Washington, D.C., 1896), pp. 192–218.

10. *Wall Street Journal*, 22 March 1906, p. 2.

11. Barnes and Morgan, *Foreign Service*, p. 350; Paterson, "American Businessmen," p. 94.

12. *Proceedings of the National Board of Trade*, December 1897, pp. 67–70.

13. Ibid., January 1895, p. 45; Henry Cabot Lodge to Elihu Root, 19 April 1906, 23 June 1906, 17 November 1906, and Root to Lodge, 18 December 1905, The Papers of Elihu Root, Library of Congress; "Consular Reform," *Nation* 59 (29 November 1894): 398–99; Paterson, "American Businessmen," pp. 86–87.

14. NBT, *Proceedings*, January 1905, pp. 128–29; Paterson, "American Businessmen," p. 88; George Smart, "Good Consuls and Good Consular Service," *American Industries*, 15 February 1906, p. 11; Edward B. Grubb, "The Consular Service and the Spoils System," *Century Magazine* 48 (June 1894): 308.

15. *Congressional Record*, 3 April 1894, p. 3410; 25 April 1894, p. 4104; Ilchman, *Professional Diplomacy*, pp. 65–67; Jones, *Consular Service*, p. 29; Werking, *Master Architects*, p. 35; Paterson, "American Businessmen," p. 89.

16. Herbert Croly, *Marcus Alonzo Hanna* (New York, 1923), pp. 297–301; H. Wayne Morgan, *William McKinley and His America* (Syracuse, N.Y., 1963), pp. 287–92; Van Riper, *History*, 169–70; Paterson, "American Businessmen," p. 90; Foulke, *Spoilsmen*, pp. 104–5; Ilchman, *Professional Diplomacy*, p. 64.

17. Paterson, "American Businessmen," p. 91.

18. Ibid., p. 92; Werking, *Master Architects*, pp. 94–98, 108–9.

19. Flood quotation in Paterson, "American Businessmen," p. 93; *Congressional Record*, 19 March 1906, pp. 3971–75; U.S. Congress, House, Committee on Foreign Affairs, *Reorganization of Consular Service*, Rep. No. 2681, 59th Cong., 1st sess., (1906); Werking, *Master Architects*, pp. 94–98.

20. "The First Examination under the Reform Law," *Outlook* 85 (20 April 1907): 866; Paterson, "American Businessmen," 94; Werking, *Master Architects*, pp. 247–49.

21. Werking, *Master Architects*, pp. 22–23, 35–36, 45–46; Robert D. Schulzinger, *The Making of the Diplomatic Mind: The Training, Outlook, and Style of United States Foreign Service Officers, 1908–1931* (Middletown, Conn., 1975), pp. 15–39.

22. "Report of Convention of Consuls General and Treasury Agents at Paris," August, 1890, State Department Records, Record Group 59, E93 National Archives, Washington, D.C.

23. Werking, *Master Architects*, pp. 44–46.

24. Ibid., pp. 35–36, 49.

25. Ibid., pp. 44–67.

26. Jerry Israel, "A Diplomatic Machine: Scientific Management in the Department of State, 1906–1924," in Jerry Israel, ed., *Building the Organizational Society: Essays on Associational Activities in Modern America* (New York, 1972), p. 190.

27. Ibid., pp. 189–90. The Diary of Wilbur Carr, 18 June 1896, 28 July 1896, 8 August 1896, 11 August 1896, 12 August 1896, 28 October 1896, 30 October 1896, 3 November 1896, 4 November 1896, 8 March 1897; Wilbur J. Carr Papers, Library of Congress. Hereafter referred to as Carr Diary.

28. Carr Diary, 5 June 1896, 30 July 1896, 13 August 1896, 22 August 1896; Werking, *Master Architects*, pp. 89–90.

29. Carr Diary, 21 June 1896, 20 July 1896, 18 August 1896, 22 August 1896, 2 January 1901, 30 November 1901.

30. Ibid., 25 January 1901, 13 September 1901.

31. Ibid., 15 November 1901, 10 December 1902.

32. Ibid., 10 December 1902. On politicians, see Carr Diary, 24 December 1903.

33. Richard W. Leopold, *Elihu Root and the Conservative Tradition* (Boston, 1954), pp. 24–26.

34. Theodore Roosevelt to Elihu Root, 2 June 1904; Root to Henry Cabot Lodge, 25 October 1905; Root to Charles W. Eliot, 5 December 1905; Root to George S. Hastings, 11 December 1905, Root Papers.

35. Root to Roosevelt, 29 November 1905, Root Papers.

36. Carr Diary, 12 December 1905; John A. DeNovo, "The Enigmatic Alvey A. Adee and American Foreign Relations, 1870–1924," *Prologue* 7 (Summer 1975): 69–80; Lawrence E. Gelfand, "A Merit System for the American Diplomatic Service, 1896–1930," paper delivered at the April 1976 meetings of the Organization of American Historians.

37. Carr Diary, 7 February 1906, 26 February 1906, 30 March 1906; Edwin Denby to Root, 20 March 1906; Root to Carr, 22 March 1906, Root Papers.

38. U.S. Congress, Senate, Committee on Foreign Relations, *Hearings on Reorganization of the Consular Service*, 59th Cong., 1st sess., 13 December 1905.

39. Carr Diary, 12 December 1905; Root to Lodge, 18 December 1905; Lodge to Root, 19 December 1905; Lodge to Root, 23 June 1906; Lodge to Root, 17 November 1906; Lodge to Root, 19 April 1906. For further information on how Root handled business organizations and the press, see Root to H. H. Benedict, 17 January 1906; Root to James F. Coyle (president of the Latin-American Club and Foreign Trade Association of Saint Louis), 20 March 1906; Root to Joseph P. Reed, 10 November 1905, Root Papers.

40. Root to George E. Foss (member of Congress from Illinois) 14 December 1905; Root to Higginson, 8 October 1906, Root Papers.

41. Carr Diary, 20 January 1906.

42. Ibid., 14–15 March 1907, 18–20 April 1907, 8 May 1907, 27 November 1907; Israel, "Diplomatic Machine," pp. 189–90.

43. Katherine Crane, *Mr. Carr of State: Forty-seven Years in the Department of State* (New York, 1960), pp. 66–76.

44. U.S. Congress, House, H.R. 20044, 62d Cong., 3d sess., 13 February 1913; U.S. Congress, House, *To Improve Diplomatic and Consular Service*, Rep. No. 840, 62d Cong., 2d sess., 5 June 1912; U.S., *Statutes at Large*, 38:805–7; Werking, *Master Architects*, pp. 247–48.

45. Werking, *Master Architects*, p. 249; Ilchman, *Professional Diplomacy*, pp. 176–85; Waldo Heinrichs, "Bureaucracy and Professionalism in the Development of Career Diplomacy," in *Twentieth-Century American Foreign Policy*, ed. John Braeman et al., (Columbus, Ohio, 1971), pp. 119–206.

46. U.S. Congress, House, Committee on Foreign Affairs, *Hearings on Diplomatic and Consular Service*, 62d Cong., 2d sess., 15 January 1912; House, Committee on Foreign Affairs, *Hearings on Diplomatic and Consular Appropriation Bill, 1917*, 64th Cong., 2d sess., 19 January 1916. Trade expansion, to be sure, was not the only reason to request higher appropriations. When war broke out in Europe in 1914, the department used the greater demands on the Department of State's services to justify increases in its funds. U.S. Congress, House, Committee on Foreign Affairs, *Hearings on Diplomatic and Consular Appropriations Bill, 1915–1916*, 63d Cong., 3d sess., 17 December 1914.

47. Carr Diary, 29 January 1913.

48. Wilbur J. Carr, draft speech, undated, pp. 1–2, 5, Box 17, Papers of Wilbur J. Carr, Library of Congress.

49. Carr Diary, 28 May 1914.

50. Department of Commerce and Labor, Bureau of Manufacturers, *Monthly Consular and Trade Reports*, no. 304 (January 1906), p. 25; Paterson, "American Businessmen," p. 96; C. Arthur Williams, "Consular Reform" *World To-Day* 21 (April 1906): 396; Albert Halstead, "A Neglected Factor in Our Commercial Expansion," *North American Review* 174 (January 1902): 21; U.S. Congress, Senate, *Reorganization of Consular and Diplomatic Service*, Rep. No. 1202, 56th Cong., 1st sess., 1900; *Reports*, no. 222 (March 1899), p. 445; Jones, *Consular Service*, 117.

51. Wilbur J. Carr, draft of speech to National Board of Trade, 18 January 1911, Box 17, Carr Papers.

52. Werking, *Master Architects*, pp. 229–30; Elizabeth C. Pickering, "The International Harvester Company in Russia: A Case Study of a Foreign Corporation in Russia from the 1860's to the 1930's" (Ph.D. diss., Princeton University, 1974), pp. 45–103.

53. Robert Bruce Davies, *Peacefully Working to Conquer the World: Singer Sewing Machines in Foreign Markets, 1854–1920* (New York, 1976), pp. 116–18.

54. Werking, *Master Architects*, pp. 229–30.

55. Frederick Emory to Chief Clerk Edward I. Renick, 17 March 1897, Report of the Chief Clerk, State Department Records. John Osborne, "The American Consul and American Trade," *Atlantic Monthly* 99 (February 1907): 161–64.

56. "Memoranda on the History and Organization of the Office of the Economic Adviser," 23 October 1911, State Department Records; Osborne, "American Consul," p. 162; Werking, *Master Architects*, pp. 76–81.

57. Werking, *Master Architects*, pp. 81–84.

58. Ibid., pp. 138–40; U.S. Congress, House, Committee on Appropriations, *Hearings before Subcommittee in Charge of the Legislative, Executive and Judicial Appropriation Bill for 1909*, 60th Cong., 1st sess., 9 January 1908, pp. 44–45 (hereafter cited as *Hearings on LEJ*); Richard C. Baker, *The Tariff under Roosevelt and Taft* (Hastings, Neb., 1941), pp. 70–72.

59. Werking, *Master Architects*, pp. 145–49; U.S. Congress, Senate, *Foreign Trade and Treaty Relations*, 61st Cong., 1st sess., Doc. No. 150, July 31, 1909, pp. 4–5.

60. Werking, *Master Architects*, p. 149.

61. Ibid., pp. 150–51.

62. Werking, *Master Architects*, pp. 152–53, 164–65; "History, Organization and Activities of the Bureau of Trade Relations," May 1912, State Department Records, File 111.26; Address of John Osborne to the American Manufacturers Export Association, September 29, 1911, in *Pan American Union Bulletin* 33 (December 1911): 1136. *Hearings on LEJ for 1912*, 61st Cong., 3d sess., 29 November 1910, pp. 40–41.

63. U.S. Senate, Committee on Appropriations, *Bureau of Trade Relations in Department of State and Domestic Bureau in Department of Commerce and Labor*, 62d Cong., 2d sess., Senate Doc. 761.

64. Werking, *Master Architects*, pp. 206–10; U.S. Congress, Senate, *Hearings on the Legislative, Executive and Judicial Appropriation Bill for 1913*, H.24023, 62d Cong., 2d sess., 23 May 1912.

65. Charles M. Pepper, Memorandum, 8 August 1912, State Department Records, file 162./27.

66. Acting Trade Adviser A. C. Millspaugh to Assistant Secretary of State Fred M. Dearing, "Memorandum on the Place of the Foreign Trade Adviser's Office in the Department of State," 31 January 1922; Departmental Order 68, 31 January 1916, State Department Records.

67. Millspaugh to Dearing, State Department Records.

68. Ibid.

Six

1. James D. Richardson, ed., *Messages and Papers of the Presidents* (20 vols.; Washington, D.C., 1917), 13:6646.

2. Theodore Roosevelt to Knute Nelson, 21 July 1906, in Elting E. Morison, et al., *The Letters of Theodore Roosevelt* (8 vols.; Cambridge, Mass., 1951–54), 5:334; Arthur M. Johnson, "Theodore Roosevelt and the Bureau of Corporations," *Mississippi Valley Historical Review* 45 (1959): 571–77; Robert Wiebe, *Businessmen and Reform: A Study of Progressivism* (Cambridge, Mass., 1964), pp. 40–44.

3. U.S. Industrial Commission, *Reports of the Industrial Commission on Trusts and Industrial Combinations* (19 vols.; Washington, D.C., 1900–1902), 19: 575–76; Lawrence F. Schmeckebier and Gustavus A. Weber, *The Bureau of Foreign and Domestic Commerce: Its History, Activities, and Organization* (Baltimore, 1924), pp. 23–28; U.S. Senate, *Department of Commerce and Industries*, Rep. No. 321, 56th Cong., 1st sess., 1900; the National Association of Manufacturers devoted much attention to such a department; see National Association of Manufacturers' Proceedings of the Annual Convention for the years 1895–1902 and especially National Association of Manufacturers' *Proceedings of the Fourth Annual Convention for 1898* (Philadelphia, 1899), pp. 3–16. Further information about the NAM's views can be found in NAM, *A Department of Commerce and Manufacturers*, Circular of Information No. 4 (Philadelphia, 1896), and *A New Federal Department*, Circular of Information No. 36 (Philadelphia, 1900); Wiebe, *Businessmen and Reform*, p. 44.

4. Richard Hume Werking, *The Master Architects: Building the United States Foreign Service, 1890-1913* (Lexington, Ky., 1977), pp. 173–76.

5. *Congressional Record*, 57th Cong., 1st sess., 1903, 36:945–46, and 57th Cong., 1st sess., 1902, 35:761–65; for an example of bureaucratic squabbling see General Records of the Department of Commerce, Office of the Secretary, General Correspondence, Record Group 40, National Archives, file 66651; hereafter cited as DOC Records; Werking, *Master Architects*, pp. 178–80.

6. Werking, *Master Architects*, p. 181; Department of Commerce and Labor, *Report, 1905* (Washington, D.C., 1906), pp. 62–65.

7. U.S. Congress, House, Committee on Appropriations *Hearings Before the Subcommittee in Charge of the Legislative, Executive and Judicial Appropriation Bill for 1908*, 59th Cong., 2d sess., 30 November 1906, p. 319; and for 1911, 61st Cong., 2d sess., 27 January 1910, p. 299; hereafter these hearings will be referred to as *Hearings on LEJ*.

8. Department of Commerce and Labor, *Report, 1906* (Washington, D.C., 1907), p. 55; U.S. Congress, House, *Hearings on LEJ for 1908*, 59th Cong., 2d sess., 20 November 1906, p. 391; for 1909, 60th Cong., 1st sess., 29 January 1908, p. 466; for 1912, 61st Cong., 3d sess., 2 December 1910; U.S. Congress, Senate, *Hearings on LEJ for 1909*, 60th Cong., 1st sess., 28 February 1908, p. 11; Werking, *Master Architects*, pp. 181–84.

9. Department of Commerce and Labor, *Report, 1905* (Washington, D.C., 1906), pp. 63–64 and for 1907, p. 53; Werking, *Master Architects*, pp. 184–85.

10. Werking, *Master Architects*, pp. 185–87; see the file Wilbur Carr assembled on "duties of foreign consular officers in connection with reporting on the standing of commercial firms," 20 January 1909, which included information obtained from American ambassadors in London, Paris, Vienna, and Berlin, case 17643, State Department Records, Record Group 59, National Archives.

11. Werking, *Master Architects*, pp. 188–89.

12. Schmeckebier and Weber, *Bureau of Foreign and Domestic Commerce*, p. 27; Charles Donaldson to Oscar S. Straus, 3 May 1907, DOC Records, 70328.

13. Department of Commerce and Labor, *Reports for 1908, 1909, 1910, 1911 and 1912* (Washington, D.C., 1907–13); Werking, *Master Architects*, pp. 189–90.

14. Oscar S. Straus to Isidor Straus, 5 October 1907, Oscar S. Straus Papers, Library of Congress; see also Oscar S. Straus, *Under Four Administrations: From Cleveland to Taft* (Boston and New York, 1922), p. 236; Naomi W. Cohen, *A Dual Heritage: The Public Career of Oscar S. Straus* (Philadelphia, 1969), pp. 19–20, 39–40; Alan L. Seltzer, "Progressive Politics and the Idea of the Enlightened Businessmen" (Ph.D. diss., University of Chicago, 1972), p. 157.

15. New York *Times*, 7 October 1907, p. 8; *Who Was Who in America* (New York, 1897–1942) 1:1092; Chamber of Commerce of the State of New York, *Annual Report, 1907–1908* (New York, 1908), pp. 4–7, 16–17; Gustav Schwab to Oscar S. Straus, 22 June 1907, DOC Records, 66419; Seltzer, "Progressive Politics," pp. 157–58.

16. Schwab to Straus, 25 September 1907; Straus to Schwab, 26 September 1907; Straus to Schwab, 2 December 1907, DOC Records, 66419; Wiebe, *Businessmen and Reform*, p. 34; Seltzer, "Progressive Politics," p. 159.

17. Department of Commerce and Labor, *National Council of Commerce* (Washington, D.C., 1907), pp. 24–30.

18. Ibid., pp. 14–15, 26–27, 35; N. I. Stone, *Promotion of Foreign Commerce in Europe and the United States* (Washington, D.C., 1907), pp. 9–14; Straus to Robert Filene, 7 November 1908, DOC Records, 66419; Oscar S. Straus, *The American Spirit* (New York, 1913), p. 189; Seltzer, "Progressive Politics," pp. 161–64.

19. Boston *Herald*, 22 February 1908, p. 1, quoted in Seltzer, "Progressive Politics," p. 164.

20. Department of Commerce and Labor, *Report, 1908* (Washington, D.C., 1909), p. 54.

21. Department of Commerce and Labor, *Report, 1907* (Washington, D.C., 1908), p. 6; Straus, *American Spirit*, pp. 84, 130–89; *National Council of Commerce*, pp. 22–24; Richardson, *Messages and Papers*, 15:7137; Seltzer, "Progressive Politics," pp. 164–66.

22. Department of Commerce and Labor, *Report, 1908* (Washington, D.C., 1909), p. 54; Seltzer, "Progressive Politics," pp. 165–70.

23. "Remarks of Secretary Nagel before the Conference of Executive Committee of the National Council of Commerce," 7 April 1909; National Council of Commerce, *Bulletin to*

Members, no. 1 (14 June 1909); Schwab to T. L. Weed (chief clerk, Department of Commerce and Labor), 23 October 1909, DOC Records, 66419; *American Industries*, 1 July 1909, p. 20; 5 October 1909, p. 9; Wiebe, *Businessmen and Reform*, p. 35.

24. "Report of the National Association of Manufacturer's Committee on Reorganization of the National Council of Commerce," 11 March 1910, DOC Records, 66419.

25. *National Council of Commerce*, pp. 5–8; NAM, *Proceedings*, 1907, pp. 5, 24–27; A. B. Farquhar, "Tariff Revision from the Manufacturer's Standpoint," *Popular Science Monthly* 74 (May 1909): 448; Francis B. Loomis, "Notes on Our Tariff Relations with Mexico," *Annals of the American Academy of Political and Social Science* 32 (September 1908): 343–47; Wiebe, *Businessmen and Reform*, p. 34; N. I. Stone, *One Man's Crusade for an Honest Tariff* (Appleton, Wis., 1952), pp. 23–34.

26. Richardson, *Messages and Papers*, 15:7675; Seltzer, "Progressive Politics," pp. 182–84.

27. Charles Nagel (Secretary, Commerce and Labor) to Charles D. Hilles, 13 April 1912; A. H. Baldwin to R. Wheeler (telegram), 12 April 1912, DOC Records, 70503; Otto Heller, ed., *Charles Nagel: Speeches and Writings* (2 vols.; New York, 1931), 1:246–47; Seltzer, "Progressive Politics," pp. 183–91; Wiebe, *Businessmen and Reform*, p. 36.

28. Heller, *Nagel*, 1:xviii, 288; Kenneth M. Sturges, *American Chambers of Commerce* (New York, 1915), p. 63.

29. Harwood L. Childs, *Labor and Capital in National Politics* (Columbus, Ohio, 1930), pp. 110–19, 157–71.

30. See Seltzer, "Progressive Politics," pp. 192–206 for an excellent discussion of both Taft's and Nagel's views of the relationship between public and private power. After leaving office, Nagel joined the Board of Directors of the Chamber of Commerce; Heller, *Nagel*, 1:273.

31. Werking, *Master Architects*, p. 191.

32. Department of Commerce and Labor, *Reports for 1909, 1910 and 1911*; Werking, *Master Architects*, pp. 191–93.

33. Burton I. Kaufman, *Efficiency and Expansion: Foreign Trade Organization in the Wilson Administration, 1913–1921* (Westport, Conn., 1974), pp. 69–70; William C. Redfield, *The New Industrial Day* (New York, 1912), pp. 52–63, 72–73.

34. A. H. Baldwin to Redfield, 16 April 1913; Redfield to Frank Taussig, 29 September 1913; Redfield to Woodrow Wilson, 17 November 1913; A. H. Baldwin to Redfield, 5 January 1914, DOC Records, 70801/46; Schmeckebier and Weber, *Bureau of Foreign and Domestic Commerce*, pp. 27–28; Kaufman, *Efficiency and Expansion*, pp. 76–80.

35. The department was to face problems in the future. By 1917 its employees had declined to 129. See the drafts of material to be included in annual reports, DOC Records, 74974; memo of 19 January 1915, 70801/137; Department of Commerce, *Annual Report of the Secretary of Commerce, 1915* (Washington, D.C., 1915), pp. 29, 44; Redfield to Farrell, 24 December 1915, DOC Records, 71737/1.

36. Assistant Secretary E. F. Sweet to Secretary of State Bryan, 11 November 1913, DOC Records, 70801/59; "handout" of "Suggestions to Manufacturers and Exporters," October 1914, 70801/119; *Annual Report of the Secretary of Commerce, 1915*, pp. 44–50.

37. "Suggestions of Manufacturers and Exporters"; Acting Secretary of Commerce Sweet to Bryan, 9 August 1915, DOC Records, 70801/15.

38. Department of Commerce, *Annual Report of the Secretary of Commerce, 1915*, p. 40.

39. "Form letter" to Midwest manufacturers, 13 June 1914, DOC Records, 70801/88; Bernard Feinstein (Cincinnati Chamber of Commerce), "Some Weak Points in the United States' Consular System with Hints and Suggestions to Improve the Service," in Redfield's files, DOC Records, 70801/58; Redfield to Francis S. White (Alabama senator), 26 October 1915 and lists of the work of field agents, 18 November 1915, DOC Records, 70801/163.

40. E. E. Pratt (director, Bureau of Foreign and Domestic Commerce) to Redfield, 13 November 1914, DOC Records, 70801/88.

41. See, for example, Redfield to Rosenwald and Weil, 6 July 1914, DOC Records, 70801/88 and Redfield to D. R. Francis, 17 April 1916, 70801/104; Henry D. Baker, Attaché, to Pratt, 29 May 1915, 70801/104; and Baker to Redfield, 10 June 1916, 70801/110.

42. Feinstein, "Some Weak Points in the United States Consular System."

43. Department of Commerce, *Annual Report of the Secretary of Commerce, 1915*, p. 45; Redfield to Fred Lavis (Pan American Engineering Committee), 13 March 1916, DOC Records, 70801/108; Redfield to Henry L. Rosenfeld (Equitable Life Assurance Society of the United States) 16 July 1919, 70801/114; Pratt to Redfield, 2 December 1915, 70801/110.

44. Pratt, memorandum, to Redfield, 10 June 1916, DOC Records, 70801/173. Critics accused Redfield of enjoying too much of the limelight. He thought of the public attention that he received, however, as helping in his "missionary" effort. American Manufacturers Export Association, "Resolutions," *Eighth Annual Convention* (1917) DOC Records, 72155/53.

45. "Form letters" to 47 Midwest manufacturing companies, 13 June 1914, DOC Records, 70801/88. Other form letters are in this file, too. Robert Patchin (secretary of National Foreign Trade Council) to Redfield, 27 December 1915 and 5 February 1916, 71737/1; see descriptions of the work of field agents, 18 November 1915, 70801/163.

46. There was extensive correspondence begun in the spring of 1915 among trade associations, the office of the secretary and between the secretary's office and that of the department's legal adviser. See the memoranda in DOC Records 70801/138; Sweet to Redfield, 23 January 1915, 71737/1; Pratt to Redfield, 14 October 1915, Redfield to Claude Kitchin, 9 October 1915, Kitchin to Redfield, 14 October 1915, Redfield to Kitchin, 29 October 1915, 70801/158; Redfield to Francis S. White, 26 October 1915, 70801/160.

47. Simmons to Redfield, 10 March 1914, Redfield to Simmons, 12 March 1914, and Redfield to Simmons, 14 March 1914, DOC Records, 70801/84; Redfield to Director of Census, 4 December 1917, 74974.

48. Redfield to Congressman John M. Morin, 22 January 1914 and Redfield to Senator Boies Penrose, 15 January 1914, DOC Records, 70801/82.

49. Acting Secretary E. F. Sweet to Willys-Overland Inc., Export Department, 8 January 1917; Sweet to Lee S. Overman (Senate Appropriations Committee) 8 January 1917, Sweet to Simmons, 8 January 1916; Sweet to F. N. Poe (Philadelphia Chamber of Commerce), 23 January 1917, DOC Records, 70801/113.

50. Letters pertaining to and speeches given at conference of 4 and 5 February 1916, DOC Records, 70801/168.

51. Patchin to Sweet, 11 May 1916, DOC Records 71737/1; Redfield to Baldwin, memorandum of 13 April 1914, 70801/86. Redfield to Patchin, 19 December 1914, 71377/1; for a similar problem, see Redfield to Patchin, 25 October 1916, 717737/1.

Seven

1. American Manufacturers Export Association, *Resolutions of the Seventh Annual Meeting*, 31 October 1916, in Department of Commerce, Bureau of Foreign and Domestic Commerce Records, Record Group 151, file no. 800, National Archives, Washington, D.C.; hereafter cited as BFDC Records.

2. D. F. Houston (Secretary of Agriculture) to Redfield, 22 March 1917; Redfield to Houston, 24 March 1914; Redfield to L. L. Bracken (secretary, Federal Trade Commission), 4 April 1917, General Records, Office of the Secretary, General Correspondence, Department of Commerce in Record Group 40, file no. 70801/76; hereafter cited as DOC Records.

3. William J. Harris (director, Bureau of Census) to Redfield, 13 April 1914; Redfield to Houston, 15 April 1914; Redfield to Franklin K. Lane (Secretary of Interior) 15 April 1914, DOC Records, 70801/76.

4. Robert F. Rose (foreign trade adviser) to Redfield, 17 November 1913; Redfield to Rose, 18 November 1913; Secretary of State William Jennings Bryan, Order No. 57 (6 November 1913); E. F. Sweet (Assistant Secretary of Commerce) to Bryan, 24 November 1913, and 15 December 1913; E. E. Pratt (director, Bureau of Foreign and Domestic Commerce) to Redfield, 8 July 1916; Redfield to Frank H. Polk (Department of State), 8 July 1916, DOC Records, 70801/63.

5. Secretary of Commerce Joshua W. Alexander to Secretary of State Bainbridge Colby, 8 October 1920, DOC Records, 70801/63.

6. Redfield to Polk, 8 July 1916; Redfield to Secretary of State Robert W. Lansing, 15 July 1916; Polk to Redfield, 25 July 1916; Redfield to Lansing, 29 July 1916; Redfield memorandum of 27 June 1918 to the Bureau of Foreign and Domestic Commerce; Redfield to Acting Secretary of State Polk, 13 June 1919; Alexander to Colby, 20 May 1920, DOC Records, 70801/63.

7. Redfield to A. S. Phelps, 18 May 1914, DOC Records, 71737/1; Burton I. Kaufman, *Efficiency and Expansion: Foreign Trade Organization in the Wilson Administration, 1913–1921* (Westport, Conn., 1974), pp. 82–84; Martin J. Sklar, "Woodrow Wilson and the Political Economy of Modern United States Liberalism," in *A New History of Leviathan*, ed. Ronald Radosh and Murray N. Rothbard (New York, 1972), pp. 28–51.

8. Alan Seltzer, "Woodrow Wilson as Corporate-Liberal: Towards a Reconsideration of Left Revisionist Historiography," *Western Political Science Quarterly* 30 (June 1977): 183–212.

9. *Proceedings of the Sixteenth Annual Convention of the National Association of Manufacturers, 1911* (New York, 1912), pp. 76–77. Robert H. Wiebe, *Businessmen and Reform: A Study of Progressivism* (Cambridge, 1962), p. 37; Alan L. Seltzer, "Progressive Politics and the Idea of the Enlightened Businessman" (Ph.D. thesis, University of Chicago, 1972).

10. New York *Times*, 11 May 1914, p. 13.

11. New York *Times*, 13 July 1914, p. 11; National Foreign Trade Council, *The National Foreign Trade Council: Its Purpose, Personnel, Accomplishments* (New York, 1918), pp. 3–4.

12. New York *Times*, 27 May 1914, p. 9; 8 May 1914, pp. 9, 19; NFTC, *Purpose, Personnel, Accomplishments*, pp. 3–4.

13. E. V. Douglass (secretary, American Manufacturers Export Association) to Redfield, 19 October 1917, DOC Records, 72155/53.

14. See *Final Declaration of the Fourth National Foreign Trade Convention*, 25–27 July 1917, pp. 3–5 in DOC Records, 70801/182; an excellent and useful study of attitudes toward big business is Louis Galambos, *The Public Image of Big Business in America, 1880–1940: A Quantitative Study in Social Change* (Baltimore, 1975).

15. Robert H. Patchin (secretary, NFTC) to Redfield, 28 July 1914, and the enclosed "news release" quoting remarks of NFTC president, James A. Farrell, DOC Records, 71737/1.

16. Redfield, although substantially more sympathetic to the interests of those with an established stake in export markets than his predecessors Straus and Nagel, nevertheless reflected on occasion the prejudices of many smaller producers toward the larger role of the "trusts" in foreign markets. Writing to the chairman of the Federal Trade Commission on the need to loosen restraints on antitrust laws to allow cooperation in the deployment of foreign trade, Redfield noted that "the present [antitrust] law plays into the hands of the larger concerns and shuts out smaller ones from very important markets" (Redfield to Joseph E. Davies, 11 October 1915, DOC Records 72441).

17. Federal Reserve Act, Pub. Law No. 43, 38 STAT 378; National Foreign Trade Coun-

cil, *The War and South American Trade* (New York, 1914), pp. 9–11; Kaufman, *Efficiency and Expansion*, pp. 74–76. Clyde W. Phelps, *The Foreign Expansion of American Banks* (New York, 1927), p. 105; a useful study of the background of the Federal Reserve Act and its implementation is Robert C. West, *Banking Reform and the Federal Reserve, 1863–1923* (Ithaca, N.Y., 1974).

18. James C. Baker and M. Gerald Bradford, *American Banks Abroad: Edge Act Companies and Multinational Banking* (New York, 1974), pp. 25–29.

19. Phelps, *Foreign Expansion*, pp. 106–8; Kaufman, *Efficiency and Expansion*, pp. 243–47.

20. Kaufman, *Efficiency and Expansion*, pp. 243–47; Michael J. Hogan, *Informal Entente: The Private Structure of Cooperation in Anglo-American Economic Diplomacy, 1918–1928* (Columbia, Mo., 1977), pp. 79–80; Carl P. Parrini, *Heir to Empire: United States Economic Diplomacy, 1916–1923* (Pittsburgh, 1969), pp. 104–12; Joan Hoff Wilson, *American Business and Foreign Policy, 1920–1933* (Lexington, Ky., 1971), pp. 17–18; Phelps, pp. 106–8.

21. National Foreign Trade Council, *European Economic Alliances* (New York, 1916), pp. 7–36, 69–81; "News Release" sent by Patchin to Redfield, 28 July 1914; copy of minutes of the meeting of the National Foreign Trade Council, 16 September 1918; and AMEA, *Bulletin*, 1 April 1914, in DOC Records, 717737/1.

22. Kaufman, *Efficiency and Expansion*, pp. 155–57 estimates that 15,000 businessmen were interested in trade expansion. U.S. Cong., Senate, *Cooperation in American Export Trade*, Doc. No. 426, 64th Cong., 1st sess., May 1916, pp. 2–3.

23. Senate, *Cooperation in American Export Trade*, p. 3; Gerald D. Feldman and Ulrich Nocken, "Trade Associations and Economic Power: Interest Group Development in the German Iron and Steel and Machine Building Industries, 1900–1933," *Business History Review* 49 (Winter 1975): 413–45. Senate, *Cooperation in American Export Trade*, p. 3.

24. Senate, *Cooperation in American Export Trade*, p. 3.

25. Ibid., pp. 3–4. Peter Mathias, "Conflicts of Function in the Rise of Big Business: The British Experience," in Harold F. Williamson, ed., *Evolution of International Management Structures* (Newark, Del., 1975), pp. 40–58.

26. Douglass to Redfield, 19 October 1917, transmitting copy of AMEA resolutions and reports of committees on legislation; see also copy of the undated minutes of the National Foreign Trade Council received in Redfield's office, 3 April 1917, DOC Records, 71737/1.

27. Redfield to Lansing, 11 July 1917, DOC Records, 72155/53.

28. National Foreign Trade Council, *Official Report of the Proceedings of the Second Annual Convention* (New York, 1916), pp. 53–93; hereafter cited as NFTC, *Proceedings*. New York *Times*, 25 May 1914, p. 17; American Iron and Steel Association, *Bulletin*, 15 January 1913.

29. Webb Act was approved 18 April 1918; E. F. Sweet (Assistant Secretary, Department of Commerce) to Patchin, 19 February 1916; see testimony on Webb bill in U.S. Congress, Senate, *Hearings on H.R. 17350*, 64th Cong. 2d sess., 1917, passim; Kaufman, *Efficiency and Expansion*, pp. 155–57; Galambos, *Public Image*, pp. 119–20.

30. U.S. Congress, House, Committee on the Judiciary, *Hearings on Trust Legislation*, 63d Cong., 2d sess., 1914, pp. 1567–83; U.S. Congress, Senate, Committee on Interstate Commerce, *Hearings on Bills Relating to Trust Legislation and Interstate Trade*, 63d Cong., 2d sess., 1914, pp. 1009–1201. Gabriel Kolko, *The Triumph of Conservatism: A Reinterpretation of American History, 1900–1916* (Chicago, 1963), pp. 261–67. NFTC, *Proceedings*, 1916, pp. 285–87; Kaufman, *Efficiency and Expansion*, pp. 155–56.

31. Redfield to Charles Muchnic, 14 May 1914; Redfield to Bryan, 28 November 1914; DOC Records, 7173, 72626, Redfield to Edward N. Hurley, 7 June 1916; Redfield to

Woodrow Wilson, 7 June 1916; Hurley to Redfield, 22 June 1916, DOC Records, 7173, 72626, 72236, 74302. Kaufman, *Efficiency and Expansion*, pp. 156–58; Edward N. Hurley, *Awakening of Business* (New York, 1916), pp. 158–68; Federal Trade Commission, *Report on Cooperation in American Export Trade* (Washington, D.C., 1916), 1:98–99, 378–79.

32. *Congressional Record*, 64th Cong., 1st sess., 1916, pp. 13676–727; 65th Cong., 1st sess., 1917, pp. 2784–91, 3563–85, 7324–7328; 65th Cong., 2d sess., 1918, pp. 68–75, 4723–24. Kaufman, *Efficiency and Expansion*, pp. 158–59, 214–15; William F. Notz and Richard S. Harvey, *American Foreign Trade as Promoted by the Webb Pomerene and Edge Acts* (Indianapolis, 1920), pp. 149–52.

33. Notz and Harvey, *American Foreign Trade*, pp. 152–53; New York *Times*, 5 December 1917, p. 1; *Congressional Record*, 65th Cong., 1st sess., 1917, pp. 3584–85; *Congressional Record*, 65th Cong., 2d sess., 1917, pp. 168–86.

34. Chamber of Commerce of the United States, *Referendum No. 26: The Federal Trade Committee of the Chamber Regarding Trust Legislation* (Washington, D.C., 1919), pp. 12–14; Notz and Harvery, *American Foreign Trade*, pp. 157–60; Kaufman, *Efficiency and Expansion*, pp. 215–16.

35. B. S. Butler (director, BFDC) to Redfield, 4 May 1918, and James A. Farrell, "Foreign Trade Aspects," 19 April 1918, copy of speech in DOC Records 71737/1.

36. Farrell, "Foreign Trade Aspects"; National Foreign Trade Council, *Ocean Shipping: The Basic Principles of Maritime Transportation, with Particular Reference to the Foreign Trade of the United States* (New York, 1915), passim.

37. John G. B. Hutchins, *The American Maritime Industries and Public Policy, 1789–1914: An Economic History* (New York, 1941), pp. 49–60; Jeffrey J. Safford, *Wilsonian Maritime Diplomacy, 1913–1921* (New Brunswick, N.J., 1978), pp. 1–16.

38. Safford, *Wilsonian Maritime Diplomacy*, pp. 32–38; NFTC, *Proceedings*, 1914, pp. 144–45.

38. Safford, *Wilsonian Maritime Diplomacy*, pp. 47–51; John J. Broesamle, *William Gibbs McAdoo: A Passion for Change, 1863–1917* (Port Washington, N.Y., 1973), pp. 225–28.

40. Broesamle, *McAdoo*, pp. 228–31; Safford, *Wilsonian Maritime Diplomacy*, pp. 38–51; National Foreign Trade Council, *Effect of the War upon American Foreign Commerce* (New York, 1915), passim.

41. Broesamle, *McAdoo*, pp. 222–25.

42. Ibid., pp. 213–24.

43. Ibid., p. 215.

44. Ibid., p. 216.

45. Ibid., pp. 214–15, 226–30; Arthur S. Link, *Wilson: The Struggle for Neutrality, 1914–1915* (Princeton, N.J., 1960), pp. 86–87; New York *Times*, 20 August 1914, p. 1.

46. Broesamle, *McAdoo*, p. 222; Chamber of Commerce of the United States of America, *Referendum Number 9: The Buildup of the Merchant Marine* (Washington, D.C., 1915), pp. 3–5.

47. New York *Times*, 7 October 1919; *Journal of Commerce*, 15 October 1915; Broesamle, *McAdoo*, p. 222.

48. Broesamle, *McAdoo*, pp. 223–28; Link, *Neutrality*, pp. 149–51, 155–58.

49. Broesamle, *McAdoo*, p. 225; Farrell, "Foreign Trade Aspects," and NFTC, *Ocean Shipping*, pp. 3–7.

50. Wiebe, *Businessmen and Reform*, pp. 145–47; Broesamle, *McAdoo*, p. 229.

51. Broesamle, *McAdoo*, pp. 230–33.

52. Edward N. Hurley, *The New American Merchant Marine* (New York, 1920), p. 22; Broesamle, *McAdoo*, pp. 233–34.

53. NFTC, *Proceedings*, 1917, pp. 455–60.

54. Hurley, *Merchant Marine*, pp. 158–68; NAM, *Proceedings*, 1918, pp. 132–43; Kaufman, *Efficiency and Expansion*, pp. 157–87. Redfield to Hurley, 7 June 1916; Redfield to Wilson, 7 June 1916; Wilson to Redfield, 8 June 1916; Hurley to Redfield, 22 June 1916, DOC Records, 74302, 72237. Safford, *Wilsonian Maritime Diplomacy*, pp. 24–25.

55. *Annual Report of the United States Shipping Board, 1918* (Washington, D.C., 1918), pp. 7–15; Darrell H. Smith and Paul V. Betters, *The United States Shipping Board* (Washington, D.C., 1931), pp. 8–18; Kaufman, *Efficiency and Expansion*, pp. 188–89.

56. Safford, *Wilsonian Maritime Diplomacy*, pp. 141–67; Kaufman, *Efficiency and Expansion*, pp. 192, 240–41.

57. John G. B. Hutchins, "The American Shipping Industry since 1914," *Business History Review* 28 (Spring 1954): 110.

58. Safford, *Wilsonian Maritime Diplomacy*, pp. 221–29.

59. U.S. Congress, House, *Hearings before the Subcommittee on the Merchant Marine and Fisheries*, 66th Cong., 1st sess., 1919, pp. 8–11; Arthur E. Cook, ed., *A History of the United States Shipping Board and Merchant Fleet Corporation* (Baltimore, 1927), pp. 10–13; Paul M. Zeis, *American Shipping Policy* (Princeton, N.J., 1938), pp. 116–19; Safford, *Wilsonian Maritime Diplomacy*, pp. 230–31.

60. Safford, *Wilsonian Maritime Diplomacy*, pp. 244–46.

61. Hutchins, "The American Shipping Industry," pp. 110–11.

62. Redfield to McAdoo, 12 October 1918, DOC Records, 75024/56.

63. Farrell to Redfield, 21 May 1917, DOC Records, 75024/42. One of the points of this letter is that Latin American trade should be kept up so that raw materials could still be bought there. The largest producers of locomotives, steel products, agricultural machinery, etc., had substantial sales in Latin America already. They did not have to be encouraged to sell there; indeed they were concerned with protecting and continuing their trade with Latin America.

64. See the extensive correspondence on this issue in June 1917 in DOC Records, 75024/56; War Trade Board, *Report of the War Trade Board* (Washington, D.C., 1920), pp. 1–13.

65. Redfield to Acting Chief of the BFDC, 20 August 1917; Wilson to Redfield, 21 August 1917; Redfield to Wilson, 22 August 1917; and Wilson to Redfield, 22, 23 August 1917, DOC Records, 75024/56. Although the large increases of exports were no doubt the major reason for bureaucratic changes, there might have been other reasons for the removal of responsibility from the Department of Commerce. Redfield had involved himself in an ugly public quarrel with the head of the BFDC, E. E. Pratt, in 1915. Redfield's prestige was damaged by this episode. Furthermore, the high turnover in the department had raised questions about Redfield's administrative abilities. See Henry D. Baker to E. E. Pratt, 20 May 1916; Baker to Redfield, 12 June 1916, DOC Records, 70801/104. Also see Philip D. Kennedy, Chief, BFDC, to Redfield, 18 September 1919 and Redfield to Pierce C. Williams, 18 September 1919, DOC Records, 70801/103.

66. Ernest L. Bogart, "Economic Organization for War," *American Political Science Review* 14 (November 1920): 587–606; Thurmon (the Department of Commerce's solicitor) to Sweet (Acting Secretary of Commerce when Redfield was out of town), DOC Records, 75024/56.

67. B. S. Cutler to Redfield, 2 November 1917, DOC Records, 70801/175.

68. *Report of the War Trade Board*, pp. 1–13; NFTC, *Proceedings*, 1918, p. 108; Kaufman, *Efficiency and Expansion*, pp. 184–85.

69. Business attitudes toward the War Trade Board can be found in the Daily Digest of News and Comments in Papers of the War Trade Board, Record Group 154, National Archives, Box 1503. Patchin to Redfield, 16 May 1917 and Redfield to Patchin, 19 May 1917, DOC Records, 75024/56. (Patchin was, at the time these letters were written, a

former executive secretary of the NFTC.) See also Redfield article in *Weekly Export Bulletin* of Philadelphia Commercial Museum, 2 June 1917 in DOC Records, 75024/56. Acting Secretary of Commerce Sweet to C. M. Woolley (Commerce Department's representative on the War Trade Board), 17 August 1918 and Sweet to P. J. Phillips (Federal Export Corporation), 26 September 1918, DOC Records, 75024/56.

70. Redfield to McAdoo, 18 October 1918 and Davis (executive secretary, NFTC) to Redfield, 19 October 1918, DOC Records, 75024/56 and Cutler to Redfield, 25 April 1918, DOC Records, 71737/1.

71. Redfield to McCormick (WTB chairman), 27 July 1918 and Redfield's memorandum to the Department of Commerce, 30 July 1918, DOC Records, 75024/56. Other information about disputes among businessmen, the Commerce Department and the WTB are found in Cutler to Redfield, 24 July 1918; Alfred H. Benjamin to Redfield, 17 June 1918 and Redfield to W. A. Forman, 6 August 1918; Redfield to Treadway, 12 August 1918, DOC Records, 75024/56.

72. Redfield to Bernard Baruch, 24 September 1918, DOC Records, 75024/56. *Wall Street Journal*, 16 February 1918, p. 8; NFTC, *Proceedings*, 1918, pp. 111–13.

Eight

1. Mira Wilkins, *The Maturing of Multinational Enterprise: American Business Abroad from 1914 to 1970* (Cambridge, Mass., 1974), pp. 43–52.

2. Michael J. Hogan, *Informal Entente: The Private Structure of Cooperation in Anglo-American Economic Diplomacy, 1918-1928* (Columbia, Mo., 1977), pp. 20–21. Robert H. Van Meter, "The United States and European Recovery, 1918-1923: A Study of Public Policy and Private Finance" (Ph.D. diss., University of Wisconsin, 1971), pp. iii-v, 1–26.

3. Joseph L. Tulchin, *The Aftermath of War: World War I and U.S. Policy toward Latin America* (New York, 1971), pp. 38–39; Charles W. Phelps, *The Foreign Expansion of American Banks* (New York, 1927), pp. 86–87; M. F. Jolliffe, *The United States as a Financial Centre, 1919-1933* (Cardiff, 1935), p. 3; U.S. Department of Commerce, *Statistical Abstract of the United States for 1925* (Washington, D.C., 1926), pp. 449–60.

4. Wilkins, *Maturing*, p. 51; League of Nations, *Industrialization and Foreign Trade* (New York, 1945), p. 134; U.S. Department of Commerce, Bureau of Foreign and Domestic Commerce, *American Trade With Germany 1914, 1921, 1922* by C. Herring and Edward G. Eichelberger, *Commerce Reports*, Supplementary, Trade Information Bulletin no. 150 (Washington, D.C., 1923), pp. 8–16.

5. An excellent discussion of the exchange problems can be found in Fred I. Kent, "Foreign Exchange," in National Foreign Trade Council, *Official Report of the Proceedings of the Seventh National Foreign Trade Convention, May 12, 13, 14, 15, 1920* (New York, 1920), pp. 38–55; hereafter cited as NFTC, *Proceedings*.

6. William Ashworth, *A Short History of the International Economy Since 1850* (3d ed.; London, 1975), pp. 204–7.

7. *Proceedings of the Twenty-Fifth Annual Convention of the National Association of Manufacturers* (New York, 1920), pp. 5–91; hereafter cited as NAM, *Proceedings*; Michael J. Hogan, "The United States and the Problem of International Economic Control: American Attitudes toward European Reconstruction, 1918-1920," *Pacific Historical Review* 44 (February 1975): 84–103; Paul Abrahams, "American Bankers and the Economic Tactics of Peace," *Journal of American History* 46 (December 1969): 572–83; Carl P. Parrini, *Heir to Empire: United States Economic Diplomacy, 1916-1923* (Pittsburgh, 1969), pp. 47 ff.

8. Hogan, *Informal Entente*, pp. 24–27; Abrahams, "American Bankers," pp. 572-83.

9. Hogan, *Informal Entente*, pp. 26, 29; Van Meter, "United States and European Recovery," pp. 238–40.

10. Van Meter, "United States and Economic Recovery," pp. 114–57, 180–85.

11. Tulchin, *Aftermath*, pp. 38–40; Department of Commerce, *Statistical Abstract for 1925*, pp. 449–460.

12. Department of Commerce, *Statistical Abstract for 1925*, pp. 45–46; Hogan, *Informal Entente*, pp. 20–21; Van Meter, "United States and European Recovery," pp. 23–25.

13. Tulchin, *Aftermath*, pp. 53–54; Diary of Wilbur J. Carr, 23 March 1920, Papers of Wilbur J. Carr, Library of Congress, Washington, D.C.; hereafter cited as Carr Diary.

14. Hogan, *Informal Entente*, pp. 32–35; Tulchin, *Aftermath*, pp. 160–61; Van Meter, "United States and European Recovery," pp. 124–26, 152–57.

15. W. W. Ewing to C. C. Kochenderfer, 15 February 1921, 21 February 1921, and 28 April 1921; O. V. Brown to Department of Commerce, 21 February 1921; O. P. Hopkins to O. V. Brown, 26 February 1921, Department of Commerce, Records of the Bureau of Foreign and Domestic Commerce, Record Group 151, file no. 220, National Archives, Washington, D.C.; hereafter cited as BFDC Records; also see the Minutes of the Economic Liaison Committee Meetings, BFDC Records, 151.2. The papers of the committee are to be found in Department of State, General Records, Records of the Office of Economic Adviser, Record Group 59, E 557, E 558, National Archives, Washington, D.C.; hereafter cited as Records of the Economic Adviser. Tulchin, *Aftermath*, pp. 45–46.

16. See drafts and internal memoranda concerned with the preparation of the Commerce Department's annual report for 1919, General Records, Office of the Secretary, General Correspondence, Department of Commerce, Record Group No. 40, file no. 79266; hereafter cited as DOC Records and Redfield to Henry L. Rosenfeld (Equitable Life Assurance Society of the United States), 16 July 1919; Hoover to W. B. Price, 10 December 1921, DOC Records, 70801/114.

17. "Minutes of Economic Liaison Committee," Third Regular General Meeting, 9 April 1919, BFDC Records, 151.2; Lawrence E. Gelfand, *The Inquiry: American Preparations for Peace, 1917–1919.* (New Haven, Conn., 1963), pp. 184–86; Robert D. Cuff, *The War Industries Board: Business-Government Relations during World War I* (Baltimore, 1973), pp. 241–64.

18. Tulchin, *Aftermath*, pp. 57–60.

19. Ibid.

20. Daniel M. Smith, *Aftermath of War: Bainbridge Colby and Wilsonian Diplomacy, 1920–1921* (Philadelphia, 1970), pp. 1–31, 155–59.

21. Redfield to O. K. Davis, 13 May 1919; DOC Records, 70737/1.

22. Davis to E. F. Sweet (Assistant Secretary of Commerce), 3 May 1919 and Davis to Redfield, 23 May 1919, DOC Records, 71737/1.

23. See DOC Records, 7502456, for a discussion of Wilson's Executive Order No. 3086A (12 May 1919), which set up the procedures by which the WTB was to be gradually turned over to the Department of State; also see the unsigned draft of a response to an inquiry about the transition of the WTB, 7 December 1919, DOC Records, 75025/56. Tulchin, *Aftermath*, pp. 57–60.

24. Redfield to Thomas R. Marshall (President of the Senate), 20 October 1919, DOC Records 79818.

25. Ibid.; Tulchin, *Aftermath*, p. 113.

26. Redfield to Marshall, 20 October 1919, DOC Records, 79818.

27. R. E. Magie to J. W. Alexander (Redfield's successor), 21 January 1920; Alexander to William H. Harris (senator from Georgia), 13 March 1920, DOC Records, 79818.

28. Ibid.

29. Alexander to Harris, 13 March 1920, DOC Records, 79818; Carr Diary, 1 and 3 March 1920.

30. O. K. Davis to Redfield, 26 January 1920; J. Roberts (Acting Secretary of Commerce) to Davis, 30 January 1920, DOC Records, 71737/1.

31. NAM, *Proceedings*, 1918, pp. 77, 144; NAM, *Proceedings*, 1919, pp. 115-33, 189; NAM, *Proceedings*, 1920, pp. 114-15, 118-20, 125-26; NAM, *Proceedings*, 1921, pp. 140, 143.

32. Harvey E. Fisk, "The Flow of Capital–Canada," *Annals of the American Academy of Political and Social Science* 107 (May 1923): 175.

33. NFTC, *Proceedings*, 1919, pp. 148-49, speech by William E. Peck.

34. Ibid.; NFTC, *Proceedings*, 1920, pp. 142-43.

35. NFTC, *Proceedings*, 1919, pp. vii, xix.

36. Ibid., p. vii.

37. Ibid., pp. 3-4, 31-35.

38. See, for example, confidential weekly report of the Department of State, "Economic Conditions in Foreign Countries," Office of Foreign Trade Adviser, no. 22 (10 January 1920) and no. 26 (7 February 1920), Records of Economic Adviser; NFTC, *Proceedings*, 1919, pp. 388-89.

39. NFTC, *Proceedings*, 1919, pp. 389-91.

40. Ibid., p. 473.

41. NFTC, *Proceedings*, 1920, passim.

42. Ibid., pp. 13-23, 76-81.

43. Ibid., pp. 63-66.

44. Ibid., pp. 66-67.

45. Ibid., p. 67.

46. Ibid., p. 68.

47. Ibid., p. 160.

48. Ibid., p. 15.

49. Ibid., pp. 385-89.

50. Ibid., pp. 6-7, 147; Abrahams, "American Bankers," pp. 578-83.

51. NFTC, *Proceedings*, 1920, pp. 304-9.

52. Ibid., pp. 307-8.

53. NFTC, *Proceedings*, 1919, p. 6; NFTC, *Proceedings*, 1920, pp. 40-41.

Nine

1. Mira Wilkins, *The Maturing of Multinational Enterprise: American Business Abroad from 1914 to 1970* (Cambridge, Mass., 1974), pp. 49-52; Cleona Lewis, *America's Stake in International Investments* (Washington, D.C., 1938), pp. 309-10; National Association of Manufacturers, *Proceedings of the Annual Convention for 1918*, p. 148; for 1919, p. 189; for 1920, pp. 118-20, 125-26, 140; for 1922, pp. 143, 148-50.

2. Department of Commerce, Bureau of Foreign and Domestic Commerce, Record Group 151, National Archives. File 163 contains much information about the bureau's and the department's attitude toward what was referred to as the "branch factory movement." See also Wilkins, *Maturing*, pp. 52-53; Joseph S. Tulchin, *The Aftermath of War: World War I and U.S. Policy toward Latin America* (New York, 1971), pp. 110-11; Joseph Brandes, *Herbert Hoover and Economic Diplomacy: Department of Commerce Policy, 1921-1928* (Pittsburgh, 1962), pp. 151-69.

3. Wilkins, *Maturing*, pp. 50-53, 63, 68-69; Robert H. Van Meter, "The United States and European Recovery, 1918-1923: A Study of Public Policy and Private Finance," (Ph.D. diss., University of Wisconsin, 1971), pp. 180-84.

4. Burton I. Kaufman, *Efficiency and Expansion: Foreign Trade Organization in the Wilson Administration, 1913-1921* (Westport, Conn., 1974); Joan Hoff Wilson, *American*

Business and Foreign Policy, 1920-1933 (Lexington, Ky., 1971); Michael J. Hogan, *Informal Entente: The Private Structure of Cooperation in Anglo-American Economic Diplomacy, 1918-1928* (Columbia, Mo., 1977); Ellis W. Hawley, "Herbert Hoover, the Commerce Secretariat, and the Vision of an 'Associative State,' 1921-1928," in Martin Fausold and George T. Mazuzan, eds., *The Hoover Presidency: A Reappraisal* (Albany, 1974); Grant McConnell, *Private Power and American Democracy* (New York, 1966).

Bibliography

I. Primary Materials

A. Archival and Manuscript Collections

Aldrich, Nelson W. Papers. Library of Congress. Washington, D.C.
Carnegie, Andrew. Papers. Library of Congress. Washington, D.C.
Carr, Wilbur J. Papers. Library of Congress. Washington, D.C.
Lansing, Robert. Papers. Library of Congress. Washington, D.C.
McAdoo, William Gibbs. Papers. Library of Congress. Washington, D.C.
National Association of Manufacturers. Papers. Eleutherian Mills Historical Library. Green-ville, Delaware.
Redfield, William C. Papers. Library of Congress. Washington, D.C.
Roosevelt, Theodore. Papers. Library of Congress. Washington, D.C.
Root, Elihu. Papers. Library of Congress. Washington, D.C.
Straus, Oscar S. Papers. Library of Congress. Washington, D.C.
U.S. Department of Commerce. Bureau of Corporations Records. Record Group 122. National Archives. Washington, D.C.
_____ . Bureau of Foreign and Domestic Commerce. Record Group 151. National Archives. Washington, D.C.
_____ . General Records of the Office of Secretary of Commerce. Record Group 40. National Archives. Washington, D.C.
U.S. Department of State. Consular Bureau Decisions and Precedents. Record Group 59. National Archives. Washington, D.C.
_____ . Foreign Service Posts (Russian-Diplomatic). Record Group 84. National Archives. Washington, D.C.
_____ . General Records. Records of the Office of Economic Advisor. Record Group 59. National Archives. Washington, D.C.
U.S. Tariff Commission. Papers of the Tariff Board. Record Group 81. National Archives. Washington, D.C.
U.S. War Trade Board. Records. Record Group 182. National Archives. Washington, D.C.
Wilson, Woodrow. Papers. Library of Congress. Washington, D.C.

B. Government Documents and Publications

League of Nations. Economic Intelligence Service. *Industrialization and Foreign Trade.* New York, 1945.
U.S. Congress. *Congressional Record.*
_____ . House. Committee on Appropriations. *Hearings before Subcommittee of House*

Committee on Appropriations... in Charge of Sundry Civil Appropriation Bill for 1913. 62d Cong., 2d Sess. 1912.

————. House. Committee on Foreign Affairs. *Hearings on Diplomatic and Consular Appropriations Bill, 1915-1916, 1917.* 63d Cong., 1914; 64th Cong., 1916.

————. House. Committee on Investigation of the United States Steel Corporation. *Hearings on United States Steel Corporation.* 62d Cong., 1st Sess. 1911.

————. House. Committee on the Judiciary. *Hearings on Trust Legislation.* 63d Cong., 2d Sess. 1914.

————. House. Committee on Appropriations. *Hearings before Subcommittee in Charge of Legislative, Executive and Judicial Appropriation Bills, 1908-1912.* 59th Cong. to 61st Cong. 1906-12.

————. House. *Department of Commerce and Industries.* Report No. 321. 56th Cong., 1st Sess. 1900.

————. House. *To Improve Diplomatic and Consular Service.* Report No. 840. 62d Cong., 2d Sess. 1912.

————. Senate. Committee on Appropriations. *Bureau of Trade Relations in Department of State and Domestic Bureau in Department of Commerce and Labor.* 62d Cong., 2d Sess. 1912.

————. Senate. Committee on Foreign Relations. *Reciprocity Convention with France.* 56th Cong., 1st Sess. 1899.

————. Senate. Committee on Interstate Commerce. *Hearings on Bills Relating to Trust Legislation and Interstate Trade.* 63d Cong., 2d Sess. 1914.

————. Senate. *Cooperation in American Export Trade.* Document 426. 64th Cong., 1st Sess. 1916.

————. Senate. Committee on Foreign Relations. *Hearings on Reorganization of the Consular Service.* 59th Cong., 1st Sess. 1905.

————. Senate. *Foreign Trade and Treaty Relations.* Document 150. 61st Cong., 1st Sess. 1909.

————. Senate. *Hearings on H.R. 17350* (Webb Legislation). 64th Cong., 2d Sess. 1917.

————. Senate. *Reorganization of the Consular and Diplomatic Service.* Senate Report 1202. 56th Cong., 1st Sess. 1900.

————. Senate. *The Tariff Board.* Document 463. 61st Cong., 2d Sess. 1910.

U.S. Department of Commerce. *Annual Report of the Secretary of Commerce, 1915.* Washington, D.C., 1915.

————. Bureau of the Census. *Historical Statistics of the United States, Colonial Times to 1957.* Washington, D.C., 1961.

————. Bureau of the Census. *Statistical Abstract of the United States, 1925.* Washington, D.C., 1926.

————. Bureau of Foreign and Domestic Commerce. *American Trade with Germany 1914, 1921, 1922,* by C. E. Herring and Edward G. Eichelberger. *Commerce Report.* Suppl. Trade Information Bulletin, No. 150. Washington, D.C., 1923.

U.S. Department of Commerce and Labor. Bureau of Corporations. *Beef Industry. Report of the Commissioner of Corporations on the Beef Industry, March 3, 1905.* Washington, D.C., 1905.

————. Bureau of Corporations. *Report of the Commissioner of Corporations on International Harvester.* Washington, D.C., 1913.

————. Bureau of Corporations. *Report of the Commissioner of Corporations on the Petroleum Industry.* Part 3: "Foreign Trade." Washington, D.C., 1909.

————. Bureau of Corporations. *Monthly Consular and Trade Reports 1905-1910.* Washington, D.C., 1905-10.

————. Bureau of Corporations. *Report of the Commissioner of Corporations on the Steel Industry.* 3 vols. Washington, D.C., 1911.

Bibliography

_____ . Bureau of Corporations. *Report of the Commissioner of Corporations on the Tobacco Industry.* Washington, D.C., 1909.

_____ . Bureau of Manufactures. *Monthly Consular and Trade Reports.* Washington, D.C., 1890–1910.

_____ . Bureau of Statistics. *Consular Reports, 1903–1905.* 12 vols. Washington, D.C., 1903–05.

_____ . *National Council of Commerce.* Washington, D.C., 1907.

_____ . *Reports, 1905–1912.* Washington, D.C., 1906–13.

U.S. Department of Interior. U.S. Census Office. *Report on the Manufactures of the United States at the Tenth Census.* Washington, D.C., 1883.

U.S. Department of State. Bureau of Foreign Commerce. *Commercial Relations of the United States with Foreign Countries, 1902.* Washington, D.C., 1902.

_____ . Bureau of Foreign Commerce. *Consular Reports, 1885–1903.* Washington, D.C., 1886–1904.

_____ . *Regulations Prescribed for Use of the Consular Service of the United States.* Washington, D.C., 1896.

U.S. Federal Trade Commission. *Electric-Power Industry, Supply of Electrical Equipment, and Competitive Conditions.* Washington, D.C., 1928.

_____ . *Report on Cooperation on American Export Trade.* Washington, D.C., 1916.

U.S. Industrial Commission. *Reports of the Industrial Commission on Trusts and Industrial Combinations.* 19 vols. Washington, D.C., 1900–1902.

U.S. Shipping Board. *Annual Report of the United States Shipping Board, 1918.* Washington, D.C., 1919.

U.S. Tariff Commission. *Reciprocity with Canada: A Study of the Arrangement of 1911.* Washington, D.C., 1920.

U.S. War Trade Board. *Report of the War Trade Board.* Washington, D.C., 1920.

C. Periodicals and Proceedings

American Industries.
American Iron and Steel Association, *Bulletin.*
American Manufacturers Export Association, *Proceedings of the Annual Conventions.*
American Trade.
Hardware, Review of the American Hardware Market.
Iron Age.
National Association of Manufacturers. *Proceedings of the Annual Conventions.*
National Board of Trade. *Proceedings.*
National Foreign Trade Council. *Proceedings of the Annual Conventions.*
New England Cotton Manufacturers Association. *Transactions.*
New York *Commercial and Financial Chronicle.*
New York *Times.*
Proceedings of the National Reciprocity Convention, 1901. Washington, 1902.
Wall Street Journal.

D. Contemporary Books, Articles, and Reports

Adams, Frederick Upham. *Conquest of the Tropics.* Garden City, N.Y., 1914.

Belcher, Wallace E. "Industrial Pooling Agreements." *Quarterly Journal of Economics* 19 (November 1904): 111–23.

Berglund, Abraham. "The United States Steel Corporation and Price Stabilization." *Quarterly Journal of Economics* 38 (November 1923): 1–30.

Bibliography

Bogart, Ernest. "Economic Organization for War." *American Political Science Review* 14 (November 1920): 587-606.

Bridge, James Howard. *The Inside History of the Carnegie Steel Company.* New York, 1903.

Carr, Wilbur J. "The American Consular Service." *American Journal of International Law* 1 (October 1907): 894-907.

Chamber of Commerce of the State of New York. *Annual Report, 1907-1908.* New York, 1908.

Chamber of Commerce of the United States of America. *A Permanent Tariff Commission.* Washington, D.C., 1915.

————. *Referendum No. 2: On the Question of a Permanent Tariff Commission.* Washington, D.C., 1913.

————. *Referendum No. 9: The Buildup of the Merchant Marine.* Washington, D.C., 1915.

————. *Referendum No. 26: The Federal Trade Committee of the Chamber Regarding Trust Legislation.* New York, 1914.

"Consular Reform." *Nation* 59 (29 November 1894): 398-99.

Depew, Chauncy, ed. *1795-1895: One Hundred Years of American Commerce.* New York, 1895.

Dingley, Edward Nelson. *The Life and Times of Nelson Dingley, Jr.* Kalamazoo, Mich., 1902.

Emery, Henry C. *The Tariff Board and Its Work.* Washington, D.C., 1910.

Export Trade Directory, 1912, 1919-1920. New York, 1912, 1920.

Farquhar, A. B. "Tariff Revision from the Manufacturer's Standpoint." *Popular Science Monthly* 74 (May 1909): 67-71.

Filsinger, Ernest. *Exporting to Latin America: A Handbook for Merchants, Manufacturers, and Exporters.* New York, 1919.

"The First Examination under the Reform Law." *Outlook* 85 (20 April 1907): 864-67.

Foster, John W. *The Practice of Diplomacy.* Boston, 1906.

Foulke, William D. *Fighting the Spoilsmen.* New York, 1919.

Grubb, Edward B. "The Consular Service and the Spoils System." *Century Magazine* 48 (June 1894): 307-308.

Halstead, Albert. "A Neglected Factor in Our Commercial Expansion." *North American Review* 174 (January 1902): 20-29.

Houston, David F. *Eight Years with Wilson's Cabinet.* 2 vols. Garden City, 1926.

Hurley, Edward N. *Awakening of Business.* New York, 1916.

————. *The New American Merchant Marine.* New York, 1920.

International Harvester. *Annual Report 1911.* Chicago, Ill., 1911.

Johnson, Emory R., et al. *History of Domestic and Foreign Commerce of the United States.* 2 vols. Washington, D.C., 1915.

Jones, Chester L. *Consular Service of the United States.* Philadelphia, 1906.

Kasson, John A. "Impressions of President McKinley, with Special Reference to His Opinions on Reciprocity." *Century* 63 (December 1901): 269-75.

Loomis, Francis B. "Notes on Our Tariff Relations with Mexico." *Annals of the American Academy of Political and Social Science* 32 (September 1908): 342-47.

McKenzie, Fred A. *The American Invaders.* London, 1901.

Osborne, John. "The American Consul and American Trade." *Atlantic Monthly* 99 (February 1907): 159-70.

National Association of Manufacturers. *A Department of Commerce and Manufacturers.* Philadelphia, 1896.

National Foreign Trade Council. *Effect of the War upon American Foreign Commerce.* New York, 1915.

_____ . *European Economic Alliances: A Compilation of Information on International Commercial Trade Policies after the European War and Their Effect upon the Foreign Trade of the United States*. New York, 1916.

_____ . *The National Foreign Trade Council: Its Purpose, Personnel, Accomplishments*. New York, 1918.

_____ . *The War and South American Trade*. New York, 1915.

_____ . *Report of the Committee on Foreign Trade of the National Foreign Trade Council*. New York, 1915.

National Tariff Commission Association. *The National Tariff Commission Association Convention*. Washington, D.C., 1911.

Notz, William F., and Harvey, Richard S. *American Foreign Trade as Promoted by Webb Pomerene and Edge Acts*. Indianapolis, 1920.

Richardson, James D., ed. *Messages and Papers of the Presidents*. 20 vols. Washington, D.C., 1917.

Ripley, William Z. *Trusts, Pools, and Corporations*. Boston, 1916.

Roosevelt, Theodore. "Six Years of Civil Service Reform." *Scribner's Mazagine* 18 (August 1895): 238-247.

Smart, George. "Good Consuls and Good Service." *American Industries* 5 (February 15, 1906): 11.

Stanwood, Edward. *American Tariff Controversies in the Nineteenth Century*. New York, 1903.

Stevens, William S., ed. *Industrial Combinations and Trusts*. New York, 1913.

Stone, N. I. *One Man's Crusade for an Honest Tariff*. Appleton, Wis., 1952.

_____ . *Promotion of Foreign Commerce in Europe and the United States*. Washington, D.C., 1907.

Straus, Oscar S. *The American Spirit*. New York, 1913.

_____ . *Under Four Administrations: From Cleveland to Taft*. Boston, 1922.

Sturges, Kenneth M. *American Chambers of Commerce*. New York, 1915.

Thwaite, B. H. *The American Invasion*. London, 1902.

United States Steel Corporation. *Annual Reports, 1904-1914*. Hoboken, N.J., 1904-14.

Vanderlip, Frank A. *The American "Commercial Invasion" of Europe*. New York, 1902.

Washburn, Albert H. "Some Evils of Our Consular Service." *Atlantic Monthly* 74 (August 1894): 241-52.

Williams, C. Arthur. "Consular Reform." *World To-Day* 21 (April 1906): 396.

II. Secondary Materials

A. Books

Ashworth, William. *A Short History of the International Economy since 1850*. 3d ed. London, 1975.

Baker, James C., and Bradford, Gerald M. *American Banks Abroad: Edge Act Companies and Multinational Banking*. New York, 1974.

Barnes, William, and Morgan, John H. *The Foreign Service of the United States: Origins, Development and Functions*. Wasington, D.C., 1961.

Bass, Herbert J., ed. *State of American History*. Chicago, 1970.

Berenson, Conrad, ed. *The Chemical Industry*. New York, 1963.

Berglund, Abraham. *The United States Steel Corporation: A Study of the Growth and Influence of Combination in the Iron and Steel Industry*. New York, 1907.

Birr, Kendall. *Pioneering in Industrial Research: The Story of the General Electric Research Laboratory*. Washington, D.C., 1957.

Bibliography

Black, Max, ed. *The Social Theories of Talcott Parsons: A Critical Examination.* Englewood Cliffs, N.J., 1961.

Bowers, Claude G. *Beveridge and the Progressive Era.* Cambridge, Mass., 1932.

Braeman, John, ed. *Twentieth Century American Foreign Policy.* Columbus, Ohio, 1971.

Bright, Arthur A. *The Electric Lamp Industry.* New York, 1949.

Broesamle, John J. *William Gibbs McAdoo: A Passion for Change, 1863-1917.* Port Washington, N.Y., 1973.

Brown, E. H. Phelps, and Browne, M. H. *A Century of Pay.* London, 1968.

Cameron, Rondo E. *France and the Economic Development of Europe, 1800-1914.* Princeton, N.J., 1961.

Candler, Charles H. *Asa Griggs Candler.* Atlanta, 1950.

Casson, Herbert N. *Cyrus Hall McCormick, His Life and Work.* Chicago, 1909.

Chandler, Alfred D., Jr. *Strategy and Structure: Chapters in the History of the American Enterprise.* Cambridge, Mass., 1962.

_____ . *The Visible Hand: The Managerial Revolution in American Business.* Cambridge, Mass., 1977.

Chandler, Alfred D., Jr., and Salisbury, Stephen. *Pierre S. DuPont and the Making of the Modern Corporation.* New York, 1971.

Clark, Victor S. *History of Manufactures in the United States, 1869-1893.* 3 vols. New York, 1929.

Cleland, Robert G. *A History of Phelps Dodge, 1834-1950.* New York, 1952.

Cochran, Thomas C. *The Pabst Brewing Company.* New York, 1948.

Cohen, Naomi. *A Dual Heritage: The Public Career of Oscar Straus.* Philadelphia, 1969.

Conan, A. R. *Capital Imports into Sterling Countries.* London, 1960.

Condliffe, J. B. *The Commerce of Nations.* London, 1951.

Cook, Arthur E., ed. *A History of the United States Shipping Board and Merchant Fleet Corporation.* Baltimore, 1927.

Coon, Horace. *American Tel & Tel: The Story of a Great Monopoly.* New York, 1939.

Crane, Katherine. *Mr. Carr of State: Forty-seven Years in the Department of State.* New York, 1960.

Croly, Herbert. *Marcus Alonzo Hanna.* New York, 1923.

Crowther, Samuel. *John H. Patterson, Pioneer in Industrial Welfare.* New York, 1926.

Cuff, Robert D. *The War Industries Board: Business-Government Relations during World War I.* Baltimore, 1973.

Davies, Robert B. *Peacefully Working to Conquer the World: Singer Sewing Machines in World Markets, 1854-1920.* New York, 1976.

Day, Clive. *A History of Commerce.* Rev. ed. New York, 1922.

Day, Richard E. *Breakfast Table Autocrat: The Life and Times of Henry Parsons Crowell.* Chicago, 1946.

Depew, Chauncey, ed. *One Hundred Years of American Commerce.* New York, 1895.

Dunning, J. H. *Studies in International Investment.* London, 1970.

Dyer, Frank L., and Martin, Thomas C. *Edison: His Life and Inventions.* 2 vols. New York, 1929.

Eichner, Alfred S. *The Emergence of Oligopoly: Sugar Refining as a Case Study.* Baltimore, 1969.

Ellis, L. Ethan. *Reciprocity, 1911.* New Haven, Conn., 1939.

Eysenbach, Mary Locke. *American Manufactured Exports, 1879-1914: A Study of Growth and Comparative Advantage.* New York, 1976.

Fausold, Martin, and Mazuzan, George T., eds. *The Hoover Presidency: A Reappraisal.* Albany, N.Y., 1974.

Feis, Herbert. *Europe, The World's Banker 1870-1914.* New Haven, Conn., 1930.

Bibliography

Galambos, Louis P. *Competition and Cooperation: The Emergence of a National Trade Association.* Baltimore, 1966.

————. *The Public Image of Big Business in America, 1880-1940: A Quantitative Study in Social Change.* Baltimore, 1975.

Gates, William B. *Michigan Copper and Boston Dollars.* Cambridge, Mass., 1951.

Geist, Walter. *Allis-Chalmers: A Brief History of 103 Years of Production.* New York, 1950.

Gelfand, Lawrence E. *The Inquiry: American Preparations for Peace, 1917-1919.* New Haven, Conn., 1963.

Gibb, George Sweet, and Knowlton, Evelyn H. *The Resurgent Years, 1911-1927.* New York, 1956.

Grace, Peter J. *W. R. Grace and the Enterprises He Created.* New York, 1953.

Gras, N. S. B., and Larson, Henrietta. *Case Book in American Business History.* New York, 1939.

Gray, James. *Business without Boundaries: The Story of General Mills.* Minneapolis, 1954.

Hacker, Louis M. *The World of Andrew Carnegie, 1865-1900.* Philadelphia, 1968.

Hammond, John W. *Men and Volts: The Story of General Electric.* Philadelphia, 1941.

Haynes, William. *The American Chemical Industry: Background and Beginnings.* 6 vols. New York, 1945-54.

Heller, Otto, ed. *Charles Nagel: Speeches and Writings, 1900-1928.* 2 vols. New York, 1931.

Hendrick, Burton, J. *The Life of Andrew Carnegie.* 2 vols. New York, 1932.

Hidy, Ralph W., and Hidy, Muriel E. *Pioneering in Big Business, 1882-1911.* New York, 1955.

Hogan, Michael J. *Informal Entente: The Private Structure of Cooperation in Anglo-American Economic Diplomacy, 1918-1928.* Columbia, Mo., 1977.

Hutchins, John G. B. *The American Maritime Industries and Public Policy, 1789-1914: An Economic History.* New York, 1941.

Hutchinson, William T. *Cyrus Hall McCormick.* 2 vols. New York, 1930, 1935.

Ilchman, Warren. *Professional Diplomacy in the United States, 1779-1939: A Study in Administrative History.* Chicago, 1961.

Imlah, A. H. *Economic Elements in the Pax Britannica.* Cambridge, Mass., 1958.

Israel, Jerry, ed. *Building the Organizational Society: Essays on Associational Activity in Modern America.* New York, 1972.

Jenkins, Resse W. *Images and Enterprise: Technology and the American Photographic Industry, 1839-1925.* Baltimore, 1975.

Jessup, Philip C. *Elihu Root.* 2 vols. New York, 1938.

Joliffe, M. F. *The United States as a Financial Centre, 1919-1933.* Cardiff, 1935.

Kaufman, Burton I. *Efficiency and Expansion: Foreign Trade Organization in the Wilson Administration, 1913-1921.* Westport, Conn., 1974.

Kemp, Tom. *Industrialization in Nineteenth-Century Europe.* London, 1969.

Kenwood, A. G., and Lougheed, A. L. *The Growth of the International Economy, 1820-1960.* London, 1971.

Kolko, Gabriel. *The Triumph of Conservatism: A Reinterpretation of American History, 1900-1916.* Chicago, 1963.

LaFeber, Walter. *The New Empire: An Interpretation of American Expansion, 1860-1898.* Ithaca, N.Y., 1963.

Landes, David S. *The Unbound Prometheus: Technological Change and Industrial Development in Western Europe from 1750 to the Present.* Cambridge, 1969.

Lauren, Paul Gordon. *Diplomats and Bureaucrats: The First Institutional Responses to Twentieth-Century Diplomacy in France and Germany.* Stanford, 1971.

Leffler, Melvyn P. *The Elusive Quest: America's Pursuit of European Stability and French Security, 1913-1933.* Chapel Hill, N.C., 1979.

Bibliography

Lewis, Cleona. *America's Stake in International Investments*. Washington, D.C., 1938.

Lief, Alfred. *The Firestone Story*. New York, 1951.

―――――. *"It Floats": The Story of Procter and Gamble*. New York, 1958.

Linder, Staffan Burenstam. *An Essay on Trade and Transformation*. New York, 1961.

Link, Arthur S. *Wilson: The Struggle for Neutrality, 1914-1915*. Princeton, N.J., 1960.

Lipsey, Robert E. *Price and Quantity Trends in the Foreign Trade of the United States*. Princeton, N.J., 1963.

McConnell, Grant. *Private Power and American Democracy*. New York, 1966.

McCormick, Cyrus. *The Century of the Reaper: An Account of Cyrus Hall McCormick*. Boston, 1931.

Manchester, Herbert. *The History of the Diamond Match Company*. New York, 1935.

Maizels, Alfred. *Industrial Growth and World Trade*. Cambridge, 1963.

Marcosson, Isaac F. *Wherever Men Trade*. New York, 1945.

Marquette, Arthur E. *Brands, Trademarks, and Good Will*. New York, 1967.

Minger, Ralph E. *William Howard Taft and United States Foreign Policy: The Apprenticeship Years, 1900-1908*. Urbana, Ill., 1975.

Mintz, Ilse. *American Exports during Business Cycles, 1879-1958*. National Bureau of Economic Research, Occasional Paper 76. New York, 1961.

Morgan, H. Wayne, ed. *The Gilded Age*. Syracuse, N.Y., 1970.

―――――. *William McKinley and His America*. Syracuse, N.Y., 1963.

Morison, Elting E., et al. *The Letters of Theodore Roosevelt*. 8 vols. Cambridge, Mass., 1951-54.

Nelson, Ralph L. *Merger Movements in American Industry, 1895-1956*. National Bureau of Economic Research, General Series No. 66. Princeton, N.J., 1959.

O'Connor, Harvey. *The Guggenheims*. New York, 1937.

Output, Employment, and Productivity in the United States after 1800. National Bureau of Economic Research, Studies in Income and Wealth, No. 30. New York, 1966.

Parrini, Carl P. *Heir to Empire: United States Economic Diplomacy, 1916-1923*. Pittsburgh, 1969.

Parsons, Talcott. *Essays in Sociological Theory*. Rev. ed. Glencoe, Ill., 1954.

―――――. *The Social System*. Glencoe, Ill., 1951.

―――――. *Structure and Process in Modern Societies*. Glencoe, Ill., 1960.

―――――. *The Structure of Social Action*. New York, 1937.

―――――. *Toward a General Theory of Action*. Cambridge, Mass., 1951.

Parsons, Talcott, and Smelser, Neil. *Economy and Society*. Glencoe, Ill., 1957.

Passer, Howard C. *The Electrical Manufacturers, 1875-1900: A Study in Competition, Entrepreneurship, Technical Change, and Economic Growth*. Cambridge, Mass., 1953.

Peterson, L. A. *Elisha Graves Otis, 1811-1861*. New York, 1945.

Phelps, Clyde W. *The Foreign Expansion of American Banks*. New York, 1927.

Platt, D. C. M. *Latin America and British Trade, 1806-1914*. London, 1972.

Porter, Glenn. *The Rise of Big Business, 1860-1910*. New York, 1973.

Porter, Glenn, and Livesay, Harold. *Merchants and Manufacturers: Studies in the Changing Structure of Nineteenth Century Marketing*. Baltimore, 1973.

Prout, Henry G. *A Life of George Westinghouse*. New York, 1921.

Richardson, James D., ed. *Messages and Papers of the Presidents*. 20 vols. Washington, D.C., 1917.

Richardson, Leon B. *William E. Chandler: Republican*. New York, 1940.

Ripley, William Z., ed. *Trusts, Pools, and Corporations*. Rev. ed. Boston, 1916.

Rosenberg, Nathan. *Technology and American Economic Growth*. New York, 1972.

Safford, Jeffrey J. *Wilsonian Maritime Diplomacy, 1913-1921*. New Brunswick, N.J., 1978.

Saul, S. B. *Studies in the British Overseas Trade, 1870-1914*. Liverpool, 1960.

Bibliography

Scammell, W. M. *The London Discount Market.* London, 1968.

Schlöte, Werner. *British Overseas Trade from 1700 to the 1930's.* W. O. Henderson and W. H. Chaloner, trans. Oxford, 1952.

Schmeckebier, Lawrence F., and Weber, Gustavus A. *The Bureau of Foreign and Domestic Commerce: Its History, Activities, and Organization.* Baltimore, 1924.

Scholes, Walter V., and Scholes, Marie V. *The Foreign Policies of the Taft Administration.* Columbia, Mo., 1970.

Schroeder, Gertrude G. *The Growth of Major Steel Companies, 1900-1950.* Baltimore, 1953.

Schulzinger, Robert D. *The Making of the Diplomatic Mind: The Training, Outlook, and Style of United States Foreign Service Officers, 1908-1931.* Middletown, Conn., 1975.

Simonds, William Adams. *Edison: His Life, His Works, His Genius.* Indianapolis, 1934.

Smith, Daniel M. *Aftermath of War: Bainbridge Colby and Wilsonian Diplomacy, 1920-21.* Philadelphia, 1970.

Smith, Darrell H., and Betters, Paul V. *The United States Shipping Board.* Washington, D.C., 1931.

Steigerwalt, Albert K. *The National Association of Manufacturers, 1895-1914: A Study in Leadership.* Ann Arbor, Mich., 1964.

Stephenson, Nathaniel W. *Nelson W. Aldrich: A Leader in American Politics.* New York, 1930.

Stocking, George, and Watkins, Myron W. *Cartels in Action.* New York, 1946.

Stork, John, and Teague, Walter D. *Flour for Man's Bread.* Minneapolis, 1952.

Stuart, Graham H. *American Diplomatic and Consular Practice.* New York, 1936.

Taussig, Frank W. *The Tariff History of the United States.* 8th ed. New York, 1931.

Temin, Peter. *Iron and Steel in Nineteenth-Century America: An Economic Inquiry.* Cambridge, Mass., 1964.

Tennant, Richard B. *The American Cigarette Industry.* New Haven, Conn., 1950.

Terrill, Tom E. *The Tariff, Politics, and American Foreign Policy.* Westport, Conn., 1973.

Thimm, Alfred. *Business Ideologies in the Reform-Progressive Era, 1880-1914.* University, Alabama, 1976.

Throton, Harrison J. *The History of the Quaker Oats Company.* Chicago, 1933.

Tilley, Nannie May. *The Bright-Tobacco Industry, 1860-1929.* Chapel Hill, N.C., 1948.

Tulchin, Joseph L. *The Aftermath of War: World War I and U.S. Policy toward Latin America.* New York, 1971.

Urofsky, Melvin I. *Big Steel and the Wilson Administration: A Study in Business-Government Relations.* Columbus, Ohio, 1969.

Van Riper, Paul R. *History of the United States Civil Service.* Evanston, Ill., 1958.

Vernon, Raymond, ed. *The Technology Factor in International Trade.* New York, 1970.

Wall, Joseph Frazier. *Andrew Carnegie.* New York, 1970.

Watson, Thomas J. *Men—Minutes—Money.* New York, 1934.

Wells, Louis T., Jr., ed. *The Product Life Cycle and International Trade.* Boston, 1972.

Werking, Richard Hume. *The Master Architects: Building the United States Foreign Service, 1890-1913.* Lexington, Ky., 1977.

West, Robert C. *Banking Reform and the Federal Reserve, 1863-1923.* Ithaca, N.Y., 1974.

Whittlesey, C. R., and Wilson, J. S. G., eds. *Essays in Money and Banking in Honour of R. S. Sayers.* Oxford, 1968.

Wiebe, Robert H. *Businessmen and Reform: A Study of the Progressive Movement.* Cambridge, Mass., 1962.

Wilkins, Mira, and Hill, Frank Ernest. *American Business Abroad: Ford on Six Continents.* Detroit, 1964.

Wilkins, Mira. *The Emergence of Multinational Enterprise: American Business Abroad from the Colonial Era to 1914*. Cambridge, Mass., 1970.

―――― . *The Maturing of Multinational Enterprise: American Business Abroad from 1914-1970*. Cambridge, Mass., 1974.

Williams, William Appleman. *The Roots of the Modern American Empire: A Study of the Growth and Shaping of Social Consciousness in a Marketplace Economy*. New York, 1969.

―――― . *The Tragedy of American Diplomacy*. Rev. ed. New York, 1962.

Williamson, Harold F., ed. *Evolution of International Management Structures*. Newark, Del., 1975.

Williamson, Harold F., and Daum, Arnold R. *The American Petroleum Industry: The Age of Illumination, 1859-1899*. Evanston, Ill., 1959.

Williamson, Jeffrey G. *American Growth and the Balance of Payments, 1820-1913*. Chapel Hill, N.C., 1964.

―――― . *Late Nineteenth Century American Development: A General Equilibrium History*. New York, 1974.

Wilson, Charles M. *Empire in Green and Gold*. New York, 1947.

Wilson, Joan Hoff. *American Business and Foreign Policy, 1920-1933*. Lexington, Ky., 1971.

Woytinsky, W. S., and Woytinsky, E. S. *World Commerce and Governments*. New York, 1955.

Younger, Edward. *John A. Kasson, Politics and Diplomacy from Lincoln to McKinley*. Iowa City, 1955.

Zeis, Paul M. *American Shipping Policy*. Princeton, N.J., 1938.

B. Articles

Abrahams, Paul. "American Bankers and the Economic Tactics of Peace." *Journal of American History* 56 (December 1969): 572-83.

Becker, William H. "American Manufacturers and Foreign Markets, 1870-1900: Business Historians and the 'New Economic Determinists.'" *Business History Review* 47 (Winter 1973): 466-81.

―――― . "Foreign Markets for Iron and Steel, 1893-1913: A New Perspective on the Williams School of Diplomatic History." *Pacific Historical Review* 44 (May 1975): 233-62.

―――― . "The Political Economy of American Expansionism, 1898-1920: A Parsonian Perspective." *Proceedings of the Program of the American Historical Association Meetings, December 1977*. Ann Arbor, Mich., 1978.

Berglund, Abraham. "The United States Steel Corporation and Price Stabilization." *Quarterly Journal of Economics* 38 (November 1923): 1-30.

Chandler, Alfred D., Jr. "The Beginnings of 'Big Business' in American Industry." *Business History Review* 33 (Spring 1959): 1-31.

―――― . "The Structure of American Industry in the Twentieth Century: An Historical Overview." *Business History Review* 43 (Autumn 1969): 255-98.

Davies, Robert B. "Peacefully Working to Conquer the World: The Singer Manufacturing Company in Foreign Markets, 1854-1889." *Business History Review* 43 (Autumn 1969): 299-346.

DeNovo, John A. "The Enigmatic Alvey A. Adee and American Foreign Relations, 1870-1924." *Prologue* 7 (Summer 1975): 69-80.

Dozer, Donald M. "Secretary of State Elihu Root and Consular Reorganization." *Mississippi Valley Historical Review* 29 (December 1942): 339-50.

Edwards, Richard C. "Stages in Corporate Stability and the Risks of Corporate Failure." *Journal of Economic History* 35 (June 1975): 428-57.

Bibliography

Feldman, Gerald D., and Nocken, Ulrich. "Trade Associations and Economic Power: Interest Group Development in the German Iron and Steel and Machine Building Industries, 1900–1933." *Business History Review* 49 (Winter 1975): 413–44.

Fisk, Harvey E. "The Flow of Capital–Canada." *Annals of the American Academy of Political and Social Science* 107 (May 1923): 170–86.

Gould, Lewis L. "Diplomats in the Lobby: Franco-American Relations and the Dingley Tariff of 1897." *Historian* 39 (August 1977): 659–80.

Hawke, G. R. "The United States Tariff and Industrial Protection in the Late Nineteenth Century." *Economic History Review* 28 (1975): 84–99.

Hogan, Michael J. "The United States and the Problem of International Economic Control: American Attitudes toward European Reconstruction, 1918–1920." *Pacific Historical Review* 44 (February 1975): 84–103.

Hutchins, John G. B. "The American Shipping Industry since 1914." *Business History Review* 28 (Spring 1954): 105–28.

Jenkins, Reese W. "Technology in the Market: George Eastman and the Origin of Amateur Photography." *Technology and Culture* 16 (January 1975): 1–19.

Johnson, Arthur M. "Theodore Roosevelt and the Bureau of Corporations." *Mississippi Valley Historical Review* 45 (March 1959): 571–90.

Kaufman, Burton I. "Organization for Foreign Trade Expansion in the Mississippi Valley, 1900–1920." *Business History Review* 46 (Winter 1972): 444–65.

_____. "The Organizational Dimension of United States Economic Foreign Policy, 1900–1920." *Business History Review* 46 (Spring 1972): 17–44.

_____. "United States Trade and Latin America: The Wilson Years." *Journal of American History* 58 (September 1971): 342–63.

Kramer, Helen M. "Harvesters and High Finance: Formation of the International Harvester Company." *Business History Review* 38 (Autumn 1964): 284–301.

Kujovich, Mary Yeager. "The Refrigerator Car and the Growth of the American Dressed Beef Industry." *Business History Review* 44 (Winter 1970): 460–82.

Leffler, Melvyn P. "Political Isolationism, Economic Expansionism, or Diplomatic Realism: American Policy toward Western Europe, 1921–1933." *Perspectives in American History* 8 (1974): 413–64.

Lewis, William Arthur. "International Competition in Manufacturers." *American Economic Review* 47 (May 1957): 578–609.

Lewis, William Arthur, and O'Leary, P. J. "Secular Swings in Production and Trade, 1870–1913." *Manchester School of Economics and Social Studies* 23 (May 1955): 113–51.

Litterer, Joseph A. "Systematic Management: Design for Organizational Reform in American Manufacturing Firms." *Business History Review* 47 (Winter 1973): 369–91.

_____. "Systematic Management: The Search for Order and Integration." *Business History Review* 35 (Winter 1961): 461–76.

Livermore, Shaw. "The Success of Industrial Mergers." *Quarterly Journal of Economics* 50 (November 1935): 68–96.

Massmouth, Michael. "Technological and Managerial Innovation: The Johnson Company, 1823–1898." *Business History Review* 50 (Spring 1976): 46–68.

Navin, Thomas R. "The 500 Largest American Industrials in 1917." *Business History Review* 44 (Autumn 1970): 360–86.

Parsons, Talcott. "A Sociological Approach to the Theory of Organizations." *Administrative Science Quarterly* 1 (June–September 1956): 63–85, 225–39.

Peterson, Thomas G. "American Businessmen and Consular Service Reform, 1890's to 1906." *Business History Review* 40 (Spring 1966): 77–97.

Penrose, Edith. "Foreign Investment and the Growth of the Firm." *Economic Journal* 64 (June 1956): 220–35.

Porter, Patrick G. "Origins of the American Tobacco Company." *Business History Review*

43 (Spring 1969): 59-76.

Porter, Patrick G., and Livesay, Harold C. "Oligopoly in Small Manufacturing Industries." *Explorations in Economic History* 7 (Spring 1970): 371-79.

Richter, F. Ernest. "The Amalgamated Copper Company." *Quarterly Journal of Economics* 29 (February 1915): 400-406.

Richter, J. H. "The Place of Agriculture in International Trade Policy." *Canadian Journal of Agricultural Economics* 12 (January 1964): 1-9.

Rosenberg, Nathan. "Technological Change in the Machine Tool Industry, 1840-1910." *Journal of Economic History* 23 (December 1963): 414-43.

Simon, Matthew, and Novack, David E. "Some Dimensions of the American Commercial Invasion of Europe, 1871-1914." *Journal of Economic History* 24 (December 1964): 591-605.

Seltzer, Alan L. "Woodrow Wilson as Corporate Liberal: Towards a Reconsideration of Left Revisionist Historiography." *Western Political Science Quarterly* 30 (June 1977): 183-212.

Thompson, J. A. "William Appleman Williams and the 'American Empire.'" *Journal of American Studies* 7 (April 1973): 91-104.

Varg, Paul A. "The Myth of the China Market, 1890-1914." *The American Historical Review* 73 (1968): 742-58.

Vernon, Raymond. "International Investment and International Trade in the Product Life Cycle." *Quarterly Journal of Economics* 80 (May 1966): 190-207.

Vietor, Richard H. K. "Businessmen and the Political Economy: The Railroad Rate Controversy of 1905." *Journal of American History* 64 (June 1977): 46-66.

Wilkins, Mira. "An American Enterprise Abroad: American Radiator Company in Europe, 1895-1914." *Business History Review* 43 (Winter 1969): 326-46.

III. Unpublished Materials

Abrahams, Philip. "The Foreign Expansion of American Finance and Its Relationship to the Foreign Economic Policies of the United States, 1907-1921." Ph.D. diss., University of Wisconsin, 1967.

Engelbourg, Saul. "International Business Machines: A Business History." Ph.D. diss., Columbia University, 1954.

Galambos, Louis. "The Economic Effects of the Reorganization of the Sources of Knowledge in America, 1870-1920." Paper presented at the Smithsonian Institution, March 1976.

Gelfand, Lawrence E. "A Merit System for the American Diplomatic Service, 1896-1930." Paper delivered before the Organization of American Historians, April 1976.

Goldman, Michael A. "The War Finance Corporation in the Politics of War and Reconstruction, 1917-1923." Ph.D. diss., Rutgers University, 1976.

Harrison, Benjamin T. "Chandler Anderson and American Foreign Relations (1896-1928)." Ph.D. diss., University of California, Los Angeles, 1969.

Kenkel, Joseph. "Tariff Commission Movement: The Search for a Non-Partisan Solution of the Tariff Question." Ph.D. diss., University of Maryland, 1962.

Kujovich, Mary Yeager. "The Dynamics of Oligopoly in the Meat Packing Industry: An Historical Analysis." Ph.D. diss., Johns Hopkins University, 1973.

Mayer, Robert Stanley. "The Influence of Frank A. Vanderlip and the National City Bank on American Commerce and Foreign Policy." Ph.D. diss., Rutgers University, 1968.

Pickering, Elizabeth C. "The International Harvester Company in Russia: A Case Study of a Foreign Corporation in Russia from the 1860's to the 1930's." Ph.D. diss., Princeton University, 1974.

Seltzer, Alan L. "Progressive Politics and the Idea of the Enlightened Businessman." Ph.D. diss., University of Chicago, 1972.

Snyder, John R. "Edward P. Costigan and the United States Tariff Commission." Ph.D. diss., University of Colorado, 1966.

Terleckyj, Nestor E. "Sources of Productivity Advance: A Pilot Study of Manufacturing Industries, 1899–1953." Ph.D. diss., Columbia University, 1960.

Van Meter, Robert H. "The United States and European Recovery, 1918-1923: A Study of Public Policy and Private Finance." Ph.D. diss., University of Wisconsin, 1971.

Index

Index